Manhattan

Cadogan Books plc
27–29 Berwick Street, London W1V 3RF, UK
e-mail: guides@cadogan.demon.co.uk

Distributed in North America by
The Globe Pequot Press
6 Business Park Road, PO Box 833, Old Saybrook,
Connecticut 06475–0833

Copyright © Vanessa Letts 1997
Illustrations © Kicca Tommasi 1997
Cover design by Animage
Cover photographs:
      front: James Davis Worldwide Photographic Travel Library
      back: Eye Ubiquitous/Michael George

Maps © Cadogan Guides, drawn by Map Creation Ltd

Series Editor: Rachel Fielding

Editing and proofreading: Linda McQueen
Indexing: Isobel McLean
Production: Book Production Services
Editorial and DTP assistance: Joanna West and Adrian McLaughlin

A catalogue record for this book is available from the British Library
ISBN 1-86011-072-X

Printed and bound in Great Britain by Redwood Books Ltd.

*The author and publishers have made every effort to ensure the accuracy of the infor-
mation in this book at the time of going to press. However, they cannot accept any
responsibility for any loss, injury or inconvenience resulting from the use of information
contained in this guide.*

About the Author

Vanessa Letts was born and brought up in London. She has lived and worked in Manhattan and lectured on New York on board the QE2. In 1990 she won the Shiva Naipaul Memorial Prize for travel writing; since then she has been a film reviewer on the *Spectator Magazine* and a writer on *Punch* .

Please help us to keep this guide up to date

Every effort has been made to ensure the information in this book is accurate at the time of going to press. However, practical details such as opening hours, travel information, standards in hotels and restaurants and, in particular, prices are liable to change. We will be delighted to receive any corrections and suggestions for improvement which can be incorporated into the next edition.

We intend to keep this book as up-to-date as possible in the coming years, so **please do write** to us. Writers of the best letters will receive a free copy of the Cadogan Guide of their choice.

Contents

An Architectural Compendium   69–86

The Walks   87–174

Introduction

New York—*synonym for big, great,
astounding, miraculous!*

New York—*mecca which lures the brightest
minds, the most brilliant writers,
the most masterful artisans to
its gates!*

New York—*!!! What visions of magnitude,
variety and power the name
New York conjures up for human
comprehension!!*

*MILLIONS and BILLIONS, instead of 100s
and 1000s are the figures
constituting the basis for calculation
nowadays in this WONDER CITY!!!!*

W. Parker Chase
New York The Wonder City,
1931

In the Great Depression, W. Parker Chase—self-made impresario, master of hyperbole, and owner of several troupes of show-girls—wrote a Vision of New York in the Future for his guidebook *New York The Wonder City*. By the 1990s, Parker Chase tells readers, Manhattan will have a population of 50 million; buildings will soar 250 storeys into the air; Manhattanites will crunch up their meals and cocktails in pills and pellets; ladies will fling away their dowdy outer-garments for sensational bathing costumes; roads will be noise-less; and 'business depressions, Wall Street crashes, Communistic upheavals and other disturbances will be a thing of the past'. Best of all, scientists will have perfected a life-perpetuating serum.

Not one prediction has come true. Spirited into the future with a suitcase of serum, Parker Chase would find a surprisingly old-fashioned Wonder City. He would touch down in streets which still smell of laundry soap and subways, and be stranded in traffic which still deafens with klaxons, sirens and cab-dispatchers' whistles. As he walked he might trample on a cockroach whose shape has hardly altered from forebears who inhabited jungles in various parts of the planet 250 million years ago. Towering above him he would recognize the world's most eccentric skyscrapers; and everywhere he went he would encounter the same quick-witted Manhattanites. To the great Parker Chase, Manhattan would be a familiar place, as unperfect as ever, and fortunately just as scintillating.

For the newcomer, too, the Wonder City captivates instantly: inspires and elevates one minute, alarms and depresses the next. Prepare yourself for a cloudland and sinkhole, paradise and pande-monium; for the most oxymoronic of cities, depending on your mood. Amongst the millions and billions you will find 8 million citizens, 8–15 million rats, 2.4 million trees, 1 million illegal immigrants, nearly 1 million buildings, 12,000 miles of streets and sewers, 600–1000 residents *per acre*, 17 million tourists and 700–1000 murders a year, 3.5 million commuters (the population of Havana) and 30,000 tons of rubbish a day. Not least among the world-famous attractions of Gotham (Manhattan was first christened 'Gotham' by Washington Irving, in honour of an old nursery rhyme about Gotham, an English village in Nottinghamshire which was proverbial for the folly of its inhabitants) are streets shuddering with movement, free-falling litter and a seaside light which transfigures towers and scrapers into pink, lemon and lime-green confections;

and, of course, Manhattanites themselves, who wisecrack and curse their way through life with enviable swagger. They make Manhattan a peculiarly verbal place. Keep your ears pricked at all times and you will be as entertained as much by what you hear as by what you see. Behind the gruff exteriors, Manhattanites are a wistful, open-hearted lot and, perhaps because over 40 per cent are immigrants, they have a knack of muscling newcomers into instant conversations which can culminate in lifelong friendships.

Is Manhattan New York or New York Manhattan? No one, from the first settlers to Parker Chase, has made up their minds. What we do know is that Manhattan is the world's metropolis, and what's more that the world's metropolis is a curiously parochial place, made up of discrete neighbourhoods, small diners and shops, and original residents. In a city as intimate as this the best entertainments are the simplest: the ordinary restaurants and bars, where Manhattanites eat the ice in their drinks; the bookstores, where women queue up with a poodle in one hand and a pile of books in the other; Central Park, with its afternoon nannies and roller-bladers; the gridlocked traffic, with its police-officers on scooters and pristine Dodge Ram trucks; and Sunday brunch, when Manhattanites lug all 5lbs of the *New York Times* to the nearest diner to be scrutinized over French toast and coffee.

Before you step into the metropolis, remind yourself that the very things that make Manhattan unbearable—the incivilities, the hurry and congestion—are the ones that make it the most exhilarating, the most energetic and the most challenging Wonder City in the world. Only one thing is guaranteed, and that is that after you've been here, nowhere else on earth will scramble your brains so totally.

To Betsy Sosland

Acknowledgements

Heartfelt thanks go to Robert Mantho and Michael Pauls, the mentors responsible for any intelligence to be found in this book. Special thanks also go to quintessential New Yorker and true friend Betsy Sosland, (who fed, clothed and advised me on everything, put me up and generally put up with me); to Dibbs Locksmith and Willie Olivieri, who both gave inspiring advice; to Bonnie Mark and Heather Carr; to Sarah Pinto and Aidan Mantho; to Francisca and Mizpy, Goldie, Randy and Karen Williams, Debs and Joe Trump, Christopher Ash and James Soane, Matthew Barac, Ritu Birla, Frank Chirico, Sam King, Paddy O'Hara and Eric Thurnauer who all looked after me in New York; to my mother and father; to my excellent editors on both editions, Vicki Ingle and Linda McQueen; to Kicca, who did the pictures; to the ever-wise Rachel Fielding; and most of all to David, for making me happy always.

Thanks to George Sassoon for permission to use the quote from Siegfried Sassoon's poem 'Storm on Fifth Avenue' on p.190, and to the Monacelli Press of New York for permission to use two extracts from *Delirious New York* by Rem Koolhaas in the **Architecture** chapter.

Travel

Getting There

'Nearly all th' most foolish people in th' country an' manny iv th' wisest goes to Noo York. Th' wise people ar-re there because th' foolish wint first. That's th' way th' wise men make a livin'.'

Finley Peter Dunne, *Mr Dooley's Opinions*, 1901

From the UK
By Air

Heathrow to JFK is the world's busiest international air route. Flights leave three times daily from Heathrow and Gatwick, Manchester (daily), Glasgow (three times a week) and Prestwick (once a week). Unless you're flying on Concorde, flights take 7–8hrs there and, thanks to prevailing winds, 6–7hrs back. Flights mostly leave Europe and the UK mid-morning to mid-afternoon UK time, arriving late evening in New York; they generally return from New York overnight, arriving early the next morning in the UK. Make sure you drink plenty of water, and if you want to sleep ask for a window seat so you have something (rather than someone) to lean on. If the flight isn't too crowded, ask the hostess if you can bag a row of seats to lie down on.

Fares are at their most expensive in the peak season (Christmas and Easter) and in the high season (late June until the very end of September). If you plan to travel during these times, be sure to book a month in advance at *least*. Flights will be cheaper mid-season (April to early June, October and sometimes August too), and rock bottom from November to March (except Christmas). Flights are cheaper Monday to Friday than at weekends. If you really want to travel in style, the full fare on **Concorde** is £6678, which is discounted by £1000 or so in the summer, but you may find yourself in the company of people like Michael Jackson and Oprah Winfrey. For reservations call ✆ (0345) 222100. If you book with a good discount travel agent on Air France you can fly out business class from Paris, returning on Concorde, for something like £4000.

All the **airlines** will get you there in the end but some will get you there in better shape than others. For comfort, reliability, food, fine wines, seat-width and completely civilized service, **KLM** beats the others by a clear margin. The airline does daily flights to New York from 19 UK airports via Amsterdam (a 40-minute flight): for more information call ✆ (0181) 750 9200 in the UK or ✆ 31 20 4 747 747 directly to Holland. Otherwise it's much of a muchness. **British Airways** has slightly wider seats than Virgin. **Virgin** provides slightly better food and hand massages, and if you're flying on your birthday will make a special on-board anniversary announcement (plus, for a fee, cake, champagne and/or chocolates—call between 2 days and 2 months in advance on ✆ (01293) 747691). **Air India** consistently offers the cheapest flights to New York; service is good and food is excellent. However, economy airlines are more crowded and hence more prone to delays than the others.

For the latest **bucket-shop prices**, which can be very low, it's worth having a look at the *Evening Standard*, London listings magazines or the Sunday papers. The Air Travel Advisory Board, ✆ (0171) 636 5000, gives numbers of travel agents currently offering good deals.

travel agents/students

Europe Student Travel, 6 Campden St., London W8, ✆ (0171) 727 7647. Small, unusually helpful travel agent, who'll research the cheapest flights to New York as well as Europe with total thoroughness. For non-students as well as students.

Trailfinders, 42 Earls Court Road, London W8, ✆ (0171) 938 3366/5400. Cheap flights and good deals, and absurdly long waits on the telephone.

Campus, ✆ (0171) 730 2101. Cheap BA and Virgin flights.

Airline Network, ✆ (01772) 727272. For unusual stopovers, e.g. Reykjavik.

airlines in London

Air India:	✆ (0181) 745 1000/✆ (01753) 684828
Air Canada:	✆ (0990) 247 226
American Airlines:	✆ (0181) 572 5555
British Airways:	✆ (0345) 222111
Continental:	✆ (0800) 776464
Delta:	✆ (0800) 414767
KLM:	✆ (0181) 750 9200
TWA:	✆ (0171) 439 0707
United:	✆ 1 (800) 888555 or in UK ✆ (0181) 990 9900
Virgin Atlantic:	✆ (01293) 747747

From the USA and Canada

Practically all the big US airlines do flights to the New York area. Before booking, make sure you know whether flights include stops or changes of aircraft, which may reduce the price of your ticket but will greatly increase the length of your journey. Check in at least half an hour before departure.

major US carriers serving New York

America West	✆ 1 (800) 235 9292
American	✆ 1 (800) 433 7300
Continental	✆ 1 (800) 525 0280
Delta	✆ 1 (800) 221 1212

Northwest	✆ 1 (800) 225 2525
TWA	✆ 1 (800) 221 2000
United	✆ 1 (800) 241 6522
US Air	✆ 1 (800) 428 4322

Airports

New York has two main international airports, John F. Kennedy (JFK) and Newark and a third, LaGuardia, used mostly for domestic flights. Kennedy and LaGuardia are considered to be the two worst airports in America. JFK and LaGuardia lie to the east of Manhattan in Queens, and Newark to the west in the state of New Jersey. Although high-speed rail links between Manhattan and the airports have been planned since the 1960s they do *not* as yet exist. All three are a 30–90min taxi ride away from Manhattan, depending on the appallingness of the traffic.

JFK

General information	✆ 1 (718) 244 4444
Complaints	✆ 1 (800) 498 7497
Currency exchange	✆ 1 (718) 656 8444
Customs	✆ 1 (718) 553 1824
Lost and found	✆ 1 (718) 244 4225
	(but contact individual airline for lost luggage)
Medical clinic	✆ 1 (718) 656 5344
Emergency	✆ 1 (718) 244 4225/6

Newark

General information	✆ 1 (201) 961 6000
Currency exchange	✆ 1 (201) 961 6633
Customs	✆ 1 (201) 645 3409
Police	✆ 1 (201) 961 6230
Disabled	✆ 1 (201) 961 6154

LaGuardia

General information	✆ 1 (718) 533 3400
Currency exchange	✆ 1 (718) 533 3400
Customs	✆ 1 (718) 476 4378
Medical office	✆ 1 (718) 476 5575
Police	✆ 1 (718) 533 3900
Traveler's aid	✆ 1 (718) 476 5575

Getting To and From the Airport

Arriving in New York is not necessarily a soothing experience. If you're arriving after 10pm, have some American currency on you in case the bureaux de change are closed (don't panic if you don't have any dollars, as most shops and even cab drivers will accept dollar traveller's cheques). Remember: if you need to make a phone call to Manhattan from the airport add © 1 (212), the Manhattan area code.

Immigration

Unless you get out of the plane first and barge to the front of the queue, allow 30 minutes to an hour to get through. The officers can seem peevish, but this is more pose than reality, and any display of politeness from you will melt the most vinegary exterior. Even so, if you don't have traveller's cheques, credit cards or cash to prove you have enough money to stay in the country unaided (calculated at about $300–400 a week), you may find your visit is restricted to 6 weeks, especially if you don't have a return ticket. The officials usually ask where you'll be staying, so have the name, address and telephone number of your hotel or friends in the city handy, or explain, with conviction, that you're 'touring'.

Transport From the Airports

by cab

Getting to Manhattan is the next hurdle. The best and easiest way is to take a cab. This costs a flat fare of $30, not including tips. Taking a cab is more expensive than taking a bus, but you can quarter the price by asking the taxi dispatcher to fix you up with a group of people who want to share. More simply, make friends with the lonely person standing in the queue next to you, and ask if they mind sharing. Make sure you go to a taxi rank, take a regular yellow cab and let the driver know that you're aware of the official $30 flat fare. Steer clear of amiable-looking characters who offer to take your bags and ferry you to Manhattan by glamorous-looking mini-cab. The ride will cost more than the official flat fare, and if anything goes awry, you won't have anyone to complain to.

If queues for yellow taxis are slow, ring for a private cab from a public telephone. **Tel Aviv**, © 1 (212) 777 7777, claims to be able to pick up airport passengers in minutes for a fare of around $25.

by boat (LaGuardia only)

The **Delta Water Shuttle**, © 1 (800) 54 FERRY, operates Mon–Fri between La Guardia airport and 34th Street and the East River and Pier 11 at Wall Street. Fares cost $20 one way and $30 return; the trip takes less than 25 minutes.

by Carey Bus or Olympia Trails

If you're travelling on a budget and don't have too much luggage, a cheap and reliable option is to take a privately operated bus. The efficient **Carey Bus System**, © 1 (718) 632 0500, leaves JFK and La Guardia every 20mins 6am–midnight, dropping passengers at Grand Central Station on the east side of Midtown at 42nd Street and Park Avenue. From Grand Central the bus continues on round the main hotel districts; however, if your accommodation is more out of the way, it will be easy to get a cab from Grand Central. (Cabs are yellow; a lit sign on the roof means they're vacant; *see* p.17.) From Newark, **Olympia Trails** buses, ✆ (1 212) 964 6233, run every 15mins 6am–midnight to the World Trade Center in downtown Manhattan, or else to Grand Central Station in Midtown. Tickets to Manhattan cost around $13 for a Carey bus from JFK, around $10 for a Carey bus from La Guardia, and around $7 for an Olympia bus from Newark. Allow 45 minutes for the trip, but up to 1½hrs during rush hours.

by helicopter (JFK only)

If you need to get into the city extra quickly, take a helicopter from Kennedy. The ride takes 10 minutes, costs about $58 and choppers leave JFK terminals for the East Side Heliport on 34th Street and the East River in Midtown every half-hour between 1.30pm and 7.30pm. (Call **New York Helicopter**, ✆ 1 (800) 645 3494, ✆ (1 516) 756 2643, for more information.)

by subway (JFK only)

This is the last resort, to be undertaken only if you have 90mins, no luggage and no money. From JFK, either take a free shuttle bus to Howard Beach and get on the A subway train (this costs $1.50, and you'll need to buy a subway token); or, Plan Z: from JFK take the Q10 green bus from JFK to the Union Turnpike-Kew Gardens subway station (costing $1.50), and then catch an E train into the city. This costs a total of $3, and the potential nightmare of travelling between Manhattan and JFK this way has been well exploited in a number of Hollywood screenplays.

by New York Transit Authority bus (LaGuardia only)

This is also the last resort. From the terminal follow signs that say 'Ground Transportation' and look out for an M60 bus sign. You'll need $1.50 in change in the form of six quarters (6 x 25¢) or else a subway token, not forgetting that subway tokens can only be purchased in subway stations and never on buses.

Transport to the Airports

Unfortunately the $30 flat fare does not apply to cab rides back to the airports, and if you catch an ordinary cab you will probably have to pay a few dollars extra, depending on where you are in Manhattan. However, you can save money if you can order a car from a cab service company (preferably 24 hours before you leave the city). The cab will pick you up from a specified address for a fare of around $30 or sometimes as low as $25.

Always allow extra time for traffic jams and confusion. JFK is enormous, sprawling and illogically designed. At both international airports most airlines have individual terminals. If your airline is at the end of the line, add an extra 15 minutes to your journey. If it's raining, add another hour.

For up-to-date **information** on traffic and weather conditions, and convenient transportation to the airports, call ℭ (1 (800) AIR RIDE. Finding out information about flight arrivals and departures can be infuriating, especially if you're travelling on one of the more obscure airlines, because there is no central bureau of information. Most of the major carriers have their own numbers, and are reluctant to give out the phone numbers of their rivals (call ℭ 411 for directory enquiries).

airlines in New York

Air France: ℭ 1 (212) 247 0100 (reservations) or 1 (800) 237 2747
Alitalia: ℭ 1 (800) 223 5730
American Airlines: ℭ 1 (800) 235 9292
British Airways: ℭ 1 (800) 247 9297
Continental: ℭ 1 (800) 525 0280
Delta: ℭ 1 (212) 239 0700 or 1 (800) 221 1212
El Al: ℭ 1 (212) 768 9200 or 1 (800) 223 6700
KLM Royal Dutch Airlines: ℭ 1 (800) 374 7747
Lufthansa: ℭ 1 (800) 645 3880
Northwest: ℭ 1 (800) 225 2525 (domestic) or ℭ 1 (800) 447 4747 (international).
Swissair: ℭ 1 (800) 221 4750 or 1 (718) 995 8400 (reservations), or ℭ 1 (718) 995 5112 (flight information)
TWA: ℭ 1 (212) 290 2121 (domestic), or 290 2141 or ℭ 1 (800) 892 4141 (international)
United Airlines: ℭ 1 (800) 241 6522
US Airways: ℭ 1 (800) 428 4322
Virgin Atlantic: ℭ 1 (800) 862 8621

By Sea

If you've got lots of wonga, a harp and Mercedes to transport, and a cast-iron stomach, travelling by ocean liner is the obvious alternative. On the **QE2** you may take unlimited baggage (Cunard charges a fee for more than eight suitcases); and once on board you may eat unlimited amounts of food, or immerse yourself in free classes on the intricacies of deck quoits and skittles, embroidery and pet care, as well as lectures by some of the world's most scintillating authors and personalities. The QE2 was re-refitted in 1996 (after the infamous botch-job of 1994); and these days a one-way 6-day trip from Southampton to New York in the QE2's most expensive suite will set you back around £12,540, whilst an economy class off-season cabinette will be around £1200. Make reservations/package deals through a travel agent or directly through Cunard: New York, ℭ 1 (212) 880 7500; London, ℭ (01703) 716634.

Entry Formalities

Passports and Visas

Citizens of the **UK, New Zealand, Japan** and most of **Western Europe** should take a valid 10-year passport. If you're visiting the US for less than 90 days and have a return ticket on a major airline, you do not need a visa. To stay longer apply for a visa from the US Embassy. (In London, from the Visa and Immigration Department, 5 Upper Grosvenor St, London W1A 2JB, ✆ (0891) 200290; calls cost a whopping 50 pence per minute). Unless you queue up outside the embassy in person, a written application takes four weeks. You need a passport, a photograph and evidence that you'll return to your native land (a note explaining that you are tied to a job, college, child or dog is usually enough). On the application form, you must swear you're not a communist, fascist, criminal or drug-dealer, and if customs find any incriminatingly subversive literature on you they can refuse admission on the grounds that you swore falsely.

Canadians need ID with a photograph, but no passport.

Citizens of **Ireland, Australia** and the **rest of the world** need a visa. Before you travel, apply for a B2 visa from a US consulate by post or in person. Bring or send in your passport and separate passport photographs.

Customs

'I have nothing to declare except my genius.'
Oscar Wilde, arriving at the New York Custom House in 1918

In fact foreigners are allowed to enter with **duty-free** gifts valued at up to $100, plus 200 cigarettes, 50 cigars or 3lbs of tobacco, and 1 litre of alcohol. Returning Americans may bring gifts worth up to $400, whilst returning Britons can enter with goods worth up to £420.

If you have a foreign passport and make it conspicuous, customs officials will mostly wave you straight on—if they do decide to inspect, they may be rigorous and will swiftly relieve passengers of drugs, plants, fresh food (especially fruit and meat), chocolate liqueurs, obscene publications, items purchased in Libya, Haiti or Cuba, switchblade knives, fireworks and even, and inexplicably, lottery tickets.

US Customs: ✆ 1 (800) 697 3662.

Getting Around

Like most ancient Greek and Roman cities, and 13th-century Peking, Manhattan is built on a grid. This makes getting around on foot rather simple, except for certain anarchic areas such as Brooklyn and Lower Manhattan (below 14th Street) where the grid goes doolally. Fifth Avenue runs straight down the middle of Manhattan, neatly dividing the island into east and west. Broadway, following an Indian trail, is the only real confusion, since it runs diagonally from top to bottom slicing up avenues and creating irregular chequers.

How to Find an Address

Here is a magic system for locating the nearest cross-street to a building: cancel the last digit of the building's number (328 8th Avenue becomes 32), divide it by two (= 16), and then add or subtract the relevant number listed below (+10 = 26, so the nearest cross-street is West 26th Street).

Avenue A: add 3
Avenue B: add 3
Avenue C: add 3
Avenue D: add 3
1st Avenue: add 3
2nd Avenue: add 3
3rd Avenue: add 10
4th Avenue: add 8
5th Avenue: 1–200 add 13
      201–400 add 16
      401–600 add 18
      601–775 add 20
      776–1285 subtract 18
      1287–2000 add 45
      2000+ add 24
6th Avenue: subtract 12
7th Avenue: add 12
8th Avenue: add 10

9th Avenue: add 13
10th Avenue: add 14
Amsterdam Avenue: add 60
Audubon Avenue: add 165
Broadway: subtract 30
Columbus Avenue: add 60
Convent Avenue: add 127
Central Park West: divide by 10 and add 60
Edgecombe Avenue: add 134
Lenox Avenue: add 110
Lexington Avenue: add 22
Madison Avenue: add 26
Manhattan Avenue: add 100
Park Avenue: add 34
Riverside Drive: divide by 10 and add 72
St Nicholas Avenue: add 110
West End Avenue: add 59
York Avenue: add 4

Maps

It's important to get a good street map. The best available is the purple plastic-covered *Streetwise Manhattan* map, published by Streetwise Maps Inc. It's small and sturdy, and stands up to physical abuse and rain. More importantly, it shows the exact locations of subway stations. You can get Streetwise maps in most bookshops (and discounted, along with huge and detailed Rand McNally maps, in the Strand Bookstore on 12th Street and Broadway). The other alternative is the excellent *Van Dam* fold-out map, or the *Flashmaps Instant Guide to New York* which comes in a wallet. Some shops sell attractive-looking thumbnail maps and magnifying glasses. Don't buy these as they are useless.

It's also useful to get **subway** and **bus maps**. These are free from token booths (but they tend to run out), from tourist information centres, some hotels, and from the information booths at Grand Central and Penn Stations.

On Foot

Cars drive on the right-hand side of the road. Luckily, most streets are one-way; even-numbered streets run east, odd-numbered streets run west.

In Manhattan, crossing the road can be an ordeal. Car drivers may screech past pausing only to hurl out such abuse at pedestrians as 'Walk when it says walk, Four Eyes'. Bicycle messengers bike the wrong way down streets at breakneck speeds. Even on one-way streets or avenues, make a mental note to look the other way as you cross. Watch out in particular for cyclists dressed as comic-book superheroes with long Lycra sleeves, leggings, thick gloves, plastic headgear and epaulettes. These are the X-MEN, emulators of the comic-book mutants, and in real life of a man known only as 'X-MAN'—a cycle messenger who became legendary in the 1980s after he developed a method of hanging on to vehicles with one glove, allowing him to travel from Brooklyn to Manhattan at speeds of 80mph.

New Yorkers are always delighted to help out with directions, but may do so in a hurry and sometimes in code. The words 'street' and 'avenue' are redundant. '42nd-n-Park' means, 'The place you are looking for is on 42nd Street, between Park and Lexington Avenues.' Be prepared, as well, for directions reduced, to your untrained ear, to a minimalist 'Grr-rr-rrr'. Once you've been in the city a short time you will be used to judging distances in blocks. Blocks in Manhattan are mostly rectangular, and it takes about 1½ minutes to walk along a short side, from one street to another; and about 3–5 minutes to walk a long side, from one avenue to another. One mile is roughly equal to 20 north–south blocks or 8 crosstown blocks.

roller blade hire

Blades West, 120 West 72nd St., at Columbus Ave., ☎ 787 3911
Blades East, 160 E. 86th St., between 3rd and Lexington., ☎ 996 1644

By Subway

Bus and subway information: ☎ 1 (718) 330 1234, 6am–9pm daily
Non-English-speakers: ☎ 1 (718) 330 4847
Travel for the disabled: ☎ 1 (718) 596 8585, 6am–9pm daily
Customer complaints and enquiries: ☎ 1 (718) 330 3322

Since 1991 crime on subways has dropped by 64.3%. Travelling by subway is pleasanter as well as safer than in the 1980s, and more people than ever are using the subway's 469 stations and 700 miles of track: 3.5 million in 1996 (as opposed to 2.5 million in London). All carriages have been air-conditioned, police are more conspicuous, trains more punctual, Victorian tiles and mosaics reconditioned and, after a long-obsessed battle, graffiti and the homeless ('mole people') wiped off the face of the earth. These days the NYC Transit Authority cares about its image.

But Moscow Manhattan is not. Subway platforms are humid and crowded. Rows of ugly iron girders are an eyesore. Maps are scarce and hard to read. Arrivals aren't announced and the only way to anticipate a long-delayed train is to wait for a breeze. Interchanges are as intricate as a fantasy by Piranesi. Train doors are prone to closing rather suddenly and dragging strap-hangers along platforms (despite modernization there were 70 such incidents in 1996).

On the plus side, travelling by subway is the fastest, cheapest, most convenient way of getting around: if all goes to plan, an express can whisk passengers from 14th to 96th Street in ten minutes. Some people savour the ride: the subway has 10 separate fan clubs, and architecture buffs frequently go into raptures over the machine-age aesthetics and uncompromisingly functional material integrity of exposed girdering. Meanwhile in their quest to beautify the system, MTA are commissioning new art installations for stations. Less beautifully, the Authority is considering a plan to sell advertising space on subway train exteriors and platform floors.

As you judder around the city, keep an eye out for the following new art works:

> *A Canal Filled with Water*—a new art installation in Canal Street.
>
> *Parts of the Brooklyn Bridge*—a sculpture in Brooklyn Bridge constructed out of tangled cables salvaged from the actual bridge.
>
> *Trompe l'œil murals*—in Spring Street station.

On majolica-tiled walls on Victorian platforms you'll see graceful depictions of:

> *Beavers*—decorating Astor Place station in bas-relief, in deference to John Jacob Astor, who made his first fortune selling beaver furs.
>
> *Sloops*—at South Ferry commemorating the boats which sailed to markets up the Hudson in the 1850s.
>
> *Crowstepped gables*—at Wall Street station, showing Dutch gables and the wooden fence or 'wall' built to keep out Indians in the 17th century.
>
> *Peter Stuyvesant's house*—in a mosaic at Whitehall Street station. Originally whitewashed, it was derided as the 'White Hall' by the English Governor.
>
> *Steamboats*—at Fulton Street station, actually the Clermont which Robert Fulton designed in 1807, six years after he invented the submarine.
>
> *The City Gaol*—depicted in mosaic at Christopher Street, originally New York's principal penitentiary before it moved to Sing Sing.
>
> *Brooklyn Bridge*—in bas-relief at Chambers Street Station.

Incidentally, the word 'sub-way' was a New York coinage, first used in 1864 to refer to the underground tunnels for cars (and originally carriages) under Central Park.

Slits and Slots—for Newcomers

Newcomers to Manhattan will manage well, as long as they have a subway map and remember whether they're going 'uptown' (north) or 'downtown' (south). Above ground, Gaudíesque green and red lollipops signify subway entrances. A green globe means the entrance is open and staffed 24 hours a day; a red globe that the entrance is sometimes closed, usually at night.

The fare is presently $1.50, no matter how far you go. There are no ticket machines: instead each station has a booth manned by a sullen-looking clerk in a really bad mood. Avoiding eye contact, and, enunciating your request as clearly as possible, ask for either a **Metrocard** (encoded electronically with fares from $6 to $96) or a **subway token** (a brass coin 'good for one fare', sold singly or in packets of 15). Apart from being cross, clerks won't accept bills over $20 or pennies. If you use a Metrocard, you can transfer free of charge between subway and bus and subway. Next, swipe the Metrocard through the slit on the turnstile, or drop the token in a slot in the turnstile, then make your way down to the track, unless you're travelling late at night in which case it's safer to stay in the yellow off-hours waiting area. It's possible to leap over the turnstiles without paying and cops, waiting for you on the other side, know this.

Trains are referred to by **letter** (as in Duke Ellington's A train) or **number** (1–7); the two most efficient lines are the red 1, 2 and 3 trains (taking you up and down the West side of Manhattan, and the green 4, 5 and 6 trains (taking you up and down the East Side of Manhattan). Lines have several other names (like the Lexington Avenue Express, the IRT, or BMT), but as no one can remember these it's simpler to stick to letters and numbers. Express trains (e.g. green 4 and 5 trains and red 2 and 3 trains) are good for getting around in a hurry, but you must keep your wits about you. As well as being fast, expresses are wilful and prone to not stopping where they're supposed to. Which was what the garbled announcement was all about. If you make a mistake, bear in mind that at many stations it's not possible to get to the other side of the track without leaving the station completely and paying the fare all over again. If you miss your stop, get off at one of the bigger stations, such as 14th Street or Grand Central, where you can change over.

By Bus

Bus and subway information: ✆ 1 (718) 330 1234, 6am–9pm daily
Non-English-speakers: ✆ 1 (718) 330 4847
Travel for the disabled: ✆ 1 (718) 596 8585, 6am–9pm daily
Customer complaints and enquiries: ✆ 1 (718) 330 3322

New York's buses are schizophrenic: in the daytime they're packed and so slow that a lot of the time it's quicker to walk; at night, James Bond-types take over the wheel and you zoom along at breakneck speeds basking in the sunshine charisma of your hero-driver. For women, catching a bus late at night is one of the safest options. By day, if you have time to spare, buses are a good way of seeing the city and getting to know New Yorkers. Buses travelling up and down avenues can be excruciatingly slow, cross-town buses are faster even on busy streets like 42nd or 14th. If the bus says 'Limited' on the front, it's an express bus, stopping at major intersections, but still at the mercy of gridlock stagnation.

Bus Etiquette

Bus drivers are a higher breed and will appreciate it if you thank them as you disembark (one is said to salute his passengers with 'Get'cher smile on, folks; nobody rides dis bus today widdout a smile.') The fare is the same as for the subway and you need a subway token (not sold on buses), a Metrocard (not sold on buses) or exact change in quarters (6 x 25¢). If you don't have any of these on you, sometimes a kindly person in the bus queue will offer to sell you a token.

As you pay the fare, ask the driver for a transfer, so you can change from a north–southbound to an east–westbound bus, or vice versa. Transfers cost nothing and last several hours, allowing you to get off, do a spot of shopping, then board your next bus free. Enjoy your ride: passengers on New York buses are entertaining and very chatty: if you're not sure where you're going, your neighbour will gladly help out. Exit the bus from the door in the middle, which you push open yourself. Note that if you do not keep a tight hold on the door it's liable to swing backwards and knock you unconscious.

By Taxi and Limo

NYC Taxis and Limousine Commission (complaints): ℂ 221 8294, 🖷 840 1607

Cabs are about half the price of London or Paris, and it can be cheaper to share a taxi between four than travel by subway. Legitimate taxis are yellow with a medallion on top; gypsy cabs are banned below 79th Street, but are not necessarily dodgy, especially if you negotiate in advance. Many yellow cabs refuse to go to places like the Bronx (though legally they must). Taxis in Manhattan are plentiful; around 11,000 roam the streets each day.

When a taxi is empty the central light on the roof is illuminated and you can hail it from the street. Get in, then tell the driver your destination, stating the intersection (ie '42nd and 5th Avenue'). New York taxi drivers are notoriously vague about addresses: they do a maximum of 10–20 hours' training before going on to the road, and many are absolutely new to the city. Try not to let on that you don't know where you're going: an unscrupulous taxi driver may reward you with a long, expensive detour. Tips are 15%, but unless the trip is *very* short native New Yorkers tip a lot less.

If it starts to rain, go to a coffee bar and wait, in a philosophical frame of mind, for the rain to stop. You won't get a taxi even if you pray. On the other hand, if an old-fashioned **Checker cab** stops for you, count it as a miracle: these huge, luxurious and loveable heffalumps are the kings of Manhattan cabs and nowadays so ancient there are only about ten left on the road. Most of New York's 11,000 yellow taxis are owned by cab companies: to buy one of the coveted medallions costs up to $200,000 and consequently less than a score are privately owned.

Limousines are mostly not limos at all, but large cars run by cab companies for air-port service. If you see a proper limousine waiting in a stupor of boredom outside a prestigious hotel or restaurant it may be a hired limo—in which case you can try asking the chauffeur if he'll take you to your destination for around twice the usual taxi rate. Chauffeurs will occasionally agree to this highly unorthodox arrangement.

car service companies

Useful for booking taxis to the airport. Try the following:

> **All City**, ✆ 1 (718) 402 2323, ✉ 1 (718) 993 1471
> **Bell Radio**, ✆ 691 9191, ✉ 366 4489
> **Carmel**, ✆ 666 6666
> **Tel Aviv**, ✆ 777 7777, ✉ 505 6004

By Motorbike and Scooter

Except for the police hardly anyone rides motorbikes or scooters, mostly because it's considered too dangerous. However, in fashionable circles owning a rare or very expensive motorcycle is considered to be the ultimate in trendiness, and there are even two bike-themed clubs, The Harley Café and Handlebars.

By Helicopter

> **NY Helicopter**, ✆ (1 800) 645 3494
> **Downtown Manhattan Heliport**, ✆ 248 7240
> **East 34th Street Heliport**, ✆ 889 0986
> **West 30th Street Heliport**, ✆ 563 4442

By Ferry

NY Hoboken Ferry: connecting Erie-Lackawana Terminal New Jersey to World Financial Center, Manhattan, 7am–11pm weekdays, 10am–10pm weekends, ✆ 1 (800) 53 FERRY.

Staten Island Ferry: at the foot of Whitehall Street, Battery Park, 24 hours, ✆ 806 6940.

Even New Yorkers avoid driving in the city. Parking is a nightmare. If you do find a space, remember it's illegal to park in front of a fire hydrant, and parking often alternates from one side of the road to the other from morning to evening.

car hire

Avis: ✆ 1 800 331 1212
Budget Rent-a-car: ✆ 807 8700
Enterprise: ✆ 1 800 325 800.

By Bicycle

If you too have the death wish you can pick up second-hand bikes cheaply from junk stores and thrift shops or the Chelsea fleamarket.

bicycle hire

Metro Bicycles: 1311 Lexington Avenue, at 88th Street, ✆ 427 4450, ✉ 427 4452.
Midtown Bicycles: 360 West 47th St., at 9th Ave., ✆ 581 4500, ✉ 581 4503. One of the cheapest.

Long Distance Train and Bus Trips from Manhattan

Penn Station: West 34th Street, between 7th and 8th Aves., ✆ 582 6875.
Long Island Rail Road: trains to Brooklyn, Queens and Long Island leaving from Penn Station, ✆ 1 (718) 217 5477.
Amtrak Information, ✆ 1 (800) 872 7245: express trains to Washington DC and all over the US.
PATH, ✆ 1 (201) 216 2677: trains to New Jersey from Penn Station and the Lower West Side.
Port Authority Bus Terminal, 8th Ave and West 41st St., ✆ 564 8484.
Greyhound Trailways, ✆ 1 (800) 231 2222.

Guided Tours

By Boat, Yacht and Helicopter

If you're new in New York, the best way of orientating yourself is to take the Petrel or Circle Line boat trips round the island (about $20), or, more expensively, a helicopter flight over the top. Otherwise, taking an ordinary bus from one end of Broadway to the other ($1.50) or the Staten Island Ferry (50¢) will be illuminating as well as fun.

Circle Line Cruise: Pier 83, West 42nd Street and 12th Ave., ✆ 563 3200, ✉ 630 8118, *www.circleline.com* (*sailing April–Nov; adm $20, senior* *citizens $16, under 12s $10*). Trips are 3hrs, with a highly recommended 2hr express tour (for $17) or a 2hr evening cruise June–Aug.

Petrel: Battery Park, ✆ 825 1976, 📠 425 4982 (*sailing May–Nov; tickets $8–26*). An elegant 70ft racing yacht, first launched in 1938. Book sailings at least two weeks in advance.

Island Helicopter: leaves from the East River Heliport at 34th Street and the East River, ✆ 683 4575, 📠 564 9574 (*open 9am–9pm, tickets from $44 upwards. No reservations necessary*).

Staten Island Ferry: Staten Island Ferry Terminal at South Ferry, ✆ 806 6940 (*24 hours a day, daily; 50¢*). Ferries to Staten Island and back every half-hour (*see* **Walk IV**, p.161).

Trolleys Round Central Park: ✆ 397 3809 (*leaving weekdays 10.30am, 1pm and 3pm, April–Oct*). 90-minute tours of Central Park.

Specialist Walking Tours

These are mostly high quality and often attended by native New Yorkers, who are keen students of their city.

Big Apple Greeter, 1 Center St., New York NY 10007, ✆ 669 2896, 📠 669 4900, *email 76026.3625@compuserve.com*, volunteer New Yorkers who will meet newcomers and show them a specific part of the city. 'Tours'/meetings last a few hours, and you should specify in advance the area or aspect of Manhattan you would like to be introduced to.

Grand Central Terminal: organized by the Municipal Art Society, 457 Madison Avenue, ✆ 935 3960, 📠 753 1816. The best tour in New York. Tours last an hour, are free and meet every Wed at the station at 12.30pm at the Chemical Commuter Bank. The Municipal Art Society also organizes tours of other Manhattan curiosities, including an abandoned subway tunnel.

Radio City Music Hall: 50th Street, at 6th Avenue, ✆ 247 4777 (*open Mon–Sat 10–5, Sun 11–5, adm around $12*). Tours of Radio City's wonderful Art Deco interior, leaving frequently.

Federal Reserve Bank of New York: 33 Liberty Street, ✆ 720 6130. Free and fascinating tour of the largest underground gold vault in the world, including distressing glimpses of deceased dollar bills being shredded at the rate of $40 million a day (*see* p.168). Phone a week in advance for tickets.

Wild Man Steve Brill: ✆ 1 (718) 291 6825. Botany courses in the field, in parks throughout New York including Central Park. Eccentric, but never boring.

The 92nd Street Y: 1395 Lexington Avenue, at 92nd Street, ✆ 996 1100. Excellent ever-changing programme of Sunday tours all over the city: from visits to the Hasidic community in Williamsburg and photographers' studios in the Flatiron District, to jaunts over the George Washington Bridge into New Jersey.

Lower East Side Shopping Tour: meet Sundays at 11am April–December outside Katz's Deli at the corner of Ludlow and East Houston Sts., ✆ 1 (800) VALUES 4 U (*adm free*).

NBC Studio Tour: 30 Rockefeller Plaza, ✆ 664 4444, (*see* **Walk I**, p.106).

Tours of Harlem

Although thousands of tourists visit Harlem independently, the sights are spread out and difficult to see all in one day. Unless you have lots of time in Manhattan, you may see more of the black metropolis if you join in one of the tours recommended below. Otherwise make sure that you at least visit Harlem for Sunday brunch (*see* **Food and Drink**, p.220).

Harlem Your Way!: 129 West 130th Street, ✆ 690 1687, ✆ 866 7133. Packaged Harlem, including evening knees-ups described as 'champagne jazz safaris'.

Harlem Spirituals, Inc.: 1697 Broadway, at 53rd St., ✆ 757 0425, ✆ 757 0435, from $29 upwards. Religion gets a slice of the tourism market: visits to gospel services on Sunday mornings, also evening cabarets, nightclubs and restaurants, and historical tours including shops and museums.

Penny Sightseeing Company: 1565 Park Avenue, ✆ 410 0080. The oldest Harlem tour-company: owner-operated coach rides round Harlem, also walking and gospel tours from $18. Reserve a day in advance.

Tour Operators and Special-interest Holidays

in the UK

American and Worldwide Travel, 45 High Street, Tunbridge Wells, Kent TN1 1XL, ✆ (01892) 511894, ✆ 5166001. Tailor-made holidays.

Bon Voyage Travel and Tours Ltd., 16–18 Bellevue Road, Southampton SO15 2AY, ✆ (01703) 330332, ✆ 220248.

British Airways Holidays, Astral Towers, Betts Way, Crawley, West Sussex RH12 2TB, ✆ (01293) 722742, ✆ 722702. Short breaks and mini packages, theatre tickets booked on arrival.

Celebrity Cruises (UK) Ltd., 17 Old Park Lane, London W1Y 3LG, ✆ (0171) 355 0680, ✆ 412 0908. Week-long cruises from New York to Bermuda and back.

Crystal Holidays, Crystal House, Arlington Road, Surbiton, Surrey KT6 6BW, ✆ (0181) 240 1000, ✆ 255 6406. 2–3-day stopovers as well as skiing holidays in Vermont, Boston and Maine.

David Dryer Sports Tours, 4th Floor, 73 Farringdon Road, London EC1M 3JB, ✆ (0171) 831 7799, ✉ 831 8482. Trips arranged that take you to American football, baseball and ice hockey matches. Uses 3–4 star hotels in Madison Square Gdns.

Funway Holidays International, 1 Elmfield Park, Bromley, Kent BR1 1LU, ✆ (0181) 466 0333, ✉ 313 3547.

Mainstreet USA, Ouston House, Ouston Lane, Ouston, Co. Durham DH2 1QX, ✆ (0191) 410 6333, ✉ 410 2299. Tailor-made helicopter tours, weekend breaks and shopping trips.

North America Travel Service, 7 Albion Street, Leeds, W.Yorks LS1 5ER, ✆ (0113) 246 1466, ✉ 244 0481. Weekend breaks dinner cruises, helicopter rides arranged.

Osprey Holidays, Broughton Market, Edinburgh EH3 6NU, ✆ (0131) 557 1555, ✉ 557 1676.

STA Travel, Priory House, 6 Wrights Lane, London W8 6TA, ✆ (0171) 361 6379, ✉ 376 2335. For young independent travellers.

Titan Travel, 26–30 Holmethorpe Ave, Redhill, Surrey RH1 2NL, ✆ (01737) 760033, ✉ 779288. Escorted coach tours to Montreal and Washington via New York for the over-50s.

Trailfinders Ltd., 42–50 Earls Court Road, London W8 6GU, ✆ (0171) 937 5400, ✉ 937 0555. Discounted stays at top hotels.

Up and Away Holidays, 19 The Mall, Bromley, Kent BR1 1TT, ✆ (0181) 289 5050, ✉ 466 9099. Weekend breaks including shopping trips, helicopter filghts and dinner cruises.

Worldwide Journeys, 243 Euston Road, Lonodn NW1 2BU, ✆ (0171) 383 3898, ✉ 383 3848. City breaks and fly-drive holidays.

in the USA

Dailey-Thorp Travel, 330 West 58th Street, New York, NY 10019, ✆ 1 (212) 307 1555, ✉ 974 1420. Music and opera tours.

New World Travel Inc., 780 Third Avenue, 27th Floor, New York, NY 10017, ✆ 1(212) 754 9100, ✉ 888 2375. Study tours, languages and cultural programmes, ecology and parks programmes.

Practical A–Z

NB: to the British, Americans write dates backwards, so 2/14/47, for example, means 14th February 1947.

For precise dates, times and details, consult *Time Out*, the *Village Voice*, or the Metropolitan section in the Friday edition of the *New York Times*.

For information on events and activities celebrating the **Millennium** call the New York Convention & Visitors' Bureau on ✆ 484 1234.

September

The year starts in September. A fungoid Manhattan suddenly comes to life after a long, somnolent summer: everyone scurries back to work, and the city feels almost spring-like as the racing, football, hockey, basketball, theatre, opera and art gallery seasons get airborne.

First Mon   **Labor Day Weekend**. Supposed to honour the American worker, Labor Day signifies the end of the summer and is observed with some reverence: crowds mob beaches on Long Island, which from then onwards will be deserted until Memorial Day in May.

A highlight of Labor Day Saturday is **Wigstock** (✆ 213 2438, and ✉ 213 0204 for information): an anti-matter Woodstock, held on the 54th Street piers (and orignally in Tompkins Square Park), in which drag queens and kings and transvestites mime to back-up tapes in front of a wig-wearing audience. The nutty festival has now become so big and popular that there are plans to hold it in Central Park or the Christopher Street piers in the West Village. Meanwhile all weekend in Brooklyn, near the museum, there is the festive **West Indian Carnival** with floats, dancing and concerts.

19   **Festa San Gennaro**, held in Little Italy on Mulberry Street, over two weekends. Festival in honour of the patron saint of Naples, fire accidents and plagues, who miraculously walked out of a furnace unscathed in AD 305. The climax of the Manhattan festival is when a bronze effigy of the saint, stuck with dollar bills, is paraded down the street. The crowds, burgers, goldfish bowls and doughnuts are uncannily reminiscent of a pier resort on the east coast of England.

Late Sept   **New York Film Festival**, until early October. Excellent festival which in the past has premiered Bertolucci's *The Conformist*, Buñuel's *The Discreet Charm of the Bourgeoisie* and Truffaut's *Day for Night*. To be sure of getting tickets, apply to Lincoln Center about 5 weeks in advance. If you haven't, it's not impossible to get returns on the day (✆ 875 5050 or 877 1800 ext 489 for details).

Last Sun	**Atlantic Antic**, along Atlantic Avenue in Brooklyn (✆ 1 (718) 875 8993. Authentic *casbah*, courtesy of Brooklyn's exuberant Middle Eastern community on Atlantic Avenue, with belly dancers, *durbek* drums and even camels, as well as exotic foods and spices— *babaganouj*, myrrh, frankincense, and pastries streaming honey.

October

12 (or nearest Mon)	**Columbus Day**, a national holiday commemorating October 12th 1492 and the first sighting of the Bahamas. New York Italians are proud of their murderous ancestor but much to their fury Spanish-Americans persist in claiming him as a relative. The Columbus Day Parade up 5th Avenue from 44th Street to 72nd is a mainly Italian event, lasting from early afternoon to dusk and featuring about 20,000 marchers, 28 bands, marching Catholic schoolgirls and 18 floats; also a tableau of Ligurian flowers (✆ 397 8222).
Third Sun (or there- abouts)	**New York Marathon**. Watching the sweating armpits on television, you will be relieved you're not there. Starting on the Staten Island side of the Verrazano Narrows bridge and finishing at the Tavern on the Green in Central Park, the ill-assorted joggers puff 26.3 miles through all five boroughs (✆ 860 4455).
31	**Hallowe'en**. Children pelt each other and passers-by with eggs and shaving foam. Trick-and-treating is thought dangerous in Manhattan but is more common in Queens, the Bronx and Brooklyn. All over the city, residents decorate their houses with pumpkins, bunches of red maize or cobwebs, ghouls and witches. If you're in Manhattan don't miss the Village **Hallowe'en Parade**, when 50,000 revoltingly clad revellers thread their way through the West Village to Washington Arch.

November

Last Thurs	**Thanksgiving**. Macy's department store organizes a parade of cartoon characters (Snoopy, Buzz Lightyear, Superman) from the Natural History Museum down Broadway to their shop in Herald Square. Across the country, 37 million people watch this on TV. More amusing than the parade is **'Inflation Eve'** when Donald Ducks and Minnie Mouses are inflated with helium in the Natural History Museum park from 6pm onwards on the night before. A surreal sight (✆ 494 4495 for more information).

Thanksgiving is supposed to commemorate the first harvest of the European settlers, but these days is more of a dress rehearsal for Christmas. The day after

Thanksgiving, Manhattan is saturated with festive jollity. New Yorkers try to carry on with normal life whilst immersing themselves in a frenzy of shopping and socializing.

Last Fri   The day after Thanksgiving, and the biggest shopping day of the year in America (which is why Macy's throws a parade).

December

New Yorkers get hysterical as shopping turns into a city-wide addiction.

Early Dec   On the first Thursday after Thanksgiving) there is the ritual **lighting of the Christmas tree in Rockefeller Center** with 5 miles of lights (✆ 632 3975 for more information). 5th Avenue is spruced up with the country's classiest Christmas trees and decorations, including the massive 57th Street snowflake and the Rockefeller Center angels. Piquant window displays in shops like Barney's and Bergdorf Goodman's reinforce the feeling that Christmas in Manhattan is as delectable and glamorous as it is expensive. Carol singers are discreetly everywhere, chafing delicate nerve-endings with their insidious omnipresence. Meanwhile Lincoln Center launches a long run of *The Nutcracker*, (✆ 870 5570).

Mid-Dec   More singing: this time a **Messiah Sing-In** at Avery Fisher Hall led by 21 conductors and involving 3000 participants.

31   On **New Year's Eve** fascinated revellers gather to watch an intrinsically unthrilling ritual invented by the New York Times in 1908 in which an ambiguous ball descends from the top of Times Tower, in Times Square, to the bottom. People get drunk, and the New York Roadrunners Club organizes a **midnight run** in Central Park. There's a beautiful **firework display** in Central Park (call ✆ 360 3456 for details); in **St Marks Church** on 10th Street and 2nd Avenue a hundred poets read in the New Year with extracts from their own work (✆ 228 9682).

January

Mid-Jan   An oppressive and deadening month in which an atmosphere of depression everywhere is only slightly relieved by fantasies of finding a bargain at the **Winter Antiques Show** at the Seventh Regiment Armory, Park Avenue at 67th Street (✆ 1 (718) 665 5250 for more details).

Last week   **Chinese New Year** (✆ 397 8222 for exact date and details). Parades, firecrackers, dancing dragons, spring rolls and prawn toast.

February

Black History Month: Interesting events all over the city highlighting important aspects of African-American history.

Early Feb   At the **Empire State Building Run-Up** heavily insured fitness fanatics dash to the 86th floor in as little as 12 minutes.

22   **Sales** in stores on Washington's birthday. More sales on 12th February (Lincoln's birthday) and 14th February (St Valentine's).

March

Early March   **New York Flower Show**: on Pier 92 by the Hudson and Broadway and 59th Street, for a week and a half (call ✆ 696 3941 for information and watch the press). In 'odd' years there's also the **Whitney Biennial** showing the best of contemporary American art on all floors of the Whitney Museum until June. In 1999 only the Biennial will be replaced by a Century Show of works from the permanent collection on all five floors of the museum. Not to be missed.

Mid-March   **New Directors, New Films**: a festival of 25 new films at the Museum of Modern Art (✆ 708 9480).

17   **St Patrick's Day Parade**. Now one of the biggest holidays in US cities—a knees-up in which New York's rowdiest Irish-Americans paint their faces green and descend on 5th Avenue and the bars in Manhattan. Not a day for heated political debates (✆ 397 8222).

20/21   **Earth Day**. Ecological happenings involving street fairs, guitars, homemade bread, arnica, and the ringing of the good old UN Peace Bell.

25   **Greek Independence Day Parade**. A more upscale affair, with elegant floats, bands and majorettes.

April

1st weekend   The **Coney Island** freak show opens for the summer season.

Easter   New York celebrates **Easter** with typical gusto, another parade and an Easter Show at Radio City (✆ 247 4777). Children hard-boil eggs and colour them with special dying kits, and on the Saturday before Easter there is an **egg-rolling contest** on the Great Lawn in Central Park.

Mid-April   Extravagant and beautiful **cherry tree blossom** in the Conservatory Garden in Central Park and also the Brooklyn Botanical Gardens.

15	Income-tax deadline: on the steps outside the General Post Office, Hebrew National hand out free **hot dogs** at midnight to anyone making last-minute submissions.
23	A parade in Columbia Heights to celebrate **St George's Day**.

May

2nd Sun	**Brooklyn Bridge Day** and **Mother's Day**—the latter established by the US Congress in 1914 as a secular version of the Christian festival of Mothering Sunday. Father's Day was also invented in America four years before in Spokane, Washington, and various greetings card companies have since decreed a Grandad's Day and Stepmother's Day. Celebrations on Brooklyn Bridge.
Mid May	**Ukrainian Festival** on East 7th Street between 2nd and 3rd Avenues. One of the city's jolliest street festivals with tombolas, Ukrainian wooden toys, food and painted eggs or *pysansky*.
17	**Martin Luther King Jr. Memorial Day Parade** celebrating the achievements of the Atlantan civil rights leader, assassinated in 1969 by James Earl Ray.
3rd week	**9th Avenue Food Festival**. Two-day street festival of food. Stalls and shops between 37th Street and 54th sell food made by communities from all over the city—Italian, Argentinian, Greek, Indian, Ukrainian, Mexican, West Indian, Spanish, Japanese and Haitian.
Last Mon	**Memorial Day**. Beaches officially open; summer begins in earnest; Manhattanites retreat to the country.

June

All month	The **Metropolitan Opera** puts on free performances in the Sheep Meadow in Central Park attended by over 100,000 people (✆ 360 6000 for more details) and at the **Central Park Summerstage** musicians as various as Suzanne Vega, Queen Latifah and Carlota Santana perform numerous free afternoon gigs from June–August (✆ 360 CPSS). Also in Central Park, the outdoor Delacorte Theatre puts on two plays for its June–Sept **Shakespeare in the Park** festival. Free tickets are distributed at 6pm on the day of the performance, one per person (✆ 598 7100). Bring a picnic.
First Sun	**Puertorriqueño Day Parade**, one of the largest and most riotous parades, involving flags, floats, city politicians and Puerto Rican celebrities including Celia Cruz and Willy Colon—up 5th Ave from 44th to 86th Streets. For dates and times of all parades, ✆ 397 8222.

2nd Tues	**Museum Mile Festival**. *Free* entrance to the museums between 82nd and 102nd Street, plus street performers.
Early June	**Toyota Comedy Festival** (℘ 1 (800) 79 TOYOTA). Comedians from all over the US gather in Manhattan.
10	**Feast of San Antonio**. A smaller version of the Feast of San Gennaro in September.
Late June	**Lesbian and Gay Pride Day Parade**. Starting at Columbus Circle, marchers wend their way down 5th Avenue to Washington Square, and from there all over the West Village. The celebrations commemorate the 1968 Stonewall Riot, and last a week, culminating in open-air dancing on the Chelsea and West Village piers.

July

As temperatures rise, New Yorkers get crosser than usual.

All month	Juilliard School students perform a mixed bag of free **MoMA summergarden concerts** at the Museum of Modern Art (℘ 708 9500).
First week	**Restaurant Week**. Some of Manhattan's smartest restaurants do prix fixe lunch for $20–25.
4	**Independence Day**. Organized firework displays all over the city, and in less well-off areas like the Lower East Side projects, firecracker wars. View it all from a rooftop, or from Riverside Park. The next day most people abandon Manhattan for Long Island beaches.
2nd Sun	**Fiestas de Loiza Aldea**. A version of the Festival of St James the Apostle held in the Puerto Rican town of Loiza Aldea. Mass is held at the Church of San Pueblo on Lexington Avenue and East 117th Street, and an effigy of St James is carried to Ward's Island via the footbridge on 102nd Street. After the procession there is a Latin American festival on the island.
Full Moon	**Feast of O-Bon**: Japanese festival of music and dancing held in Riverside Park on the Saturday nearest the Full Moon. On the night itself New Age moon-gazers gather in Central Park.

August

As humidity levels rise, most New Yorkers leave Manhattan. The ones who stay behave in an erratic, eccentric manner—some say because the shrinks are all on holiday.

Early –mid Aug	**Harlem Week. Parades**, exhibitions, music, art, food and sports events in Harlem (℘ 427 7200).

Climate and Best Time To Go

'A cloudy day, or a little sunshine, have as great an influence on many constitutions as the most real blessings or misfortunes.'

Joseph Addison, 1711

Manhattan has more interesting temperature fluctuations than London or Paris. Winters can be bitterly cold and summers disconcertingly moist. Although the winter period is nowhere near as freezing as Boston or Chicago, Manhattan's sky-scraper canyons get windy and quite icy, forcing pedestrians to mince along sidewalks in a way that explains why penguins evolved a way of walking on the sides of their feet without falling over. As soon as the Christmas festivities are over Manhattanites tend to lie low in centrally heated apartments, avoiding full expo-sure to the elements as much as possible. (A lot of New Yorkers know how to get from 34th Street to Central Park via department stores, atriums and underground walkways without even going outside, but the route is quite complex.)

In the summer Manhattan can be very humid, even in temperatures of around 75°F. The only respite if you don't have air-conditioning is to loiter in freezing department stores—bear in mind, however, that this practice can bring on colds and bronchial conditions. In July and August Manhattan gets quite tropical and electric thunderstorms may break out. If this happens, go to the top of the Empire State Building or on to your roof. You have about half an hour before a flash flood drenches you from head to toe. If you can, visit Manhattan in the spring, between April and June, or in the autumn, from September to November. The weather at these times varies between congenial and exquisite. Seasons change abruptly: one day it can be snowy and cold, the next leaves on every tree will be fully out and restaurant tables cluttering every sidewalk. The light—reminding you that Manhattan is an island on the sea—can be startlingly beautiful at these times.

New Yorkers are just as obsessed by the weather as the British, the only difference is that their forecasts are accurate. It's worth switching on the weather channel before leaving an apartment building or hotel, as air-conditioning and central heating are always misleading.

Consulates

Australia: 636 5th Ave., ✆ 408 8400
Britain: 845 3rd Ave., ✆ 745 0200
Ireland: 515 Madison Ave., ✆ 319 2555
India: 3 East 64th St., ✆ 879 7800
Iceland: 370 Lexington Ave., ✆ 686 4100
New Zealand: 630 5th Ave., ✆ 586 0060

Crime

Police and emergency: ✆ 911
Nearest police station: ✆ 374 5000
US Secret Service: ✆ 637 4500
FBI: ✆ 384 1000
NYPD Sex Crimes Report Line: ✆ 267 7273
Crime Victims Hotline: ✆ 577 7777
Gay and Lesbian Anti-Violence Project: ✆ 807 0197
The New York Task Force Against Sexual Harassment: ✆ 274 3210

New York is one of the safest cities in the USA. In the mid-1990s crime hit its lowest levels since the 60s: in 1996 the annual murder tally was 983, slashing in half the record total of 2245 homicides in 1990; shootings in the city were down 21%; and only 19% of victims were killed by strangers, compared with 37% in 1993. In the first six months of 1997 killings fell another 30% to levels last seen in the 50s and New York dropped out of the FBI's league of America's 200 most violent cities...

Broken Windows and 'Quality of Life'

In 1990 a right-wing think tank called the Manhattan Institute started publicizing theories about crime and how to improve 'quality of life' on the streets of New York. Some of these ideas were taken up by William Bratton, New York's charis-matic Police Commissioner until 1996. Thanks to Bratton the NYPD now holds regular gun amnesties. Thousands more arrests are made for small offences (smoking marijuana, jumping turnstiles, urinating in the street), and anyone who is arrested has any guns or other weapons in their possession confiscated on the spot. As long as offenders are in custody they can be checked out for any outstanding warrants and taken to court on other more serious offences. Finally under Bratton's 'broken windows' policy the NYPD has collaborated with communities and busi-nesses to reduce 'visible signs of decay' and improve 'quality of life' on the streets, the theory being that a neglected neighbourhood full of broken windows, litter and graffiti is an invitation to commit crime. Bratton's 'quality of life' policies have been so successful that they are fast catching on with police forces as far afield as Glasgow and politicians all over Europe. The NYPD avoids using the term 'zero tol-erance', mostly because the phrase implies an atmosphere of crackdowns, intolerance and possible racism and infringement of civil liberties. One upshot of new quality of life policing techniques in New York is that currently 1.6 million people are incarcerated in jails in New York State.

The Manhattan Institute was also a major influence on Mayor Giuliani. In 1993 Giuliani made 'quality of life' the buzzword of his election campaign, and in the last few years Giuliani has articulated more often and more effectively than anyone else the message that safety on the streets is a fundamental civil right. In Manhattan especially crime wins votes: most New Yorkers believe that Giuliani manoeuvred Bratton out of office in 1996 (replacing him with Howard Safir) because he thought the Police Commissioner was getting too popular. In the same year polls showed that about 50% of New Yorkers disliked Giuliani, but 75% supported his policies on crime. In November 1997, Giuliani looks sure to be re-elected as mayor for his handling of the crime issue alone.

In reality, of course, many factors have helped to bring crime rates down. The crack epidemic (always associated with crime and violence) has slowed up and heroin, which sends addicts into an incapacitating lethargy, is taking its place. Real estate is booming and property owners in Manhattan are banding together into BIDs ('business improvement districts'), which pay up to $6m annually to private security and sanitation firms to keep districts safe and clean. Community boards are being given increased powers to refuse licences to rowdy clubs and bars. Finally, under former mayor David Dinkins the NYPD significantly increased in size by 11,000 into a force of 38,000. The falling crime rate has had a profound impact on life in New York, especially in Manhattan. On streets and in subways the city feels safer and looks cleaner. Nevertheless things haven't changed so utterly that you should completely relax (a symptom of this is the average New Yorker and his tabloid's obsession with juicy crime stories). Organized crime is still big, from Vietnamese and Chinese tongs in Chinatown, to Colombian, Haitian, Jamaican and even Albanian gangs in the Bronx. The Latin Kings is a 3000-strong gang which operates a policy of BOS or Beating On Sight (even though their leader recently went religious). Manhattan itself still has thousands of pickpockets and petty thieves who prey on tourists. Be wary at all times, and as a rough guide:

- *Don't wander alone at night.*
- *Don't dawdle in obvious danger-spots. The Port Authority Bus Terminal on 8th Avenue is a favourite haunt of chicken-hawks—named after a kind of vulture from the mid-West. Crime has fallen in Times Square, but crowded, touristy areas like this will always attract hustlers and pickpockets. One trick is to bump into a victim with an ice-cream, mop up his or her jacket and incidentally lift a wallet.*
- *Don't believe anyone who tells you an intricate story involving cars, women or money. Pickpockets have a trick of pointing at a potential victim and bawling 'Stop, thief!'*
- *Some people suggest carrying a spare $40 on your person as 'mugger's money'. Statistically the chances of being mugged are quite slim (around 30,000 to one) and about 95% of victims are unharmed.*
- *Mace is outlawed (but available over the counter in some shops).*

Report any thefts to the nearest police station (call © 374 5000 to find out where). Police in New York can look frightening, with their riot bats, guns, beer guts, mostly Caucasian faces and names like Serge and Rollo. Remember, while you're taking all this in, to ask for a statement so you can claim back the theft from your insurance.

Curtness

Except in streetcars one should never be rude to a lady.'

O. Henry, *Strictly Business*, 1910

New Yorkers are mostly very polite. However, at some point you may brush up against a stereotypically gruff New Yorker (usually a driver or shopper in a mood). If you're good at being rude, let rip, remembering that New Yorkers are better at rudeness than anyone else and telling them they are wrong will only inflame their powers of vitriol and invective. Sometimes this can be quite fun. Alternatively, you can take refuge in politeness: confronted with a kind word or an English accent the average New Yorker will melt.

In private, New Yorkers are *spectacularly* polite: they open doors, shake hands, help you on with coats and pay for meals. They use coasters and mats on tables; they hardly ever swear in front of ladies, and if they do they apologize. They pretend not to notice clumsiness and uncouth behaviour, and on the whole they have nicer manners than the British.

As far as being a business person in New York goes, remember that PR types, and anyone else with a vested interest in the 'image' of the city, sometimes react defensively to what they think is criticism—'We don't have more litter than anyone else,' one said bitterly. 'It's just that the wind blows it around more.'

Disabled Travellers

A few years ago, a Federal judge ordered the transport system to provide city-wide access for the disabled. In reply the city facetiously proposed a plan allocating a chauffeur-driven limousine for every citizen with a disability—and they proved this would be cheaper than remaking all the buses and subway stops.

These days Manhattan is still not the most accessible of cities, but things are improving. There are currently only a score or so of accessible subway stations, and to get around the system in a wheelchair you'll still need some assistance. Buses, on the other hand, are fully accessible: since 1993, all buses have been able to 'kneel' (or tilt hydraulically to the kerb), and all have been fitted with special wheelchair lifts at the centre of the bus. If you have a collapsible wheelchair taxis must stop by law; if a driver does not stop, take down the medallion number (if possible) and complain to the Taxi Commission on © 221 8294.

According to the Americans with Disabilities Act, all public buildings built after 1993 must be accessible, and all buildings erected before then must be modified as far as possible. Most public buildings in New York do at least have ramps and other basic facilities for the disabled: to find out which ones don't, check in the HAI's free *Access for All* guide (*see* below).

Travel Information for People with Disabilities: ✆ 1 (718) 596 8585. Information including subway maps in Braille.

Travel Information for People with Impaired Hearing: with access to a teletypewriter, ✆ 1 (718) 596 8273.

Big Apple Greeter, 1 Center St., New York NY 10007, ✆ (1 212) 669 3602, ✉ 1 (212) 669 4900, TTY 1 (212) 669 8273, *76026.3625@compuserv.com*. Free service linking non-disabled as well as disabled visitors with volunteer greeters who will show you the city on arrival. With special information on accessibility in Manhattan.

The Society for the Advancement of Travel for the Handicapped, 347 5th Ave., New York NY 10016, ✆ 1 (212) 447 7284, ✉ 1 (212) 725 8253: for more information worldwide, also regular newsletters.

Lighthouse Inc., 111 East 59th St., between Park and Lexington Avenues, ✆ 1 (800) 334 5497: advice for blind people visiting Manhattan and guidebooks in Braille.

The NY Society for the Deaf, 817 Broadway, at 12th St., ✆ 1 (212) 777 3900.

Mayor's Office for People with Disabilities, 52 Chambers Street, Office 206, New York NY 10007, ✆ 1 (212) 788 2830. Ask for the free *Access Guide for People with Disabilities*, as well as general information.

Access for All, Hospital Audiences Inc., 220 West 42nd St., New York NY 10036, ✆ 1 (212) 575 7663, TTY 1 (212) 575 7673. A free and very detailed guide describing the accessibility of Manhattan's cultural institutions.

State Commission for the Blind and Visually Handicapped, ✆ 1 (212) 961 4440.

Theatre Access Project for the disabled at 1501 Broadway, ✆ 1 (212) 221 1103 or TTY ✆ 1 (212) 719 4537.

Domestic Hazards

American locks are quite tricky. Interior doors have small buttons in the centre which can slip into place and lock you in by accident. Front doors have at least two or three different locks, and sometimes police locks as well (sliding iron bars designed to keep out intruders equipped with battering rams).

> **Emergency locksmiths**, Champion Locksmiths, ✆ 362 7000, open 24 hours. You will need proof of residence, naturally.

Cockroaches can be dealt with in various ways: sprays will kill them instantaneously; Roach Motels, cardboard boxes full of glue where 'roaches check in, but they *don't* check out', will stop them in their tracks forever; poisons (with names like Combat and Black Flag) will stupefy them; exterminators (or pest controllers) will blast them to kingdom come; finally Javan geckos (bought from a pet shop and allowed to roam free) will eat them.

Roach Busters, open 24 hours, ✆ 1 (718) 232 5507.

Gas, steam and electrical emergencies at the Con Ed Emergency Line: gas, ✆ 683 8830; electrical or steam, ✆ 683 0862, open 24 hours for leak-reportage and emergencies.

Electricity

It's hard to electrocute yourself in New York as the voltage is only 110. You can buy transformers for razors and hairdryers in pharmacies or drugstores. If you're taking a computer, purchase an adaptor in advance from the company you bought it from. You should also invest in something called a power buster, since New York suffers from power spikes, or surges of electricity, which gradually destroy the brain of the machine till it dies. Plugs are two-pronged and you will need an adaptor.

To foreigners, light switches can be confusing. To turn a light on, you put the switch up, not down; bedside lamps have switches that you turn clockwise.

Electrical emergencies: ✆ 683 0862.

Emergency Services

Police, ambulance and fire: call ✆ 911.

Complaints about emergency services: Department of Health Emergency Medical Service, ✆ 1 (718) 416 7000.

Precincts: ✆ 374 5000 to find the location of the nearest police precinct station.

Domestic Violence, call 1 (800) 942 6906, open 24 hours.

Sex Crimes Report Line of the NYPD, ✆ 267 RAPE, open 24 hours. Immediate help plus referrals on a line managed by women-only.

Bellevue Rape Crisis Service, ✆ 561 3755, open 9–5. Free emergency treatment for rape victims, counselling and referrals.

The Samaritans, ✆ 673 3000, 24 hours.

Alcoholics Anonymous, ✆ 683 3900.

Cocaine Anonymous, 1 (800) COCAINE.

Poison Control Center, ✆ 764 7667.

Animal Bites, ✆ 566 2068.

Homeless New Yorkers

Nobody is sure how many people are homeless in Manhattan: estimates range from 50,000 to 60,000, and sometimes as high as 90,000. In the summer especially you'll come across beggars and homeless people in the smartest as well as the most run-down parts of town. Some are mentally ill or disabled, some are war veterans, many have simply fallen on hard times. Some New Yorkers give beggars money (or food), and some do not, on the principle that the money would be better distributed by a charity for homeless people.

Insurance

It is **wise** to take out an insurance policy before leaving home. There is no health service in the States and breaking a leg there can end up costing an arm here. Once you're in the USA, keep your insurance policy in a safe place and travel with a credit card so you can be sure of getting immediate medical attention if you fall ill.

Campus Travel, at London Student Travel, ℗ (0171) 730 2101, has one of the cheapest deals, covering students and anyone aged under 35 for medical costs up to £2m—for around £20 for ten days without baggage, and £30 for ten days with baggage. Campus will also insure over-35s for medical costs up to £5m, plus baggage and personal money, at around £40 for 10 days. It has offices with USIT in New York, ℗ 663 5435.

All travel agents will offer some kind of travel insurance.

Laundry

Hotels charge high rates for laundry. If you can't afford these, hunt out a local launderette. These charge by the pound and are wonderfully cheap and efficient: wash 'n' fold for a sack of dirty clothes can cost under $10 and takes a couple of hours.

Lavatories, Restrooms and Bathrooms

For the uninitiated foreigner, **bathrooms** are minefields. 'Bathroom' can mean a loo, or the whole shebang: showers, bidets, jacuzzis, plus deluxe self-flushing loos. 'Restrooms', however, only have lavatories. Occasionally they don't have handles for flushing, but disconcerting rubber knobs on the floor which you step on.

Baths and showers are more difficult. A tap (called a faucet in America) diverts water from the shower to the bath. Usually the water comes out of one faucet, not two, and to change the temperature you turn a knob. In theory, flow automatically reverts to the bath when the shower is turned off. Instead of plugs, some baths have a lever, located somewhere next to the tub, which you lift and twist.

Manhattan used to be all right for **lavatories**. In the 19th century one of the city's most innovative vendors ever patrolled the streets with a bucket and a billowing cloak. In 1857 Joseph Gayetty (another Manhattanite) marketed the world's first commercial loo paper, made of hemp, 'medicated' and good supposedly for keeping piles at bay. In the 1940s, under the far-sighted LaGuardia administration, loos in New York reached a pinnacle of excellence: there were weekly inspections of 1676 public conveniences, and in the final report only 12 of these were found to be dirty.

In *recent* years, loos have not been New York's forte: so much so that in 1990 four homeless people filed a lawsuit against the city for failing to provide public conveniences. Since then, councillors have been planning to spend $3 million on 100 high-tech automatic loos modelled on those of London and Paris. At the time of going to press, however, only a handful of these have materialized: one, conveniently enough, is around the side of City Hall; others are rumoured to be in Central Park and Battery Park. In Manhattan, finding a loo can be harder than you imagine: in places like the East Village some restaurants lock their toilets and only hand out keys to patrons. Finally, in your frenzy to relieve yourself, don't forget that lavatories/toilets are referred to by a variety of euphemisms including bathroom, restroom, even sitting room, comfort station and men's/ladies' room. Your main options are as follows:

- *Scout out WCs in public institutions (libraries, hospitals, museums, universities and municipal offices). The best are in the New York Public Library.*

- *Swagger into the lobby of a big hotel, department store or public atrium (places like Trump Tower and the Sony Building). The swankiest loos in New York are in the International Center of Photography on 94th Street, Macy's on 34th Street, and Barney's department store in Chelsea.*

- *Every time you stop at a restaurant or café, remind yourself to use the lavatory.*

- *For those with weaker bladders, invest in a copy of* Where to Go, *a useful guide to Manhattan's toilets, available in most bookshops.*

Left Luggage

You can leave luggage at Grand Central Station, on 42nd Street and Park Ave., ℂ 340 2555 at a cost of around $2 a day. However, *try not to forget that the luggage department has restricted opening hours*: 7am–8pm weekdays, and 10am–6pm weekends.

Medical Matters

If you need to see a doctor, look up 'Clinics' and 'Physicians and Surgeons' in the *Yellow Pages*. The Stuyvesant Polyclinic on 2nd Avenue and East 9th Street is one of the cheapest.

Remember that in America, you say 'I am sick', not 'I am ill'; but 'sick' can also mean repellent or revolting, as in 'pornography is sick'. Also, 'gas' means wind, 'mucus' means catarrh, 'cramps' are period pains, and 'jock itch' is a nasty rash around the testicles. The doctor will send you to a 'pharmacist' or chemist to get 'medication' or medicine, and this will come in the form of 'tablets' or pills.

Ambulances: ✆ 911

Doctors On Call: 24-hour house-call service, ✆ 1 (718) 238 2100

Emergency dentists: ✆ 1 (800) 439 9299, 24 hours

Roosevelt Hospital: has a 24-hour emergency room at 458 West 59th Street, ✆ 523 4000

St Vincent's Hospital: has a 24-hour emergency room at 7th Avenue and 11th Street, ✆ 604 7998

Rape Help Line: ✆ 267 7273

AIDS Information Hotline: ✆ 447 8200

Gay Men's Health Crisis Hotline: ✆ 807 6655

Herpes Hotline: ✆ 213 6150

NYC VD Hotline: ✆ 427 5120

24-hour pharmacy: Kaufman's at Lexington Avenue and 50th Street, ✆ 755 2266

Planned Parenthood at The Margaret Sanger Center: 380 2nd Avenue and East 17th Street—for sympathetic family planning, contraception and abortion advice, ✆ 677 3320

Animal bites: ✆ 566 8611

Contagious disease: ✆ 788 4199

Food poisoning: ✆ 566 8611

Lead poisoning: ✆ 334 7893

Fifth Avenue Center for Counseling and Psychotherapy: 43 5th Avenue, ✆ 989 2990

New York Psychoanalytic Institute: Discount therapy by psychiatrists-in-training, 247 East 82nd Street, 879 6900

Television

At first watching television in America is quite mesmerizing; however, it soon gets boring. One of the problems is that listings are complicated—whether you consult an apparently straightforward daily paper or the bible of America, the monthly *TV Guide*. There are scores of channels, but none of the letters and numbers listed correspond to the letters and numbers on the remote control. None of which matters, because most of the channels show the same dreary ragoût of commercials, game shows, talk shows, cop shows, soap operas, sitcoms and more commercials.

The world's first television commercial, showing a ticking Bulova watch, was broadcast by a New York television station on 1 July 1941. Nowadays, commercials dominate everything else and these can be charmingly artless. Films are chopped up into 15-minute slots so companies can squeeze in as many commercials as possible; sitcoms and TV dramas have commercials sandwiched *in between* credits.

CBS, on channel 2, NBC on 4 and ABC on 7 do **news**. With the exception of the *News Hour* show on public television and CBS' popular *Sixty Minutes* (Sundays at 7pm), analysis is inclined to be sketchy, especially with international news stories. NY1 concentrates on local New York news and despite the irritating presenters is good for minute-by-minute **weather forecasts**. Channels 13, 21 and 31 are the only non-commercial stations and they show a curious mix of well-intentioned instructional programmes (on sewing, painting, sociology etc.); nature programmes (Goldie Hawn pursuing a half-blind elephant through Africa); plus a mishmash of imports from Britain (*Crossroads*). On the whole, shows gaining the highest television audiences are sitcoms (*Seinfeld*, *Murphy Brown*, *Sabrina the Teenage Witch*), hospital dramas (*ER*), talk shows (a national addiction with hundreds a day on such scintillating subjects as 'Wives treated like servants' and 'Mates who primp excessively'), quizzes (*Jeopardy!*), and finally Fox's *America's Most Wanted* which has captured nearly 500 fugitives since the show started in 1988.

free TV show tickets and standbys

Geraldo, CBS, 524 West 57th St., New York NY 10019. Apply a month in advance enclosing a stamped addressed envelope or queue for standbys before noon at 530 West 57th Street on Tuesdays or Thursdays.

NBC, 30 Rockefeller Plaza, New York NY 10112. One standby ticket per person distributed from 9am onwards from the 49th Street entrance to Rockefeller Center for *Late Night with Conan O'Brian* and on Saturdays for the ailing *Saturday Night Live*.

David Letterman, Ed Sullivan Theatre, 1697 Broadway, New York, NY 10019. Apply three to four months in advance by post, or wait for standby tickets before noon at the Ed Sullivan Theatre.

Sally Jessy Raphael Talk Show, PO Box 1400, Radio City Station, New York NY 10101. Send a stamped addressed envelope three to four months in advance, or wait for standbys from 10am at 515 West 57th Street.

cable

Most apartments and hotels have cable TV, which can be a lot more palatable than broadcast TV, if sometimes quite bizarre. HBO, TMC and MAX show recently released movies; CNN shows 24-hour news reports; C-SPAN shows live sessions from Congress and the House of Commons; COM or Comedy Central shows comedy ranging from *Absolutely Fabulous* to the *Daily Show*, a nightly programme of crazy-but-true Americana; TNT is a blissful channel specializing in old films and revivals. Other cable channels focus specifically on subjects including the arts (BRV or Bravo), home shopping, weather, Latin American soap operas (featuring television's most inept actors), prayer (preachers with a knack for making money) and pornographyPublic Access television, on channels 16, 17, 34 and 69, lurks at the bizarrest and most disconcerting end of the cable TV spectrum.

Radio

Despite the dull-sounding names, New York radio is excellent. AM stations play mostly country music, talk, salsa and religious shows. Below is a random selection of the most interesting:

FM stations

WNYC (*93.9 FM*): The best news bulletins, and entertaining as well as informative talks on New York's politics and arts, the much-loved *New York & Co.* weekday discussion from noon to 2pm (with guests ranging from the art critic Robert Hughes to actress Janet McTeer), and *All Things Considered*, portraits of ordinary Americans by radio journalist David Isay.

WBLS (*107.5 FM*): At the end of the dial: popular, black-owned and playing funk and soul plus disco and hip-hop classics on Friday and Saturday nights, and jazz Sun–Thurs midnight–5am.

WCBS (*101 FM*): Rock and roll oldies and the Top 40.

WKCR (*89.9 FM*): Columbia University's own station, best for jazz and dance.

WQXR (*96.3 FM*): Conservative classical music station, big on 19th-century orchestral works and opera.

WPAT (*93.1 FM*): Popular salsa and Spanish language station.

WXRK (*92.3 FM*): Known as K-Rock and featuring electronic rock and a 4½hr morning chat show by Howard Stern, New York's top shock jock.

AM stations

WWRL (*1600 AM*): Rhythm and blues.

WINS (*1010 AM*): Public radio with all-day news, weather and traffic round-ups and no advertisements. Its two rivals are **WABC** (*770 AM*), which offers medical advice and theological discussions as well as weekly wrap-ups, and **WCBS** (*880 AM*).

short-wave

BBC World Service: Available on the 49-metre short-wave band.

Newspapers and Magazines

Only three daily papers remain: two tabloids, the *New York Post* and the *Daily News* (printed in the world's grubbiest newsprint); and one broadsheet, the *New York Times*, dubbed the 'grey lady' because of its prehistoric appearance and dread of all things new-fangled. The *Times* is nevertheless well-written and a surprisingly gripping read—and whereas the tabloids are guaranteed to sustain your rapt attention for at least three seconds, the *Times* will actually tell you what's going on in the world. In September 1997 the *Times* opened printing plants in Boston and Washington DC as well as Queens, New York, in a move towards turning the newspaper into a national that will rival the terminally dull *USA Today*. It also takes the daring step of introducing much more colour to its news and sports pages. For visitors to Manhattan it's useful for arts and restaurant reviews and listings: there's the excellent *Science Times* on Tuesdays, a daily Metro section and on Sundays the corpulent *Sunday Times*, currently weighing in at 5lbs.

The two tabloids have both been ravaged by television and plummeting circulation figures. In the eighties the *Daily News* lost over $100m and a bitter five-month strike culminated in the newspaper (and its pensions) falling into the slippery hands of Robert Maxwell. Over at the *New York Post* ownership disputes and equally heavy debts led to the *Post*'s being acquired by Australian press baron Rupert Murdoch. Although the *Post* was originally slightly more liberal than the *News*, both papers are now a similar mix of crime stories, Hollywood gossip, excellent funnies (up to 30 strip cartoons a day) and 20–30 pages a day of sports reports. The *Daily News* has the edge, especially since Pete Hamill—a lovable 'Daily Planet' breed of hack who started his career on the *Post*—was appointed the *News'* editor in 1997. Hamill is attempting to gussy up the *News* with crispier headlines, juicier muckraking and highbrow writers such as William Goldman and Norman Mailer.

New York's only 'alternative' paper was the weekly *Village Voice*. This once fearless and provocative journal is nowadays **free**, owned by a pet-food millionaire and marginalized by its unrelenting politicization of everything, especially as it struggles to compete with the glossier London-owned listings magazine *Time Out*, a clone of which arrived in New York in 1995.

The *New Yorker*, under revolutionary British editor Tina Brown, is more glamorous in concept than reality, and astutely indulges its readership's preference for a fuddy-duddy 1920s look, serious articles, elegant cartoons, highbrow fiction and wryly written reviews and capsule listings. The glossy and gossipy *New York Magazine* is a diverting mix of articles on local politics and jaunty goings on about town, plus listings, shopping bargains and strange advertisements for role-play escorts such as sensuous governesses and upscale nurses. By strong contrast, *Union Jack— America's Only National British Newspaper* contains month-old news about Britain written by journalists called Quentin and Ronald.

'You mention it, we got it' is the slogan of the Hotalings news-stand on 42nd Street and in Manhattan you will of course able to get hold of practically any newspaper or magazine in the world. Most of the news-stands in Manhattan are owned or managed by Indian or Pakistani vendors, who bought up many of the concessions in the sixties and seventies when immigrants from the Indian subcontinent were allowed into New York in large numbers for the first time.

At supermarket checkouts, you will see copies of the *National Enquirer*, and battalions of rivals including the *National Examiner* and the *Weekly World News*. These are worth buying for the headlines alone: 'Brave Doctors Remove Live Bomb From Man's Chest', 'JFK Was Related To King Arthur', 'Pit Bull Savages Killer Shark', 'Top Model Eats Herself To Death', and 'Your Shoe Size Tells How Long You'll Live'.

Internet

Emailers can get their name in electronic lights in Times Square by sending a message c/o ***timesquare@joeboxer.com***. A drawback being that messages are displayed on a billboard advertising underpants.

The following may mean something to readers:

äda 'web: *www.adaweb.com*. New York-based art gallery.

Bianca's Smut Shack: *shack.bianca.com/shack/*. On-line sex, drugs and chat c/o Bianca.

Business and Leisure Information on NYC, email: *nyc@mediabridge.com*.

The East Village: *www.theeastvillage.com*. Soap opera chronicling the lives of typical East Villagers.

Hedda Lettuce Worldwide: *www.hedda.com/*. A New York drag queen on-line.

Netizens Cyberstop New York: *www.columbia.edu/~hauben/nyc-guides. html*. Comprehensive list of websites on New York City.

New York Yellow Pages: *www.bigyellow.com.*

Pseudo Online Network: *www.pseudo.com/*. Weekly listings of websites.

Sublets Online: *www.aprtsforrent.com or www.aptguides.com.* Limited listings of apartments for rent in Manhattan and the boroughs.

Urban Diary: *getrude.art.uiuc.edu/ludgate/*. Fictional diary about life in the city.

View from the 77th floor of the World Trade Center: *www.wtca.org/view. html*. A 'Webcam' site, bringing visitors live views from a camera set on the 77th floor of the World Trade Center.

Money

Take double the amount you think you will need. Apart from having shops full of things you'll want to buy, Manhattan is slightly more expensive for groceries, medicines and other essentials than anywhere else. At a pinch you can get by on $30 a day; to feel comfortable you need about $60–70.

Take some dollars for when you arrive (most bureaux de change close at 6pm), and the rest in **traveller's cheques**. Buy cheques in dollars: most large shops and restaurants in Manhattan will accept these (especially if they're American Express) instead of cash. Don't bring cheques in sterling or other currencies: changing them in banking hours is a bore, and you might find that some banks refuse to cash them in any case. If you run out of cash completely, arrange for money to be transferred from abroad to branches of Thomas Cook and American Express. Alternatively, you can sell your own blood (look up 'Blood Donations' in the *Yellow Pages*).

Banks are open between 9am and 3 or 3.30pm, and closed on weekends.

lost or stolen traveller's cheques

American Express: ✆ 1 (800) 221 7282

Visa: ✆ 1 (800) 227 6811

Thomas Cook: ✆ 1 (800) 223 9920

The financial cogs of America turn on plastic, and **credit cards** are invaluable, not just for emergencies and getting instant cash from ATM machines, but also for all hotels, restaurants and shops.

Currency

American **currency** is straightforward. There are $1, $5, $10, $20, $50 and $100 notes or bills. When New Yorkers hand over change, they say 'six-fifty', not 'six dollars fifty'. There are 100 cents to the dollar and four types of coin:

Penny: small copper coin equal to one cent (¢). Practically useless, and by the time you go home you will have half a dozen of the little devils jangling around in your pockets. This is because of a 8¼% city and state sales tax which is added on to nearly everything.

Nickel: zinc-nickel coin worth 5 cents. Almost as useless as pennies.

Dime: or 10 cents; silver, much smaller than the nickel, but worth double.

Quarter: or 25 cents; a large silver coin with rough coppery edges. Save these up to use in public telephones and on buses.

changing money out of banking hours

American Express Travel Service: 65 Broadway, between Rector Street and Exchange Place, ✆ 493 6500. There are nine other American Express counters in Manhattan. Call and ask for details of their locations.

Chequepoint USA: 609 Madison Avenue at 58th St., ✆ 750 2255 or 1 (800) 544 9898 (*open weekdays 8–8, Sat 10–8, Sun 10–7*). Ask for branches in other locations if necessary.

Harold Reuter & Co: Met-Life Building, 200 Park Avenue, Room 332 East, ✆ 1 (800) 258 0456 or 661 0826 (*open weekdays 8.30–4*).

Thomas Cook: 41 East 42nd St., ✆ 757 6915 (*open weekdays 9–5*). Will transfer money from abroad, for a fee.

Packing

New Yorkers like to dress up, and you won't feel out of place in your snazziest togs. At work, dress codes are surprisingly formal and in some companies women are banned from wearing trousers or skirts above the knee. Bow ties and braces (in the US: suspenders), are a status symbol—only those at the very summit of the corporate ladder wear them. Outside the office anything goes, no matter how casual or strange. Be sure, however, to bring at least one pair of comfortable walking shoes (most women and men in Manhattan wear revolting-looking sneakers on their way to work and do a quick change at the entrance). If you're a man and plan to eat in certain restaurants you'll need a jacket and tie and long trousers. In the winter in Manhattan woman *and* men wear stuff like black furry hats, pink earmuffs, orange plastic galoshes, yellow raincoats and red balaclavas. Woolworths sell plastic skins which fit over shoes and high heels, useful in the rain.

Except for Gentleman's Relish, you'll be able to buy more or less anything in New York. Bring a small pair of binoculars, if you like, for looking at views and skyscraper tops. Camera film, pharmaceuticals and medicines are expensive unless you buy them from discount stores all over the city. Plastic knapsacks, earmuffs, cosmetics, dark glasses, computer disks, cameras, electric razors and collapsible umbrellas are very cheap.

Post Offices

> 'I travelled along a portion of the frontier of the United States in a sort of cart, which was termed the mail. From time to time, we came to a hut in the midst of the forest; this was a post-office.'
>
> Democracy in America, 1835, Rev. Francis Bowen, trans. Henry Reeve 1862

The post office is one of America's last nationalized businesses, and it's notoriously inept. To get an impression of this you need only visit Manhattan's main GPO (on 33rd Street and 8th Avenue)—a monolithic monument to bureaucracy, open 24 hours and containing over 5000 rooms, including hospitals, wheezing elevators, and a hopeful inscription from Herodotus: 'Neither snow nor rain nor heat nor gloom of night stays these couriers from the swift completion of their appointed rounds'. Totalitarian confusion reigns supreme here; immersing yourself in it can be fun, especially if you go to **auctions** of year-old unclaimed parcels, held once a month in the GPO basement (© 967 8585 for times and dates: bidders aren't allowed to open the lots, but can shake and prod at the 'viewing'). If you're in the city on 15 April at midnight, you may also like to join the impromptu gathering of TV cameramen on the steps of the GPO when Hebrew National hands out **free hot-dogs** to New York desperadoes hurrying to meet the deadline for income-tax returns.

Sending and Receiving Mail

At the time of going to press, sending a postcard anywhere in the world costs 50¢. An airmail letter costs a minimum of 60¢.

Stamps are available at news-stands, delicatessens and some supermarkets, as well as from Manhattan's 59 post offices (*open Mon–Fri, 9–5, and Sat 9–12*). Avoid buying stamps from **vending machines** in shops, hotels, drugstores or supermarkets, as these charge three times a stamp's face value.

Post boxes are blue and look like rubbish bins. Letters posted at post offices will get to their destinations more quickly than letters 'thrown away' in post boxes. Remember, mail can take between three to five days to get from state to state, and there's only one postal delivery a day. Make sure you write a return address *and a zip code* on the top lefthand corner, or your parcel stands a fair chance of turning up in at the GPO auction. Sending parcels by **overseas surface mail** is quite cheap, but the speed of arrival depends on the caprices of the weather. Usually it takes about two months to get to Europe: in case it doesn't get there at all, you can insure it. Rules and regulations verge on the absurd: above all, make sure the parcel is wrapped in brown paper and stuck together with gummed paper.

Finally, if you're visiting Manhattan in the summer, keep an eye out for Manhattan postmen and women, who look startlingly handsome dressed in regulation navy shorts and peaked caps.

Poste restante: c/o General Delivery, General Post Office, 421 8th Ave., New York NY 10001. If you don't pick up mail within ten days it will be returned; arrive at the GPO well before 1pm bringing photographic ID.

Public Holidays and Opening Hours

Contrary to the belief that Manhattan is open all the time, banks, shops and some businesses are liable to close on the following days:

> **1 January** (New Year's Day)
> **Third Monday in January** (Martin Luther King's Birthday)
> **Presidents' Day** (Usually second or third Monday in February and commemorating George Washington and Abraham Lincoln's birthdays)
> **Third Monday in May** (Memorial Day)
> **4 July** (Independence Day)
> **First Monday in September** (Labor Day)
> **Second Monday in October** (Columbus Day)
> **11 November** (Veteran's Day)
> **Fourth Thursday in November** (Thanksgiving)
> **25 December** (Christmas Day)

Banks are open Monday to Friday only and usually close at 3 or 3.30pm.

Museums are mostly closed on Mondays and open late on Tuesdays or Thursdays when with any luck admission may be free. Exceptions include MoMA, which is open late on Thursdays and Fridays and closed on Wednesdays, the Guggenheim which is open late on Fridays and Saturdays and closed on Tuesdays, and the Natural History Museum which is open daily and late on Fridays and Saturdays.

Churches are mostly closed except on Sundays and weekday evening services.

Shops in Midtown and the Financial District keep business hours; drugstores are open till late; shops in the East and West Villages and Upper West Side and Chelsea stay open until 9 or 10.

Smoking

You may love New York but if you smoke New York will hate you. Smokers are the pariahs of Manhattan: everywhere you go you'll see groups of them, huddled together outside buildings, shunned as scrupulously as a colony of lepers. Anyone who rashly lights up in a confined space or walking along a street can expect torrents of revulsion, and the odd swipe. Smoking is banned on all public transport, and in banks, hotel lobbies, airports, sports stadiums, restrooms, all enclosed public areas, taxis, theatres and supermarkets. Under a law passed in 1995, smoking is also banned from all restaurants, except those seating fewer than 35 people (although smoking *is* allowed in some larger restaurants, as long as the bar is a minimum of 6 feet away from dining tables—for more detailed information *see* **Food and Drink** p.191).

In a city where perversity is the norm, Manhattanites have recently developed a thing about cigars. The craze has been aggressively marketed in *Cigar Aficionado*, a preposterously glossy magazine launched in 1993 by New York publisher Marvin Shanken and currently boasting one million readers. Riding on the marketing wave, 'cigar bars' have been flourishing in Manhattan; cigar shops have opened up inside restaurants; and many clubs feature a glamorous in-house cigar lounge. Between 1993 and 1997 cigar sales in the US rose from 2.1 billion to 3 billion. Women, spurred on by seeing the likes of Linda Evangelista, Demi Moore and Whoopi Goldberg posing on the front cover of *Cigar Aficionado*, have been especially susceptible to the hype.

For detailed listings of smoking restaurants see *The Smoker's Guide to Dining— Lighten Up New York* by Michael Leo, also available on the Internet at *www.lighten-up.com.*

Steam

Wherever you go in Manhattan, you'll come across city steam: billowing out of a Cup Noodle sign on Times Square; cooking oysters in the Grand Central Oyster Bar; broiling pleasure-seekers in the 10th Street Turkish baths; creating artificial clouds at the Metropolitan Opera and Radio City; and most obviously of all, swirling everywhere out of manholes, brickwork and ruptures in the tarmac on streets and sidewalks.

Steam heating was first introduced to downtown Manhattan in 1882, six months before Thomas Edison brought electricity to New York. Nowadays fifty miles of steam mains lie under the city streets and 500°F steam courses through Manhattan at 15 million lbs an hour, supplying office blocks, schools and businesses all over the city with a very economical form of central heating. On the downside, much of the steam still whisks round the city via a network of original 19th-century pipes, which have an alarming tendency to erupt in lethal explosions. In 1989 a jet of steam gorged through concrete and paving on Gramercy Square, causing several injuries, denting cars, and coating an apartment and a tree with asbestos snow.

Steam emergencies: © 683 0862

Telephones

The New York telephone system is decentralized and ultra-efficient. Telephone operators are civil and have names like Dwight, Caspar and Marlon. A ringing tone is a single doleful moan whereas an engaged tone is fast and chirrupy. Distant muzac means you've been put on hold and you'll probably stay that way for some time.

Pay Phones

It costs 25 cents to make a local call from a **public telephone** and **pay phones** can be found on practically every street corner in Manhattan. The pay phones are owned by different telephone companies, and you'll be charged a different rate accordingly. As a rule, NYNEX phones offer cheaper rates and slightly more reliable service. If you need to find a number call **directory enquiries** on © 411 (for New York City) or © 1 + area code + 555 1212 (outside New York City).

Pay phones do not include *Yellow Pages* (businesses and services) or *White Pages* (private numbers and businesses). To consult these you can try a pay phone in a hotel, restaurant or department store.

Area Codes and Calling Outside Manhattan

The **area code** for Manhattan and the Bronx is © (212) and the area code for Brooklyn, Queens and Staten Island is (718). **Whenever you use an area code make sure you preface it with a 1 (i.e. dial 1 (718) to call Brooklyn from Manhattan).** 1 (800) numbers are 'toll free' and cost nothing. Some numbers come in letters: a good old-fashioned system in which the letters correspond to an alphabet printed on the telephone dial (so phone sex lines have numbers like 970 INYA; whereas the New York Aquarium is 1 (718) 265 FISH).

In this book, if no code is given, assume the number is in Manhattan, © 1 (212).

Long Distance Calls and Phone Cards

To call Manhattan from the UK, dial © 00 1 (212), and to call Brooklyn, © 00 1 (718). In New York you can dial **long distance and international calls** directly from any public or payphone. To make an international call from New York dial © (011) followed by the country code. These include:

Australia: 61	**Papua New Guinea**: 675
France: 33	**Russia**: 7
Germany: 49	**Spain**: 34
Ireland: 353	**Switzerland**: 41
Italy: 39	**UK**: 44
Netherlands: 31	**Vatican City**: 39
New Zealand: 64	**Zimbabwe**: 263

The operator (✆ 0) will tell you any other country codes you may need.

To find out the cost of a long distance or international phone call, dial the number without putting coins in and a voice will tell you how much you need to deposit. You can pay by credit card or with coins, but remember that to pay in coins you'll need about 22 quarters. Apart from the troublesomeness of getting hold of so much change all at once, you may find that 22 quarters really weigh down your pockets.

A better idea is to buy a **phone card** from a deli, grocery store, supermarket or newsagent. NYNEX phone cards are useful for local cards; and **long distance phone cards** issued by a number of different telephone companies offer very cheap international rates for calls abroad. Using one of these cards, a 30-minute phone call to Europe costs $5–$10 (the best for the UK is the PTI Phonetime card). The cards come with instructions, which usually involve calling a 1 (800) number and punching in a pin code. They're especially useful for making telephone calls from hotels, which often charge high rates for local as well as international calls.

Call Collect/Reverse Charge Phone Calls

To reverse the charges, call the operator (✆ 0) and ask to make a 'collect' call. To call an operator in your own country from the US free, dial one of these numbers:

UK: ✆ 1 (800) 44 55 667
Ireland: ✆ 1 (800) 562 6262
Australia: ✆ 1 (800) 682 2878
New Zealand: ✆ 1 (800) 248 0064

The cheap rate for calls is from 11pm to 8am weekdays and all day on weekends, although your European friends won't be too pleased if you forget the 5-hour time difference.

Useful Numbers

Operator: ✆ 0
Directory Enquiries: ✆ 411 (for numbers in Manhattan) or ✆ 1 + (area code) + 555 1212 (for numbers in other area codes).

Pay Services:
Speaking clock: ✆ 976 1616
Sportsphone: ✆ 976 1313
Weather: ✆ 976 1212
Stock Market prices: ✆ 976 4141
Jokes: ✆ 976 3838

Traffic: ✆ 830 7666
Dial-a-Dinner: ✆ 779 1222
Insomniacs' Hotline: ✆ 337 4790
Dial-a-Prayer: ✆ 246 4200
Dial-a-Hearing-Test: ✆ 737 4000

Time

It is 3500 miles across the Atlantic, and New York is 5 hours behind London. For a few weeks in March, however, it is 6 hours behind, since London changes to British Summer Time (Daylight Saving Time) about three weeks before America. Australia is 16–18hrs in front of New York. Chicago, which operates on Central Time, is an hour behind New York and California, operating on Pacific Time, is three hours in front of New York, eight hours behind London.

Tips on Tipping

Remember to tip the good-looking barman who sells you your pint, the grinning bell-hop who carries your luggage, the grouchy concierge who hands you a towel in the restroom, the unctuous captain who shows you to your table and the chatty taxi driver who drives you to your door. Waiters, waitresses and barmen are all underpaid, and rely on tips to top up their salaries. If they don't get a tip they will sometimes turn nasty. Tips in restaurants are between 15 and 20%, which can be calculated in seconds by doubling the sales tax (8¼%) and adding or subtracting for good or bad service. Between 15 and 20% also applies to barbers and hairdressers. Unless the journey is very short, New Yorkers tip taxi drivers a lot less than 15%. Delivery men, doormen who find you a taxi, restroom attendants, coatcheck girls and boys, porters and shoeshiners will also give you the beady eye. Tip them a dollar at least, or dodge their glances and run.

Tourist Information

The official New York State Tourism Office is at 633 3rd Avenue, 32nd floor, New York, NY 10017, ✆ 803 2246, ✉ 803 2279. For information on New York City contact the New York Convention and Visitors Bureau, 2 Columbus Circle, ✆ 397 8222. It has thousands of free leaflets and subway and bus maps. Or try the information stand at 1465 Broadway in Times Square. The Restaurant Hotline (888 FOOD) answers questions about prices and menus, and *New York Magazine* has recorded listings about current attractions, ✆ 880 0755. For listings of theatre, film, and the arts and for classified ads see the free weekly *Village Voice*, the daily press or *Time Out New York*.

History

'...though I have kind invitations enough to visit America, I could not, even for a couple of months, live in a country so miserable as to possess no castles.'

John Ruskin, *Fors Clavigera*, vol. I, letter 10, 1871

More and more, too, the old name absorbs into me—MANAHATTA, 'the place encircled by many swift tides and sparkling waters'. How fit a name for America's great democratic island city! The word itself, how beautiful! how aboriginal! how it seems to rise with tall spires, glistening in sunshine, with such New World atmosphere, vista and action!

Walt Whitman, 1819–92

Manhattan sits on a bed of three-billion-year-old rock. You can see chunks of it in Central Park, black Manhattan schist glittering with slivers of mica. This close-packed hard rock is practically the only thing in Manhattan which is durable.

In the Pleistocene Period two glaciers steam-rollered down from the Arctic, grinding to a halt over Manhattan. Later on, sabre-toothed tigers, giant beavers, bisons, sloths and tapirs meandered up from the tropics. Not long ago workers dug up a mastodon, a kind of 15ft-long elephant with tusks and shaggy auburn hair, at what is nowadays 141st Street and Broadway.

Discovery, and Early Profiteering

Nearly one and a half million years after the glaciers and the mastodons, ancestors of the American Indian migrated to North America across the Bering Straits from Siberia via Alaska. They roamed Manhattan for several thousand years—until **Giovanni da Verrazano**, searching out a mythical Northwest Passage to the East, stumbled on New York Bay. There, he found 'a very agreeable place between two small but prominent hills', populated by friendly 'Indians' dressed in birds' feathers who 'came towards us joyfully, uttering loud cries of wonderment'.

About six different **Algonquin** tribes lived in the area, planting maize, beans and tobacco, and hunting reindeer, bobcats, otters and wild turkeys. Virgin Manhattan had fish, game and berries in abundance: at the south end of the island were flat salt marshes; in the middle, hills, forests and streams; and at the far end Harlem was filled with fertile plains and meadows.

Strong currents forced Verrazano back to his caravel before he had a chance to step ashore, and nearly a century passed before the first European set foot on Manhattan. On 6 September 1609 **Henry Hudson** anchored the *Half-Moone* in the Lower Bay. Hudson was an Englishman, working for the Dutch East India Company, but supposedly the first tribe he encountered thought he was a Supreme Being who lived in a floating house. 'Strong drink was offered which made all gay and happy', and the unknown land was christened Mannahattanink: 'island of general intoxication'. So runs a story told to a credulous Moravian missionary by a tribe of Delaware Indians in 1790. The genuine derivation is obscure, but probably comes from the Algonquin and means 'island', or 'Island of the Hills'.

Hudson was more intent on discovering a passage to the Orient than finding land, so he immediately sailed upriver, charting its course as far as the present-day state capital, Albany. He did not find the spice route, but he did find something just as precious: beaver, mink and otter furs, and Indians willing to trade them. This was enough to convince the Dutch that the area was worth colonizing, and in 1610 and 1614 a group of Amsterdam merchants dispatched several boats on reconnoitering trips, and a trading post was established at Fort Nassau in Albany. Hudson himself returned in 1610, this time under the British flag, only to find himself icebound with a starving crew who finally mutinied, abandoning him to a chilly death in the depths of New York Bay.

The first settlers came over in 1619 and 1624. There were 30 families in all, a mix of Dutch, French-speaking Walloons and black slaves. The main settlement was upstate, at Fort Nassau, but eight families and some cattle were left behind under the walnut trees of Nut Island, nowadays called Governor's Island. In 1625 a larger group settled at the south end of Manhattan. Finally in 1626 **Peter Minuit**, the Director-General of the Company, purchased Manhattan for trinkets worth 60 guilders, which 19th-century historians calculated as worth $24. The deal was hardly a purchase, however, since the tribe Minuit dealt with didn't come from Manhattan, and anyway the Indians, who had land in abundance, had completely different notions of ownership from that of Europeans.

Speculation became and remained the city's *raison d'être*. While the rest of the early colonies were started by settlers escaping religious and political persecution abroad, New Amsterdam was founded on hopes of commerce and trade. The first, urbanized settlers set up Nieuw Amsterdam in the image of their fatherland. They could have picked a better spot on the island—with brooks, ponds and lakes—but instead they chose flat, swampy land more reminiscent of Holland. The infant city had a windmill, a canal (the Heere Gracht or Gentleman's Canal), and narrow crow-stepped houses built gable-end to the street, with Dutch *stoeps*, or stoops: steep-stepped porches leading to a raised ground floor.

Colonial New York: Free Trade, Strong Drink and Riots

You will have heard of our taking of New Amsterdam... 'Tis a place of great importance to trade. It did belong to England heretofor, but the Dutch by degrees did drive our people out and built a very good town, but we have got the better of it and now 'tis called New York.

King Charles II

By the 1660s, Dutch New York was already a busy trading post. In 1644 the West India Company opened up the station to traders outside the corporation. Eight English merchants emigrated to the city, and the first black settlement, owned by freed slaves, developed in today's SoHo. The next year a Jesuit missionary was told that 18 languages were spoken on the island. The early colonists paid scant attention to the strictures of their governors and were indifferent to religion, and so exasperated one pastor that he denounced them all as 'uncivil, and stupid as garden poles'. Trade thrived, however: in only a few years the Dutch transformed Manhattan from countryside into a grubby, prospering, entirely man-made city. By 1670, the Englishman Thomas Denton wrote a eulogy to Manhattan describing the island as a new commercial Canaan 'where the land floweth with milk and honey'.

In the 1640s bloody wars broke out with the Indians as a result of the high-handed policies of the governor, **William Kieft**. He organized a protection racket, imposed a tax on the Indians, and built a barrier, actually a wooden fence, across today's Wall Street to protect the city. To set things back to rights, in 1647 the Company sent in **Peter Stuyvesant**. New Amsterdam, Stuyvesant said sneeringly on arrival, was 'more a mole hill than a fortress'.

Stuyvesant had come hot-foot, as it were, from the Dutch colony in Curaçao where Portuguese sailors had blown off his leg with a cannonball in a naval tussle. Nicknamed Old Peg Leg behind his back, Stuyvesant tramped around New Amsterdam on a wooden stump with silver attachments for ceremonial occasions. Authoritarian, priggish and quick-tempered, Stuyvesant administered the colony with a rod of iron. His first act was to close pubs on Sundays and at 9 o'clock on other nights, a reckless move, since the settlers were keen drinkers and nearly a quarter of the colony's thriving businesses were grog shops. Stuyvesant then tried to exile a group of Brazilian Jews who arrived in the colony in 1653, and had Quakers lashed and beaten. However, commerce was king in New Amsterdam, and the Company, who insisted on religious tolerance, told Stuyvesant to desist. Under Stuyvesant's 17-year administration New Amsterdam matured into a city and in 1653 got its first rudimentary representative government when a common council was set up under orders from the Hague.

In 1664, in the middle of Dutch trade wars with England and France, Charles II gave the Dutch colony to his brother, the Duke of York. In March a 'ragged troup' of British warships duly raided Dutch towns on Long Island. Their justification for the assault was a dodgy claim based on John Cabot's voyages of 1498. Eventually a fleet under **Colonel Richard Nicolls** blockaded New Amsterdam Harbor and demanded surrender. Stuyvesant defiantly tore the letter to shreds and held out for 11 days. Unfortunately the city's fortifications were in a wretched state, and its citizens phlegmatic and impassive. On 8 September, the British took the city without a shot; New Amsterdam became New York; instead of going back to Holland, a disconsolate Stuyvesant retired to a farm on the Bowery.

Under the English, Manhattan clung to its slipshod morals and loose lifestyles. In 1692 a shocked Anglican chaplain described a city addicted to flip (a rum and beer toddy that smelt of ammonia) and 'cursing & Swearing, some doing it in that frequent horrible & dreadfull manner as if they prided themselves both as to the number and invention of them'. It seemed that typical Manhattanites lived together out of wedlock, and were only able to have conversations with each other in loud voices while constantly interrupting one another. Governors were notoriously spineless, especially the lackadaisical **Edward Hyde**, who went about dressed as a woman and had his portrait painted wearing a décolleté gown cut in the latest fashion. Eventually Hyde was arrested and ended his days in a debtors' gaol.

In 1688, inspired by the Glorious Revolution, **Jacob Leisler** and a group of Protestant radicals seized the fort. The group took over government of the city for nearly two years, during which time they called Manhattan's first municipal elections. Leisler was an unflinchingly loyal partisan, but when William of Orange finally sent a new governor in 1789, he was unfairly tried and hanged for treason.

In the next few years rumbling dissatisfaction with the administration voiced itself in uprisings, fires and robberies which were blamed on Negro slaves. The most important event of the period, however, was the trial of the newspaper editor, **Peter Zenger**. In 1725 the city's first newspaper, the *New York Gazette*, was published, but in no time at all this mutated into a mouthpiece for Willam Cosby, the city's corrupt governor. Zenger and his colleagues formed an oppositional faction, and published a newspaper of their own, the *New York Weekly Journal*. When the *Journal* took to satirizing government officials as circus animals and exposing the desperate poverty of city-dwellers, Zenger was clapped into gaol. Andrew Hamilton, Pennsylvania's brilliant attorney general (and also, incidentally, the architect of Independence Hall), came to his defence, acquitted Zenger, and struck a critical blow for freedom of speech in America.

Revolution and its Rewards

In 1763 the Treaty of Paris concluded the Seven Years' War with the French, who conceded most of their American possessions to England. Relieved of the French menace, the colonies suddenly united in resentment of the English. New York had more Tories than any of the other colonies, but it also had a vociferous contingent of militant patriots. When the British tried to pay off debts from the war with provocative new taxes like the Sugar, Stamp and Townshend Acts, the **Sons of Liberty** took to the streets. They declared independence in City Hall Park, burnt an effigy of Governor Colden and ripped up and melted down a statue of George III on Bowling Green. In January 1770, a few days before the Boston Massacre, the Battle of Golden Hill broke out near Wall Street. Though it was really no more than a scuffle, New Yorkers think of it as the first engagement of the American Revolution.

New York occupied a critical position between the southern colonies and New England, and the British went all out to grab control. In the spring of 1776, while **Washington** made his headquarters in Greenwich Village, General Howe moved 200 ships into the harbour. Later that summer the two sides met near Brooklyn Heights at the Battle of Long Island, in which Washington's troops were outnumbered by two to one. Under the cover of fog, Washington managed to retreat up Manhattan Island to Washington Heights, while a Quaker matron called Mrs Murray supposedly distracted Howe and his troops with her hot cakes and songs. At the next confrontation, the Battle of Harlem Heights, Washington beat the British and escaped to White Plains with his ragged troops.

The British occupied the city and for the next seven years New York became a thriving Tory town. The British played cricket, went whoring, and, on a more cultural level, listened to concerts and watched plays. They kept thousands of rebel soldiers in prison ships moored on the Hudson, where many of the prisoners starved to death in intolerable conditions. In 1781 there was excitement when Prince William Henry, the first member of the royal family to set foot in America, paid a visit to the garrisoned city. But in 1783 **Lord Cornwallis** surrendered New York and Washington triumphantly marched from Harlem down to the Bowery. As British troops evacuated, their parting gesture was to grease the flagpole to prevent Revolutionaries raising the flag of the new Republic.

For a short time New York became the capital of the USA. Congress members met in the old City Hall, which was revamped by **Pierre L'Enfant** (who later designed Washington DC). In 1789 George Washington was elected and inaugurated in a new Federal Hall as President. The capital then moved to Philadelphia. In the next decade, however, New York's population doubled to 60,515, turning it into the largest city in the nation. The first stock exchange and the first bank were organized, and Tammany Hall, founded in 1786 as a friendly society, developed into a powerful Democratic Party machine which would later dominate New York politics.

At the same time **Alexander Hamilton** published *The Federalist* with John Jay; 85 essays on the new democracy that have become part of America's secular scriptures. An outstanding mover and shaker in New York life in this period, Hamilton was as romantic a figure as any Treasury Secretary could be (he was America's first, and his face is on the $10 bill). Born in the West Indies, he met an untimely end in a famous duel with Aaron Burr; however in a brilliant career he oversaw the beginnings of American industry and personally did much to ensure that New York, and not Philadelphia or Boston, became the nation's financial capital.

By 1809, New York's population topped 100,000. The city continued to prosper in spite of the 1812 War when a British fleet once again blockaded the harbour and cut off foreign trade. To direct its growth, in 1811 the commissioners laid out Manhattan in a chequerboard of 2028 rectangular blocks, at a point when practically the whole of Manhattan north of City Hall was still rural. Anticipating that traffic would run between docks on the east and west sides of the island, the commissioners laid out 155 cross-streets with only 12 north-south avenues along its length. The only vestige retained of pre-colonial Manhattan was the diagonal Broadway, once an Indian trail.

Dawn of the Metropolis; Immigrant Waves and Tammany Sachems

The Erie Canal opened in 1825 at a cost of $7million. Connecting Albany and Buffalo, the canal gave the east coast access to trade with the Midwest and the Great Lakes, and massively boosted the economy of New York Harbor, making it easily the most important port on the whole eastern seaboard. By the middle of the century, according to one recent historian, maritime trade made New York 'the unchallenged metropolis of America'.

While the port expanded and prospered, it also started to bear the brunt of the first of the great tidal waves of European immigrants that swept America via New York from the early 19th century until the 1920s. In 1819 the first 19,000 immigrants, mostly Irish Catholics, appeared on the scene. Between 1840 and 1857 another three million followed: Irish escaping the potato famines and Germans fleeing the failed Revolution of 1848.

New York was unprepared for the influx. Slums mushroomed all over the city and from 1818–40 poor water supplies and sewage systems led to a series of yellow fever and cholera epidemics. Although business thrived, the gap between rich and poor began to gape. In the financial panic of 1837 about 50,000 people became unemployed, and there were a series of riots in which thousands of people convened on City Hall and then ransacked a warehouse, tumbling barrels of flour on to the streets.

Between 1840 and 1860, with the population more than doubling again, a committee including **William Cullen Bryant**, the newspaperman and nature poet, pressed for the building of a central park to relieve the congested city. But in the same year as work began on the park, there was another financial crisis leaving 40,000 unemployed. In Tompkins Square in today's East Village, there were hunger demonstrations. Elsewhere troops and howitzers were enlisted to protect buildings like the Customs House and Subtreasury from looters led by violent Irish gangs, like the Dead Rabbits, the O'Connell Guards, the Hudson Dusters, and the Gopher Thugs.

The gangs flourished under **Fernando Wood**, so-called grand sachem, or leader, of Tammany Hall, and Mayor from 1850 until the outbreak of the Civil War in 1861. Wood turned politics into a profession, and was one of the first in a long line of Tammany bosses who got into power by exploiting the immigrant vote (at a time when a third of the voters in the city were Irish). He was a shifty character who entered the city on the back legs of an elephant in a circus procession and went on to make his fortune selling bootleg liquor in the Gold Rush.

In the Civil War, the city divided between Wood's Democratic faction (which opposed the war since the immigrant vote was reluctant to serve in the military) and those who sided with the Union against the Confederates in the South. While **Abraham Lincoln** enthused Abolitionists with his famous 'Might Makes Right' speech against slavery at Cooper Union, Fernando Wood gave his full-hearted support to the South and even went to such ludicrous lengths as proposing New York's secession from the Union.

Disaffection with the war finally erupted in the Draft Riots, after Congress passed a compulsory Conscription Act in 1863. The rioters were incensed by a clause in the act exempting the well-off from compulsory military service upon payment of $300 for a substitute. Street battles with the police raged for four days, and a rabble rampaged through the city, burning down the enrolment office, sabotaging telegraph wires and storming the Colored Orphan Asylum. Meanwhile businesses and banks shut down and public transport ground to a halt. In all about 50,000 rioters took to the streets, bringing well-to-do New Yorkers face to face with its own hoi-polloi. Over a thousand people were killed and property worth between $2 and $5 million was destroyed.

After the war, Wood was soon upstaged by the most spectacularly crooked of all Tammany's bosses, **William Marcy 'Boss' Tweed**. During his six-year reign, the Boss and his accomplices pocketed $200 million between them. Tweed shot up the ladder of caucus politics. He left school at 14, joined a riff-raffy gang and a volunteer fire company, the 'Americus'. By the time he was 21, he was thoroughly ensconced in the Tammany machine. He became an alderman, won a seat on the corrupt City Council dubbed the 'Forty Thieves', and eventually got himself elected as grand sachem.

At last, in 1871, the kickbacks, graft and bribes which Tweed nurtured for so long were exposed by George Jones, editor of the *New York Times*, and Thomas Nast, a cartoonist who lampooned Tammany with 'those damn pictures', as Tweed called them. Tweed was subsequently tried and sent to jail, but escaped and made off for Chile and Cuba. Eventually Tweed was re-captured in Spain by Spanish authorities, who sent him back to the Manhattan prison he himself had built, inside which he finally died of double pneumonia.

1865–1918: The Four Hundred and the Four Million

After the Civil War, New York matured into a full-blown metropolis. It was a land of opportunity not just for Tweed and his plundering crew, but also for go-getters who ranged from Eastern European immigrants to parvenues and robber barons who made fabulous fortunes out of commodities such as sugar, rubber and gas. Central Park, the Metropolitan Museum, Brooklyn Bridge, New York Public Library, and the laying of the Trans-Atlantic Cable were all completed in the years before the turn of the century.

By 1863 several hundreds of millionaires lived in the city, whereas two decades previously there were twenty in the whole nation. In these halcyon days before taxation the rich indulged themselves in conspicuous consumption as well as philanthropy. New York's new department stores, (A. T. Stewart's, Arnold Constable's, Macy's and Lord & Taylor), began catering to the first consumers. By 1900, New York gobbled up four times as much electricity and five times as much water as London. Châteaux and mansions started their northern march up 5th Avenue, pushing back shantytowns of thovering poor as far as 89th Street.

Society moulded itself into the Four Hundred, the maximum number of guests who could squeeze into Mrs Astor's 5th Avenue ballroom. The Astors, Vanderbilts and Whitneys were the film stars of their day and their extravagances and parties were written up in salivating detail for the general public to devour. One report describes an evening in Sherry's Restaurant hosted by C. K. G. Billings, where guests sitting on horses ate a lavish supper in between sucks of champagne delivered to them via rubber tubes.

At the turn of the century a new wave of immigrants swept into the city from Southern and Eastern Europe and China. Eighty per cent of New Yorkers were now either first or second generation immigrants. In 1907 a record 1,285,349 were admitted in a single year; in 1908 a British Zionist called Israel Zangwill wrote a play about American immigration called *The Melting Pot*. Those immigrants who stayed in New York's melting pot mostly found themselves on the Lower East Side, the most densely populated place on earth with a density of 334,000 people per square mile, or less than 10 square yards (including sidewalks and streets) per person. In this urban purgatory, the Jewish Lower East Side evolved an intellectual and cultural life which was entirely its own. Workers became politically aware, and began publishing their own newspapers and striking. In 1911 a tragic fire at the Triangle Shirtwaist Factory in SoHo killed 145 sweatshop workers; this was the spur that at last forced through New York's first legislative reforms. At the same time, a Danish immigrant called Jacob Riis arrived in Manhattan fully expecting to see bisons and Indians roaming a rural landscape. Instead he found squalor and congestion which was unprecedented in history. Riis' book, *How the Other Half Lives*, brought the slums, sweatshops, street urchins, 'misery and vice' into the front parlours of the well-to-do in the form of the world's first documentary photographs.

Congestion was such an issue that in 1870 someone called Melville Smith suggested the city build elevated pedestrian walkways or 'arcades' over the streets. The bizarre idea was rejected, but in the 1880s New York did get a 'vertical railway', known as the El or Elevated, and in 1904, an infant subway system, the IRT. The subway opened up expanses of New York to commuters, in particular Brooklyn, Queens and the Bronx which were consolidated into the city in 1898. A construction boom followed and in 1913 the Woolworth Building became the tallest in the world. While the skyline metamorphosed into a toothy jaw, New Yorkers evolved a completely 20th-century lifestyle, living in apartment houses and working in skyscrapers.

When America entered the war in 1917, 1.5 million soldiers were dispatched from New York Port and a steel net was laid across the Narrows to keep out German U-Boats. Flags flapped from every window and the city bubbled with patriotism: New York became the headquarters of US propaganda; there were attacks on German Americans on the Upper and Lower East Side.

The Twenties: New York at the Top of the World

America emerged triumphantly from the war as a world power. However, economic and politcal policies remained strongly isolationist and in 1921 and 1924 new immigration laws put such a squeeze on quotas that immigration all but ceased. Within Manhattan, however, Harlem doubled its population from 83,000 to over 200,000. Most were black Americans fleeing the rural south where farmers were devastated by a world surplus of grain and other agricultural products. Although Harlem was overcrowded with a population density twice that of the rest of Manhattan, the black metropolis flourished. The next decade saw the Harlem renaissance when writers, artists and musicians like the poet Langston Hughes and the novelist Claude McKay gravitated to what became the capital of black America.

Twenties New York was a curious mix of dutiful morality and joyful decadence— epitomized in Anita Loos' recollection of when 'we flappers patronized a beauty parlor where a lady barber used to shave certain hirsute areas into the shape of either a heart or a derby hat (the emblem of Al Smith, a political idol of the day)'. While women got the vote, an alliance of the Women's Christian Temperance Union, the Anti Saloon League and the Methodist Church succeeded in imposing Prohibition of the 'manufacture, sale or transportation' of alcohol over the whole country. New Yorkers responded with predictable gusto. One hundred thousand speakeasys opened for business, and alcohol was as easy to come by as before, except that the lucrative trade was controlled by the criminal underground, making the fortunes of such big-time gangsters as Big Bill O'Dwyer, Dutch Schultz, Lucky Luciano and Louis Lepke. The 21 Club on 52nd Street was one of the more sophis- ticated speakeasys, with an underground cellar holding 5000 cases of booze, and an automatically disappearing bar.

Embodying the optimism of post-War New York was 'Beau James' aka **Jimmy Walker**, the raffish, dandified new mayor. The author of 'Kiss All the Girls for Me', 'There's Music in the Rustle of a Skirt' and 'In the Valley Where my Sally Said Goodbye', the mayor was the most charming in the city's history. Having started out in Manhattan as a songwriter on Tin Pan Alley, Walker carried on in much the same milieu during his administration, freely indulging his passion for nightclubs, sports, gambling, showgirls and clothes (he designed his own clothes, including pearly spats, cravats and suits which he changed as many as five times a day; and he once packed 100 ties and 20 new waistcoats on a trip to Europe). Walker was another Tammany man, and he won the heart of New York when he legalized boxing and Sunday baseball. He remained popular even when a series of Tammany scandals over graft and bribery crumpled his administration. In 1932, Walker finally resigned and fourteen years later was given a requiem mass with all the trim- mings in St Patrick's Cathedral on 5th Avenue.

Twenties New York was fantastical place with inhabitants who loved spectacle. At Rudolph Valentino's fortnight-long funeral in 1926, mobs turned out to cheer on the stars and a rose-petalled coffin. At weekends millions left the city for Dreamland and Luna Park at Coney Island. They canoodled in the Tunnel of Love, laid bets at a 25-acre mechanical race course, went to Midget City (inhabited by 300 dwarfs) and gaped at a lifelike reconstruction of the Creation. In Manhattan, the entertainment king was 'Roxy'—a man called Samuel Lionel Rothapfel who at first opened chains of bowling alleys and cleaners in Manhattan and then hosted his own radio show, *Roxy's Gang*. In 1926, he spent $15 million building a Cathedral of the Motion Picture called the Roxy. Here New Yorkers were wafted to an air-conditioned arcadia of electric fountains, multicoloured flickering lights and Louis Quatorze furniture.

The rollicking jollity was accompanied by the economic boom which engendered the Chrysler Building, the Empire State and Rockfeller Center. By 1929 the US GDP was greater than that of Britain, Germany, Japan, France and 18 other countries put together. Money saturated the stock exchange, and speculation fed on a mixture of its own momentum and cheery events like Lindbergh's Trans-Atlantic flight in 1927. At its peak in 1929 tickers were unable to keep up with the pace of business as the market reached an all-time peak. Then suddenly the market lost its nerve and the enormous bubble burst. On Black Thursday 13 million shares were sold and 11 speculators killed themselves; five days later, on Tuesday 29 October, another 16.4 million shares were dumped as Wall Street crashed.

The Thirties: The Little Flower and the Evil Gnome

For the next six years New York suffered the worst economic depression in its short history. By 1932 one in three New Yorkers in the workforce were unemployed and 1.6 million were on public relief. Many found themselves in shantytowns branded 'Hoovervilles' after the US President. They slept in 'Hoover blankets' made of newspaper and rummaged the garbage bins for scraps of food. One of the biggest Hoovervilles was next to the Reservoir in Central Park with a main thoroughfare dubbed Prosperity Street. Another at the foot of East 10th Street was so organized it elected its own mayor and laid on special police and sanitation services.

Coincidentally in 1934 the city elected **Fiorello La Guardia** as mayor. It was a timely move and the 'Little Flower' is remembered to this day as the most clean-cut mayor New York ever had (and also as the stocky, fatherly figure wearing an enormous Stetson who chatted to New Yorkers over Sunday radio broadcasts, and dramatized the comics in a squeaky voice to children during a newspaper strike). The son of a Jewish mother and a Protestant Italian father, La Guardia lived in Italian East Harlem and spoke six languages, which he used at Ellis Island where he worked as an interpreter to support himself at law school.

As soon as La Guardia moved into office he had Lucky Luciano arrested and set about cracking down on the criminal underworld, cleaning up the police, and breaking Tammany boss rule. Most importantly of all, La Guardia got money flowing back into the city via the New Deal, Franklin D. Roosevelt's reform package designed to set the country back on its feet. The deal laid down $500 billion dollars for emergency relief and allocated $4.8 billion to WPA or Works Project Administration to create new jobs.

In New York, WPA soon became the most vigorous engine for economic recovery, creating as many as 7000 assignments or jobs a day, from street cleaning and park labour to projects like civic murals and WPA guidebooks specifically created for artists and writers. Since Roosevelt saw New York as a key testing ground for the New Deal programmes, his support was unstinting. Along with the president and his wife, La Guardia was at the forefront of a new era of liberal politics in America. Between 1934 and the end of his administration in 1945, La Guardia pumped dollars into welfare, housing, highways, parks and a new airport. Reforms were massive, ranging from banishing salacious magazines and organ grinders from the street, to creating tens of thousands of acres of new parks.

Overseeing the latter was La Guardia's right-hand man, the civil servant **Robert Moses**. While mayors merely came and went, Moses stayed. He stayed for nearly four decades, assuming La Guardia's mantle of reform in the 1940s, and keeping a vice-like grip on it until 1968, by which time Moses was one of the most powerful and power-hungry men in the city. In the end the imperious Moses emerged as an angel-devil, compelled simultaneously by misplaced vision, zeal and megalomania. He is sometimes said to have been the greatest single influence over the car-ensnared present-day shape of American cities. Certainly he did more than any other person to recast physical New York into the city we see today.

The achievement was immense. During Moses' half-century reign the city got 627 miles of roadways, seven bridges, Lincoln Center, the World Trade Center and the parks and beaches of Long Island. All worthy causes, but all achieved at the cost of laying waste expanses of the Bronx and Brooklyn for freeways; uprooting and evicting an estimated quarter of a million people from their homes and replacing whole neighbourhoods with anonymous tower blocks—new, vertical slums where lids for toilets were considered an unnecessary expense. 'No law, no regulation, no budget stops Bob Moses in his appointed task,' La Guardia once said.

The Post-War Period: Decay and Bankruptcy

Between the 1939 and 1964 World's Fairs, both Moses creations, New York filled out with a population of 7.5 million. Exhibits at the 1939 World's Fair heralded the triumph of the new consumer society and its emblems—televisions, sheer nylon stockings, cars, and family. But it took the Second World War to create the economic conditions for the dream to become a reality. During the war New York once again became a take-off point for American troops and soldiers. Lights were dimmed in Times Square; while at Columbia University a nuclear experiment by Dr Robert Oppenheimer code-named the 'Manhattan Project' led to the atomic bomb which ended the war against Japan in August 1945.

In the same year, La Guardia stepped down, and a Democratic candidate, **William O'Dwyer**, became mayor. After the War, the city became suddenly affluent, and there was a burst of construction. Moses talked O'Dwyer into giving the United Nations a permanent home in Manhattan, saying it would fix New York forever as capital of the world. In 1948 the complex was built on land worth $8.5 billion which John D. Rockefeller bought and donated.

In the next decade, neo-classical residences along Park Avenue were bulldozed and replaced by a slick glass skyscrapers with bland plazas and concourses, the most presentable of which were Lever House and the Seagram. In 1947 Stuyvesant Town and Peter Cooper Village were built as middle-income housing, initially for war veterans, on the Lower East Side. They proved such an inspiring success that the city brought in huge tax abatements to encourage schemes like the Manhattan Urban Renewal Project on the Upper West Side (which all but collapsed in a scandal over finances and tax abatements). O'Dwyer himself suddenly resigned in disgrace over his connections with the criminal underground and a crooked bookie called Harry Gross. Ironically, years before he became mayor, O'Dwyer the District Attorney had helped crush crime syndicates including the famed Brooklyn hit squad, Murder Inc.

O'Dwyer left for Mexico, tail between his legs. Meanwhile New York experienced a third wave of immigration. Between 1950 and 1970, 1.6 million new faces arrived in the city, many black, Hispanic and Puerto Rican. A combination of oafish urban planning and a construction boom in the business sectors of Manhattan drove the newcomers into a continually shrinking pool of run-down housing. These evolved into inner-city ghettos, depressing places which entangled those who lived in them in coils of poverty.

As crime and vandalism escalated, the middle classes and working families left in droves. In the great 'White Flight' of the 50s and 60s more than a million fled New York, and big corporations like Mobil and Union Carbide decamped for the sub-urbs. The city erupted in terrible riots in Harlem and Bedford-Stuyvesant in 1964, and East Brooklyn and the South Bronx in 1967. These were part of a wave of violent battles between police and ghetto dwellers which devastated cities all over America in the sixties. Molotov cocktails and bottles filled with petrol were thrown in the streets; buildings and refuse bins were incinerated; everywhere there were fresh allegations of police brutality.

New York staggered through a succession of strikes including a transit strike by 34,400 workers in 1966 which cost $70 million to resolve. Spending on social welfare rocketed, and the city imposed higher and higher taxes only to find that the exodus of businesses and the middle classes had shattered the tax base. Though the mayor, **Abe Beame**, was an accountant, by 1975 he was spending $12.8 billion and receiving only $10.9 billion. By 15 October, New York was only hours away from bankruptcy. As panic struck, everyone looked to the White House to bail them out. But the intractable Ford administration sat on its hands and refused to part with a cent of federal aid, prompting the famous *Daily News* headline: 'Ford to New York—Drop Dead!'

In the end New York was rescued by last-minute loans from teachers and sanitation unions. In the next few months the city got a new fiscal programme courtesy of Big MAC, or the Municipal Assistance Corporation, which was formed to act as a watchdog over spendthrifts at City Hall. Washington was impressed enough to offer the city a short-term loan of two and half billion dollars, and a year later a consortium of bankers headed by David Rockefeller raised a further $600 million.

New York in the Eighties and a Mayor Called Ed Koch

New York hobbled through the next three years. More than 65,000 workers lost jobs in municipal government; teachers, police and firemen took wage freezes; the poor were worst hit by cutbacks in basic services and welfare allowances.

However, with the election of **Ed Koch** in 1978 Manhattan revived a little. In an administration that lasted 12 years and the whole of the eighties, Koch's robust and sometimes abrasive utterances on smashing crime, getting tough on unions and tightening belts generally won back the confidence of New York's economic movers: the real estate boys, Wall Street's money men and Washington. Thanks to a newly buoyant economy, Koch paid back federal loans a year ahead of schedule, and in 1985 he announced the miracle of a budget surplus. This was at the height of another construction boom, subsidized by more tax abatements and low-interest loans. Sixty new skyscrapers sputtered up into the Manhattan skyline, including the quirky AT&T Building, the grisly Trump Tower, and the four glittering blue-glass prongs of the World Financial Center in Battery Park City.

Born in the Bronx, Koch was New York's most charismatic mayor for many years. He had a witty, outspoken style which attracted world-wide media attention; he was endearingly proud of his hometown and during his three terms he commissioned the song 'I Love New York' and wrote two books about himself, one of which was turned into a Broadway musical. (Now in his mid-seventies, Koch is a living mascot of New York: he hosts a daily radio show, writes a daily column, does film reviews for six papers, and has completed eight books, including a whodunnit with a hero called Ed Koch.) As mayor Koch's dry humour saw him through several crises, including the suicide in 1986 of Donald Manes (Democratic borough president of Queens), a complicated bureaucratic scandal which could have sunk a weaker administration.

Koch, however, made little impact on the more fundamental problems afflicting New York City, and by the late eighties middle-class as well as minority voters began to perceive him as no more than an accomplished rhetorician. In the eighties the co-existence of opulence and chronic poverty in New York (encapsulated in Tom Wolfe's bestseller *The Bonfire of the Vanities*) characterized a nation divided into haves and have-nots; and in this atmosphere Mayor Koch's brash style seemed to be symptomatic of hubris in American politics generally.

In 1989 Koch lost his Democratic nomination to **David Dinkins**, ex-marine and borough president of Manhattan. In the 1989 elections Dinkins narrowly beat attorney Rudoloph Giuliani (then famous for leading successful prosecutions against police corruption and the mafia). Under Dinkins, New York became one of the last big cities in America to elect a black mayor.

New York had boomed in the mid-eighties; previously scummy areas had been massively gentrified, but at the expense of the poor, who got poorer. Dinkins inherited an economic crisis (as companies continued to leave) and a crime explosion. By the time he began his administration in 1990 one in four New Yorkers were living below the poverty line: there was a 70 per cent drop-out rate in high schools, an estimated 300,000 people were homeless and in Harlem the infant mortality rate was the same as in a Third World country. A crack epidemic contributed to violent crime: meanwhile AIDS and an outbreak of multi-drug-resistant tuberculosis strained health services.

With recession kicking in hard and a budget deficit reaching $500 million, Dinkins had no hope of satisfying the expectations of his supporters. Although he increased the size of the NYPD by nearly 25%, he was forced at the same time to cut aid programmes and lay off city workers. Despite these ruthless measures, in 12 months the budget deficit reached $1.5 billion. As the deficit rose Dinkins' popularity ratings slid. The press lambasted Dinkins for being inept and ineffectual particularly on racial issues; in the 1993 elections Dinkins lost, by another small margin, to Rudolph Giuliani.

The Knotty Nineties

Giuliani became New York's first Republican mayor for 28 years. With his stony face and generally low entertainment quotient, Giuliani is not the most lovable mayor in city history. Despite this, older New Yorkers, including Italian, Irish and Slav minorities and the establishment, respect and admire him. Younger, liberal and anti-establishment New Yorkers think of him as an power-mad egomaniac, but even they concede that because of Giuliani's attempts to improve 'quality of life' on city streets, Manhattan is now more liveable-in.

The novel idea that New Yorkers might actually deserve a 'quality of life' on safe, clean streets was first mooted in 1990 by the Manhattan Institute, a privately funded right-wing think tank which promotes ideas on crime, education and downsizing government generally in a magazine and through the press, and also at deluxe lunches attended by such prominent New Yorkers as novelist Tom Wolfe and future mayor, Rudy Giuliani.

In 1993 Rudy Giuliani made 'quality of life' the vote-winning catchphrase of his election campaign; since 1993 Giuliani has mostly turned a blind eye to New York's ailing schools and social services, but he has visibly sanitized Manhattan. New Yorkers still think of the Port Authority Bus Terminal (where Ratso Rizzo stepped off a Greyhound bus in John Schlesinger's *Midnight Cowboy*) as the lavatory of Manhattan, but even this is now a sparklingly clean lavatory with kinetic art installations, murals and string quartet muzac. Riff-raff such as hookers, pushers and petty criminals have been ejected from grotty areas like Times Square; in their place big businesses like Disney and Madame Tussaud's have moved in. But while brand-name corporations like these are injecting much needed dollars into the economy and stimulating vital tourism, Manhattan is becoming expensive for normal people to live in and working families are being pushed out to places like East New York.

Rising living costs have also taken their toll on Bohemian Manhattanites. Types like these also complain that Disneyfication of the city has been a catalyst for 'crackdowns on fun' by the mayor's administration, and 'bohophobia' or a lack of interest in anything that seems too challenging, unconventional or weird in general. These days licensing regulations are more strictly enforced than ever and clubs and bars have had to shut down under the pressure of heavy fines. At the same time community groups, composed of 'respectable' residents, have powers to stop new clubs opening up altogether. The tough proscriptions have aggrieved and politicized such unlikely figures as Murray Hill, New York's first drag king mayoral candidate, and Misstress Formika, who runs a free speech organization called Freedom from Giuliani and Censorship. In what is traditionally the most liberal big city in America, 'quality of life' is perceived as a double-edged sword: as the only effective way of reclaiming Manhattan from the hoods, perverts and low-lifes who took over the city in the 1970s and 80s; and also as an increasingly used euphemism for intolerance generally.

New York will almost certainly vote Giuliani in for a second term. Even though the mayor remains an enigma, one aspect of Giuliani's personality of which voters are certain is that he relishes the limelight. Publicity-mad district attorneys based on Rudy Giuliani are now stock characters in Hollywood movies. In Manhattan itself, everywhere you go Giuliani's name is there. When crime rates miraculously fell to levels last seen in the sixties, Giuliani took all the credit for himself and many people believe that in 1996 he manoeuvred the charismatic Police Commissioner William Bratton into resigning because he thought Bratton was getting too popular. Giuliani's political ambition means that he will gamble for the interests of New York City over everything and everyone else, and sometimes at New York's expense as well. In the 1994 gubernatorial elections, this kind of gambling went wrong when Giuliani endorsed Democratic State Governor Mario Cuomo instead of George Pataki, his own party's less impressive candidate. If Cuomo had won, Giuliani would have gained precious leverage for himself and a political IOU for New York. Instead Pataki's victory has left Giuliani having to pay court to Republicans whose real political interests hinge on diverting money and prestige away from New York City to the suburbs and upstate New York.

In 1996 ex-Mayor Ed Koch withdrew *his* endorsement of Rudy Giuliani. Even so Giuliani looks invincible: not because he is idolized, but because convincing opponents for the elections in November 1997 have been slow to come forward. New Yorkers like to think of themselves as living in a city of 10 million mayors, but as the millennium approaches it seems that most of the 10 million would rather *not* take on a city as wayward as New York.

An Architectural Compendium

ECSTASY

Manhattan has generated a shameless architecture that has been loved in direct proportion to its defiant lack of self-hatred, has been respected exactly to the degree that it went too far.

*Manhattan has consistently inspired in its beholders **ecstasy about architecture.***

In spite—or perhaps because—of this, its performance and implications have been consistently ignored and even suppressed by the architectural profession.

DENSITY

*Manhattanism is the one urbanistic ideology that has fed, from its conception, on the splendors and miseries of the metropolitan condition—hyper-density—without once losing faith in it as the basis for a desirable modern culture. **Manhattan's architecture is a paradigm for the exploitation of congestion.***

Rem Koolhaas, *Delirious New York*, 1978

Architecture in Manhattan is a fusion of two conflicting American dreams: a desire for egalitarianism, and a yearning for the original, idiosyncratic or unique. Instead of rows of skyscrapers laid neatly on a grid, the first thing that strikes a visitor is an atmosphere of planned chaos; what Le Corbusier called the 'beautiful catastrophe'. In Manhattan buildings can be brutal, harmonious, utilitarian, whimsical, minimal, decadent—all at the same time. Architecture here is more anarchic than anywhere else, but the anarchy is always governed by an invisible two-dimensional grid. Like a stormy marriage, Manhattan seemed like a good idea at the time.

This compendium contains a brief chronology of Manhattan's architecture from the Dutch settlement onwards. Although Manhattanites like to think that their city is much more modern than anywhere else, it's a pleasant paradox to find that ghosts of New York's past can be found all over the island, lovingly tended and usually in the least expected places.

Internet Architecture: *For a continuously updated site on New York skyscrapers see www.geocities.com/CapeCanaveral/3366/nyc.html. The site includes Webcam views of and from the Empire State Building. For a site on Otis Odyssey Elevators see www.otis.com.*

New Amsterdam

Like Manhattan nowadays, New Amsterdam was congested and small. It was hemmed in to the north by Wall Street, a ramshackle wooden fence which developed eventually into Manhattan's first cross-street. Unlike most colonies, the Dutch settlement was not grandiose. Instead it was filled with reassuring reminders of Old Amsterdam—canals and windmills, clogs and neat rows of traditional Dutch houses built gable-end to the street with steeply pitched crow-stepped roofs and Dutch '*stoeps*' or stoops.

It's sometimes said that Manhattan's most impressive architectural structures (Brooklyn Bridge, Grand Central Terminal, Central Park, the Statue of Liberty, the Grid) are above all feats of engineering. Appropriately, Manhattan's first architect—**Cryn Fredericksz**—was actually an engineer. He was sent over by the East India Company in 1623 to lay out a typical Dutch town, tidy and rectangular, with farms, gardens, orchards, and an intimidating fort in the middle. However, the East India Company's plans made no allowance for the complicated island terrain. The New Amsterdam which was eventually built was much more haphazard and medieval in spirit, laid out on higgledy-piggledy streets, with a modest fort below Wall Street which was liable to collapse in rainstorms. Despite this, maps and pictures sent back to the Hague portrayed the settlement as a proud walled city of Renaissance grandeur. Today, although no relic of New Amsterdam and its colonists remains, there is the street plan of downtown Manhattan, a ghostly X-ray with roads and sidewalks marking long-gone paths and canals, and skyscrapers towering in place of Dutch farmsteads.

English New York

The British destroyed most of Dutch New Amsterdam, and in its turn English New York was obliterated in the Revolution. Though New Yorkers recall the Dutch settlement with affection, the English period is seldom mentioned except for the fact that English New Yorkers encouraged pigs to roam the streets and eat away the garbage. In fact it was the English who in 1664 initiated the very Dutch practice of 'landfill', which persists to this day: in the late 1980s Battery Park City was built on landfill from the World Trade Center foundations. In the 17th century, to raise revenue from real estate, the city began selling 'water lots' on land exposed at low tide. The merchants who bought them built cribs which they sunk into swampy soil below and filled with 'landfill': garbage, debris, soil and ship's ballast.

Ironically most of English New York ended up as landfill. Today the only pre-Revolutionary building remaining from British rule is St Paul's, an exceptionally elegant Georgian church built in fields next to Broadway in 1766 by Thomas McBean, a pupil of the great English church builder James Gibbs.

The Federal Style

Between the 1760s and 1830s the Federal style, a swanky Americanized version of English-Georgian, held sway in New York. Classical details harked back to the Roman republic, making the style particularly appropriate for civic buildings and monuments. The supreme example of Federal style in Manhattan is **Joseph Mangin** and **John McComb's** City Hall (*see* p.171). Mangin was an engineer from Paris who had worked on the Place de la Concorde. City Hall when it was finished was reminiscent of a French château and smacked more of Mangin's native panache than of the Scotsman McComb's predictable restraint. The interior is outstanding: filled competely by a cantilevered marble staircase with coffered dome and Adam-style decoration. Apart from civic buildings, the Federal style produced Manhattan's most charming townhouses ever. Semi-detached Federal residences were a model of simplicity, assembled for the most part by carpenters (rather than architects) who randomly nabbed details from English pattern books. These 'row houses' were two or three storeys tall, and usually had two 'eyes', a pair of dormer windows peeping out of a pitched roof. Entrances featured a Dutch stoop and front door decorated with classical columns and a fan-light illuminating the hallway inside. The best examples today are in TriBeCa's Charlton, King and Vandam Streets, and Brooklyn Heights.

Eclecticism: Mixed-up New York

> *'New York is mixed-up! The confusion of styles can be mad and dynamic! And it is exactly this which demonstrates the creative power of the city.'*
>
> Reinhart Wolf, *Interview with Andy Warhol*, 1980

The Classical Revival of the 18th century and the Greek War of Independence in 1821 naturally appealed to Jeffersonian ideals of democracy and also to architects searching out a definitively American style. Translated to the New World, the 'Greek Revival' caught on in a climate of economic euphoria following the construction of the Erie Canal in 1825. The style itself was democratic: its columns, porticoes and pediments could be tacked on to a mixed bag of buildings—from courts, churches, banks and businesses to well-to-do town and country houses—immediately conferring dignity, urbanity and confidence. Perhaps the best example of Greek-Revival New York is 'The Row', a fleet of aristocratic townhouses connected by an unbroken cornice on Washington Square, built by developers in the 1830s and home to Henry James' grandmother.

The American Greek Revival sparked off a silent 30-year war of styles and a succession of neo-Gothic, Romanesque, Renaissance, Italianate, even Federal Revivals. 'Though New Yorkers imitate the dead and gone of Italy and Greece,' wrote one satirist, 'they will not copy their next-door neighbors.' Practically all the different styles can be seen in Brooklyn Heights which was divided up and sold off in lots from the 1820s until the end of the century and remains New York's finest encyclopedia of the 19th-century townhouse.

The Brownstone

By the 1850s Italianate styles came out on top, and the New York brownstone, which Edith Wharton referred to as a disgusting cold chocolate sauce, triumphantly dribbled over Manhattan. Nowadays the brownstone is regarded with great affection and priced accordingly sky-high, but right up until the 1950s it was snubbed by New Yorkers as the worst kind of parvenu.

Mined in New Jersey and Connecticut, brownstone was cheap to quarry and easy to carve. It could be slapped like daub on to an even cheaper brick structure below. Brownstone lots were narrow and deep, and because space was limited, they filled up the whole area available. Instead of back entrances and alleys, their fronts had stoops—steep steps leading up and down to entrances on the ground and basement floors. A descendent of the Dutch *stoep*, an anti-flooding device, the New York stoop was useful in New York because it meant that tradesmen and guests could use the same entrance and savings made on ever more valuable real estate.

Another advantage was that once a client had a basic template, he could tart up his brownstone with all sorts of grandiose embellishments, such as heavy overhanging Renaissance cornices (resembling the eaves on a Dutch farmhouse) and fancy cast-iron railings, lamps and banisters (some even dispensed with stoops in an attempt to look fashionably English). Carving on most brownstones is usually clumsy and amateurish, and fire escapes are often the most conspicuous feature.

In the 1880s, the brownstone was humbled by sophisticated Queen Anne and Romanesque townhouses built on the Upper West Side. In the thirties most brownstones were demolished to make way for apartment houses and department stores. But a good deal do survive, especially on Lexington and 3rd Avenues, in Harlem, and on the east and west fringes of Midtown. Indeed, the style is perceived as being so ubiquitous in the city, that the term 'brownstone' often refers to any old townhouse, whether it's faced with brownstone or not.

Geometrical New York: The Grid

The chequerboard blocks, the recurrent regularity of the streets, you admit, point to something planned: but the buildings are eruptive and the whole city abnormal—something again that apparently just 'happened'.

John Van Dyke, *The New New York*, 1909

In 1811 the city commissioners devised a grid for Manhattan: a chessboard super-imposed on a city that did not yet exist. 'It may be a subject of merriment,' the report admitted, 'that the Commissioners have provided space for a greater popula-tion than is collected on any spot this side of China'. It was the most reckless real estate venture in the history of New York. At the time the island was almost com-pletely rural, and though there was a smattering of hamlets in Greenwich Village and Harlem, Manhattan town occupied a space barely a mile long at its butt-end (to skimp on costs, the back of City Hall was faced in brownstone rather than marble—it was unimaginable at that time that the city could grow any further).

An engineer, **John Randel Jr.**, was contracted to survey Manhattan. Though he was frequently attacked for trespassing and was once even arrested by a sheriff, Randel eventually covered the whole island. His grid plan was an imitation of 13th-century Peking. Ignoring the natural terrain, hills, valleys and lakes, Randel sliced Manhattan into a horizontal plane of 2028 rectangular blocks of busy avenues (for commerce and business) and quieter cross-streets (for residences). In one stroke, Randel created the pre-conditions for Manna-hatta (the Indian 'island of hills') to evolve into today's geometrical mountain range of scrapers.

The commissioners were not interested in planning a beautiful city of parks and boulevards in the style of Sixtus V's Rome or Haussmann's Paris, and they made no provision for a Central Park except for a meagre 'Parade' on 34th Street. Like their Dutch forebears, New York's planners were concerned with getting the most real estate at the highest value into the smallest area possible. As the report bluntly put it, 'a city is composed principally of the habitations of men, and straight-sided, and right-angled houses are the most cheap to build and the easiest to live in'.

Because it laid down no aesthetic restrictions, the grid gave unexpectedly free rein to architectural improvisation. This affected the development of New York in two ways. First the grid encouraged vertical growth, creating a ladder which New York's social pioneers scampered up to flee the relentless encroachment of com-merce and business. And secondly it functioned and still functions as a unchanging skeleton in a city which in every other respect is permanently changing. In Manhattan, as nowhere else, buildings can float: the Waldorf-Astoria has moved twice, Madison Square Garden has changed location four times. 'Within the grid, architectural conformity to a general design is something not required, not planned, not even contemplated,' wrote Van Dyke. 'Nothing shall be like anything else, nothing shall conform except by the law of contrariety.'

Central Park

By the middle of the 19th century the only recreational space in New York was Green-Wood Cemetery, 478 acres of rolling hills and lakes in Brooklyn, popular with weekenders and tourists. Central Park on the other hand was planned at the last minute in 1858, eighteen years after Green-Wood, just as Manhattan was on the point of being engulfed forever in a tidal wave of real estate.

Designed by two men—**Frederick Law Olmsted** (another engineer), and an English designer, **Calvert Vaux**—Central Park is an extraordinary creation: an 840-acre carpet of countryside rolled across the centre of Manhattan and filled with sample landscapes for the urban rambler. Though it looks natural, the park is entirely synthetic, and in fact was carved out of scrubland used by squatters. The project was a feat of engineering: 10 million cartloads of muck and stone were removed for the landscaping, and transverse roads from west to east sides of Manhattan were sunk into the ground so pedestrians were hardly aware of them.

Red New York: Apartment Houses and Tenements

The genealogy of the famously palatial New York apartment house is in fact quite lowly. The notion of living in apartments germinated in the first place from tenements built from the 1840s onwards to contain the massive influx of immigrants from Ireland, Germany, Italy and Eastern Europe in the 19th century (a good deal of whom gravitated initially to squalid slums in the Bowery and a dingy disreputable area known as the Five Points).

The first tenements striped New York in red and green bricks and cornices, like an Edward Hopper painting. Nice to look at, but ghastly to inhabit, they would have been more bearable had they not been so horrendously congested. Five- or six-storey walk-ups took up 90ft of the standard 100 by 25ft lot ordained by Randel's grid plan. Ventilated by a narrow airshaft (which stank because it was used for garbage), each building held at least 20 families sharing a bathroom per floor and lavatories in the basement which were aerated by grates in the street. The worst horrors of the slums were tenement-lodging houses; these were so impossibly overcrowded that signs outside advertised 'Standing Room' or space in hallways between 3¢ and 5¢ a night.

In 1901 a law was passed on 'Old Law' tenements demanding stricter regulations on air, light and people density. It was weakly enforced, and in the end only the stringent legislation of 1929 fazed out tenement construction altogether. Even so, great numbers of tenements survive all over the city, particularly on the less well-off perimeters: on the Lower East Side, in Alphabet City, Harlem, Amsterdam Avenue and the Bronx. Many have been gentrified, many remain hopelessly overcrowded, and some in the most desperate areas are merely empty shells, blackened and gutted by fire. Typically, façades are draped with a tangle of fire escapes (Henry James' ghastly 'little world of bars and perches and swings for human squirrels and monkeys'). Meanwhile the roofs, Manhattan's very own 'costa del tarmac', are covered in wires, cables and television aerials resembling seaweed. Lurking beneath the fire escapes and wires, you will see fine plaster carvings and crude gargoyles, all executed in the 19th century by Italian immigrants.

By the turn of the century, congestion and real estate prices had reached such a pitch that the middle classes reluctantly vacated their brownstones. They moved into the middle class equivalent of tenements, called 'apartment-hotels' or 'French flats'. Although the first proper apartment house was built down on East 18th Street in 1869, the first of Manhattan's apartment pioneers settled on the Upper West Side. Here, establishments like the Ansonia, the Dakota and the Dorilton imitated French châteaux and Baroque castles, except that their interiors were equipped with all mod-cons, from the usual central heating, primitive air-conditioning and refrigerators, to pneumatic pipes for polishing top hats, seals splashing in fountains, and bakeries, restaurants and servants.

After the First World War it was the turn of the rich to evacuate their free-standing mansions on 5th Avenue and squeeze into 22-room apartment-palazzi on the newly created Park Avenue, then known as New York's 'gold-digger's lane'. These buildings were at first conservative in design, but later during the twenties massive and exuberant Art Deco apartment houses were developed on Central Park West. The twin-pronged towers of the Majestic, the Beresford, the San Remo, the Eldorado and the Century Building still stud the Manhattan as theatrically as a stage backdrop.

The Chicago World's Fair and Beaux-Arts Civic Monuments

Orchestrated by **Daniel Burnham**, who designed the Flatiron Building on Madison Square, the Chicago World's Fair of 1893 envisaged an American renaissance of buildings designed in richly classical beaux-arts styles, with cities laid out according to urbane beaux-arts ideals of pomp and circumstance. The Fair had a big impact on Manhattan. The influence of the more radical Chicago school of skyscraper architects was quashed, and Manhattan evolved into a sugar-white city of civic buildings and monuments. This style dominated the period between the 1890s and the 1920s when Manhattan got its most magnificent and aristocratic civic architecture, from the great New York Public Library on 42nd Street to Park Avenue to the aptly named Grand Central Terminal (*see* pp.110–12).

One of the quirks of these buildings is that they are so well versed in the art of surprise. Because the grid precludes vistas (which beaux-arts buildings rely on for their grandiose impact) Manhattan's civic monuments lurk round corners, then leap into view. The only New York building with a proper approach is **Cass Gilbert's** Custom House, a stupendous Paris Opéra adapted for commerce, which sits on Bowling Green on European-style streets devised originally for 17th-century New

Amsterdam (see pp.163–4). By strong contrast, the grid plays strange tricks on conventional beaux-arts designs: most spectacularly on the sumptuous façade of **Warren & Wetmore's** Grand Central Terminal, where the three great arched windows and the central sculpture group are almost entirely upstaged by a road—Park Avenue—sticking out of the middle storeys of Grand Central like an enormous tongue.

Spurring on the New York renaissance were a clutch of American architects who had trained at the École des Beaux Arts in Paris, and most of whom had exhibited at the Chicago World's Fair. One, **Richard Morris Hunt**, had worked on the north façade of the Louvre. Back in America he embarked on several 5th Avenue mansions, including Mrs Astor's gargantuan ballroom on 61st Street; a swaggering baroque front for the city's stately home, the Metropolitan Museum of Art; and a huge pedestal for the Statue of Liberty. The designs of the beaux-arts school of architects drew eclectically on a range of European styles, interpreted them with a lot more verve, then adapted them to an extraordinary variety of functions. For example, **George Post** adapted a sturdy Roman temple for Wall Street's Stock Exchange (see p.167), and a replica of the Château de Blois for Mrs Vanderbilt. The team of **Carrère & Hastings** produced a version of Charles Girault's Petit Palais in Paris for a beaux-arts swimming pool which is still open in Hamilton Fish Park on the Lower East Side; and a second look at their most famous work, the New York Public Library, reveals that it is actually a free-wheeling Versailles (see p.97). Sometimes designs were downright eccentric, as in **Whitney Warren's** batty New York Yacht Club on West 44th Street, with its three bay windows carved to resemble the sterns of 18th-century clippers and gushing stone waves.

New York's pre-eminent civic architects were the McKim, Mead and White triumvirate: **Charles Follen McKim**, the austere classicist of the group, **Stanford White**, the brilliant, romantic genius with a flair for the picturesque and a penchant for chorus girls (he was shot in the end on the roof of his own Madison Square Garden, then in the Flatiron District, by the deranged husband of an ex-mistress and chorus girl, Evelyn Nesbit; see below); and **William Rutherford Mead**, a relatively pedestrian worker, eclipsed into permanent obscurity by his more colourful partners.

Stanford White was short with red hair, but he managed to seduce the 16-year-old Evelyn Nesbit with the aid of a lavish pied-à-terre designed by himself and featuring wall-to-wall mirrors, green velvet sofas, sketches of nudes in suggestive poses, and a red velvet swing trailing smilax. The architect sat Nesbit on the swing and sent her reeling up to the ceiling where he told her to kick out all the panels in a rotating paper parasol. Next door was a red velvet room with a mirrored four-poster bed illuminated by multicoloured fairy lights. 'It's all over, kittens, don't cry,' White said when Nesbit came to.

'Now you belong to me.' After he had murdered White, Evelyn Nesbit's husband was committed to an asylum. Madison Square Garden was demolished and a second Madison Square Garden was built in a completely different location on 9th Avenue. Evelyn Nesbit became a heroin addict, and died in 1966 in a brothel in Panama.

Although this odd trio worked outside the city (the Mall in Washington DC, a rebuilding of the White House, and the campuses of Harvard and the University of Virginia), they were firmly rooted in New York. Scores of projects commissioned for the city included churches, mansions and hospitals, stations, offices and restaurants. Perhaps their greatest work of all, alas no more, was Penn Station, an immense and grand space based on the Roman Baths of Caracalla, and replaced by a bland new Madison Square Garden kettle drum in 1966. Despite this McKim, Mead and White's impact on New York is still impossible to ignore—from clubs based on outsized Florentine palazzi on 5th Avenue, to Washington Arch in Greenwich Village, Brooklyn Museum, Columbia University, and a towering Municipal Building on Centre Street which so impressed Stalinist architects that they copied it for Moscow University tower, then reproduced it again for the 800ft tall Palace of Culture in Warsaw.

Embryonic Skyscrapers

> *This is the first sensation of life in New York—you feel that the Americans have practically added a new dimension to space. When they find themselves a little crowded, they simply tilt a street on end and call it a skyscraper.*

William Archer, *America Today*, 1899

When it rose up to loom down Wall Street in 1846, the 284ft Gothic Revival spire of Trinity Church was the tallest in the city: tourists were encouraged to climb to the top, where the great height made 'the people in the streets seem like pygmies, and the vehicles like so many toys'. Seven years later, Manhattan got its first prototypical skyscraper: the Latting Observatory, a 350ft tower of timber and iron erected on 42nd Street along with a Crystal Palace as part of the 1853 World's Fair. Taller than the Statue of Liberty, it was one of the highest structures ever built in Manhattan (until the 390ft 31-storey Park Row Building in 1899). The Observatory was equipped with a steam elevator and in the style of the Empire State Building today, tourists bought ice-creams from shops at the base and then took elevators to look through telescopes on the first and second floors. Meanwhile over in the Crystal Palace a mechanic from Yonkers called Otis demonstrated the world's first safety elevator by standing on a platform and slashing the cable that held him up with a razor-sharp dagger.

The invention of the elevator, and the introduction of cast and wrought iron, first made skyscrapers feasible; and both inventions came together in New York in 1857. Peter Cooper, the iron-works owner and developer of the *Tom Thumb* locomotive, installed wrought-iron railway tracks as beams in his building on Astor Place, the Cooper Union For the Advancement of Science and Art (*see* p.151–2). In the same year, Elisha Graves Otis installed the world's first passenger elevator in the Haughwout Building, a newly cast-iron palazzo-department store in SoHo. The Haughwout was one of hundreds of cast-iron warehouses built in SoHo from the 1850s onwards. Cast-iron was quick to assemble and cheap to manufacture, and unlike traditional load-bearing walls, cast-iron frames were strong enough to support a seemingly infinite number of storeys.

Manhattan's first elevator building and skyscraper proper was the 12-storey Tower Building, constructed in 1889 at 50 Broadway. Most New Yorkers now spend an average of one week every year travelling in Manhattan's 32,000 elevators, but when the Tower Building was completed people were so nervous the architect had to live on the 11th storey to prove it was safe. It was not the tallest building on the island, but it was the first to use a steel skeleton and stone curtain-wall construction. Other pioneering scrapers, like the Park Row Building of 1899, shot up near City Hall on Printing House Square.

In 1898 Chicago's most radical skyscraper designer, **Louis Sullivan**, designed the Bayard-Condict Building on Bleecker Street. The iconoclastic work rejected the neoclassical 'rules' formulated at the Chicago World's Fair of 1893. Instead it fulfilled Sullivan's dictum that 'form follow function': that buildings should express their purpose (in this case offices) and their structure (a steel-cage skeleton). However, the anti-historical functionalism did not go down a treat with New Yorkers (who have always had a traditionalist side to them), and Sullivan received no more commissions in Manhattan.

Evolution of the Skyscraper I: Sodom by the Sea

> *Manhattan is the twentieth century's Rosetta Stone.*
>
> *Not only are large parts of its surface occupied by architectural mutations (Central Park, the Skyscraper), utopian fragments (Rockefeller Center, the UN Building) and irrational phenomena (Radio City Music Hall), but in addition each block is covered with several layers of phantom architecture in the form of past occupancies, aborted projects and popular fantasies that provide alternative images to the New York that exists.*
>
> Rem Koolhaas, *Delirious New York*, 1978

New York's infant scrapers are peculiar creatures, based loosely on the classical column, with sensible bottoms and fantastically flamboyant tops. The fancy hats are shamelessly eclectic, stolen from Gothic, Romanesque, Renaissance and beaux-arts styles, by architects to whom the words 'aesthetic' and 'integrity' were meaningless. The architect Rem Koolhaas has put forward the delightful and utterly convincing theory that the fantastical buildings of early theme parks in Coney Island (over in Brooklyn) in fact created the Manhattan skyscraper. Dubbed a latter-day 'Sodom' by its many detractors, turn-of-the-century Coney Island was a complex of extraordinary amusement parks. A developer, **George Tilyou**, began in 1881 with an Observation Tower that he bought from the 1876 Centennial Exhibition in Philadelphia. At 300ft, the skeletal structure was taller than anything across the water in Manhattan. It was accompanied by Brazilian and Japanese pavilions from the same exhibition, a hotel constructed in the shape of a 150ft-high elephant, and a replica of a ferris wheel built for the Chicago World's Fair of 1883.

The island's second developer was a showman **Fred Thompson**, also a drop-out from the École des Beaux Arts in Paris. In 1903 he designed **Luna Park**, complete with 1214 electrically illuminated minarets and towers, and a skyline straight out of *The Arabian Nights*. Luna Park was a spookily accurate premonition of the finialed Manhattan that emerged two decades later in the twenties. Anticipating the eclecticism of later Manhattan skyscrapers, Thompson announced that his buildings rejected all set forms of architecture, and that the architect 'must dare to decorate a minaret with Renaissance detail or to jumble Romanesque with *l'art nouveau* always with the idea of keeping his line constantly varied, broken, and moving, so that it may lead gracefully into the towers and minarets of a festive sky-line'.

A year later a real estate promoter and former state senator **J. R. Reynolds** opened **Dreamland**, illuminated by a million electric lights and with a Renaissance tower in the centre which soared 375ft into the air. The tower bore an uncanny resemblance to the Metropolitan Life Tower built five years later on Madison Square in Manhattan. For Dreamland, Reynolds employed a New York architectural firm who produced a white city resembling the 1893 Chicago World's Fair (*see* 'Beaux-Arts', above, for its influence on Manhattan architects). Completing the circle, a quarter of a century after Dreamland, Reynolds became the developer responsible for Manhattan's most whimsical Christmas tree of all, the Chrysler Building.

Evolution of the Skyscraper II: Manhattan Palazzi

Meanwhile, in Manhattan the race to build the tallest building began in earnest. In 1902 **Daniel Burnham**, a brilliant skyscraper builder from Chicago and director of the World's Fair, built one of Manhattan's most irresistible skyscrapers on Madison Square. An extruded Renaissance palazzo, it was constructed out of a steel cage and stood on a triangular site the shape of an iron. Looking like an ocean liner sailing up Broadway, it was immediately nicknamed the Flatiron Building (*see* p.94). At 300ft the Flatiron was a little shorter than the Park Row Building on Broadway, but dwarfed its neighbours. New Yorkers found its shape so disturbing that many were convinced it would collapse in the wind.

The Flatiron was followed in 1908 by another composite palazzo-tower, **Ernest Flagg's** wonderful Singer Building, double the height of the Flatiron and, unfortunately, a magnet for suicides. Demolished in 1970, it still holds the record as the tallest building ever blown up. A year later, however, in 1909 the Singer was beaten in height by the Metropolitan Life Tower, a bizarre 712ft version of the Campanile of St Marks in Venice built opposite the Flatiron and now dwarfing it.

By 1908 skyscrapers were promoted as miniature cities: the idea had been a New York obsession ever since Melville's Bartleby the Scrivener preferred not to move out of his Wall Street office. In the skyscraper, architects had at last created a totally autonomous environment which rivalled nature.

In 1913, the skyscraper reached full maturity with **Cass Gilbert's** Woolworth Tower, the tallest building in the world at 792ft, and a monumental advertisement for Frank Woolworth's great chain of five-and-dime stores (*see* pp.170–71). A fan of Napoleon and of Barry's Houses of Parliament in London, Woolworth commissioned and received a Gothic Revival masterpiece of imperial proportions.

Zoning

In 1915 the Equitable Building loomed up on Broadway, containing offices for 15,000 workers and 45 acres of space on a plot just bigger than an acre. It was blatantly greedy, and ate up light and air from the streets around it. The building added fuel to calls from real estate owners and city planners alike for restrictive legislation, culminating in the Zoning Law of 1916.

The new zoning laws imposed a vertical grid plan on Manhattan. Instead of rising sheer from their sites as the Equitable Building did, at a certain height skyscrapers had to step back from the plotline or area on which they stood. A tower could then rise as high as the builder could take it, so long as it filled no more than 25 per cent of the plot. The laws did not impose aesthetic ambitions on designs: as long as buildings made space for light and air, architects could design what they like. For the next half-century, however, zoning laws transformed Manhattan. In only a few years its skyline began to mirror exactly the fanciful finials, pyramids and ziggurats of Luna Park.

Art Deco Aerodynamics

Despite the world-beating height of some of its towers, New York was slow to catch up with design innovations taking place in Chicago and Europe. The two catalysts for change were zoning laws and the emergence of Art Deco at the Paris *Exposition des Arts Decoratifs* in 1925. The skyscrapers that resulted were new and imaginative in style and decoration, and they gave New York its extraordinary skyline. However, they were not fundamentally iconoclastic.

The obsession was with aerodynamics: like fireworks, nearly all the futuristic scrapers of the twenties and thirties imitated rockets or referred in some way to flight. Most famously, the Empire State Building had a mast for dirigibles, then being hyped as the transport of the future. The American Radiator Building caught green-coloured fire at the top, like an upended firecracker; the Waldorf-Astoria had an electrically retractable roof, and stood on stilts wedged between the tracks of Grand Central. The architect of the Chrysler meanwhile hid a spire in the roof, which he tacked on at the last minute to beat the briefest Tallest Building in the World, at 40 Wall Street. The Chrysler itself was dressed in icons of the automobile and four years later Walter Chrysler brought out a streamlined and finned 'Airflow' car looking like a speed car (and also available with the same engine and chassis, and a 'traditional' body).

New York's architects quickly began experimenting with the zoning laws: one, **Hugh Ferriss**, actually gave up architectural practice in order to concentrate on drafting an imaginary New York of the air, with the tops of skyscrapers as hangars, airports and runways. In 1923 **Harvey Wiley Corbett** (who later worked on Rockefeller Center) put a proposal into the Regional Plan Association of New York for 'a modernized Venice'. In this, pedestrians would be elevated on to overhead bridges and walkways, and surface levels abandoned to trucks and cars. In 1929 the architect **Raymond Hood** came up with a scheme that was similar in spirit, for a city of apartment buildings to be built along the spans of the East River bridges.

Rockefeller Center: Manhattan's Utopian City-Within-A-City

Plans for a new New York eventually surfaced in Rockefeller Center, an unparalleled example of urban planning built in the midst of the Depression (*see* pp.104–5). Here at last New York planners created a true city-within-a-city: an organic complex whose underground concourses magically absorbed pedestrians, cars, tourists, delivery trucks and businessmen, and whose scrapers functioned as offices, theatres, cinemas, museums, television studios and plazas which doubled as showcases for modern sculpture. It was a brilliant achievement, vindicating at last the whimsicality of Art Deco.

Raymond Hood and the International Style

In the 1930s **Raymond Hood** emerged as New York's most innovative skyscraper architect. His two best scrapers, the Daily News and the McGraw-Hill, stood as sentinels of the avant-garde at either end of 42nd Street. The Daily News Building at the east end is New York's earliest (many would say superior) version of the slabs that proliferated across post-war Manhattan. Pinstriped in brown and white brick, with spandrels set close together, it emphasizes the vertical thrust of the building in a way that culminated in New York's supreme skyscraper, the soaring RCA Building in Rockefeller Center, designed a few years later by a consortium including Hood.

The McGraw-Hill Building also spans the gap between pre-war Art Deco and modernism. It is one of the city's most appealingly extravagant skyscrapers, with a sleek Art Deco lobby, and a matchless glimmering green terracotta exterior tipped with gold which turns from a greeny-blue at the bottom to a lighter leafy green at the top, making the scraper look taller than it really is.

Though they piously denounced its Deco details, the architect Philip Johnson, then only 26, and the critic Henry Russell Hitchcock, hailed the McGraw-Hill as the only New York building to merit inclusion in their compendium of 1932 called 'The International Style'. Their own coinage, the 'international style' referred loosely to the work of the Viennese architects Loos and Hoffmann, the radical Dutch group, de Stijl, and also to the founder of the Bauhaus, Walter Gropius— well before the First World War, all of these had rejected ornament for abstract, cubist designs, curtain walls and corner windows. Hitchcock and Johnson saw the new movement as a universal style; a successor to the anonymous but standardized architecture of the Middle Ages. Scandalized by the brazen caprice of Art Deco, the authors proclaimed the McGraw-Hill as the only structure in Manhattan which— thanks to its horizontal bands of windows—came close to 'achieving aesthetically the expression of the enclosed steel cage'.

The Rise and Fall of the Glass Box

Along with exhibitions organized by Philip Johnson at New York's temple of modernism—the new Museum of Modern Art on 53rd Street—'The International Style' paved the way for the supremacy of the glass slab. The war, of course, brought construction to a halt, but it also brought an influx of architects fleeing Europe. In the hiatus, the Bauhaus boys infiltrated all the important American schools: Gropius became head of architecture at Harvard; Mies van der Rohe (at that time Johnson's mentor) took a similar position at the Illinois Institute of Technology; Moholy Nagy founded the Chicago Institute of Design; Josef Albers became a director of Yale.

After the war, the architecture of Manhattan was transformed. A marriage of reinforced concrete and air-conditioning created office space which was infinite, and in which only the nobs got to sit next to a window. In 1952 the first International Style glass curtain-wall arrived, (courtesy of the new United Nations buildings, a project initiated by Le Corbusier), and the fully fledged glass box was born. Slabs invaded Midtown and Lower Manhattan's streets and avenues, blunting the delicately jagged skyline of the pre-war years. The only exception to their homogeneity was **Frank Lloyd Wright's** enigmatic snail-shell, the Guggenheim Museum (*see* pp.179–80), the second and last of his commissions in Manhattan (which was still twice as many as his mentor, Louis Sullivan, received half a century earlier).

Not all the boxes were bland, however. **Mies van der Rohe's** Seagram Building and **Skidmore, Owings & Merrill's** Lever House (*see* pp.107–8) rank as two of Manhattan's finest scrapers. Unfortunately for such buildings, imitation has been the sincerest insult: in the 50s and 60s whole avenues of New York filled with queues of slipshod replicas. Done on the cheap, these clones could not compete with buildings like the Seagram which relied on the highest quality materials (bronze and walnut panelling), meticulous detail (to preserve uniformity on the exterior, window blinds could only be drawn halfway up), and lastly on sophisticated sleight of hand which can elegantly 'express' the scraper's internal construction.

Finally, in 1977, New York got the ultimate in glass boxes, the gigantically boring, technologically innovative twin-towered World Trade Center, begun in 1962 and finished 15 years later, at unthinkable cost. In recent years, New Yorkers have grown fond of these plain-faced towers.

Post-modernism in the Eighties and Nineties

In Manhattan, Post-modernism was a useful catch-all term for buildings built in the seventies and eighties which weren't glass boxes. Conveniently for both critic and architect, post-modernism described what new buildings were not, not what they were. By the mid-1970s, some areas of Midtown New York had turned into a Hall of Mirrors where glass skyscrapers were endlessly repeated and distorted in each other's reflecting skins. Films or photographs set in Manhattan habitually luxuriated in the reflections of skyscraper windows until the reflections themselves came to symbolize the essence of New York.

Manhattan was slow to rebel against the glass curtain wall, and the first serious challenge came with **Hugh Stubbin's** Citicorp Center, a chisel-shaped scraper dressed in white aluminum and standing on stilt-like columns. Built on 53rd Street in 1977, its distinctive angled crown was supposed to double as a solar generator, but the panels for these were never, in the end, installed.

In the eighties and nineties, a hundred years after the city's first skyscraper was built downtown, Manhattan's architects reverted to what New York has always excelled at: extravagant, feckless, aesthetically aimless eclecticism. **Philip Johnson**, once a star in the International Modern stable, turned coat and in 1984 designed the Madison Avenue AT&T (now the Sony) Building—topped by a

Chippendale highboy crown and containing an enormous out-of-proportion Gothic/Romanesque atrium at the bottom. The AT&T was followed in 1986 by John Burgee and Philip Johnson's 385 Third Avenue, an elegant beige-pink office building resembling a stick of lipstick, and **Kevin Roche's** E. F. Hutton building with serrated top hat and neo-Egyptian columns on the ground floor.

Post-modernism, as with any 'ism', has been a hit-and-miss affair. Skyscrapers flirted with what was snobbishly thought kitsch, and sometimes themselves became kitsch. Built in the late 1980s, Cesar Pelli's hideous **World Financial Center** in Battery Park City is a complex of four high-rise office towers which sum up everything that is a liability in post-modern architecture, from the fast-food design and concept to outright pretentiousness, exemplified in Pelli's **Winter Garden**, an oversized DIY-style conservatory with palm trees and red marble.

In the thirties commentators predicted that Manhattan would evolve into an unflinchingly futuristic city: H. G. Wells thought it would go underground; others thought it would shoot 250 storeys into the sky. But if anything the buildings of recent years make neurotic gestures to the past. In 1989 **Skidmore, Owings & Merrill** designed a pioneering new skyscraper for Citicorp in Queens. At 663ft, this was the tallest structure outside Manhattan. Land has always been plentiful outside Manhattan, and although space within Manhattan is significantly more expensive, few skyscrapers have been built outside of Manhattan island in places like Brooklyn or New Jersey. The pioneering Queens Citicorp Building boldly went beyond the pale. Like the first gabled Dutch houses built by the colonists in the 17th century, its top was crow-stepped. Similar Dutch allusions can be seen at 100 United Nations Plaza, a residential building with an eight storey crow-stepped crown built by Der Scutt on East 48th Street in 1992.

An Odyssey into the 21st Century

> '...the wonders of 1908 will be far outdone, and the 1,000 foot structure realized; now nearly a million people do business here each day; by 1930 it is estimated the number will be doubled, necessitating tiers of sidewalks, with elevated lines and new creations to supplement subway and surface cars, with bridges between structural heights. Airships, too, may connect us with all the world. What will posterity develop?'

Moses King, *King's Views of New York*, 1912

> '...the only thing Yankee Ingenuity [has] not yet accomplished... the successful passing of two car-loads on a single line of tracks.'

Mark Twain, 1835–1910

No one has any idea how Manhattan will develop, except that the grid will stay the same, skyscrapers will probably get taller, and the strictures of architectural theorists will mostly be ignored. If Manhattan develops into the futuristic 50-million-people city-in-the-sky that New Yorkers predicted early this century, it will be thanks to technological inventions like the Odyssey, a sideways elevator developed by Otis in 1996 and scheduled to go into production in 1998.

With Otis' revolutionary elevator system, super-skyscrapers rising more than half a mile into the skies will be viable for the first time in history. Like the Leap Frog railway cars in Coney Island (which had rails on their backs so they could slide over and under each other) Odysseys will be able to glide smoothly out of the way of oncoming elevators, liberating precious space wasted in conventional elevator shafts. Odysseys will also be able to travel diagonally, and developers, previously unable to build over 1800ft because elevator cables could not take the strain, will be able to reach heights of over 3500ft. Passengers, travelling horizontally and vertically in 'Transitor' cabs, will be able to commute between skyscrapers thousands of feet above street level, or diagonally from ground level to the far-away tops of hyper-tall scrapers.

With the Odyssey elevator, 21st-century Manhattan may actually become the vertiginous metropolis-in-the-sky it always aspired to be, absorbing fantastic quantities of human beings in teeming metroplexes of towers which will soar 250 storeys into the clouds and beyond.

...tram-lines from two to three inches above street level; building materials scattered half across the street; wheeled traffic taking its chances, dray versus brougham, at cross roads; sway-backed poles whittled and unpainted; drunken lamp-posts with twisted irons... In any other land they would be held to represent slovenliness, sordidness, and want of capacity. Here it is explained, not once but many times, that they show the speed at which the city has grown and the enviable indifference of her citizens to matters of detail. One of these days, you are told, everything will be taken in hand and put straight.

Rudyard Kipling, *Across a Continent*, 1892

Walking in Manhattan...

Manhattan is not, like other cities, an amorphous sprawl. Instead it is divided into little principalities or 'neighbourhoods'—each no bigger than a small hamlet, and each quite different from the other. Broadway crosses roughly 17 separate neighbourhoods on its journey from the bottom of Manhattan to the top, and undergoes at least 17 personality swings along the way. The walks in this book take in roughly 11½ Manhattan neighbourhoods. The streets may seem noisier and more chaotic than you're used to, but in Manhattan as nowhere else in the world you are guaranteed exhilaration and adventure as you walk.

However, you will need to readjust the way you look. In Manhattan streets and avenues are gullies filled with sky and lined by mountainous buildings. You can look at the architecture close to, or from miles away, but there are no European-style vistas in between. To help you see the city inside and out, the four walks take you under the city streets, through lobbies, into elevators, across elevated walkways and up to the tops of the city's most distinguished skyscrapers. A couple of the walks involve ferry or helicopter rides and all four include views, food and drink. Bring binoculars and a change of shoes if possible, perhaps a tie if you're a man.

When to Walk

Walk I Best **Monday–Friday**, as the Oyster Bar in Grand Central is closed on Saturday and Sunday, and the Garment District is livelier in the week as well.

Walk II Good **any day except Monday**, when the Frick Collection is closed. (It includes a picnic in Central Park, but if it's rainy there are interesting restaurants along the way.)

Walk III Best for **Sunday brunch or Monday–Thursday**, avoiding the Jewish Sabbath, when some shops in the area and especially the Orchard Street Market will be closed. The East Village wakes up late and shops here are open every day from about brunchtime onwards.

Walk IV Includes a ride on the Staten Island Ferry (50¢) and a walk across Brooklyn Bridge and is good on **any day**; on a weekend if you want to avoid the office workers, on weekdays if you want to go to the court-houses.

As Groucho Marx put it, 'when it's 9.30 in New York it's 1937 in Los Angeles'; so if opening times, admission charges and restaurant prices have altered out of exis-tence, take it as a healthy sign that Manhattan is still happening.

Lastly, remember that when you come out of subway it can be difficult to work out whether you're facing uptown or downtown, until you locate a street sign. When crossing streets it's wise to obey the 'Don't Walk' signs at all times. Directions within the text are given New York style in 'blocks'. Blocks between avenues take about four minutes on foot; blocks between streets, about one and a half.

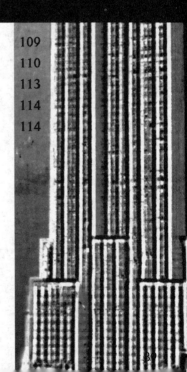

I: Vertical City

Start: *By subway, take the **N** or **R** train to West 34th Street and 6th Avenue, or the **6** to 33rd Street and Park Ave.*

Walking Time: *4 hours, but allow an extra hour for the tour round Radio City and/or the helicopter ride.*

> *They are independently new and still more independently 'novel'—this in common with so many other terrible things in America.*
>
> Henry James on skyscrapers, 1904

Midtown is quintessential Manhattan: exhilaration, glamour, vertigo—and noise, confusion, anxiety; objects plummeting from heights, leaky air-conditioners, Lycraed bicycle messengers, and traffic; the most expensive restaurants and real estate, the worst

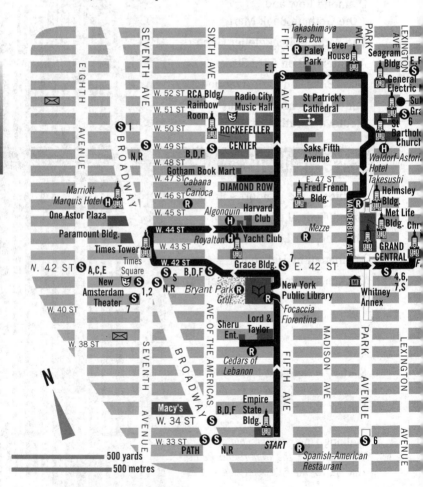

theatres and the best skyscrapers in the world. This walk through the canyons of Midtown takes you through, up and around a thoroughly vertical city.

The Midtown skyscraper, so emblematic of Manhattan and Manhattanism, is in fact only a century old, and has only slowly grown in prominence. In fact the word 'skyscraper' originally applied to the loftiest of the small triangular sails tied to rigging on 18th-century schooners, and in slang to the most memorable part of the male genitalia, the intromittent organ. In 1789 a 'Sky-scraper' won the Derby, and the word was used to refer to particularly tall horses. By 1800, skyscraper changed again: it meant a jauntily cocked hat or bonnet, and, by 1857, anyone who was tall and lanky. A few years later, it was applied sarcastically to the stupid-looking riders of penny-farthing bicycles.

A John J. Flinn first referred to *buildings* as 'sky-scrapers' in a small book about Chicago published in 1890. In Manhattan, the first 12-storey skyscraper had gone up on Broadway in 1889; Manhattanites, used to living in five-storey buildings, were so afraid of it that the architect had to move into

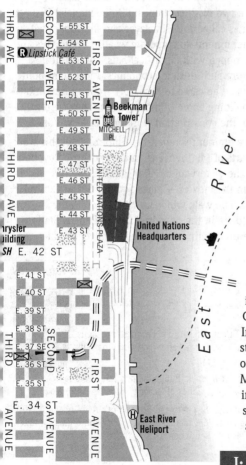

I: Vertical City

91

the 11th floor to prove it was safe. Less than three decades later, the city sprouted a futuropolis of 50-storey skyscrapers. They were touted as miniature cities: 'One can live in them, indefinitely, without going out for food, clothing or lodging', wrote one publicist. Meanwhile H. G. Wells was smugly predicting the death of the skyscraper: 21st-century New York, he assured his readers, would go underground; people would live in catacombs, and by 2055 high-rises would be as cobwebby as flying buttresses.

But as the 20th century gives up the ghost, skyscrapers are omnipresent. There are two distinct clumps: in the Financial District and Midtown, sometimes called the Himalayas and the Alps. Wall Street's scrapers are monuments to corporate wealth; Midtown's are flighty and whimsical, topped with fantastical hats, and flaunting a defiance of gravity, nature and sensible economics. Most were built by Caughnawaga Indians who came to New York from a reservation near Montreal in the building boom of the twenties. They currently make up 40 per cent of the construction workforce in New York.

Starting at the city's pre-eminent scraper, the Empire State, this walk takes in the quirkier parts of Midtown (tea in the eccentric Royalton Hotel, for instance, or the waterwall in Paley Plaza) as well as places everyone has been to in the movies—Times Square, Grand Central and Rockefeller Center. The walk winds up with lunch in the wonderful Oyster Bar (deep in the bowels of Grand Central Station) and finally, if you have time, with a helicopter ride over Manhattan.

---

lunch/cafés

Spanish–American Restaurant, 2 East 33rd Street, at 5th Ave. Basic Hispanic café: bacalao, tripe, cassava rice, omelettes and fries (from $5).

Cedars of Lebanon, 39 West 38th Street, off 5th Ave. Lebanese houmous, baba ghanouj and baked lamb with cracked wheat and pine nuts, buffet lunch from $10.

Focaccia Fiorentina, outside the New York Public Library, 5th Ave., between 40th and 42nd Sts. Twenty kinds of focaccia sandwiches (from $5).

Bryant Park Grill & Café, 25 West 40th St., between 5th and 6th Aves., ✆ 840 6500. Swanky pavilion behind the New York Library in an elegant park: brunch or lunch at the rooftop grill ($20–40) or sandwiches from the cheaper adjoining café (around $15).

Cabana Carioca, 123 West 45th St., near 7th Ave. Huge, bustling, jolly Brazilian joint. Fried eggs on steaks; *feijoada* (black bean stew); *caipirinha*—lime juice and rum cocktail ($15).

Edison Café, Hotel Edison, 228 West 47th St., between Broadway and 8th Ave. Excellent quaintly old-fashioned coffee shop in the Art Deco Hotel Edison, serving good East European blintzes, borscht and matzoh brei ($10).

Algonquin Hotel Lobby, 59 West 44th St., between 5th and 6th Aves. A good stopping-off point for tea or cocktails; avoid the food.

44, at the Royalton Hotel, 44 West 44th St., between 5th and 6th Aves., ✆ 944 8844. Pricey (around $8 for a bowl of crisps, $16 for a turkey on sourdough sandwich or $40 for camomile-cured salmon with frisée), but amusing because of its slick modern interior and clientele. You can play chess, drink martinis, have afternoon tea or sit in the lobby for nothing.

Mezze, 10 East 44th St., between 5th and Madison Aves., ✆ 697 6644; *American (AE)*. Reasonable prices for lunch or breakfast in stylish surroundings (from $7).

Paradise & Lunch, 55 West 44th St., beween 5th and 6th Aves. Salads by the quarter pound, soups and elegant sandwiches.

Dean & Deluca, Rockefeller Plaza, on 49th St., off 5th Ave. Branch of the glamorous SoHo delicatessen—top sandwiches and strong espressos (from $5).

Rainbow Promenade, 30 Rockefeller Plaza, adjoining the Rainbow Room on the 65th floor of the RCA Building, between 49th and 50th Sts. Cocktails in lovable Art Deco stratospheria from $10; also 'little meals': variable but including burgers, smoked salmon, etc.

Lyn's Café, 28 West 55th St., between 5th and 6th Aves; *American (AE)*. Happy café around the corner from MOMA and serving decently priced club sandwiches, French onion soup and fries in big portions (from $7).

Lipstick Café, 885 3rd Ave., at East 54th St. Excellent value: deluxe sandwiches, soups and salads at low prices by super-chef Jean-Georges Vongerichten ($10–15).

Takashimaya Tea Box, basement, 693 5th Ave., between 54th and 55th Sts. *Forty* kinds of tea in Midtown's second Japanese-owned department store: cucumber or smoked salmon sandwiches, *à la Japonais.*

St Bartholomew's Café, St Bartholomew's Church, Park Avenue between 50th and 51st Sts. Good outdoor café on church plaza inscribed with the words 'Your Body is the temple of the Holy Spirit.' ($10–15).

Takesushi, 71 Vanderbilt Avenue, near 45th and 46th Sts. Yellowtails, fluke and sea urchin sushi lunch from $15 in restaurant containing tatami rooms.

Grand Central Oyster Bar and Restaurant, lower level, Grand Central Terminal, at 42nd St., ✆ 490 6650 *(reservations only for the main dining room)*. Atmospheric oyster bar in the bowels of Grand Central station: 20 varieties of oysters, also soft-shelled crab and fresh fish. $20–40, but you can order clam chowder, oyster pan roast (oysters with Worcester sauce and cream) or half a dozen raw oysters for less than $6 from the nicer and more laidback luncheonette-style counter-bar.

From the subway or bus stop walk east or west to the 33rd Street/5th Avenue entrance to the **Empire State Building**, *the king of all sky-scrapers (and also the HQ of the US Soccer Federation).*

Before you go inside, look south down 5th Avenue: eleven blocks down at 23rd Street is one of the most startling and beautiful skyscrapers in Manhattan—the **Flatiron Building**.

The 300ft 22-storey triangular palazzo is Manhattan's earliest extant skyscraper and when it was built in 1902 (by Chicago architect Daniel Burnham) it galvanized the city's imagination: Ford Madox Ford and H. G. Wells wrote eulogies to it and Edward Steichen and Alfred Stieglitz photographed it obsessively—in snow, rain and fog—comparing it to a 'monster steam-liner' advancing on the onlooker. (If you have binoculars, you'll notice the exterior walls are undulated rather than flat, making the building ripple along 5th Avenue.) The Flatiron was especially fasci-nating to Peeping Toms, who flocked to the windiest corner in the city for a flash of calf, stocking and ankle. In 1905 an ankle fetishist shot a racy docudrama on the corner called *The Flat-iron Building on a Windy Day.* Meanwhile policemen tried to shoo the voyeurs away—and according to New York City legend (but not according to any etymological dictionary) this is the origin of the expression 'twenty-three skidoo' or scram!

> *Now enter the Empire State Building, buy a ticket for viewing decks only from the basement office, and take the elevator to the 86th floor (decks open 9.30am–midnight; in case you decide to walk, it's 1575 steps).*

If you're visiting New York with a friend and there happens to be a thunderstorm, the observation decks on the 86th floor are the ideal place to head for—'For if con-ditions are right' the Empire State Fact Sheet assures us, 'static electricity build-up is mammoth,' and when you stick your fingers through the observatory fence not only will 'St Elmo's fire ... stream from your fingertips' but blue electric sparks fly from the lips of kissing couples. If you're not in the mood, you can hunt out the world's highest colony of ants instead. Presumably these ants have evolved spe-cially adhesive footpads to withstand winds that are sometimes violent enough to thrash even the Empire State Building an inch and a half to the side.

In February 1997, this deck was the scene of a terrible shooting after a 69-year-old Palestinian, Ali Abu-Kamal, killed himself, a bystander and wounded six others with a semi-automatic after losing the life savings he planned to invest in the USA. Since then extra security has been added to every level of the Empire State.

> *After the 86th deck, continue up to the second observatory on the 102nd floor. This is really part of the building's 'mooring mast', a 150ft glass and metal spire which was added at the last minute, supposedly so dirigibles could dock on the roof, but mostly to make it taller and discourage rivals.*

The mast was incredibly dangerous and the idea was abandoned in 1931 after a blimp keeled over, drenching pedestrians below with water from its ballast, and nearly sweeping away celebrities who had come to watch. Nowadays the tower has a high-tech lighting system and is lit in any number of colour combinations for an enormous variety of occasions: blue and white if the Yankees win the World Series (they managed this for the first time in 15 years in October 1996); red and white for St Valentine's Day; pink and white for National Breast Cancer Day. On foggy nights in the spring and autumn the lights are turned off to prevent mesmerized migrating birds colliding with the building—the fate of a B-25 bomber when Colonel W. F. Smith crashed it 18ft into the 79th floor in 1945, killing fourteen people and causing $1 million worth of damage. One engine shot through the other side of the building; the other plummeted down an elevator shaft, taking an elevator with it.

It's odd, 102 floors in the air, to think that less than 200 years ago the ground below was a farmyard which John Jacob Astor purchased in 1827 for a mere $20,000. Things only started to change in 1857 when Astor's sons built two mansions on the farm. At a time when 'society' was straightforwardly limited to the 'Four Hundred' coat-tails that could fit in Mrs Astor's ballroom, the Astor mansions became the focal point of a nouveau riche 'Millionaire's Row'. Things changed again in 1893 when to spite his overbearing aunt William Waldorf Astor demolished his mansion and built a hotel on the site instead. He called it the Waldorf and shortly afterwards went to Europe. In an equivalent fit of pique, Mrs Astor built the Astoria Hotel next door and moved uptown to the Upper East Side.

Joined together, with the proviso that connecting corridors could be sealed off if necessary, the Waldorf-Astoria evolved into a new more potent social hub. For the next thirty years the likes of Frick and Guggenheim were elaborately received in rooms that were more like those of a private mansion than a hotel. Finally in 1929 the Waldorf moved to its present location on Park Avenue, metamorphosing this time into a skyscraper. The site on 34th Street was sold again, and plans laid down for building the Empire State.

Demolition began on 1st October 1929 and less than a month later on October 29th the Stock Market crashed. Nevertheless the architects, Shreve, Lamb & Harmon, miraculously completed the office building in a year and 45 days. Elevator cores and passenger elevators from the old Waldorf were used to build the new Empire State and spectators gathered on the sidewalk to watch the steel framework rise at the astonishing rate of 4½ storeys a week (peaking at one point to 14½ storeys in ten days). Building costs were cut by half, thanks to the Depression, but space was hard to let out and the skyscraper was dubbed the 'Empty State Building'.

Today, the offices inside are practically fully occupied; on the exterior brickwork, limestone and chrome-nickel steel (an alloy that never tarnishes) are being replaced and re-welded; and Donald Trump and Leona Helmsley, plus a group of foreign investors, now own and control the building. About 500 tenants make menswear, and there is a gentleman in a basement photocopy shop who has been working in the Empire State since it opened in 1931: 'Boy, oh boy,' he says sturdily.

> Leave the Empire State Building by the 5th Avenue entrance. If you've come to New York to shop, you can make a short detour from here to **Macy's**, supposedly the largest department store in the world. The store takes up two million square feet of floor space on a whole city block between 6th and 7th Avenues and 34th and 35th Streets: to get there, walk a block west along 34th Street as far as 6th Avenue.

Macy's sells anything from pet supplies to items you assumed were discontinued centuries ago. After the parent company went into bankruptcy protection in 1991, Macy's no longer stocks the cheapest bargains in Manhattan; however if you're looking for something like a swimming costume with a skirt attached, Macy's will probably stock it.

> From the Empire State Building, walk north up 5th Avenue to 38th Street. On the way, you brush against the fringes of the **Garment District**, more scrum than district, thanks to the vast number of clothes and manufacturing workshops and showrooms which have been here since the First World War.

The chaos of 38th and 39th Streets can be amusing, especially in the mornings. If you can handle the trundling clothes-racks, gridlocked traffic, shoulder-padded shoppers, and people bombarding you with circulars for embarrassing warts, verrucas and broken nails, then **Sheru Enterprises**, just off 5th Avenue at 49–53 West 38th Street, is well worth a visit. This gem of a shop sells trimmings, rugs, shiny beads, sequins, costume gems, ribbons, buttons and a lot of mystery objects, by the pound. Even if you don't know what it is, it's worth buying something here just to eavesdrop on the two gents who run the shop: 'I'm so busy I can't even talk,' they'll say, followed by, 'Have you got a rug at home? Have you got a man at home? Then take ME home!'

> On the northwest corner of 38th Street is another department store, **Lord & Taylor**, which was famous for introducing the world's first window displays to Manhattan in 1905.

Lord & Taylor is stylish but old-fashioned, with in-store restaurants, a big perfume hall, a bigger shoe department and 'walking talking mannequins'—chatty models who roam the store for hours at a time advertising the designer outfits they're wearing: until they get into a conversation with you, the catwalk gait, pancake make-up and unnatural facial expressions give the girls an interestingly zombified appearance.

> *Walk another two blocks up 5th Avenue as far as 40th Street and the famous bouffant stone lions of the Center for the Humanities, better known to New Yorkers as the **New York Public Library** (www.nypl.org). The lions are supposed to roar every time a virgin walks past, but according to New Yorkers the last time that happened was a long time ago.*

Libraries are not supposed to be exciting, but this is an exception. Built in 1911 by Carrère and Hastings, the Library is the finest beaux-arts building in Manhattan. Inside it's even grander, with an entrance hall based on the baths of Caracalla, white Vermont marble ceilings and floors, a Paris Opéra staircase and candlestick ballroom chandeliers.

Most of the action goes on at the top of the staircase in Rm 315: the **Bill Blass Reading and Catalog Room**, and it's worth going in here and ordering a book just to observe the Luddite ritual that ensues: dispatchers stuff requests into glass batons which are sucked up pneumatic tubes into the library's innards. Down here human pages remove the call slips and search out requested books from eight levels of stacks. An average of ten minutes later, a number lights up on an illuminated bingo board and the books are delivered to the main reading room by computer-operated dumb waiter. Quaintly antique, the system is six times faster than the British Library's.

At 11am and 2pm, there are excellent (free) guided tours. The twinkly guide is full of recherché facts, informing you that the Polaroid camera and the Xerox were invented in the science department; that the army, apparently owning no atlases of their own, resorted to the Map Room to plan the American invasion of North Africa; and finally that the library contains 25,000 menus, and has 140 miles of shelving and some six million books in the stacks below.

No one minds if you explore on your own, for the library styles itself 'The People's Library' and has **public lavatories** (the only ones on this walk) and was practically the only place Trotsky approved of when he came to New York in 1917. When you've had enough, you can join the cheerful crowd sitting on the steps outside, eating hot-dogs and reading between the lions (sculpted by E. C. Potter and later dubbed 'Patience' and 'Fortitude' by LaGuardia for the qualities New Yorkers needed to survive the Depression). Incidentally, these steps are a prime spot for strange and fascinating conversations: to keep them lively you can buy coffee and homemade cakes from **The Café Crème** on the left-hand side of the entrance.

> *From the Public Library turn left on to West 42nd Street and walk west as far as **Bryant Park**, at the back of the library on your left.*

Until 1980 this was the biggest drugs 'supermarket' in town. Now, after restorations which involved digging a maze of book stacks below ground, it's a civilized, dare one say English-looking park, with a fountain, wrought-iron chairs to sit on and London plane trees lining a formal lawn. One un-British element is the **Bryant Park Grill**, an elegant restaurant and bar with dining rooms in a pretty glass and steel pavilion (and rooftop terrace). This serves good expensive brunches (eggs and sevruga caviar for $40), also lunch and supper.

Less pleasantly, only a century and a half ago the site was a paupers' burial ground at the extreme northern reaches of a newly urbanized Manhattan. In 1853, two years after London's Great Exhibition, burials were banned in Manhattan south of 86th Street and a **Crystal Palace** was built on the potter's field as the centrepiece of the first American World's Fair. Joseph Paxton, the engineer behind London's Crystal Palace, offered a design for this, but it was rejected and a bloated version by two Germans used instead. It was 'much more beautiful as an architectural work', claimed handbooks of the time—and just as great a fire hazard because after five years it burnt to the ground (supposedly after the owners set fire to it in order to recover the insurance).

The 6000 exhibits included pumps, sewing machines and the Otis Safety Brake, a spring mechanism with gripper cogs which in a few years' time would transform the skyline of Manhattan and the rest of the world. Elisha Graves Otis had developed the safety elevator two years earlier for a New York manufacturing firm where he worked as a master mechanic. The following year Otis opened his own elevator shop in Yonkers, New York. At the Crystal Palace main exhibition hall he staged a dramatic demonstration of the Safety Elevator: an assistant presented him with a dagger on a velvet cushion; Otis climbed on a platform, hoisting himself 30 feet into the air; he then seized the dagger, slashed the cable supporting him, and miraculously stayed put. Otis was a consummate showman and toured the world with this compelling piece of theatre until his death in 1861.

Opposite the palace was the Latting Observatory, a 350ft wood and iron prototype skyscraper, 150ft shorter than the Great Pyramid of Cheops to which it was compared. Visitors bought ice-creams from the bottom and took a steam elevator to the top to observe a city which by that time had only spread as far as 42nd Street. In 1856 tragedy struck: the tower shot up in flames, creating a space which was filled in the 1970s by the ungraceful **Grace Building**, a skyscraper which actually resembles a pair of bell-bottoms.

> *A block west down 42nd Street takes you to the intersection with Broadway known as the Crossroads of the World and a Disneyfied **Times Square**.*

In the stories of Damon Runyon, this was 'Dream Street' where could you see a motley bunch of 'burlesque dolls, and hoofers, and guys who write songs, and saxophone players, and newsboys...and midgets, and blondes with Pomeranian pooches...' (and also the sacred spot where, according to instructions in his will, Runyon's ashes were decanted from an aeroplane). 'Broadway reads better than it lives,' Runyon once wrote, but he would probably be as much astonished by 'New' Times Square as the three-card monte players, pickpockets, male prostitutes and pornographers who were purged from 42nd Street in the 1990s so that the district could be reclaimed for tourists and businesses like Disney who thrive on them.

Disney's takeover of Times Square was sudden and thorough. Until 1992, the block of 42nd Street to your left between Broadway and 8th Avenue was 'Sin Street'—a sinkhole overflowing with peep shows, strip joints and porn shops with a sideline in fake IDs and publications such as *How to Get Even* and *How to Make a Bomb Out of Urine*. Now every sex parlour has gone. On the corner of Broadway and 42nd, under the American Express billboard, is a Disney Superstore. In the middle is the New Amsterdam Theater, restored by Disney for $38 million to show Disney films and theatrical productions like Tim Rice's *King David*. On Friday 13th June 1997 Disney sealed off 30 city blocks around 42nd Street for a parade the next day down 5th Avenue to the New Amsterdam Theater and the world premiere of *Hercules*. Street lights were extinguished as the floats passed each block and Disney paid $500,000 to the City for helping to stage the event. By the end of 1997 'New' 42nd Street will get a Madame Tussaud's and the largest multiplex cinema in the US with 26 screens and 17 escalators.

The urban cleansing began after the city passed new zoning laws which prevented pornography merchants opening up within 500 yards of a church, school or other merchants. Meanwhile in 1992 businesses in the area banded together into the Times Square BID or 'business improvement district'. Thanks to the BID, Times Square now smells of disinfectant instead of urine: the BID uses $6m a year (coughed up by 404 landlords in the district) to pay for private sanitation crews who vacuum and wash sidewalks and discipline smokers who 'dispose of their butts inappropriately'. The BID also finances 50 unarmed safety officers who wear cowboy hats and escort 'quality-of-life' offenders (turnstile jumpers, marijuana smokers, graffiti artists, pedlars, prostitutes and small-time drug dealers, etc.) to an autonomous community court on 54th Street. As punishment, less serious offenders are sent to work with sanitation crews cleaning streets; you can recognize these bad eggs by their jackets with '**CORRECTION**' emblazoned on their backs. Since its formation in 1992 the BID claims to have cut overall crime by nearly 50 per cent, a remarkable achievement for an area that was famous in the 1980s for being the national cesspool. (Pick-pocketing has fallen by only 30 per cent so *beware:* a notorious scam is 'swashbuckling'—passers-by have their belts slashed, their wallets whipped away and are left stranded, trousers crumpled round toes).

Times Square may be safer and more pleasant than it was in the 1980s, but many New Yorkers feel that the cleansing has gone too far. They claim that the city, and Mayor Giuliani in particular, has sold out to big business; that Pocahontas is a form of pornography in itself; that 42nd Street has been hideously transformed into a shopping mall Disneyland for suburban tourists; and finally that Times Square as a whole has been homogenized into a bland city centre the same as any other insipid city centre anywhere else. New businesses who have taken the place of the porn shops include Virgin Megastore, Conde Nast, the Gap and flocks of ersatz 'theme-u-rants' (including a Harley Davidson Café and a Jekyll & Hyde Diner as well as Planet Hollywood). Meanwhile anyone who actually misses the likes of 42nd Street's Triple XXX and the Harem House of Hores shouldn't despair too much, because a range of cheap dollar peepshows still lurk in the area, especially on 8th Avenue and the area west of 9th Avenue called Hell's Kitchen (supposedly after two police officers watched a fight there on a humid August night. 'This neighborhood is hot as hell,' one of the policemen said. 'Hell is cool,' the other replied drily. 'This here's Hell's Kitchen.')

As well as drastic drops in crime, good things have come out of the Times Square redevelopment. One is a new subway entrance on 42nd Street. (During rainstorms, the 42nd Street and 6th Avenue subway station sometimes smells of elephants. The Transit Authority only discovered why in the 1950s when they sent in James Patrick Kelly, who was mainly employed smelling out gas and water leaks. 'Smelly Kelly' realized that a water mains had leaked into the old New York Hippodrome where circuses had regularly performed and several decades' worth of elephants' dung was buried in the basement.) Other advantages include a completely new auditorium for the New York City Ballet (under construction in 1997 and 1998); the lighting of the globe on the old Paramount Building (opposite Times Tower and where Frank Sinatra rose to fame); and the restoration of several beautiful 19th-century Broadway theatres which landlords left to rot in the 1980s so that they could build modern condominiums in their place. In one engineering feat due to take place in late 1997 structural engineers will lift the Empire Theater off its foundations and roll it on steel rods 70ft down 42nd Street to make way for the AMC cini-complex. The BID organises excellent tours around some of these 19th-century theatres led by an entertaining actor called Lawrence Emilio (*12pm, Fridays, free: meet at the Times Square Visitor Center—on the north side of 42nd St between 7th and 8th Aves*).

> *In front of you on the island between 42nd Street, Broadway and 7th Avenue is* **Times Tower***, a once-elegant terracotta skyscraper dating from*

*1904 which was sheathed in marble in the 60s, and which thankfully will
be sheathed again in transparent industrial mesh in 1997/8 by architect
Frank Garry. When it was built the 476ft-high tower was the tallest in
Midtown: 'It Touches Higher Clouds than Anything within Twelve Miles',
claimed publicists. Today you can't miss it, because of its **Motogram**, a
360ft electrified 'zipper' which circles the building relaying the news in
digital letters. At the pointy end of the building is the **Sony Jumbotron**, a
giant video screen and supposedly the largest 'tron' of its kind in the
world. The building itself was originally home to the* New York Times
*which gave Times Square its name and published 'All the News that's Fit
to Print' here from December 31st 1904 until the 1930s, when it moved
round the corner to 229 West 43rd Street.*

Times Square may be sanitized nowadays but it still indulges in neon extravaganzas. By law, 'supersigns' in the square have to be big and include lights, and
from here you can see some of the most ebullient examples: a Cup Noodle billowing out real city steam, a Coke bottle with a top that comes off and a motorized
straw, and (on 42nd Street above a 3-D Concorde) a billboard for Joe Boxer boxer
shorts which flashes up e-mail from all over the world sent c/o *timesquare@joe-
boxer.com.* (In the 1950s you would have seen a man who puffed real smoke rings
out of Camel cigarettes, a penguin smoking Kools, a girl who endlessly blew her
nose on Kleenex, and soap bubbles frothing out of a packet of Lux flakes.)

Today's less whimsical signs are upstaged by evangelists of varying degrees of offen-
siveness but always with bad dress sense, who rant Eternal Damnation down
microphones at the base of the Motogram: 'You've been brainwashed with filth
and contamination, by 5th Avenue and David Letterman, God hates you so-called
Americans,' they inform the crowds who walk past in a steady oblivious stream.

*From Times Tower walk two blocks north to 44th Street. On the west side
of Broadway are two of New York's supremely ugly skyscrapers, **One
Astor Plaza** between 44th and 45th Streets (a gangling seventies sci-fi
building with a crown of concrete fins) and the **Marriott Marquis Hotel**,
a block north between 45th and 46th Streets.*

A camp blend of Star Wars and showbiz, the Marriott is the Zsa Zsa Gabor of New
York skyscrapers. At the top is Manhattan's only revolving restaurant, **The View**
(*open from 5.30pm Mon–Sun*), accessible by the city's most terrifying elevators
(worth a ride even if the restaurant is closed). These are test tubes studded with red
rhinestone lights and they plunge thrillingly through a false 1st-floor ceiling to the
45th floor. After a ride in one of these, you'll understand why a few years ago the
management slowed the lifts down after guests complained that the ride was
making them throw up.

*Walk a block and a bit east along West 44th Street back in the direction of
5th Avenue. On the second block, between 6th Avenue and 5th Avenue,
you pass the **Algonquin Hotel** at 59 West 44th Street. After the dizzy-
ments of Times Square, it might be relaxing to stop for tea either here, in
the Algonquin's tomb-like lobby, or across the road at the trendier
Royalton Hotel, diagonally opposite the Algonquin at 44 West 44th St.*

A travelling salesman called Douglas Fairbanks sold it some soap in 1902, but most
people remember the **Algonquin** as the rendezvous of the literary club known as
the Round Table. The club started in 1919, and revolved around boozy lunches,
well-rehearsed anecdotes and angel cake. The screenwriter Anita Loos called it 'a
boring set of exhibitionists' and even Dorothy Parker described it as 'just a lot of
people telling each other how good they were'. In the late 1980s the Algonquin
was bought by a Japanese corporation, who renovated it but thoughtfully preserved
the musty atmosphere (reminiscent of tweed coats which haven't been cleaned for
25 years). Previous guests have included Graham Greene, Prunella Scales and
William Faulkner, who keeled over and burnt himself on a steam pipe in a drinking
bout in the 1950s.

The actor and writer Robert Benchley was a Round Table fixture and also a perma-
nent resident in the **Royalton Hotel** opposite, where he lived in a hammed-up
Victorian suite with a library of books chosen for their titles alone, including *Forty
Thousand Sublime and Beautiful Thoughts* and *Talks on Manure*.

In 1988 the dowdy hotel was revamped to thrills and spills in the media by disco
entrepreneurs Ian Schrager and the late Steve Rubell of Studio 54 fame. You know
what you're in for as soon as you see the doormen—ladies in black crêpe trousers
and chaps wearing eyeliner—whose job is to look cryptic. Inside, a definitively
Eighties lobby features such humorous post-modern totems as conical stainless
steel 'airline' basins in the lavs and pointy mahogany tusks poking out of the lobby
walls. The hotel pulls a sparkling crowd of magazine magnates and their hangers-
on but you may also be shocked to see several beautiful but dead Japanese fighting
fish floating on their sides in goldfish bowls on plinths in the lobby. Nobody seems
to care a jot about them. 'There's no filter,' the waiters explain coldly. 'The fish die
in a few days and we forget to throw out the dead ones.' Luckily guests are treated
better and, although expensive and upsetting fish-wise, the Royalton remains an
amusing place to stop for a game of chess or a martini.

*A little way down from the Royalton on your left at 37 West 44th Street is
Warren & Wetmore's **New York Yacht Club**; 1890 beaux-arts, and until
recently home to the Americas Cup.*

Although most New Yorkers are used to it, the club is without doubt one of
Manhattan's crankiest buildings. Poseidon slobbers over the entrance, while three

17th-century ships' sterns, petrified in stone and gushing limestone water, are wedged into the window frames. Next door, at 27 West 44th Street is the **Harvard Club**, by New York's brilliant neoclassical architects, McKim, Mead & White (*see* **Architecture**, pp77–8). Hoi polloi aren't allowed, but if you sweep in with sufficient hauteur to paralyse the doorman, you will be able snoop round the baronial halls inside. The walls are studded with startled elephant-heads and echo with equally pachydermic snores from Harvardites sunk in leather armchairs; snores which contrast rather eerily with the far-off twitter of ladies playing bridge.

*Make your way to the junction of 44th and 5th and turn left, walking north up 5th Avenue, past shops with names like Objets d'Arts Inc which sell Persian carpets, telephones and reproduction antiques with price tags ranging from $10,000 for a gold-coloured bums-up goddess lampstand to 99¢ for a silver-plated coaster. As you walk you pass **535 5th Avenue**, on your right between 44th and 45th Streets, and the **Fred French Building** a block up at 45th Street.*

Craning your neck you'll see a frieze of a rising sun, bees and griffins (symbolizing thrift and integrity) in red and lime-green tiles on the roof of the Fred French, in fact a disguise for the water tower. Both scrapers resemble Mayan pyramids and are copybook examples of 'setbacks' which came in after the Zoning Laws of 1916 (*see* **Architecture**, p.81). In 1926 the *New Yorker* grumbled that 535 5th Avenue had 'the grace of an overgrown grain elevator', so enraging the litigious architect Craig Severance that he sued for a formal retraction.

*On the left at 47th Street, between 5th and 6th Avenues, is **Diamond Row**.*

The dealers and cutters on 47th Street are mostly Hasidic: diamonds are bought and sold by the Diamond Dealers' Club; deals made in the name of 'Mazel' and 'Brooch', Yiddish for good luck and disaster, and gems exchanged in ingeniously folded pieces of paper. Between Monday and noon on Friday, $400 million changes hands.

Stranger still, in the middle of all this is the **Gotham Book Mart**, a quirky bookshop with an art gallery above and a sign outside saying 'Wise Men Fish Here'. The store's late owner Frances Steloff was legendary for her Writers' Emergency Fund, which rescued the likes of Henry Miller, who sent in SOSs for food, and Theodore Dreiser, who is supposed to have inscribed all the books in the store as well as the Bible 'with the compliments of the author'. Steloff also smuggled in copies of *Lady Chatterley's Lover* and *Tropic of Cancer*, selling them under the counter and provoking a series of lawsuits which led to radical changes in American laws on censorship. The charming new owner, Andreas Brown, has a similarly courageous policy of refusing to stock cookbooks, exercise manuals or cat cartoons. The shop specializes in works by the eccentric writer and illustrator Edward Gorey, and many of them on sale here are signed by the author.

> *Continue along 5th Avenue another two blocks north to 49th Street. On your right is **Saks Fifth Avenue**—haute couture and stuffy. Opposite Saks is **Rockefeller Center** and the view down the **Channel Gardens** of the RCA Building that Gertrude Stein described in 1935 as 'the most beautiful thing I have ever seen'.*

Usually when you look down one of New York's vertiginous gorges, you see nothing but wedges of sky. The gully between 49th and 50th Streets is one of the city's few vistas, best at night when the needle-slim and spandrelled limestone slab of the RCA Building is illuminated in white. Framed by two squat buildings, the **British Empire Building** and the **Maison Française**, this vertical avenue of light seems higher than its 70 storeys and elegant as only a spectre can be.

> *Walk down the Channel Gardens, a 60ft walkway with ponds in the centre. Ahead of you a set of nereids and tritons by the sculptor René Chambellan point towards Paul Manship's golden Prometheus. At the end is a sunken plaza with clanking flags. At Christmas this plaza is flooded and frozen into a pretty but somewhat minuscule skating rink (open Oct–April, call © 757 5730 for more information).*

This is the heart of the **Rockefeller Center**, a city within a city, in which 21 buildings on eight city blocks are related to each other aesthetically as well as physically by a subterranean network of truck ramps, shop concourses, shipping rooms and car parks (once supervised by 725 attendants who slid between floors on firemen's poles). Like the Roman Forum, Rockefeller Center makes a virtue out of congestion and the Center's offices, shops, apartments, theatres and cinemas absorb up to a quarter of a million people a day. The Center is also a model of the American Way. It was the brainchild of John D. Rockefeller, who saw the complex as a synthesis of private enterprise and public interest, and a concrete embodiment of the unselfish face of making money. Rockefeller's personal credo, 'I believe in the supreme worth of the individual...', is inscribed in marble, like Moses' tablets, on a plaque above the ice rink. It came as rather a shock, therefore, when a Japanese corporation bought what the press imaginatively dubbed 'Wokafeller Center' for $400m in 1989.

The original development was announced on the same day as Black Tuesday, 1929. Soon after, Rockefeller's backers (the Metropolitan Opera) pulled out. But Rockefeller pushed on regardless, negotiating a building loan for $65m (the largest ever) and employing a cohort of architects including Hood & Fouilhoux, Reinhard & Hofmeister and Corbett, Harrison & MacMurray. Between 1931 and 1940 and during the worst ravages of the Depression, they built 13 of the Center's skyscrapers: 'tombstones of capitalism with windows', as a visitor described the empty offices in 1934.

*Walk towards the entrance to **RCA Building**, behind Prometheus on Rockefeller Plaza.*

In a way that is quite medieval the architecture was integrated with murals, sculptures and mosaics: a hundred artists and craftsmen were employed to work on the project and over the RCA entrance is one of the best examples: Lee Lawrie's bas-relief of *Genius*, a giant brandishing a pair of calipers. The figure was inspired by, if not actually snitched from, the frontispiece to William Blake's *Europe* which shows *Urizen* ('your reason'), the creator of the material world. Urizen also created the first artist, *Los*, a blacksmith of dubious morals who bound his maker in chains of iron.

Diego Rivera's mural in the RCA lobby was more blatant. The vaguest of briefs— 'Man at the Crossroads Looking with Uncertainty but with Hope...to a New and Better Future'—was a choice subject for Rivera, a committed Marxist. He immediately began a very literal depiction of the proletariat seizing the means of production. Along with scenes of police brutality, the mural showed sturdy Soviet women playing sports outside the Kremlin and ugly capitalist tarts exuding venereal miasmas over a card game. But it was only when Rivera painted in a portrait of Lenin that the Rockefellers objected.

The '*Battle of Rockefeller Center*' as Rivera recounted the affair with relish, ensued. At the opening ceremonies, Rockefeller sent in 'sappers' who covered the mural in a tarpaulin; mounted police trawled the streets; the skies 'roared with airplanes flying round the skyscraper menaced by Lenin'. When Rivera refused to capitulate, the painting was destroyed and replaced with José María Sert's bland mural *American Progress*. Soon after Rivera painted a picture called the *Billionaires' Banquet*, showing J. D. Rockefeller, Henry Ford and J. P. Morgan dining on tickertape. This is now in the National Palace in Mexico, along with a version of the destroyed mural.

By now you may need a drink or food. You can get a view as well from the **Rainbow Promenade**, an Art Deco cocktail bar adjoining the famous Rainbow Room restaurant on the 65th floor of the RCA.

The lovely Art Deco bar and restaurant reopened at the end of 1987 after being restored by 30 artists. The restaurant has a revolving dance floor and house cabaret and is full of camp and amusing waiters. From here you can make out the secret roof gardens, with pools and sloping lawns, on top of the Maison Française and the British Empire Building.

On the way out you can walk past the Today Show's *'Window on the World' on 49th Street and Rockefeller Plaza (which* Today *broadcasts live every weekday from 7.15am to 9am). It's possible in theory to pick up* **free standby tickets** *for various television recordings including* Saturday Night Live *and* Late Night with Conan O'Brian *from the NBC Studios information desk in the RCA mezzanine (tickets distributed from 9.15am onwards).*

NBC began broadcasting from the RCA in 1935 with two shows a week, and televized cookery was restricted to salads because the heat of the studio lights melted everything else. Studio tours leave every 15 minutes (*Mon–Sat 9.30–4.30, Sun 10–4; adm $10*).

Before you finally leave the Center, try to squeeze in a tour of **Radio City Music Hall** *on 50th Street and 6th Avenue. (Daily tours leave every 15 minutes; adm $6).*

This is Art Deco at its most bizarre: the brainchild of cinema impresario Samuel Rothapfel ('Roxy') and architect/designer Donald Deskey, it was also the largest theatre in the world when built in 1932. Roxy claimed he got the idea for Radio City when he was sailing on an ocean liner at dawn, and inside the theatre a vast proscenium arch is supposed to resemble a sun rising out of an ocean of 6000 red velvet seats and a carpet of Art Deco fish. Architecture critics sometimes compare the design to the *Grosses Schauspielhaus*, a German Expressionist circus built in Berlin in 1919. But Roxy's theatre was kitted out with an extraordinary array of technical gadgetry: whole landscapes could be recreated on stage thanks to artificial raincurtains made of 20ft-high walls of city steam, and four elevators which could lift scenery and orchestras 13ft above the audience and 27ft below.

Roxy's opening show at Radio City was a spectacular flop. Charlie Chaplin, Clark Gable and Toscanini all came to see an indescribably boring five-hour marathon which included a 'Symphony of the Curtain' in which the curtain performed motorized acrobatics while the orchestra played a 'Hymn to the Sun'. When people asked whether the horses on stage were mice, Roxy fainted and had to be carried away on a stretcher. He lost $180,000 in a fortnight and soon after reverted to the simple combination of movies and live acts which had made him rich in the first place.

Return to 5th Avenue, turn left and walk three blocks north past St Patrick's Cathedral and Versace, to 53rd Street. Turn right on to East 53rd Street and walk a little way down. Here, just on the left at 5 East 53rd Street, you can search out the chunks of Berlin Wall in **Paley Park***, or better still, sit down peacefully and have a rest.*

Under the shadow of Paley Park's honey locust trees, pale-faced office workers turn white plastic chairs to contemplate its altar, 'the waterwall'. The clattering water comes from nowhere and goes nowhere and temporarily obliterates all other sounds.

As you leave, look east to the end of 53rd Street which is filled by the crowstepped silhouette of the **Citicorp Building** built in 1989 across the East River in Queens. With a Dutch gable and 663ft and 48 storeys high, it stands alone on the frontier of Queens and is practically the only skyscraper that anyone has dared to build outside Manhattan.

*Now walk a block east on 53rd Street to **Madison Avenue**.*

Madison Avenue is associated with two phenomena: boring suit shops (Chipp, Orvis, Tripler, and Brooks Bros., now owned by Marks & Spencer!) and the advertising industry. Most of the agencies (including Saatchi & Saatchi) are actually based in SoHo these days, but the image persists, partly because for some reason the Madison ad-man was the hero of hundreds of films and sitcoms made in the 1950s and 60s.

*Cross Madison and walk another block east to **Park Avenue**, the only road in Manhattan featuring live plants.*

Also in the 1950s and 60s, Madison Avenue's favourite clients congregated on next-door Park Avenue in spanking-new headquarters dubbed 'the glass boxes' and designed by equally swish architects. These great galumphing corporations included Lever Bros, (soap and detergent), Colgate (toothpaste), Seagrams (distillers whose HQ is tinted the same colour as their rye whisky), Union Carbide and Philip Morris (Marlboros).

*On your left, on the northwest corner of 53rd and Park Avenue, is **Lever House**.*

Lever were so delighted with this when it was built in 1952, they put a little picture of it on all their detergent boxes. Indeed, the Lever House glass box was the parthenogenetic father and mother of all the other glass boxes you have seen anywhere; in fact it was 'as fecund as the shad', as Tom Wolfe put it in *From Bauhaus to Our House* and such an influence that nowadays it's an effort to imagine why anyone thought it iconoclastic in the first place. The man responsible was Gordon Bunshaft, a partner in America's largest architectural conglomerate (Skidmore, Owings & Merrill). His *Star Trek* mission was to boldly cut a swathe of light, air and space into Park Avenue—then a dour wall of masonry apartment blocks. Lever House by contrast was awesomely transparent, and its spandrelled curtain wall created a thrilling architectural *trompe l'œil* in which a tallish vertical slab was balanced impossibly on a longish horizontal slab on stilts.

The illusion of weightlessness had more of an impact when Park Avenue was packed with stone buildings, and with cruel irony the success of Lever House led to their eventual demolition. Today, diagonally across from Lever House on the southeast side of 53rd is Manhattan's sleekest box: the elegant **Seagram Building**, between 53rd and 52nd Streets.

This inscrutable bronze-glassed tower was designed in 1958 by Ludwig Mies van der Rohe (director of the Bauhaus until the Nazis abolished it in 1933) and is set back 90ft from Park Avenue behind a rather dull plaza with rather dull ponds. Mies was so anal that he installed blinds which could only stay in three positions—completely rolled up, completely rolled down, or exactly halfway up. What's more, the bronze outer skin has to be oiled regularly to stop it turning a snot-coloured green. Although Mies piqued himself on his integrity, architecture critics called the Seagram a 'beautiful lady with hidden corsets' because the curtain skin was actually held up by invisible supports. At any rate, Seagram's owners were not so squeaky clean that they shunned a stunt. While it was being constructed, Plexiglass portholes were set into the fencing around the site. Each was a different height—tall, medium, or short; and each equipped with a loud-speaker from which salesmen could plug their wares (and incidentally Seagram) to passing crowds.

Philip Johnson, a post-modernist ex-disciple of Mies van der Rohe, did the beautiful interiors and a staircase inside the Seagram leads to **The Four Seasons**, one of the most expensive restaurants in New York (*see* **Food and Drink**, p.212). If you are poor but not proud you can press your nose against the windows and gawp at *Le Tricorne*, an enormous stage backdrop inside the restaurant of a gory bullfight, painted by Picasso in 1919.

> *From the Seagram walk south down* **Park Avenue***. The road you're walking on is actually a hollow 18-inch asphalt skin, braced together with metal plates and rivets, which visibly judders as cars clank down to 42nd Street. The buildings on either side of Park Avenue are supported on stilts wedged between nine levels of railway tracks leading to Grand Central. If you peer between the gratings on the streets anywhere in this area, you can hear station announcements below and see trains leaving and arriving.*

> *If gratings excite you, why not make a short detour to the world's most famous* **subway grating***, a block away on Lexington Avenue between 52nd and 51st Streets? This is the very one which belched a gust of hot air up the skirts of Marilyn Monroe as she left a cinema in* The Seven Year Itch. *'Do you feel the breeze from the subway? Isn't it delicious?', chirruped Monroe. In reply the crowd who gathered to watch the shooting of the film rowdily shouted, 'Higher, higher!'*

> *Now walk two blocks south down Park Avenue to* **St Bartholomew's Church** *and the* **General Electric Building** *on the east side of 51st St.*

This is one of the most satisfactory sights in Manhattan. The phallic 570ft Gothic Art Deco needle-point of the General Electric seems to poke through the squat Byzantine dome of St Bartholomew's in front. The superposition was engineered in 1931 by the architects of the General Electric (Cross & Cross) who chose a salmon-coloured brick to match the orange-pink of St Bartholomew's (built three decades before in 1902). If you have binoculars get them out now because the crown of the General Electric is one of the best in Manhattan. Built for the Radio Corporation of America, it is a filigree nest of lightning bolts (symbolizing radio waves and electrical energy) with spooky Afro/Egyptian figures looming behind. The lobby is even more fanciful, with a ceiling of aluminum sunrays, and silver torches for lights.

> Walk a block further down to 50th Street and look up at the chrome-capped bosoms of the **Waldorf-Astoria Towers** which are set on top of the **Waldorf-Astoria Hotel** like jellies.

When the Waldorf-Astoria moved here from 34th Street in 1929–31 it realized its ambition to be the tallest, largest, flashiest skyscraper hotel in the world. The new building had 2200 rooms, 2700 telephones, a switchboard 'large enough for a good-sized city', and 16 elevators, including one big enough to take limousines. The whole lot weighed 27,000 tons, all of which balanced on stilts in Grand Central. Wine cellars had to be shifted to the 5th floor to avoid vibrations from trains below. Guests arrived in private carriages shunted to a spur in the basement, from which they took an elevator to the hotel lobby. (Except for President Clinton, no one who's anyone travels by train these days in America and the Waldorf's private siding has long since been abandoned. In the 1960s, Andy Warhol famously sent invitations to a party at '101–121 E. 49th St.', actually a 100ft staircase connecting the siding to the street. A rock group played in the storage yards below and supper was served from abandoned dining cars.)

At the top of the hotel are the Waldorf Towers, containing 113 apartments for residents. These have included the Duke and Duchess of Windsor, Marilyn Monroe, Kissinger and Presidents Hoover and Nixon. 'Folks, folks—save them adjectives—' Jimmy Durante pleaded as he stepped into an elevator bound for the Towers and was smothered with compliments '—we got thoity floors to go!' In these palmy days before the war, residents went in for extravagant parties. Elsa Maxwell, a famous gossip columnist, once challenged the management to transport a whole farmyard—apple trees, chickens, geese, donkeys, cows, hayricks, hillbilly band and all, to the Starlight Room on the 18th floor, the centrepiece being *Molly the Moët Cow*, an life-sized artificial cow that spurted champagne and whisky and soda from its udders. In the 1960s the Waldorf lost a lot of its authentic sparkle after it was slathered in gold in a pathetic attempt to make it look 'Edwardian'. Recently, however, the elegant downstairs lobbies, chrome elevators, gold-leafed peacocks and the famous Waldorf clock have been restored and a sumptuous 148,000-piece mosaic was uncovered at the Park Avenue entrance. All of which means the hotel is nowadays a delightful place to stop for tea and a pee (the Ladies is immediately on your right as you walk through to Peacock Alley). If you look purposeful you could also try taking an elevator to the 18th floor to sneak a look round the Starlight Room with its electrically retractable roof and green-lit mirrors. Even the urinals are Art Deco here.

> *Walk south to 46th Street where Park Avenue is straddled by the gold-topped* **Helmsley Building***. Cars are guzzled up into two arches at the front of the building and crepitated out on to a ramp-road at the back.*

On top is a gold pyramid, punched like the Argus with a hundred gimlet windows. This was the roost of Leona Helmsley, New York's own Imelda Marcos and 'Queen of Mean'. Twice married to ageing hotel baron Harry, Ms Helmsley wound up doing four years in Danbury women's slammer for a few million-dollars' worth of tax evasion. Leona's trial in 1989 revealed, among other things, that in a flash of anger she once slaughtered a flock of sheep grazing on her lawn and fed them to the servants. On another occasion she informed a housekeeper that only little people paid taxes. After Harry Helmsley's death at 87 in January 1997, Leona inherited his $1 billion real estate empire and nowadays owns or controls one hundred million square feet of commercial space including the Empire State Building. Leona's specific contribution to Park Avenue was gilding this pyramid and illuminating it at night.

Built in 1929 for New York Central's railway executives, the Helmsley Building was a once glorious symbol of the biggest railroad in the country and America's industrial pre-eminence. In 1963, just as the railroad was bankrupting itself, an unlucky airline headquarters burst up behind it, blotting out a lovely vista down Park Avenue in one swoop. This was the Pan Am Building, designed by a consortium including Walter Gropius, founder of the Bauhaus. Now the **Met Life**, it is probably New York's most hated skyscraper. It was the scene in 1977 of one of the most dreadful accidents in the city's history: a helicopter landed on the roof during the rush hour, its undercarriage gave way, and debris from the accident drifted as far as Madison Avenue, killing five people and injuring seven.

> *Turn right on to 46th Street and take the first left on to Vanderbilt Avenue. Walk south to 43rd Street where on the left you will find the grandest of several entrances to* **Grand Central Terminal***.*

This takes you to the top of an aquiline flight of stairs leading to a colossal 375ft by 125ft cathedral vault. But before you stomp on down, remind yourself of the wise words of the Abbé Fausse-Maigre as recorded in *Cold Comfort Farm*: 'Lost is that man who sees a beautiful woman descending a noble staircase.' Alternatively, if that sounds daunting you can have a gin and tonic in one at the civilizing **bar** at the top and from there watch the commuters hemming zigzags up and down the concourse below. They look most like ants in a man-made ant farm, however, scuttling along **glass catwalks** encased in gigantic windows either side of the concourse. These walks are on nine levels, accessible via stairs behind the bar, and people use them to cross Grand Central (and to chuck the water bombs from) without ever having to set foot on the concourse below. They may be covered up when you visit, however, as extensive renovations are currently under way in every part of the enormous station. These include washing down the concourse ceiling with soap and water, and adding new shops, restaurants and bars to the previously shabby concourses and passageways below.

Grand Central was once heart-racingly chic: in the twenties and thirties passengers boarded trains named the *Empire State Express* and the *Super Chief*, and every evening a red carpet flopped out for the *Twentieth Century Ltd* (here, en route to Chicago, the movie-writer Anita Loos encountered a witless birdbrain called Mabel Minnow, and, observing her disorganize the behaviour of every male on board, she scribbled down a character sketch of Lorelei Lee, the indomitable authoress of *Gentleman Prefer Blondes*). Inside Grand Central itself was a newsreel theatre; and CBS broadcasted from studios in the Long Gallery parallel to the main concourse, a space that nowadays houses tennis courts and a health club. Travelling from Grand Central to Los Angeles in 1947, Evenlyn Waugh wrote in his diary, 'The *Twentieth Century* is the pride of the US railways—rightly... The compartments are full of gadgets but it is all thin aluminium and one hears coarse native laughter through the walls. The dinner absolutely excellent.'

Today's more demotic Grand Central is frequented by commuters, subway riders, waifs and strays. New Yorkers rather take the station for granted, are unmoved when Jacob's ladders cast sudden flashes of sun across the concourse, and are in too much of a hurry to gaze up at the beautiful restored ceiling, painted cerulean blue and decorated with a firmament of electrically blinking constellations. (Incidentally, as far as New Yorkers know the sun sets in the *east*. A Frenchman called Paul Helleu designed the ceiling using as his template a medieval manuscript which showed the Heavens from a godly point of view with the constellations reversed. Also he forgot Orion.)

Underneath you are 27 miles of tracks, spanning 48 acres and looped around each other like intestine to save spaces. Express trains ride the top tiers, commuter trains those below. Under the main concourse is the commuters' hypogeum, below that shopping galleries vaulted with guastavino tiles.

> Walk down the 43rd Street staircase below the level of the main concourse and follow signs to the **Oyster Bar** (open Mon–Fri, 11.30am–9.30pm). The signs come and go and if you can't see them ask someone the way.

This happy leftover from the halcyon days of train travel is one of Manhattan's loveliest establishments. Inside you'll find an elegant hall of vaults, tiled in white guastavino like a shower-room. According to legend the vaults have such booming acoustics that speculators lurked in the whispering gallery outside to eavesdrop on the latest financial gossip. Nowadays the main dining room serves 20 varieties of oysters and fish including bluefish, marlin, scrod and Dover sole flown in freshly each morning, also rainbow trout, salmon and sturgeon smoked in the Oyster Bar's own kitchens. On the right-hand side as you walk in is a cheap and entertaining luncheonette-style counter bar where you can sit over a clam chowder and watch oysters broiling in custom-built pots which are heated (via pipes connecting to the pots) by city steam (the same stuff that swirls out of manholes in the streets and travels through 50 miles of pipes at 15 million lbs an hour to heat apartments, schools and businesses all over Manhattan).

Underneath the Oyster Bar are seven more storeys and tunnels containing steam pipes, mains, sewers, water pipes, a generator, and grimy machine shops serviced by motorized carts. Air is forced down funnels to these steamy, rat-infested passageways, and it's possible to walk along them from 43rd to 49th Streets and from Lexington to Madison Avenues. Although Lex Luther's empire in *Superman* was set deep in the bowels of Grand Central, the film was actually shot in Pinewood Studios outside London. Sad to say the only people who have lived down here in real life are the homeless. These so-called Mole People (featured in the underwhelming film *Extreme Measures* which was shot in Grand Central) have been relocated from the station elsewhere and nowadays only two 'permanent residents' remain. In the 1980s 400 people lived in the tunnels, stripping copper from the high-voltage cables to sell for scrap, and sleeping in areas nicknamed the Burma Road (for its unbearable steam heat), Rikers Island (because it looked like the gaol) and the Playground (with an interior decorated by graffiti artists). Incredibly, there is no complete map of the tunnels below Grand Central; it's conceivable that more will be discovered by the station's surveyors.

> *Make your way back to Vanderbilt Avenue, walk one block south and turn left on to 42nd Street.*

The trimmings on the exterior of Grand Central were by beaux-arts architects Warren & Wetmore, but the overall concept was the inspiration of the station's chief engineer, William Wilgus, plus Reed & Stem, an architectural firm from Minnesota. Reed was responsible for the ingenious way in which pedestrians, passengers, subway travellers and cars are sifted through the station, and for the 'Elevated Circumferential Plaza' (in fact a road on a ramp) circling the station outside.

If you're in the mood you could make a flying visit from here to the **Whitney Museum of American Art at Philip Morris** (*open 11–6 Mon–Fri, 11–7.30 Thurs; adm free*) opposite the outside of Grand Central at 120 Park Avenue and 42nd Street. This branch has a pleasant sculpture garden: it's also quiet and small, attributes to be cherished in a country where big is best and a little is nothing at all.

*From here walk a block east along 42nd Street to Lexington Avenue. On the north side of 42nd you will see the church-like entrance to the **Chrysler Building**, New York's barmiest skyscraper and the only one with a cult following.*

Built two years before the Empire State in 1929, the bravely modern skyscraper is a totem pole to that other American Dream, the automobile. Dressed in exposed steel, it is draped with many intoxicating talismans. Actual hub-caps are stuccoed to the walls and the brickwork is carved in bas-reliefs of motor-cars. The eagle gargoyles bolted to the top are massively enlarged Chrysler hood ornaments. In fact, in the same year as the scraper was built, Chrysler brought out a line of cars to match the building called the 'Airflow'. These were streamlined and also covered in steel: but while the skyscraper was an unprecedented success, the 'Airflow' was a flop.

Walter Chrysler began his career in humble style (designing rollerskates) and was almost fifty by the time he built the first Chrysler car in 1924. Out of this sprang the massive Chrysler Corporation, founded only a year later in 1925. Suddenly finding that he was a big cheese in a gourmet delicatessen, Chrysler decided to prolong his shelf-life forever by commissioning William Van Alen to build him the tallest building in the world, named after himself.

As works on the 'Chrysler Building' began, a secret but furious race ensued between Van Alen and his former partner, H. Craig Severance (then working on the Bank of Manhattan at 40 Wall Street). When the Chrysler's dome reached 925ft and looked as though it was finished, Severance tacked a flagpole on to 40 Wall Street, increasing its height to 927ft. In a triumphant riposte Van Alen whipped out a Nirosta metal spire he had assembled on the sly, and in 90 minutes hoisted it through a hole in the roof and bolted it on to the Chrysler.

The Chrysler was the first building to beat the Eiffel Tower. But only two years later, to Van Alen's chagrin now, the 1250ft Empire State Building towered above them both. That year, Van Alen defiantly attended the Beaux-Arts Architects and Artists Ball dressed as the Chrysler Building in a silver coat with patent leather attachments and eagle epaulettes. He was accompanied by several other buildings including the Empire State, the Daily News and an unnamed subway station; the theme was *Fête Moderne* and guests drank silver liquid and roasted marshmallows, or Miniature Meteorites.

'Its modernistic arch is almost sensational in its bizarre magnificence and regal splendor,' a devotee wrote of the Chrysler entrance in 1931. The lobby inside is even more splendid and easily the most deluxe in Manhattan. It has red-veined African marble walls, a chrome clock and lavishly exotic elevators inlaid with rich mahogany-coloured laminated woods set in a lovely jagged pattern. At one time the lobby was also a showroom for a revolving motor-car. The ceiling still has a mural depicting the Chrysler under construction and 'transportation and human endeavor', recalling an age when big corporations could aspire without a squirm. Unfortunately the Cloud Club, an observation room and restaurant on the 66th floor filled with budgies, canaries and industrial executives, is strictly off limits to visitors. Above the Cloud Club, the apex of the Chrysler spire supposedly contains Walter Chrysler's first set of tools.

> *The ideal way to finish off this skyscraper walk is to take a helicopter ride over the city. To get to the* **East River Heliport** *take a cab or an M104 travelling east on 42nd Street as far as the United Nations Headquarters and walk eight blocks south to the riverside (East River Drive/FDR Drive) and 34th Street. Prices from Island Helicopter range from $44 for 7 miles or 15 minutes, to $148 for 100 miles (open 9am–9pm, © 683 4575 for information). Although flights are very thrilling, it's advisable to take one of the shorter rides as the noise of the choppers can be seriously deafening.*

If you arrive and your courage fails you, jump on an **M15** bus travelling north up 1st Avenue. Get off at East 49th Street. You will find yourself beneath **Beekman Tower** with **Top of the Tower**, an excellent cocktail bar and restaurant at the top. Built in 1929, the lovely rust-coloured Art-Deco tower has one of the nicest and swankiest cocktail bars in the city, with wonderful views to the north and south. Look out especially for the **Queensboro Bridge**, a 50,000-ton steel hulk spanning the dingy East River. The architect endearingly exclaimed 'My God—it's a blacksmith's shop,' after it was finished in 1909. However, ever since the bridge featured as the backdrop for Woody Allen and Diane Keaton's first date in *Manhattan*, sitting with a silhouette of the Queensboro Bridge behind you has symbolized the quintessence of urban glamour.

II: Kitsch for the Rich

*(The Upper West Side,
   A Picnic in Central Park,
   & the Upper East Side)*

Start: *B, D or E trains to West 53rd
and 7th Avenue, or N, R to West 55th
and 7th Avenue.*

Walking Time: *excluding museums,
4 hours.*

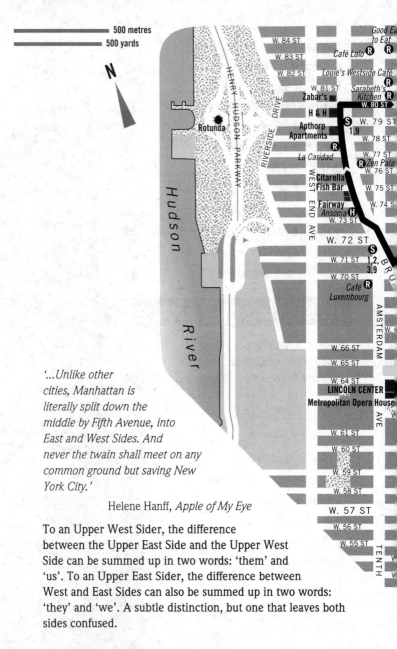

500 metres
500 yards

N

HENRY HUDSON PARKWAY

RIVERSIDE DRIVE

Rotunda

Hudson

River

WEST END AVE

AMSTERDAM AVE

TENTH AV

BRO...

W. 84 ST
W. 83 ST
W. 82 ST
W. 81 ST
W. 80 ST
W. 79 ST
W. 78 ST
W. 77 ST
W. 76 ST
W. 75 ST
W. 74 S
W. 73 ST
W. 72 ST
W. 71 ST
W. 70 ST
W. 66 ST
W. 65 ST
W. 64 ST
W. 61 ST
W. 60 ST
W. 59 ST
W. 58 ST
W. 57 ST
W. 56 ST
W. 55 ST

Good E
to Eat
Café Lalo
Louie's Westside Café
Sarabeth's
Kitchen
Zabar's
H & H
Apthorp
Apartments
1,9
La Caridad
Zen Pala
Citarella
Fish Bar
Fairway
Ansonia
1,2,
3,9
Café
Luxembourg
LINCOLN CENTER
Metropolitan Opera House

'...Unlike other
cities, Manhattan is
literally split down the
middle by Fifth Avenue, into
East and West Sides. And
never the twain shall meet on any
common ground but saving New
York City.'

Helene Hanff, *Apple of My Eye*

To an Upper West Sider, the difference
between the Upper East Side and the Upper West
Side can be summed up in two words: 'them' and
'us'. To an Upper East Sider, the difference between
West and East Sides can also be summed up in two words:
'they' and 'we'. A subtle distinction, but one that leaves both
sides confused.

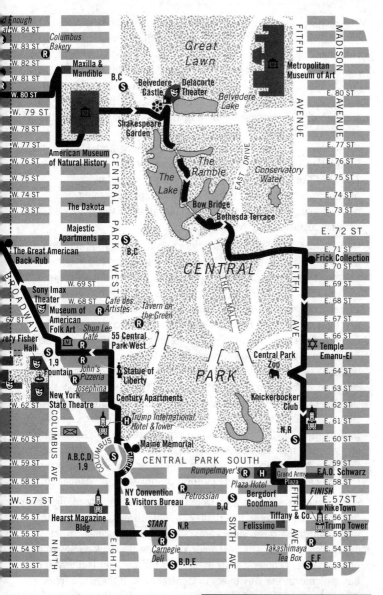

d Enough
at W. 84 ST

W. 83 ST
Columbus
Bakery

W. 82 ST

W. 81 ST
Maxilla &
Mandible

W. 80 ST

W. 79 ST

W. 78 ST

W. 77 ST

American Museum
of Natural History

W. 76 ST

W. 75 ST

W. 74 ST

The Dakota

W. 73 ST

Majestic
Apartments

The Great American
Back-Rub

W. 69 ST

Sony Imax
Theater   W. 68 ST

Museum of
American
Folk Art

ery Fisher
Hall

1,9
Fountain

New York
State Theatre

W. 62 ST

W. 60 ST

W. 59 ST
A,B,C,D
1,9

W. 58 ST

NY Convention
& Visitors Bureau

W. 57 ST

Hearst Magazine
Bldg.

W. 56 ST

START

W. 55 ST

W. 54 ST

Carnegie
Deli

W. 53 ST
B,D,E

B,C

Belvedere
Castle

Delacorte
Theater

Belvedere
Lake

Shakespeare
Garden

The
Ramble

The
Lake

Conservatory
Water

Bow Bridge

Bethesda Terrace

B,C

CENTRAL

PARK

THE MALL

EAST DRIVE

CENTRAL PARK WEST

Café des
Artistes

Tavern on
the Green

Shun Lee
Café

55 Central
Park West

John's
Pizzeria
Josephina

Statue of
Liberty

Century Apartments

Trump International
Hotel & Tower

Maine Memorial

CENTRAL PARK SOUTH

Rumpelmayer's

Petrossian

B,Q

N,R

Great
Lawn

FIFTH   MADISON   AVENUE

Metropolitan
Museum of Art

E. 80 ST

E. 77 ST

E. 76 ST

E. 75 ST

E. 74 ST

E. 73 ST

E. 72 ST

E. 71 ST
Frick Collection
E. 70 ST

E. 69 ST

E. 68 ST

E. 67 ST

E. 66 ST
Temple
Emanu-El

E. 64 ST

E. 63 ST

Central Park
Zoo

Knickerbocker
Club

E. 62 ST

N,R

E. 60 ST

E. 59 ST
F.A.O. Schwarz

Grand Army
Plaza

E. 58 ST
FINISH
E. 57 ST
NikeTown

Plaza Hotel

Bergdorf
Goodman

Tiffany & Co.
E. 56 ST
Trump Tower

Felissimo
E. 55 ST

Takashimaya
Tea Box
E. 54 ST
E,F
E. 53 ST

SIXTH AVENUE

FITH AVENUE

BROADWAY

COLUMBUS AVE

NINTH

EIGHTH

CIRCLE

67 ST

II: Kitsch for the Rich

117

The visitor, meanwhile, can make any number of brutal comparisons. The Upper West Side is, on the whole, more engaged and engaging, a lot more verbal, and slightly non-conformist. It's home to the Lincoln Center (New York's centre for performing arts), ABC's television broadcasting studios, the Sony IMAX theatre, and the enormous and eccentric Museum of Natural History. The architecture here can be exuberant, whimsical, or verging on the kitsch. The people who live here seem to suit their surroundings: Westsiders in fiction include Saul Bellow's Mr Sammler, J.D. Salinger's Glass family and Walter Matthau and Jack Lemmon's *The Odd Couple*. Stereotypically they are liberals, Jewish intellectuals, highly educated immigrants, up-and-coming professionals, writers, actors, musicians: all in all the self-styled cultural cognoscenti of Manhattan.

If the Upper West Side is somewhere you go when you think you're arriving, the Upper East Side is where you go when you know you've arrived. To an outsider, the Upper East Side means museums, in unthinkable quantities (over fifty line Museum Mile on 5th Avenue alone). To New Yorkers, the Upper East Side means status, money, prestige: items to be cherished in a city which is constantly re-inventing the past. The architecture here is competitively eclectic: Renaissance palazzi elbow for space with Gothic castles and French châteaux on land which just over a century ago was occupied by squatters living in tin-can shanties with pigs and goats. Today alongside the mansions and the apartment blocks is an Eldorado of flower shops, art galleries, boutiques, hotels, gentlemen's clubs, cinemas (but hardly a single theatre), alcoholism centres and doctors, dentists, dog-walkers, nannies and psychiatrists. The rich live on the Upper East Side in particularly splendid isolation—secure in the knowledge that they are unassailably the cultural connoisseurs of Manhattan.

For the purposes of this walk from the Upper West Side to the Upper East Side, the twain do meet: after all, only three blocks separate them, and these three blocks are a lovely green shagpile carpet called Central Park. On the Upper West Side the walk passes some of Manhattan's choicest delicatessens. If the weather is fine you can buy a picnic on the way to eat in Central Park. If there is a freak downpour (and the rain in New York really is like the stuff that falls in films: suddenly, in vertical sheets), take refuge in the wonderful

Natural History Museum, on the West Side, or, if you're feeling more cerebral, amongst the astonishing Old Masters in the Frick Collection on the East Side of Central Park.

Petrossian, 182 West 58th Street, at 7th Ave. Classic Russian gourmet restaurant with beautiful Art Deco interior. A bargain $22 *prix fixe* lunch buys smoked cod, foie gras and salmon roe *hors d'œuvres*, a choice of five entrées including salmon quenelles plus a glass of champagne.

Café des Artistes, 1 West 67th St., near Central Park West, ℂ 877 3500 (*reservations requested*). Famous for having elegant Tudor uphol-stery, quaint murals and a sophisticated atmosphere. Well into the expensive bracket, with smoking and chess in the bar (*from $30*).

Shun Lee Café, 43 West 65th Street, between Central Park West and Broadway. Hunan and Szechuan cooking, the best dim sum on the West Side but pricey (*from $20*).

John's Pizzeria, 48 West 65th Street, between Central Park West and Broadway. Branch of the famous John's on Bleecker Street run by the owner's ex-wife; slightly more elegant, but politer service (pizza from around $9 a slice).

Josephina, 1900 Broadway, at 63rd St., ℂ 799 1000. Delectable dairy-free health food in such big portions the plates are dustbin-lid-sized. Best for brunch.

Mingala West, 325 Amsterdam Ave., between 75th and 76th Sts. Rangoon Noodles, fish and lemongrass soup, tea leaf salad and thousand-layered bread in wonderful Burmese café serving lunch (*from $4.95*).

Zen Palate, 2170 Broadway, between 76th and 77th Sts., ℂ 501 7768; *Asian Vegetarian* (*AE, MC, D, V*). Ingenious vegetarian cooking, mixing Asian cuisines with flair rather than stodge: fashionable, cheap and quick—from soy paté to *Beggar's Purse*, a mixture of soy protein, chestnuts, noodles and pine nuts in a bean curd skin (*from $9–14*).

La Caridad, 2199 Broadway, between 77th and 78th Sts. Cuban-Spanish-Chinese cuisine in basic dining room: cheap, popular and big portions: good for beans, *bacalao*, devilled shrimps, *camarones*, enchiladas (*from $7–11*).

Café Luxembourg, 200 West 70th St., near Amsterdam Ave., ℂ 873 7411 (*reservations suggested*). Snazzy Art Deco sophisticates' brasserie with elegant French/Italian menu to match (*cassoulet, steak frites, crème brûlée*) (*from $27*).

Gray's Papaya, 2090 Broadway, at West 72nd St., ℂ 799 0243; (*no credit cards, 24 hours*). Papaya juice and shiny frankfurters *from $1 a go*.

Good Enough to Eat, 483 Amsterdam Avenue, between 83rd and 84th Sts. Vermont 'home cooking' (corn bread, meatloaf, pecan waffles), in small restaurant serving breakfasts including the colossal 'Lumber Jack', served until 4 (*from $10–20*).

Louie's Westside Café, 441 Amsterdam Ave., at 81st St., ℂ 877 1900, @ 877 1863. *American (MC, V, AE)*. Near the Natural History Museum, serving tasteful, deli-cious American cuisine, and excellent breakfasts (*brunches from $15*).

Sarabeth's Kitchen, 423 Amsterdam Ave., between 80th and 81st Sts. *The* brunch place for polite New York, delicious waffles, smoked salmon scrambled eggs and porridge, and an atmosphere that's Miss Jean Brodie, no longer in her prime.

Columbus Bakery, 484 Columbus Ave., between 82nd and 83rd Sts. Lovely smells in a bakery/café with good coffee, superior muffins, pastries made on the premises and what they call 'artisan' breads.

Café Lalo, 201 West 83rd St., at Amsterdam Ave. Top restaurant for pastries, desserts and good coffee (also alcohol) in a laidback conservatory-style café open from breakfast until 4am.

Dinersaurus at the Natural History Museum, Central Park West at West 79th St. Food in dinosaur shapes in a cheery cafeteria in the Natural History Museum (there's also the Whale's Lair, for cocktails and snacks, and the more expensive **Garden Café** for lunch and supper).

Fifth Avenue tea rooms

The Rotunda in the Pierre Hotel, 2 East 61st St., at 5th Ave. The nicest tea rooms in Manhattan.

The Palm Court in the Plaza Hotel, 5th Ave., at West 59th St. Equivalent of the Ritz in London, touristified tea or brunch amongst the flower-arrangements.

Rumpelmayer's in the St Moritz, 50 Central Park South, at 6th Ave. Ice-cream and hot chocolate in old-fashioned parlour that makes New Yorkers go flabby with nostalgia.

Felissimo, 10 West 56th St., between 5th and 6th Aves. Beige New Age Asian food in small tea room—30 varieties of eco-tea (the 'wine of the 90s') and a full 'haiku' tea including scones, sandwiches and biscuits served from 3pm to 5.30pm.

Takashimaya Tea Box, basement, 693 5th Ave., between 54th and 55th Sts. *Forty* kinds of tea in Midtown's second Japanese-owned department store: cucumber on rice sandwiches flavoured with wasabi, with slivers of grapefruit and butter cookies.

Start this walk (if you haven't had breakfast) with a pastrami on rye in the **Carnegie Deli** *on West 55th Street and 7th Avenue. If you've had breakfast already you may not be able to cope with the big portions and prices, in which case, start the walk at Columbus Circle (using the A, C, 1, 9, B or D subway stop)*

As New York delis go, the Carnegie stays (and the prices soar). The deli is so legendary it charges $3 extra for people to share a sandwich and plays continuous recordings of Frank Sinatra. This is the sort of restaurant where every wall is hung with signed photographs of the rich and famous. Unfortunately the hype is worth it: the pastrami on rye is delicious, the helpings the biggest in New York, and the menu the cornbeefiest (not to mention 'Carnegie Haul', 'Tongue's for the Memory' and 'Beef Encounter'). If a starlet upsets him, the owner, Sandy Levine, is apt to tear the culprit's photograph off the wall and chuck it in the bin.

From the Carnegie, walk two blocks west and turn right on to 8th Avenue. If it's sunny and warm, you may be lucky enough to pass Bertha A. Halozan, a curious 'naïf' painter from Austria (and 'freewoman of Hutt River, Australia'), famous in Manhattan for her paintings of the Statue of Liberty. This is the nutty Ms Halozan's only subject—she paints the statue again and again (always from the same view) en plein air on 55th Street.

At 8th Avenue walk a block north to 56th Street. On your left, and impossible to miss even if you're starting this walk in Columbus Circle (look one block south), is the **Hearst Magazine Building**.

A mix of Hollywood schmultz and the Viennese Secessionist details, plus sinister cowled statues, the Hearst Magazine Building is instantly spottable. As you look you will notice that the building is really a skyscraper base without a skyscraper. It was half-built in 1928 for the press baron and film and real estate giant, William Randolph Hearst. Hearst chose one of his own art directors—the set designer Joseph Urban—to design the building, but why the whole skyscraper never materialized is a mystery. These days the building continues to produce such timeless Hearst publications as *Cosmopolitan* and *Good Housekeeping*.

Continue up 8th Avenue to Columbus Circle. Here on your right you'll see one of the most excruciating buildings in Manhattan, the white marble Islamic-style **New York City Department of Cultural Affairs**.

Now an impressive monument to the American Tasteless movement of the 1960s, the Bureau was originally a Gallery of Modern Art housing the collection of Huntington Hartford, the A&P supermarket heir. Hartford was a rebel without a clue, set on starting a revolution in art: away from the abstract and post-modern, to what he called the 'beautiful'—pre-Raphaelites, Salvador Dali and Bouguereau. The gallery was a terrible flop, and the building itself derided by the whole of New York as 'Kitsch for the Rich' and 'Marble Lollipops'. It was designed by Edward Durrell Stone, one-time prophet of the international style and the architect behind its American flagship, the Museum of Modern Art. In the 1960s, Stone seriously deviated into Middle Eastern-style motifs and Islamic grilles (he was also responsible for the American Embassy in New Delhi). Today the 'New York City Dept of Cultural Affairs' inside is actually a tourist bureau, with pamphlets and maps and information on tourists' New York.

On the north side of Columbus Circle is a silver 'lollipop', a vulgar metal globe on a vulgar silver stick, and behind it a 44-storey skyscraper of excrement-coloured glass—the trademark hue of any property connected with Donald Trump.

The skyscraper originally belonged to the rapacious Gulf & Western conglomorate, but metamorphosed into the **Trump International Hotel & Tower** after a consortium of realtors bought the building in 1996 and craftily changed its address from '7 Columbus Circle' to the more prestigious '1 Central Park West'. Trump, who is these days wealthy after near bankruptcy, does not own the building and did not pay for its redevelopment; nevertheless he gave the building his brand name and refurbished it (for a fee of around $50 million). Apartments inside sold quickly for around $8 million per 5-bedroom penthouse.

On a brighter note, the northeast corner of Columbus Circle and Central Park was restored in 1997. The **Maine Memorial** in the middle was slathered in gold leaf and a seating area below was added, creating an obvious entrance to Central Park for the first time. The memorial commemorates the sinking of the US battleship *Maine*, supposed to have sparked off the Spanish-American War in 1898. It was put there at the behest of William Randolph Hearst, who claimed that newspaper editors could 'declare wars' and that the heady jingoism of his editorials had won the war for the USA.

> *Cross Columbus Circle and walk north up 8th Avenue (which at this point becomes **Central Park West**) as far as 65th Street.*

Central Park West is one of Manhattan's most fashionable addresses and it seethes with celebrities (Madonna, Robin Williams, etc) scuttling in and out of side-entrances. In fact it was rechristened in 1876 by developers who guessed that a Central Park address would lure Manhattan arrivistes. As elsewhere in New York, the by-product of speculation was spectacular architecture, and the 10-minute walk from here to 72nd Street and the Dakota building takes you past a very impressive line-up of Art-Deco semi-detacheds.

At 62nd Street look out for the Irwin Chanin company's **Century Apartments**. If the doorman likes you he will let you snoop round an amazing lobby furnished with underlit ashtray-tables, salmon-pink sofas, and shell-shaped light fittings, plus an inner courtyard with Art Deco tool huts.

Look up as you pass 64th Street and you can save yourself the bother of visiting the real thing by admiring a 55ft replica of the **Statue of Liberty**, placed on top of 3 West 64th Street in 1902.

Finally, on 65th Street is another wonderful apartment house, **55 Central Park West**, inside which a fridge exploded over Sigourney Weaver in *Ghostbusters*. In the film, a pre-Columbian temple was superimposed on to the roof of the building, turning it into one of the Mesopotamian ziggurats which the building's architects half imitated. As you look up, you will see how dramatically the brick on the outside changes from peach-red to tan, mimicking a ray of sunlight falling across the façade.

> *Cross over at 65th Street to the park side of the street and you'll also get a good view in profile of the jelly-mould towers of the **Majestic** on 71st Street. Also by Chanin, the Art Deco design was meant seriously as an*

expression of futuristic Machine Age aesthetics; the towers concealed water-tanks and so were functional as well.

If you need a stiff drink by now, walk a block up to 66th Street.

Here on the right and a little way into Central Park itself is the **Tavern on the Green**, one of the tackiest restaurants in Manhattan, with wine-gum-coloured rhinestones studding walls, ceilings and chandeliers. It's an amusing place to drop in for a cocktail or an expensive brunch ($26), as is the comparatively tasteful **Café des Artistes**, a restaurant and bar (with chess) exactly opposite at 1 West 67th Street which is so frequented by ladies who lunch that it was used as a setting for *The First Wives' Club*. Before going in, prepare yourself for mildly titillating murals (portraits of his mother, apparently) by Howard Chandler Christy, a resident in the **Hotel des Artistes** above. Tricked out like an Elizabethan manor, with shields, gargoyles and knobbly armchairs, the hotel was intended to house artists, but rapidly became expensive as rich *nouveaux pauvres* like Noël Coward, Rudolph Valentino and Isadora Duncan moved in.

*Leave Central Park West and walk one block west down 65th Street past John's Pizzeria (see 'lunch/cafés' above) as far as Columbus Avenue and Broadway (which collide at this point). Just to the right, between 65th and 66th Streets on Columbus Avenue, is the small **Museum of American Folk Art**, © 595 5933 (open 11.30–7.30pm Tues–Sun, suggested donation $3), worth a quick look for the displays of quirky naïve art, handmade toys and 'work-of-art' quilts.*

*To the left, between 64th and 63rd Streets, you'll see the five white travertine marble arches of the **Metropolitan Opera House**, one of the many halls of **Lincoln Center for the Performing Arts**, a complex of opera, ballet and concert houses which includes the New York Philharmonic, the New York City Opera, the New York City Ballet and the School of American Ballet.*

Built between 1959 and 1969, the arts centre covers 14 acres and was designed by a consortium of architects led by Wallace Harrison. The architecture may not be the most elegant you'll see in Manhattan, but it functions brilliantly, cutting a swathe of light and plazas into the Manhattan grid, where people can congregate before concerts and performances around some very beautiful fountains (one by Philip Johnson). Unfortunately in the daytime the vast and wonderful Chagall murals behind the arched windows of **Metropolitan Opera House** are protected from light damage by blinds and unless it's a really dirty day they can only be seen at night. Still, the plaza in front of the Met is pleasant to stroll around, especially the fountains which completely drown out the noise of klaxons and traffic on Broadway.

As soon as you hit **Broadway** the sidewalk becomes an obstacle course of randomly arranged second-hand books and tattered porn magazines. You might also hear and then see the singer George Jackson pushing a cart equipped with powerful speakers which booms out recordings of himself singing Frank Sinatra-style songs directly on to Broadway.

> *From 65th Street make your way two blocks north up Broadway (which forks to the left at this point) to 67th Street and, on your right, the **Sony Imax Theater** (Imax tickets $9, children $6, seniors $7.50, daily from 10.30am–10.40pm).*

You'll be amazed, after three-quarters of an hour of queer sensations (mingling vertigo with sea-sickness), to find the whole experience was pleasurable too. The 8-storey-high 3-D Imax screen is one of the biggest and most technically advanced in America. One day all feature films will be produced in Imax format; at the moment subjects are restricted to incomprehensible flights over Mars and Jupiter and concerts by the Rolling Stones pounded out over an 18,000-watt sound system. The best choice at the moment is Paul Cox's stupendous *Four Million Houseguests*, a horrifying and vomit-making journey via an illuminator supermicroscope into a fascinating world of rotting fruit, carpet communities and giant Velcro. If this isn't to your taste try *Across the Sea of Time*, a catapult through the history of New York from 1904 to modern times, told from the point of view of a Russian stowaway: for tourists but well produced.

> *Now walk four more blocks up Broadway as far as the island formed where Broadway crosses Amsterdam Avenue at 72nd Street. On the way you can stop for a massage at **The Great American Back-Rub** on the right side of Broadway between 71st and 72nd Streets. 'Rubs' start at $15 for 10 minutes, but aren't suitable for introverts as they are conducted in the shop window in full view of passers-by who tend to stop and gawp as clients bend down on their knees in preparation for the masseuses.*

As you walk, look out for the snazzy 19th century apartment houses on this stretch of Broadway, especially for the exquisite **Ansonia Hotel** on the left-hand side of Broadway at 73rd Street, and visible from 68th Street upwards. Bette Midler was discovered here, dancing in a gay spa in the basement called the 'Continental Baths'. The Ansonia's architect was a Frenchman, Paul Duboy, and when the neo-Baroque residential hotel first went up it was the most luxurious in the city with two swimming pools, air-conditioning, a pneumatic message system, and seals splashing in the lobby fountain. It is famous for its extra-thick and virtually soundproof walls, attracting a succession of musical visitors including Toscanini, Stravinsky and Caruso, who gave impromptu concerts from the balconies. However, the same walls have become structurally unsound over the years, and tragically a ceiling on the ground floor recently collapsed, killing a person in a shop below.

The small cottage with Dutch gables in the middle of Broadway at 72nd Street is one of Manhattan's two remaining **subway kiosks**, or 'control houses'. The subway came here in 1904, and led to swift development in a previously remote part of New York.

> *Continue walking north up Broadway to Zabar's Delicatessen: as you do you can buy a picnic to eat in Central Park from other classy food shops as well. On the left between 74th and 75th Streets is the grubby-looking but extremely high quality **Fairway**, famous for cheese and fresh produce grown on the shop's Long Island farm. On the same block, at 2135 Broadway, is the excellent **Citarella Fish Bar**, with artistic fish displays in the window, and a gourmet seafood and oyster bar inside, also selling appetizers such as chicken teriyaki, wild mushroom lasagne, chunks of roast salmon and scrod, fresh breads and jambalaya salads.*

> *A block further on the left corner of 77th Street is the **Hotel Belleclaire**.*

Maxim Gorki was evicted from here after he fled to New York in the wake of the failed Revolution of 1905. The visit was not a hit: he was set upon by the newspapers after it came out that the depraved Bolshevik was not married to his mistress. Gorki avenged himself in a vitriolic account of the city. New Yorkers were 'insignificant and enslaved', he vituperated; Manhattan itself was as monstrous as the 'voracious and filthy stomach of a glutton, who has grown into an imbecile from greed and, with the wild bellowing of an animal, devours brains and nerves'.

A block north, between 78th and 79th Streets, are the ornate but dull Renaissance-style **Apthorp Apartments**, built for William Waldorf Astor in 1907 on a whole city block and reeking of the opulence despised by Gorki. Ironically many of the apartments inside are rent-controlled, which means that tenants pay as little as a fifth of the going market rate to live on some of Manhattan's most expensive real estate. Part of the reason New York City is such a diverse and vital mix of high- and low-income inhabitants is because over 1.1 million apartments in the state have strictly regulated rents.

> *From the Apthorp walk a block up to 80th Street. On the left at 2239 Broadway is **H & H**, open 24 hours and the largest manufacturer of bagels in New York, selling 70,000 bagels a day, some of which are shipped as far afield as London. On the next corner, at 2245 Broadway, is **Zabar's**, the ultimate New York delicatessen.*

Originally kosher, Zabar's dates from the 1930s, when it moved here from Brooklyn. Nowadays 10,000 epicureans pile into the shop on a Saturday afternoon.

Everything is reasonably cheap, the best buy being the Nova smoked salmon, hand-picked by the Zabars. On weekends, the shop sells over a ton of smoked fish, and you can purchase 142 kinds of French cheese. Zabar's challenges its female customers—over a loud-speaker system—to think of something it doesn't stock. But it's hard to think of anything except sausages. They're everywhere you look: 15 kinds of salami hang from the ceiling like fleshy stalactites, while others lie amputated on the floor.

If the sausages are too much, go up to the mezzanine where Zabars sell bargain crockery, vacuum cleaners and Osterizers, or next door to the slightly scrotty-looking Zabar's Café. This specializes in good fresh soups, croissants and every kind of coffee from espressos to granitas.

> From Zabar's anyone who is a connoisseur of concrete can make a shortish detour to the beautiful **Rotunda** at the western end of 79th Street and Riverside Drive, near the **79th Street Boat Basin**. All sleek curves and articulated concrete lines, the Rotunda is actually an interchange on the Henry Hudson Parkway. The design is a triumph of road engineering, working on three levels, and incorporating a parking space, walkways and auto ramps. To get to the waterfront, walk through the centre, an arena circled by concrete colonnades. This rather theatrical space is used for occasional jazz concerts and as shelter in the winter to homeless people and winos, one of whom claims he wrote the musical score of Murder on the Orient Express. From spring until fall there is an excellent café here, serving simple grill food on paper plates, with outdoor seating and a good view of the 79th Street Boat Basin.

> Otherwise walk east along 80th Street in the direction of Central Park. If you like à la mode shopping you can do it now, on Columbus Avenue, and if you don't you can pay a brief visit to **Maxilla and Mandible**, a little way up on the right-hand side at 451 Columbus Avenue between 81st and 82nd Streets.

Maxilla and Mandible stuff anything in the dramatic pose of your choice, and they claim their range of skeletons and stuffed animals is unique. Customers, for some reason usually soigné young ladies, can purchase anything from pouncing antelopes, sleeping bats and 4ft-wide moose antlers, to alligator, rat and beaver skeletons and (not so nice) baby's skulls and human pelvises. The smell in the shop is quite weird—a mix of illness, fermented fruit and vinegar.

On Sunday mornings the stretch of Columbus between 77th and 76th Streets has a fiendishly over-priced **IS44 flea market**. If you're desperate for a French Empire siège d'amour or a colonial rattan armchair, this is the place to look.

*From 81st Street, walk south down Columbus Avenue to the entrance to the **American Museum of Natural History** (open Sun–Tues 10–5.45; Fri and Sat 10–8.45; suggested adm $8), four blocks down on 77th Street between Columbus Avenue and Central Park West. On the way you pass a small park in the museum grounds where residents gather once a year to watch a surreal scene in which Snow Whites and Donald Ducks are inflated with helium for floats in next morning's Macy's Thanksgiving Parade.*

When work began on the museum in 1872 it was the only building in what H. G. Wells called 'a waste of rubbish dump and swamp and cabbage garden'. The plan was to build the largest museum on the continent, and horses and carts collapsed transporting granite to the site. The curators started with a collection of 10,000 specimens from Europe, but the museum subsequently evolved into a labyrinth covering four blocks and housing 34 million exhibits.

Made of pink Vermont granite, the 77th Street wing sprouts stalactites outside the entrance. Just inside is an authentic 65ft seagoing war canoe filled with models of a Chilkat chief and members of the Haida tribe. This sets the tone for the rest of the museum, in which real and fake exhibits are presented within superbly painted dioramas, so you can never be quite sure whether you're looking at a model, a work of art or the real thing.

*Pick up a floor plan and make for **Ocean Life and Biology of Fishes**, to the right on the ground floor. The ladies on the ticket desk recommend this gallery, and they know best. On the way you pass North American Forests, containing an enormous cross-section of a Giant sequoia tree.*

*The rings are eccentrically annotated, from AD 550 when the tree was a sapling, to 1891, when 'Conan Doyle published Sherlock Holmes and the zipper was invented'. This was the year of the tree's nemesis, when two unnamed men spent 13 days hacking it down. Just to the left is a disgusting giant model of a millipede and its repulsive puling larvae, and round the corner in Invertebrates there is a 39ft squid suspended from the ceiling, a 34lb lobster, and the entrance to **Ocean Life**.*

Here, bathed in blue light, a 94ft, 10 ton whale swoops across the whole gallery in a nose dive, casting outlandish shadows in every direction. The blue whale is the largest creature known to man, and this replica is the largest museum exhibit in the world. Moulded out of fibreglass and polyurethane foam, with a steel skeleton, it cost $300,000. The dioramas round about are disturbingly gruesome. A polar bear, with its maw all bloodied, has just killed a ribbon seal; while its neighbour, a huge sperm whale with a devil-may-care look in his eyes, is munching up a trembling squid.

*Now take the elevator to the 3rd floor and walk through African Mammals to the balcony of Hall 7. From above, you see seven angry elephants stampeding the **Akeley Gallery** below.*

These were collected by Carl Akeley, after he was very nearly gored to death by an elephant in Africa in 1911, and rescued himself by swinging his body between the brute's tusks. On another occasion the redoubtable explorer strangled a leopard after he ran out of bullets. He finally died from a gnat bite which brought on a fever during an expedition to the Belgian Congo in 1926. Akeley is also renowned as a sculptor, author, and inventor of the panoramic motion picture camera, the cement gun and many revolutionary techniques in taxidermy, practised to great effect on the lifelike elephants in front of you.

*From here, take an elevator to the new 4th floor **Dinosaur Halls.***

These reopened in 1996 after a brilliant four-year renovation, which included, among other things, re-setting an incorrectly modelled Tyrannosaurus Rex so he crawled on his belly rather than walking upright on his hind legs. Up here, if you're lucky, you may encounter Mr A. Orenge, an education officer who walks the halls pushing a trolley full of bones ranging from human skulls to those belonging to bears, wolves or possums. Members of the public can pick up and handle these while, between the occasional imitation howl, Mr Orenge lectures a captive audience on post- as well as pre-historic anatomy.

*Go back to the ground floor and choose between the **Biology of Man**, where you may illuminate the Visible Woman, or the **Minerals and Gems Hall** thronged with rather freakish followers of the New Age cult for crystals and minerals.*

Although the haul was eventually retrieved, in 1964 a Californian beachbum dubbed Murph the Surf managed to break in and escape with the Star of India sapphire (the world's largest) and the DeLong star ruby, on a day when the burglar alarm wasn't working. Today the exhibits are worth over $80 million.

*The old **Planetarium** is having major renovations until 2000 when it will reopen as part of the museum's Center for Earth and Space.*

If you arrive before, go to the **Imax Theater** showing an excellent **Cosmic Voyage** in which viewers travel 15 billion light years backwards to the Big Bang; then go careering on a 'sub-atomic derby' inside a quark while a mysterious sounding voice informs us that, 'Man must understand the Universe to understand his Destiny.' If even this fails to completely satisfy you, come back in the evening for the laser show, in which 3-D laser beams groove and jive to a rock soundtrack (*open Fri–Sat, shows at 9pm and 10pm, adm $9*).

Central Park

*Leave the museum by the Central Park West exit and walk diagonally across **Central Park** in a southeasterly direction towards the Frick Collection on East 70th Street. The nearest pedestrian entrance to the park is opposite the museum entrance on Central Park West.*

*Follow the main path past the Shakespeare Garden, a scrubby rock-garden, and with any luck you'll end up at **Belvedere Castle** (accessible via a steeply winding pathway and open during daylight hours; free adm, ☎ 772 0210)*

The castle looks ever so slightly Disneyland; but in fact was built in 1858 and New Yorkers take it quite seriously. Whatever you make of it, the top has a tremendous view of the whole park and its Belvedere-less skyline; and in the Henry Luce Nature Observatory and weather station inside you'll find a useful free map for getting your bearings; also binoculars, microscopes and books on ornithology for sale.

From the turrets, the first thing you notice is a swarm of black dots; a sea of humans illustrating Brownian motion. And although it's twice the size of Monaco, Central Park is nowadays so congested and convivial that any solitary soul who has come here seeking rustic tranquillity might as well jump now.

The idea of a New York without this rectangular green carpet is horrid, and was very nearly a reality. In the original grid of 1811, surveyors had provided for a park called the 'Parade' below 34th Street. But speculators quickly built all over this and seemed likely to devour the rest of the island as well, until in the 1850s the newspaperman William Cullen Bryant launched a campaign for a park. The city bought 843 acres of land, and commissioned Frederick Law Olmsted and Calvert Vaux, America's greatest landscape architects (also responsible for Prospect Park, Boston's Fenway and the garden boulevards of Kansas City), to build a park.

From a height, Central Park looks almost artificial: the rocks, Manhattan schist that glisters in sunlight, are rubbery, and the terrain, lawns and hillocks are scorched and torn with overuse, resembling the scenery used for train sets. It's not, then, a surprise to find out that there *is* nothing natural about Central Park. In the 1850s it was a wasteland harbouring over 300 shanty huts, a garbage dump and a festering bone-boiling works. 'The valleys reeked with corruption and every possible abomination: it was viler than a hog-pen, and the habitation of pestilence,' wrote the gloomy author of *New York in Sunshine and Shadow*. Olmsted and Vaux spent 20 years destroying the natural landscape. The picturesque vistas you see now are all man-made: five million cubic yards of earth were excavated to build a network of cross-roads running beneath the park, so, as Olmsted put it, it was possible 'even for the most timid and nervous to go on foot to any district of the park.'

To the right of the East Drive is the Metropolitan Museum of Art (*see* p.181), surrounded by a group of pine trees planted there in curious circumstances in the 1970s. A reporter from the *New York Times* happened to catch a man in the act of heeling in saplings. When the reporter asked him what he was up to, the anonymous tree-fetishist remarked mildly that this part of the drive was looking a bit lacklustre and maybe a clump would cheer it up.

In amongst the pines is **Cleopatra's Needle**. Don't bother taking a closer look: the hieroglyphs on the needle, mounted on verdigris crab claws, have been completely erased by pollution. The translation below, donated by Cecil B. de Mille, reveals that the message was anyway so verbose as to be unintelligible.

For those who like taking part, there are sports and activities. To the left is the open-air **Delacorte Theater**, where you can watch movie stars like Dustin Hoffman attempt Shakespeare, between June and September (*© 861 PAPP for details*). To the north is the **Great Lawn**, an expanse of mud and caterpillar tractors for 1997–8, since the lawn, which was subjected to so much wear and tear over the last century that it started to sink, is being rebuilt from scratch and reseeded. Under normal circumstances, there are ball-games here, and on June evenings free **Grand Opera**, performed by the Met (*© 362 6000*). To the south, you can join the fireman, Nelson Cruise, head of the Empire State's Model Mariners, his fellow sea-dogs and their state-of-the-art flotilla of $1000 radio-controlled dreadnoughts every Saturday, 10am–2pm, on the **Conservatory Water and Boathouse** on the east side of the park near 73rd Street and 5th Avenue.

*Make your way down from the castle and walk south via the **Ramble** over Bow Bridge to Bethesda Terrace.*

The dense woods of tulip and gum trees, sweet-smelling sassafras, black cherries and rhododendrons, rushing gorges and intricate paths of the Ramble were intended as a secluded Jane Austen-type wilderness: beyond the perimeter of the formal gardens, where, after a chaste beating about the bush, a thrilling climax is reached when the heroine at last addresses the hero by his Christian name. However, these days the serpentine paths of the Ramble are just as congested as the rest of the park, with the addition of mountain-bikers, and Park Rangers pleading for silence down loudhailers, so their tour may listen to a traumatized woodpecker. The wildest thing you are likely to see here is **'Wildman' Steve Brill**.

The Wildman was arrested in 1983 for eating berries, which formed a substantial part of his 'half-wild' diet. After a public outcry, he was employed by the Parks Department in 1986 to lead foraging tours through the park. He is easy to spot: hirsute and rugged, trousers neatly tucked into socks because he once stepped on a hornet's nest. The tours (© *1 718 291 6825 for details*) introduce laymen to many kinds of oddities: berries which make your heart stop, and poisonous toadstools which cause death by vomiting unless the victim consumes eight frozen rabbit brains within 36 hours. 'Ask me any question,' the Wildman says not so reassuringly, 'and I'll answer it even if I don't know the answer.' You may even get invited to the annual Christmas Wild Party which features Cherokee belly dancing, a lecture on how to survive on lawns, and a banquet of dock curry, five-boro wild salad, and cream of ginkgo-nut soup. (Ginkgo trees line the sidewalks of practically every street in New York, and the prehistoric trees actually thrive on polluted air. When ripe, the nuts fall to the ground and let out a pong similar to that of excreta which is so pungent you can smell it from a distance of several feet. The nuts have to be gathered wearing rubber gloves as any contact with the skin leads to a nasty rash. Roasted, however, ginkgo nuts are absolutely delicious, tasting of a mixture of swiss cheese and green tea.)

> At the south end of the Ramble, cross the Lake via Bow Bridge and make your way to **Bethesda Terrace**. Used as a fake Florentine piazza by the great film director D. W. Griffith, the Terrace now has a small café and a jazz band; Bethesda Fountain in the middle is a lovers' rendezvous.
>
> You are now just about parallel with the Frick, but before you leave, you might like to check out Central Park's **rollerbladers' disco** which starts on Friday evenings and continues more or less the rest of the week. This occurs, of all places, on **Literary Walk**, halfway down the Mall, next to the Sheep Meadow.

Past the statue of Sir Walter Scott and his dog, and under the beady eye of Robert Burns, a big centrifuge of backward-dancing spandexed bladers gyrates round ghetto-blasters, terrorizing pedestrians. Rollerblading is now so faddish that to conserve trees and shrubbery the Parks Department has introduced free stopping classes, one of which, at 72nd Street and 5th Avenue or **Inventors' Gate**, you should walk towards now. (*Skates and lessons are available at the Central Park Wollman Rink at 62nd Street and the Dairy,* © *369 1010.*)

> From the Inventors' Gate at East 72nd Street and 5th Avenue make your way two blocks south to the **Frick Collection** on East 70th and 71st Streets (open Tues–Sat, 10–6, Sun 1–6; adm $5, students $3; there are occasional chamber music concerts and lectures).

The trustees have a policy of only admitting 200 people at a time, which means that out of all Manhattan's so-called retreats, the Frick is the best. Here, anyone suffering from New York Trauma will find everything deliciously soothing, from the plush lavatories to the elegant telephone booths upholstered in red velvet.

Henry Clay Frick was plant manager at the Homestead mill owned by Andrew Carnegie. He made his millions out of steel and coke and beating up the labour unions, most outrageously in the strike over union contracts at the Homestead steel plant in 1892. Here, Frick hired scab labour to keep the plant going and one night during a five-day sit-in smuggled in 300 armed guards to protect the scabs, provoking a horrendously bloody scrimmage in which 14 steel workers were killed. Two weeks later Emma Goldman's lover, a bookish anarchist called Alexander Berkman, tried to assassinate Frick in his office. Sadly the ultimate outcome of the strike was that for many years America's steel companies got away with paying non-union wages.

All of which goes some way to explain Frick's passion for the lost arcadia depicted by European Old Masters; in particular for those paintings showing the indomitable upper classes in emphatically unindustrialized, pastoral settings. Frick set some store by his collection and in 1914, fearing the paintings would be contaminated by pollution from the nearby steel works, moved the whole lot from Pittsburgh to this spanking new 'palazzo', a pretty mishmash decorated in the 'French eclectic Louis XVI manner' complete with Renaissance furniture and Persian carpets. According to Frick, it made 'Carnegie's place' (a mansion up the road on 91st Street and 5th Avenue, now the Cooper-Hewitt Museum) 'look like a miner's shack'. Despite this Frick had a definite slob-snob side to him and devoted Saturday afternoons to lolling in the long gallery with a copy of the *Saturday Evening Post* while a hired organist serenaded him with 'Silver Threads Among the Gold' from the landing. Frick and his paintings became so inseparable that each summer he had them specially insured and took the whole lot on holiday with him by train to his estate in Massachusetts.

It's rather trying, going round the collection, to realize that the bastards of this world not only inherit the earth but then go on to exhibit delicate tastes, for the Frick collection brings together a crème de la crème of Old Masters, from the Renaissance to the end of the 19th century, and not one of the paintings is disappointing. Even more attractively, the museum is small and the paintings so intelligently arranged there's no need for a tour. As you walk round, you will soon notice that Frick had a penchant for collecting pairs, as if playing Pelmanism. There are two portraits by Holbein, for example: the virtuous Thomas More hanging next to the shifty Thomas Cromwell, the man who hanged him for high treason. The most stupendous pair of all is El Greco's gaunt and dour *St Jerome* and an enraged Christ casting out the moneychangers in the *Purification of the Temple*. The other rooms contain Vermeers, Goyas, Whistlers, Constables and Turners, including a self-portrait of Rembrandt dressed as an emir, painted when he was in dire financial straits, and his overrated *Polish Rider*. And if this doesn't satisfy you, try the painting opposite, which features the biggest codpiece ever, smugly displayed by Lodovico Capponi, in a portrait by Bronzino.

When you have had enough, sit down in the Frick's courtyard of plants, ponds and splashing fountains, contemplate the tulip gardens, and tell yourself that you have well and truly escaped New York and all its trials and tribulations.

> *From the Frick Collection either walk the 11 blocks south to 59th Street or, if you're tired out, catch one of the M1, 2, 3 or 4 buses going down 5th Avenue (you'll need a subway token), remembering to get* off *the bus at the bottom of Central Park and East 59th Street. (If you do forget to get off the bus it won't be a disaster as one of the most delightful ways to see Manhattan in a few hours is to get on the M1 here and travel all the way down to Washington Square and the West Village at the bottom of 5th Avenue.*

> *If you're walking it's well worth stopping off at the* **Temple Emanu-El** *(open Sun–Thurs 10–5; Fri 10–4; Sat 12–5; organ recitals Fri at 5), on the left at East 65th Street.*

Temple Emanu-El is Manhattan's oldest and largest Reformed synagogue. The front is austerely Romanesque, but even Mrs Astor, whose ostentatious château stood previously on the site and boasted a marble bathtub weighing two tons, would have been moved by the interior. The synagogue hall is 150ft long with seating for 2000, although so Byzantinely dark inside that for quite a while the only thing you can see is the rose window. Once your eyes adjust you'll see the gleam of gold and blue sanctuary mosaics by Hildreth Meiere, and the bronze grille of the Ark.

> *A block south on 64th Street on the park side of 5th Avenue is the animally correct* **Central Park Zoo (Wildlife Conservation Center)** *© 861 6030 (open April–Oct, Mon–Fri 10–5, Sat–Sun 10.30–5.30, Tues 10–8; and Nov–March, Mon–Sun 10–4.30; adm $2.50 adults; $1.25 seniors; 50¢ children 3–12).*

Zoos are generally depressing, and for years Central Park Zoo was only popular with people who came to throw themselves to the polar bears. In 1988, however, $35 million was spent on a complete refurbishment by Kevin Roche. The reformed zoo is now delightfully cheerful; there is hardly a cage in sight, and the 450 or so animals are the right size for its small scale. In the centre an artificial Californian rocky outcrop is home to barking sea-lions who relish an audience. The rest of the zoo is divided into the Polar Circle, the Temperate Territory and the Tropic Zone. The Polar Circle is the most innovative, with enormous glass walls so you can watch the polar bears and two flocks of gentoo and chinstrap penguins skimming through the water an inch away from your nose. In the Tropic Zone, you walk along catwalks through a steamy fibreglass rainforest of poison-arrow frogs and Indian fruit bats. Special heating pads have been installed under the beach to keep the crocs and piranhas happy.

*From the zoo, walk down 5th Avenue past the **Metropolitan Second-hand Bookstands** to East 59th Street.*

This stretch of 5th Avenue is New York's Pall Mall and on the way you brush past palazzi housing crusty gentlemen's clubs such as the Knickerbocker and one for the ladies, the Colony. Another kettle of fish is the old **Copacabana Club** at 14 East 60th Street, immortalized in Barry Manilow's song *Lola*, and a block down at 5 East 59th Street is the New York branch of the **Playboy Club**.

*At East 59th Street is Grand Army Plaza, one of New York's few open squares, with the Pulitzer Fountain in the middle. Across the square, between 58th and 59th Streets is the **Plaza Hotel**.*

Built in 1907 in the style of a French hotel, the Plaza is a charming building, elegant and festive—the alter ego of the sinister Dakota on Central Park West by the same architect, Henry Hardenburgh. Inside, the hotel still has to outface indelible marks left behind by the Trumps, even though financially Donald now only retains a 10% interest in the building and Ivana, responsible for the mawkish refurbishments, is no longer his wife.

If you like, you can stop for afternoon tea here, in the Plaza's touristy Tiffany-ceilinged **Palm Court**. However a superior Asian high tea is served in the tea-rooms on the 4th floor of **Felissimo's** (three blocks down from the Plaza at 10 West 56th Street, just off 5th Avenue). Felissimo's is an elegant Japanese design store based in an elegant town house built at the turn of the century by Warren & Wetmore. The tea rooms are on the 4th floor and accessible by a beautiful modern birdcage-style elevator which plays birdsong recordings; in the small, ethereal tea rooms 30 kinds of tea ('the wine of the 90s') come with personalized haikus, New Age muzac and miniature scones. According to the owners of Felissimo 'most Americans have never experienced a real cup of tea'.

*Now you have got to the end of the walk, you can go shopping on **5th Avenue**.*

Manhattan's most famous toy store, **F. A. O. Schwarz**, is opposite the Plaza, at 767 5th Avenue. Children are spookily absent here but constantly heard, ululating the store's horror anthem, *Welcome To Our World Of Toys*. If this fails to drive you screaming out in seconds, have a mooch around a shop which sells more stuffed animals than you'll find in the whole Natural History Museum. More mesmerizing still are toys to placate the nastiest brats alive, including a scaled-down Ferrari which cruises at 30mph with a five-digit price tag to match.

*After Schwarz's, make your way down 5th Avenue to **55th Street**. This stretch has shops with price tags that will fur your arteries in seconds.*

On the right between 57th and 58th Street is **Bergdorf Goodman**, a much-loved, very expensive, stylish clothes store for women, with a branch for men opposite. Around the corner on East 57th Street is **NikeTown**, a 66,000 sq ft mega shoe-shop on five floors which opened on 57th Street in 1996. Nike's alleged exploitation of workers in South East Asia has been exposed by film-maker Michael Moore, but here in NikeTown shoes are elevated into an art form in a five-floor store which brazenly imitates the Guggenheim Museum and includes such mesmerizing gadgets as digital foot X-ray scanning machines, pneumatic shoe tubes, flipper score boards, and also various sports memorabilia and a 1000-gallon fish tank. Lined up sardine-style next to NikeTown on East 57th Street are Warner Bros Studio Store, Chanel, Burberrys, Hermès, Prada, Vuitton and Laroche. Further down 5th Avenue and southeast of Bergdorf Goodman's on East 57th Street you'll find **Tiffany & Co** (where, as Holly Golightly tiresomely insisted, 'Nothing bad can ever happen to you...'); **Bendel's** at 714 5th Avenue and 56th Street, an elegant department store hilariously disguised as a town house; and finally **Takashimaya** between 55th and 54th Street at 693 5th Avenue, New York's first branch of the famous Japanese department store which is so sleek it sells objects 'scoured from the top flea markets in Paris.'

> *If all this is just too unremittingly tasteful for your more abrasive and complex sensibilities, finish your walk down 5th Avenue with a baptism by fire at **Trump Tower**, next door to Tiffany's at 725 5th Avenue between 57th and 56th Streets.*

The shopping atrium inside is rather like an exhumed haemorrhoid, an effect achieved in 1983 by combining noisy cascades of water, red ashtray-marble, gleaming bronze appendages, moving staircases, piped music and ghastly shops. Donald Trump (who doggedly refused to sell the horrible building even when faced with financial ruin and debts amounting to $5 billion), Johnny Carson and Steven Spielberg have all actually chosen to live above the atrocity, in three of the tower's 263 condominiums. At the top of the escalators visitors have access to NikeTown.

It's natural to feel violent urges in surroundings like these, and anyone who does will empathize with the strange events that led to the arrest of Salvador Dali in a pool of water, blood and broken glass on this very spot in 1939. Dali was the first Surrealist to visit New York before the war, and just two weeks after his arrival he was invited to dress two windows for Bonwit Teller, a posh department store standing on the Trump Tower site. Dali started work on March 16th, working furiously through the night with the help of three mindblown Bonwit Teller assistants. In the first window—'Day/Narcissus'—an aged mannequin wearing only a red wig and green feathers stepped into a bathtub lined in black astrakhan and filled with water. Three amputated hands floated on top, holding mirrors aloft. More mirrors were set into the sides of the display and the walls were tufted with purple leather. In the next window 'Night/Sleep' a mannequin draped in charred sheets stained with trickling pigeon's blood was shown reclining on a bed of hot coals. Above her was what Dali described as 'the decapitated head and the savage hoofs of a great somnambulist buffalo extenuated by a thousand years of sleep.'

As Dali returned to his hotel the next morning, puzzled Bonwit Teller managers wondered how to dismantle the outrage. As a tactful temporary measure, the naked mannequins were clothed in tailored Bonwit Teller suits. 'It's not art,' a customer complained, 'it's perversity.' Meanwhile, Dali, a light sleeper, returned to admire his work. Seeing the adulterations, he careered into Bonwit Teller to confront the manager and the manager's lawyer. But the men only incensed the Surrealist. Shrieking loudly in Spanish and French, Dali broke away and ran amok in Cosmetics and Hats. Finally, reaching his windows, outside of which a large crowd had gathered, Dali climbed in and overturned the bath, which slid across the floor, smashed into the window and catapulted itself out on to the sidewalk, taking Dali, who lost his footing in the frenzy, in its wake. The performance won him more glory, Dali said afterwards, than if he had devoured the whole of 5th Avenue.

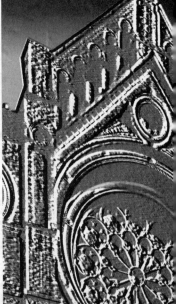

III: The Villages

(The Lower East Side, East Village and West Village)

Start: *J and F subway stop to Essex and Delancey Streets*

Walking Time: *4–5 hours*

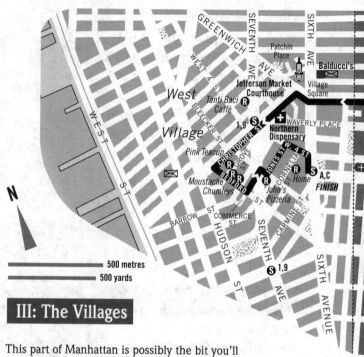

III: The Villages

This part of Manhattan is possibly the bit you'll
like best. It's low-rise, densely inhabited and
resplendent in diversity. There are no skyscrapers, no slick
museums, few tourist attractions: some parts are grimy and
impoverished, others (the East and West Villages) inhabited by a
new form of urban professional—the cyber gentry. This is 'neighbourhood Manhattan': full of distortions and shifting demographics.
It's also full of food—you'll find more of it here than anywhere in
Manhattan: from hand-held exotica to munch on as you walk, to
cheap and delicious sit-down feasts involving Chinese drag queen
waiters or what the cyber cafés call 'worldfood'. In any restaurant in
this part of Manhattan, the people around will be every bit as fascinating as the meal you eat.

The walk starts in the **Lower East Side**, a bulging belly which from
the 19th century onwards has accommodated wave after wave of
first generation immigrants—Irish and Germans escaping potato
famines in the 1850s, an estimated one-third of the entire Jewish
population of Europe between 1880 and 1900, Chinese after the

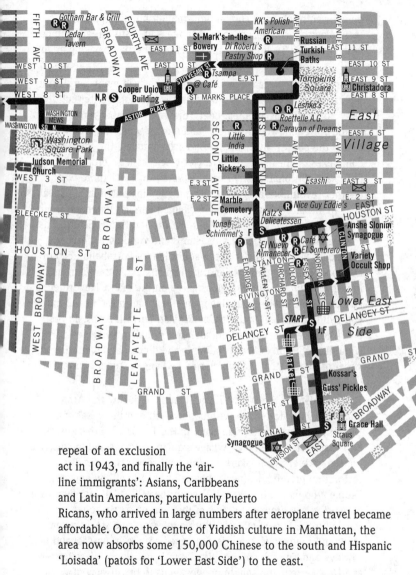

repeal of an exclusion
act in 1943, and finally the 'airline immigrants': Asians, Caribbeans
and Latin Americans, particularly Puerto
Ricans, who arrived in large numbers after aeroplane travel became
affordable. Once the centre of Yiddish culture in Manhattan, the
area now absorbs some 150,000 Chinese to the south and Hispanic
'Loisada' (patois for 'Lower East Side') to the east.

Above Houston Street is the **East Village**, another palimpsest
reflecting vacillations in immigration quotas and real estate prices.
Up here you'll find a new 'Silicon Alley' (or Nerdsville, depending

on your point of view) and an 'Information Building', a digital technology apartment house on Avenue A and 3rd Street equipped with super-fast T1 lines and inhabited by cybernauts paying up to $2500 a month rent.

In the last three decades the East Village has had many perplexing incarnations. In the sixties it became a bastion of counter-culture New York: radicals and Beat poets, drawn by cheaper rents, moved in and were followed by hippies and new-wavers. The area was then one of the poorest in Manhattan: to accommodate the 'masses' complexes of cheap antiseptic tower blocks called 'projects' were built east of Alphabet City (Avenues A–D). In 1981 there was another revolution: art galleries and nightclubs rolled in, drastically altering the East Village as they reclaimed derelict tenement buildings and launched artists like Keith Haring and Kenny Scharf. Then came gentrification: restaurants, shops and window boxes. Nowadays St Mark's Place is the equivalent of Portobello Road in London, complete with designer bohemians, PR, advertising and multimedia types, editors or journalists on the make. Nevertheless ghosts of East Villages past linger on—in amongst the newer arrivals you will find ancient and thriving Russian-Turkish baths, an Irish pub (the oldest in Manhattan), a cluster of Italian *pasticceria*, a Ukrainian church, Polish restaurants and diners, and an entire street of Indian curry houses started by Bengali students from NYU in the 1970s.

Bohemianism in the **West Village** flourished during the Armory Show of 1913, fizzled out with bobbed hair and the onset of the Depression, then spurted up again in the 1950s with the Abstract Expressionists. Greenwich Village's quaint cottages and mews once housed weavers, sailmakers, artisans and servants. Nowadays, restored to pristine neatness, they sell from $1 million apiece. People who live in the West Village in the 1990s fall into five main catagories: gay, (four out of five of the men on Christopher Street); media (in the bars); well-off (actors, professors and stockbrokers living in brownstones); tourists (dragged around in posses) and B&Ts ('Bridge and Tunnel' suburbanites from Long Island, Westchester and New Jersey who spill in on weekends to the dismay of everyone else). An oil and water combination, but one that makes the West Village one of Manhattan's most convivial and safest neighbourhoods.

Lower East Side (below East Houston Street)

El Nuevo Amanecer, 117 Stanton St., at Essex Street. Cheap verging on grotty Spanish/Mexican/American restaurant: lobsters, burritos, tortillas, quesadillas (*from $4*).

El Sombrero, 108 Stanton St., between Ludlow and Essex Sts. Jolly Mexican restaurant nicknamed 'The Hat', trendy with déshabillé East Village types.

Ludlow Street Café, 165 Ludlow St., between Stanton and East Houston Sts. Excellent for brunch: first rate cajun food, noisy bar, live music.

Katz's Delicatessen, 205 East Houston St., near Orchard St. Pastrami on rye and Dr Brown's celery soda in 'When Harry met Sally' Jewish deli.

East Village

Esashi, 32 Avenue A, at 3rd Street. Lunch from $5–20, sushi by the piece: savoury eel, urchin roe and 'tiger eye' (skate with salmon and seaweed).

Nice Guy Eddie's, 5 Avenue A, at 1st Street. Cajun food in friendly restaurant with jukebox: jambalaya and fried calamari (*from $10*).

Limbo Café, 3rd Street and 1st Ave. Cappuccinos in pudding basins, club sandwiches, dry-humoured waiters.

O.G., 507 East 6th St., between Aves. A and B, ✆ 477 4649. Fusion of Chinese, Japanese, Indonesian and Thai cooking: imaginative menu, good prices, high noise (*from $15*).

Little India on 6th St., between 1st and 2nd Aves. Thirty Bengali restaurants on one block, $5 for curry lunch, bring your own beer (the grocery store on 6th and 1st Avenue carries 400 brand names).

Caravan of Dreams, 405 East 6th St., between 1st Ave and Ave A. Fey vegetarian, low prices: angel's toast bread with almond butter.

Roettelle A.G., 126 East 7th St., between 1st Ave., and Ave. A. Foods from the Common Market. Four small rooms, plus a garden big enough for one table. High quality cold meats, rosti, sauerkraut (*from $20*).

@Café, 12 St Mark's Place, near 3rd Ave., *www.fly.net*. Cyber food, cyber music, cyber people: 18 terminals at $5 an hour.

De Robertis Pastry Shop, 176 1st Ave., between 10th and 11th Sts. Family-run Art Nouveau tea room with superior espressos and cannoli pastries.

KK's Polish-American, 1st Ave., between 11th and 12th Sts. Family-run excellent-value Polish 'Cooking like Mama Made it', best for brunch on a sunny day sitting in the attractive garden (*from $5*).

Tsampa, 212 East 9th St., between 2nd and 3rd Aves. Tibetan bistro serving sophisticated potato curry to sophisticated Buddhists (*from $5*).

West Village

Gotham Bar & Grill, 12 East 12th St., at 5th Ave., ✆ 620 4020. One of the most fashionable and best restaurants in Manhattan, with an excellent three-course lunch special for $19.97 (*rising to $19.98 in 1998*).

Moustache, 90 Bedford Street, between Grove and Barrow Sts. 'Foul'—fava beans, parsley and garlic in pitta bread—plus other cheap Middle Eastern fare, merguez sandwiches and 'loomi' iced tea (*from $7*).

Cafe Asean, 117 West 10th St., between 6th and Greenwich Aves. 'Pan-Asian' mix of Vietnamese, Thai and Malaysian: cold rice vermicelli (*bun ton*), rice paper summer rolls with shrimp and peanut sauce (*goi cuon*), in small dining room with flea market furniture.

Home, 20 Cornelia St., between Bleecker and West 4th Sts. Excellent American home-cooking and tiny back garden: pork chops crusted with cumin, sausages, apple crumb pie (*from $15–20*).

Tanti Baci Caffé, 163 West 10th St., at 7th Ave. Cheap, perfect pasta, gnocchi, salad: one of the nicest Italian restaurants in New York, bring your own alcohol (*from $10*).

The Pink Teacup, 42 Grove St., between Bleecker and Bedford Sts. Soul food. Village institution serving patties, pancakes, smothered chops, sweet potato pie, cornbread, pig's trotters (*from $10*).

John's Pizzeria, 278 Bleecker St., between 6th and 7th Aves. Manhattan's famous coal oven pizza slices in 50 varieties (*from $9*).

Lower East Side

The J and F subway stop lands you on a stretch of Delancey where all the shops (except one selling stetsons) seem to be opticians. Giant glasses dangle over the sidewalk, and in case you bump into one it's comforting to be told in extra-large lettering that Cohen's make the cheapest spectacles in Manhattan in an hour.

*The **Orchard Street Market** is a couple of blocks away. Walk west on Delancey Street to the corner of Orchard Street, where the Kool-Man ice-cream van tinkles* Fiddler on the Roof *tunes. Turn left.*

On a Sunday (when it re-opens after early closing on Friday and all day Saturday) the 300 shops and stalls of Orchard Street Market are so jam-packed it's hard to buy *anything*. Sequinned dresses, jeans, socks, T-shirts, Armani and Ralph Lauren knock-offs, fabrics and toys infiltrate themselves on to every spare inch of the street from lamp-posts to fire-escapes to nail-hooks rammed into brickwork. And as New Yorkers will admit, no one buys from Orchard Street on a Sunday. They go to look and eat; they come back on a weekday to buy. Furthermore, most of Orchard Street's Hong Kong-manufactured imitation designer clothes aren't on display: instead they are hidden away at the back. To buy them you have to go to what New Yorkers call a 'fancy schmancy' store (Lord & Taylor, Saks, Bergdorf Goodman) find a garment you want, make a note of the number on the tag, go back to Orchard Street, tell a shop assistant the number, and wait while he goes to the back to rummage. If, after this palaver, the assistant finds what you're looking for, you'll end up with the bargain of the millennium. Less dedicated shoppers can still get a thrill on Orchard Street, haggling for underwear from shops with staggering names to match—*Lady O, Climactic, Shebang* or, the enigmatic *H*.

Walk the whole way down the market to the junction of Orchard Street and Canal Street.

At the bottom of Orchard Street, where Canal Street crosses it, is one of the Lower East Side's tallest buildings, **S. Jarmulovsky's Bank**, topped by an elegant tempietto concealing a water tower. The private bank crashed in 1914 bringing about the ruin of thousands of immigrants and, after a suspended sentence for mismanagement of the bank's assets, Jarmulovsky's death.

From the junction of Orchard and Canal Streets, turn right and walk two blocks west to Eldridge Street. The Lower East Side becomes a palimpsest at this point, with a new, chaotic Chinatown overlaying the older Jewish Lower East Side. To the left, on the block between Division Street and Canal Street is the **Eldridge Street Synagogue** *(open Tues and Thurs 11.30–2.30, Sun 11–3, © 219 0888). However, as you walk down towards the synagogue, Eldridge Street is piquantly Chinese, with incense wafting on to the street from a bright storefront temple at 24 Eldridge Street ('The Palace for Mother of Saint'); and next to that, at No.26, a medicine shop with drawers and jars filled with black herbs, sea-horses, dried antelope horn and ginseng (and customers sticking out tongues for on-the-spot diagnoses). A few doors further down at No. 14 is the beautiful Eldridge Street Synagogue (open).*

Built in 1886, the synagogue fell into disrepair in the thirties, and is presently being renovated. It's exotic for the area—a high Victorian mix of Gothic and Moorish styles. The Eastern elements—pastry-cut keyhole windows and pink marble columns—have fared better over the years than the ornate Gothic finials, which have fallen off, and the vast and impressive stained-glass rose window, which was badly vandalized in the 1980s. On a Tuesday, Thursday or Sunday ring the bell and the rabbi will take you on a tour. A magnificent sanctuary inside reflects the lavish taste of Herter Brothers, a German architectural firm who specialized in 5th Avenue drawing-rooms. The rabbi reads a speech in Hebrew and English, explaining the history of the building which has been 'neglected from behind long time'. At the end, if you're lucky, he will burst into song.

Outside, the synagogue is surrounded by the kind of **tenements** (still draped with washing but now inhabited by Chinese families) which spread through the Lower East Side with vegetable speed in the 19th century. The first thing you notice is the tangle of fire escapes, which Henry James reviled in his *American Notes*. According to Arnold Bennett the buildings behind 'sweated humanity': there was a population density of 700 per acre, and the death rate in the tubercular 'lung blocks' was twice as high as the rest of the city.

The buildings with the dragon-headed newels in front of you (where the comedian Eddie Cantor—then Edward Iskowitz—grew up) are actually copybook examples of 'Old Law'-style blocks. These were built between 1879 and 1901, and laid out in accordance with the 'dumbbell' plan, in which narrow 90ft-long apartments were constructed sardine-style, with a reeking foot-wide airshaft between. Four families per floor shared a bathroom, using lavatories ventilated by street grates in the basement. By the turn of the century two-thirds of the population were already ensconced in Old Law housing. Finally in 1901, dumbbell tenements were banned, and minimally better sanitary standards set in place.

> *Go back to Canal Street and from the junction with Eldridge Street walk four blocks east along Canal. After one block you pass Allen Street, with its enormous billboard urging passers-by to 'Pray with Dignity in a Ziontalis'. A century ago Allen Street was the most notorious in the city, boasting exotic belly dancers and 'creep houses and brothels' equipped with sliding panels so thieves could sneak in and rifle through a victim's trousers. These were eventually outlawed by a Rev. Dr Parkhurst, hard-boiled chief of the Society for the Prevention of Vice. Just past the Ziontalis billboard on your right at 54–8 Canal Street is a small* **Chinese Wall Newspaper,** *a series of red banners tied to a store-front with purple, red and pink ribbons, and felt-tipped with Help Wanted columns advertising jobs. Two blocks further east, on the lefthand corner of Canal Street at 5 Ludlow Street, is the shell of the* **Kletzker Brotherly Aid Society.** *This is now a Chinese-Italian funeral home, but was originally a* landsmanshaftn *or local association established by immigrants to support new arrivals from their local* shtetl *or town; in this case, Kletz, in Russia.*

> **Straus Square,** *a block further east on Canal and Essex Streets, is the spiritual heart of Jewish Lower East Side.*

Around here are numerous store-front Orthodox synagogues, many Hasidic. A ritualarium, or *mikveh*, where married women bathe every month in rainwater, is still in use at the far east end of East Broadway at No.131 (*tours by appointment; call Mrs Bormiko on © 674 5318*). Closer to, at 145 East Broadway near Essex Street, you can peep through louvred shutters at a *yeshiva*, where students train as rabbis. Shops on Hester Street still make and repair *yarmulke*, *talith* (prayer shawls), *bar-mitzvah* sets, *mezuzahs*, *tefellin* (amulets containing prayers on Old Testament parchment) and electrically lit *menorahs*. And from the corner of Canal and Essex Streets you can't miss the **Jewish Daily Forward Building**, a tall semi-skyscraper with a clock on the tower, nowadays known as Grace Hall.

The Yiddish newspaper was founded in 1897 by a Lithuanian, Abraham Cahan, who championed writers like Isaac Bashevis Singer and Shalom Aleichem. The paper had a circulation of 125,000 and was by far the most popular of New York's dozen or so Yiddish newspapers. A column called the Bintel Brief, or 'Bundle of Letters', gave advice to readers ranging from 'The Sleepless Man'—a husband complaining about his wife's 'nocturnal concerts'—to people living in such poverty that they enquired if it was ethical to sell their children to a home where they would get a comfortable upbringing.

> *From Straus Square walk a block north along Essex Street—past wholesale dealers in barmitzvah sets, skull caps and menorahs and **Sammy's Aquarium**, a Chinese pet shop selling chinchillas, turtles and iguanas as well as bat, panther and squirrel fish—as far as **Hester Street**.*

The appetizing smell-cloud on this corner emanates partly from **Gertel's Bake Shoppe**, at 53 Hester Street, where you can sit down to a breakfast of coffee, *rugelach* and raspberry jelly doughnuts, and take advantage of the loo at the back.

> *Other seaside whiffs on the northwest corner of Hester come from **Guss' Pickles** (on the right at 35 Essex Street, between Hester and Grand Streets) selling Manhattan's sourest pickled peppers, half-sours (new pickles), sours and sauerkraut (all of which featured in Crossing Delancey). A few steps away at 5 Hester Street, the air is scented by the **Kadouri Import Co.**, where spices like cumin and cardamom are piled up in barrels alongside pistachio nuts and crystallized fruits.*

Just here was the **Khazzer-Mark** (Pig-Market) where workers gathered every morning to get jobs from 'sweaters'. The first unsensationalized account of the sweatshops they toiled in was given by Jacob Riis who in *How the Other Half Lives* described the din of sewing machines on every block, workers ankle-deep in clothes, and babies squirming on mountains of material, their faces blackened with cloth-dust.

> *From Hester Street walk a block north up Essex Street to Grand Street. On this corner on your right at 369 Grand Street is the legendary **Kossar's**, a flour-dusted bakery selling Manhattan's chewiest bagels and bialys.*

While everyone knows that the bialy, a kind of onion roll, was invented by Polish bakers in Bialystok, no one is sure about the origin of the bagel. The mystery became even more infuriating when the *Saturday Review* claimed bagels came from Turkey. A facetious man called K. Jason Sitewell replied with the theory that a Greek baker called Bagelus invented the bagel in 381 BC after he wrapped some dough round his feet to cure his gout and fell asleep in the midday sun. Others maintained that the Dead Sea Scrolls mentioned the 'legab'. The most convincing letter came from one Harry Bagel, who said his Uncle Morris invented the bagel in 1897.

> *Buy a bialy to munch on, then walk three more blocks up Essex Street as far as Stanton Street and the **Essex Street Market**.*

The right-hand side of Essex Street between Stanton and Rivington Streets is devoted to the Essex Street Market, a covered market opened in the 1930s after pushcarts were banished from the streets. The star of the market is **Julius the Candy King**, who has the stall on the corner of Delancey and Essex Streets. However, in the summer the King is elusive, and all you find is a disappointing sign saying 'Gone Fishing'. The rest of the market is very Hispanic, with fish stalls selling tripe and bacalao, and a *botánica* dedicated to Santería, an ancient African-Indian religion (in which spirits are believed to inhabit everything animate and fate is a potion or charm), practised before the Spanish arrived in Puerto Rico. Most Puerto Ricans followed Santaría rather than accept the religion of the white inter-lopers: this very small *botánica* sells the dried herbs and roots used in traditional Puerto Rican folk medicine alongside modern pregnancy tests.

> *From the junction of Rivington and Essex Streets wander two blocks north to East Houston Street. If you have time for a detour, it's easy to stroll up to Houston Street via **Clinton Street**, the high street of Hispanic Lower East Side. To get there, walk three blocks east along Rivington Street. On the way you pass a Spanish–Chinese restaurant; a kosher wine-makers (Schapiro's House of Sacremental Wines at 126 Rivington); a matzoh factory (Streit's, at 150 Rivington); and finally at 166 Rivington the **Variety Occult Shop**, another Puerto Rican bótanica specializing in evil tongues and love potion aerosol sprays. The amazing mix of shops and businesses is being complicated by the arrival of middle-class settlers who are gentrifying the area very quickly and squeezing out poorer tenants.*

Clinton Street is the Hispanic Lower East Side's high street and backbone. It's at its most energetic on Saturdays when the chihuahuas and ghetto-blasters are out in force. The shops have murals painted on their rolling gates, and signs for groceries, wash 'n' fold laundries, bridal wear or cheap telephone calls abroad are all in Spanish. Some of the stores, translating themselves simply as 'Cheap Store' or 'Variety Shop', sell *productos tropicales*—plantains, mango, *pasteles calientes* (chopped meat wrapped in leaves), and yams—and also, less exotically, plastic American eagles, loo seats, and chandeliers. In the summer, street vendors sell snow ices: scraped from a slab of ice, moulded into a cone and doused in syrup (or, occasionally, vodka or rum).

> *Walk up Clinton Street to East Houston Street and turn left. Then walk two blocks west along East Houston Street as far as Norfolk Street. A*

short way down Norfolk Street on your left at No.172 is the exquisite **Anshe Slonim Synagogue,** *nowadays home to the* **Angelo Orensatz Foundation** *(© 529 7194, email 76151.1617@compuserve.com).*

Mr Orensatz is an unconventional Spanish sculptor who works in metal and clay: you can see two of his metal sculptures standing outside the synagogue like sentries. If you ring the bell on the right-hand side of the metal gates, either Orensatz' brother or his assistant will gladly show you the extraordinarily beautiful sanctuary inside filled with many more of the curious but striking works of art..

The synagogue itself was rescued from certain demolition over a decade ago by Mr Orensatz, and is arguably the most beautiful in Manhattan. It was modelled on Cologne Cathedral and constructed in 1849 for a German congregation by Alexander Saeltzer (a German Jew) and originally was even more tremendously Gothic with pyramids, sculptures, and intricate lacework traceries. The blistering but very beautiful interior with its huge stained-glass rose window has been greatly restored since Orensatz arrived on the scene. Nowadays the space is used for performance art, opera, concerts, computer-media installations, play readings and contemporary art pieces, with the gallery above set aside as an artist's studio.

The south side of **East Houston Street**, fast and fumy with traffic, is an excellent place to buy lunch. (New Yorkers pronounce this in a English accent, as 'Howston'.) At 205 East Houston Street, on the corner of Ludlow Street, is **Katz's 'That's All!' Delicatessen**, where Meg Ryan had her virtual orgasm in *When Harry Met Sally.* Inside, purchases are punched off on old-fashioned meal tickets and signs hanging from the ceiling badger you to 'Send a Salami to your Boy in the Army' which rhymes, in New York; and in fact there is still a mailing counter to send them off from.

If you want to buy delicatessen to take home or the kind of sandwich you'll remember forever, there's the gastronome's paradise of **Russ & Daughters**, close by at 179 Houston Street, selling delicacies like golden lake smoked sturgeon, fancy chub and kippered salmon alongside barrels of sauerkraut and, on the other side of the counter, chocolates and dried fruit. Alternatively, and it is an impossible choice, try the best and tastiest knishery in Manhattan, **Yonah Schimmel's Knishes** further down at 137 Houston Street. Here fat, round hot knishes the size of croquet balls trundle up from a kitchen by dumbwaiter. The old-fashioned restaurant above is spick and span with stamped tin ceilings, friendly waitress and telly on the counter. The knishes, a savoury strudel ball of loveliness, really are wonderful: try them in potato, kasha or cherry cheese flavours with some borscht on the side.

After lunch you could suddenly make yourself feel very very ill by going to a pet shop called **JBJ Discount,** *just past Schimmel's at 153 East Houston Street between Allen and Eldridge Streets.*

JBJ's specializes in *cockroaches*, in particular 'Buy two get one free' **Madagascan Hissing Roaches**. These are the mothers of all cockroaches, 3 inches long and $15 each, and truly the most horrible things you can see in the whole of New York. Can there be a market for such brutes? Apparently there is, although the manager admits that his main customers are mostly makers of schlock horror movies and talk show hosts, to whom the cockroaches are rented out at a modest fee.

The East Village

*From here make your way into the **East Village** by crossing Houston Street and walking north. Start by walking two blocks up 1st Avenue to 2nd Street where on your left, between 1st and 2nd Avenues, you can make a brief visit to the **New York City Marble Cemetery** dating from 1830.*

This is the quietest spot in the city as the gates are permanently locked and only squirrels patronize it. President James Monroe was here briefly in 1832, but was soon removed, and now the only resident of note is Preserved Fish, a merchant from a reputable family of weirdly named lawyers. Even so, the tall, unnaturally white obelisks on pristine lawns are a haunting sight in an otherwise grubby area.

*Continue a block north on 1st Avenue to 3rd Street. On the left at 49½ 1st Avenue is a shop dealing in camp and kitsch, **Little Rickey's**, 'Where Elvis is your cashier in the cathedral of kitsch'. If you're looking for an Elvis suspender belt, a Virgin Mary scatter cushion or a Felix the Cat wagging clock, this is the place for you. If you're looking for something more rousing, try the men and their Harleys at the **New York Chapter of Hell's Angels**, round the corner from Little Rickey's on 3rd Street between 1st and 2nd Avenues.*

*Five blocks further up 1st Avenue takes you to the heart of the East Village, **St Marks Place**, which is really 8th Street. In good weather a phalanx of restaurants, bars and cafés moves tables on to the sidewalk, making St Mark's a jolly place to stop for a drink and observe the East Village in action.*

In the 19th century, St Mark's was well-to-do; the wealthiest immigrant families (mostly from East Europe) lived in its elegant Federal houses and the street had various social clubs including a German marksmen's club. In the fifties, radicals and Beat poets including Jack Kerouac, Allen Ginsberg, Frank O'Hara, William Burroughs and Norman Mailer came here from the West Village to revel in the 'Pierre-of-Melville goof and wonder of it all'. In their wake came the hippies, Bill Graham's Fillmore East concerts, and the rock group Electric Circus, at 23 St Mark's, where a community centre is now.

Nowadays the street draws a more pastel-coloured spectrum of exhibitionists, ranging from East Village culturati (dressed as New Wave punks) to preppies riding motorized skateboards with more nerve than skill. To this lot St Mark's Place is the most fashionable street in the world, so much so that beleaguered residents have painted signs on their stoops saying 'Do not sit on the stairs, please', which you can't see, because so many people are sitting on them.

As you walk along the wide sidewalk, cluttered with second-hand books, unwholesome magazines and jewellery, look out for the mosaics (by **Joe Power**) on lamp posts, walls and spare crevices like an outdoor grotto. **77 St Mark's**, on the corner of 1st Avenue, is where W. H. Auden lived from 1953 until 1972, above a basement where Trotsky had printed *Novy Mir* years before: 'God bless the USA, so friendly and so rich!' Auden optimistically announced on his arrival. Inside, however, Auden's poky apartment quickly evolved into an alpine range of egg-encrusted plates, and was beseiged by such a populous 'vertical nation of cockroaches' that the walls seemed to be moving. Auden would have appreciated the **Holiday Cocktail Lounge** opposite. This is a dark, smoke-filled and utterly nondescript bar run by a Ukrainian who seems to have been here forever. The Lounge enjoys a special mystique, partly because the dingy and drab interior never changes, striking many a weary-eyed New Yorker as the height of originality. How else do you explain the New Yorker's fondness for the English?

> *Walk to the east end of St Mark's, until you find yourself in a grotty-looking park called* **Tompkins Square**.

Tompkins Square is nevertheless the East Village's main plaza. Everyone uses it: Puerto Ricans from Loisaida, West Africans and WASPS, winos, homeless people, NYU students (who have dormitories scattered all around), ancient Ukrainians and Poles, and even the odd child. If there is one particular place in the whole of New York that sums up the feeling of different worlds obliviously colliding, it is Tompkins Square.

In its time the square has been the focal point of various community battles. After a crescendo of rioting in 1991, police expelled 300 homeless people who lived for years in a shanty town of tents in the middle, and the parks department took to locking up the area at night. Over the years rapid gentrification, an influx of NYU students and spiralling rents have caused some acrimony: and although the poor have been pushed out of sight into the mainly Hispanic tower blocks of Alphabet City, a large homeless contingent drifts into the park in the summer. Ironically Tompkins Square was a focal point of discontent years before when, in the wake of the financial panic of 1873, German socialists held a demonstration against unemployment which the police broke up so violently it was dubbed the 'Tompkins Square Massacre'. The area east of Tompkins Square has been in a state of near-permanent decline since the 1860s, when 4th Street, between Avenues A and B, was called 'Ragpickers' Row', and the two blocks of 11th Street between 1st Avenue and Avenue B had the humiliating nickname 'Mackerelville'.

The north side has a row of elegant houses with well-tended front gardens and high stoops built 12 years after the park was laid out in the style of a Bloomsbury square in 1834. On the corner of 10th Street and Avenue B is a mural by Chico, *Say no to Crack*, and round the corner on 11th Street more murals by other Loisaida artists. To the west on Avenue B the tall 12-storey Art Deco building is the **Christadora**. Originally a settlement house where George Gershwin gave his first recital, the tower was converted into luxury condominiums in 1987.

The side on Avenue A is now solid with restaurants, including **Leshko's**, a Polish diner which is a rallying point for people living in the neighbourhood as well as plump-looking police officers who seem to gather here on Fridays, when the restaurant stays open for 24 hours until Saturday

> *Leave Tompkins Square by the northwest corner, and walk west along 10th Street, where you may see a beetroot-coloured person emerging from the **Tenth Street Russian Turkish Baths** (open until 10, and later by appointment), 268 10th Street on the block between Avenue A and 1st Avenue.*

This is the last of the traditional steam baths or *shvitz* (Yiddish for sweat) which a century ago were scattered all over the Lower East Side. In the sub-basement below huge chunks of rock are heated until they turn red, at which point water is chucked on to them, releasing clouds of 'radiant' wet heat which supposedly reaches places ordinary steam can't manage. Clients can also thrash themselves with oak-branches or *platza*, take a dry Scandinavian sauna, have a sleep in a cot in the dormitories or down a Stolichnaya in the bar.

> *Walk to the junction of 10th Street and 1st Avenue and turn right. A few steps up on 1st Avenue between 10th and 11th Streets you can drop into **Di Roberti's Pasticceria** for a cappuccino, half-froth, half-cinnamon, and a cannoli (brittle pastry tubes filled with vanilla ricotta).*

The tea-rooms, built in 1904, are the finest in Manhattan, with walls tiled in white and inset with sparkly green and gold Art Nouveau mosaics suspiciously similar to the tiles in Astor Place subway station, which was built the same year.

> *After your tea, walk a block west along 10th Street to the junction with 2nd Avenue where, set back at a diagonal from the avenue, you'll see **St Mark's-in-the-Bowery**.*

St Mark's is the city's second oldest church but something of a mongrel with a 1799 Federal body topped by an 1828 Greek Revival steeple by Ithiel Town (who designed the brownstones on Washington Square), and cast-iron portico added in 1858. In 1901 Butch Cassidy lived in a boarding house around the corner, and in 1912 Big Jack Zelig was shot and killed near here by Red Phil Davidson as he was boarding a trolley car (a poster in pubs in the area offered aspiring assassins the following rewards: 'SLASH ON CHEEK WITH KNIFE—$1 to $10; SHOT IN LEG—$1 to $25; MURDER AND BIG JOBS—$10 to $100').

More pleasantly, St Mark's stands on the site of a large farm or 'bouwerie', as the Dutch called it, owned by Peter Stuyvesant, the third and final governor of New Amsterdam. Although he governed the city for 24 years, Stuyvesant is mostly remembered for having a peg leg and surrendering the Dutch colony to the British without a shot in 1664. Intriguingly, when the Staats General offered him retirement on a generous stipend in Holland, Stuyvesant refused to come home. The ex-governor spent the last eight years of his life stumping around his bowery on a silver-capped wooden leg. His chapel stood close to St Mark's and these days his statue is on the right-hand side of the entrance, and his remains in a stone vault set into in the wall of the graveyard.

To the left of the entrance is a sandstone sculpture of an American Indian, with hands that are too big. If the style looks familiar, that's because it was sculpted by Solon H. Borglum, whose more famous brother, Gutzon, carved Mount Rushmore.

St Mark's cemetery is behind the American Indian. In 1878 this was the scene of a macabre kidnapping when body-snatchers disinterred the body of A. T. Stewart and held it for a ransom of a quarter of a million dollars (Alexander Stewart had invented the department store in 1846 and his Cast-Iron Palace in SoHo became the largest retail establishment in the world). Two years passed before Stewart's widow, worth $50 million, could be persuaded to relinquish a paltry $20,000 for her husband. His putrified remains were eventually reburied in Garden City.

In the twenties the church became a centre for more unusual events under the ministry of Dr William Guthrie, who inflicted holistics, American Indian chanting, pagan murals, Eastern mantras, and a Body and Soul Clinic on East Village parishioners. The church still has a radical bent, and hosts many fascinating literary events, including 'Ontological Theater', and right up until his death in 1997 Allen Ginsberg did numerous poetry readings here. (See the *Village Voice* for listings).

> *From St Mark's walk diagonally south down Stuyvesant Street to* **Astor Place** *at the junction of 8th Street and 4th Avenue. (If you're tired catch the M8 bus, which stops all along 8th Street, from here as far as Christopher Street and the West Village.) On the left and marooned in an island between 3rd and 4th Avenues, is an enormous beached brownstone, the* **Cooper Union Building***.*

Founded in 1859, Cooper Union offered free technical, scientific and art courses to anyone 'of good moral character' (including, in 1925, Lee Krasner). Peter Cooper was an uneducated entrepreneur who made his million twice over in the glue and iron trades. He invented one of the first steam engines, the *Tom Thumb*, as well as an automatic cradle, which rocked and fanned itself and played music. Today, Cooper Union is a progressive architecture school. However the building itself is of architectural interest because it was the first in the world constructed with wrought-iron beams. Cooper built them out of railway tracks from his own iron-works, and eventually the idea evolved into the steel frames essential for supporting skyscrapers.

Between midday and through the night the sidewalk in front of Cooper Union turns into a **souk**, which comes and goes according to the movements of the police. Stuff on sale ranges from junk extracted from garbage cans to stolen bicycles.

On the traffic island in the middle of Astor Place you'll see Bernard Rosenthal's 15ft black steel cube, the '**Alamo**'. It's supposed to pirouette when pushed, but the 'weathering' apex is now so rusted that it needs a super-heroical shove.

The West Village

*Walk down Astor Place to Broadway, turn left at the junction and then right on to Waverly Place. A three-block walk along Waverly takes you to **Washington Square**, heart of the West Village. Fix it in your brain, because it's a fact of life for New Yorkers and visitors alike that before you know where you are in the West Village you're lost. Fortunately there aren't many places that are nicer to get lost in.*

Washington Square Park, in front of you, is always full of people: blubbery joggers, failed poets, social outcasts (usually musicians) and students; and, in the summer, cheery crowds and performers in all shapes and sizes, not least a man who juggles rabbits. Originally a swamp, the park first came into use as an execution ground, then as a paupers' graveyard for victims of the yellow fever that blitzed Manhattan in the 18th century. Supposedly 22,000 bodies are buried under the park and in 1965 Con Edison workers unhappily stumbled on 25 cadavers wrapped in yellowed shrouds. During the worst epidemic, in 1822, the streets round City Hall were barricaded, and the business community upped sticks and fled with their offices to the sweeter air in fields along the Hudson. Many of the refugees stayed on, and in only a few years from 1822 to 1850 a completely rural area metamorphosed into the fashionable brownstones and row-houses of Greenwich Village.

At one time, Washington Square was surrounded by these. Now only the north side of the square can be proud of its original Greek Revival row-houses. This is one of Manhattan's most eminent addresses (although inhabitants have to contend with (listed) inter-connecting doors and the constant fear that a neighbour may 'pop' into their drawing room at any moment). **1–13 Washington Square North** are the 'solid and honorable dwellings' described in *Washington Square*, though perversely No.18, the house belonging to Henry James' grandmother and the setting for the novel, was demolished. No.3 was revamped in Queen Anne style as an artist's studio in 1884, and in the 1920s John Dos Passos wrote *Manhattan Transfer* in an apartment inside shared with Edward Hopper. A few blocks north from the Row on University Place is the Cedar Tavern, innocuously spruced up and selling hamburgers these days, but years ago an anonymous bar room made legendary in the 1950s by a bunch of abstract expressionists including Pollock, de Kooning, Kline and Guston and their hangers-on—a bunch of 'washouts', 'doomed artists' and sycophants who came to spectate the parody-brawls engineered by Jackson Pollock as he lunged into alcoholic exhibitionism shortly before his death in a car crash on Long Island in 1956.

Sadly, a salient reminder that the West Village is not the hotbed of artistic iconoclasm (or even endeavour) it once was is the **Washington Square Art Show** held around the square and up 5th Avenue twice a year. Hurry past if it's on to **Washington Square Arch** in the middle. The 77ft-high triumphal arch is built on the same scale as those of antiquity. Fred Astaire danced on top of it in a forgotten film called *The Belle of New York*; and in 1916 John Sloan and Dada impresario Marcel Duchamp climbed up via stairs inside and from the top proclaimed the secession of the Village from the USA, naming the newly independent republic *'New Bohemia'*. They lit a bonfire, ate a picnic, hung up Chinese lanterns and fired toy pistols, and were presumably quite flattered when after these harmless *jeux d'esprits* they were disbanded by the militia. Nowadays, the door to the stairs inside the arch is locked (and according to one park-keeper there are no less than 28 footballs on top). Underneath the arch you might see lost souls clutching copies of *New York Magazine*, for along with the Public Library on 42nd Street, this is a popular rendezvous for blind dates.

The arch itself was designed by Stanford White (*see* pp.77–8) in 1892 to commemorate the hundredth anniversary of Washington's inauguration. White based it on the wooden arch he built for the square in 1889. This bizarre and much-loved construction was 150ft high, illuminated by hundreds of lightbulbs and crowned by a figurine of Washington painted cerulean blue.

On the south side of the square opposite you is another White creation, the **Judson Memorial Church**, a heady combination of Classical, Gothic and Romanesque, containing something that is very rare in Manhattan which is **public WCs**. The church tower also houses dormitories for **New York University**, whose campus is based in various buildings around Washington Square. NYU has had a reputation as a rapacious landgrabber since the 1960s when architects Philip Johnson and Richard Foster built three red-sandstone monoliths dubbed the 'Redskins' to the left of the Judson Church.

> From the Arch, walk up 5th Avenue, taking time to have a mooch round **Washington Mews**, a little way up on your right. Originally stables and servants' quarters for 'The Row', this humble alley has evolved into one of the most exclusive streets in Manhattan, complete with flower boxes, creepers, expensive German cars and big-wigs from NYU (which owns this as well as everything else).

> Continue walking up 5th Avenue to the next junction and turn left on to West 8th Street which specializes in cowboy boots, novelty items and T-shirts with slogans like '10 reasons why a pint of beer is better than a woman' printed on them. Walk a block west along 8th Street and turn right, on to a triangle confusingly called **'Village Square'** which is actually where 6th Avenue, Greenwich Avenue and West 8th and 9th Streets collide. At the northeast tip of the square on 9th Street and 6th Avenue is **Balducci's**, a family-owned gourmet delicatessen stocked with exotic foods.

Balducci's is one of those food shops which can make even the most depressed person realize they're glad to be alive. The store is pricey even by New York standards, but so wonderfully generous with free samples and recipe leaflets it's possible for the skilled and shameless scavenger to graze the counters without buying anything. Opposite Balducci's is the **Jefferson Market Courthouse**, a dippy-looking gothic extravaganza the colour of streaky bacon. Designed by Calvert Vaux (who also did Central Park) and Withers in 1877, it was voted the nation's fifth most beautiful building soon after. Having functioned efficiently as fire lookout, gaol and food market in one, it was ignored, neglected, almost demolished and finally rescued. Nowadays it's a public library.

Behind it, hidden away on West 10th Street between 6th and Greenwich Avenues, and invisible unless you look out for a shop selling split-gusset basques, is **Patchin Place**. This tiny mews was purpose-built in 1848 for Basque waiters, but gradually evolved into a writers' warren. Theodore Dreiser, John Reed and John Dos Passos all moved in at various times, and for 40 years e. e. cummings lived in number 4 opposite Djuna Barnes, reclusive author of the impenetrable but much admired *Nightwood*. Once in a while e. e. cummings would stick his head out of his study window to shout out 'Are ya still alive, Djuna?'.

> From Patchin Place, return to the Village Square via either 6th Avenue or Greenwich Avenue, turn right and walk east along **Christopher Street**.

Bulging with leather shops, back-room bars, and an 'erotic' bakery, Christopher Street is the main artery of **gay Greenwich Village**. At night it's swamped by crowds of goggling tourists as locals swagger past in 'alternative' streetwear. The street became a citadel for the gay liberation movement after the Stonewall Riot of 1969, when police blitzed a gay bar on the junction of Christopher Street and West 4th Street called the Stonewall Inn, provoking a riot which lasted for two days. In June the battle is commemorated in a Gay Pride march through the Village.

> As you walk you'll pass on your left the **Abracadabra** novelty store (specializing in eerie-sound door chimes and rubber roaches). A block further up, to the right, is the **Oscar Wilde Memorial Bookshop**, the world's first gay bookshop (at 15 Christopher Street).
>
> Further east at the junction with Waverly Place, Christopher Street forks to the right. As you walk make sure you continue on Christopher Street and avoid taking the left fork (which is Grove Street).

On the left at Waverley Place is the **Northern Dispensary**, famous for having two sides on one street (Waverly Place), and one side on two streets (Christopher Street and Grove Street). This was one of Manhattan's first free hospitals: Edgar Allen Poe was treated for a cold here in 1837, and the clinic remained open until 1988 when it was fined for refusing to admit two men infected with the AIDS virus. It has since been taken on by the Roman Catholic Archdiocese, who have fittingly converted it into a nursing home for AIDS patients.

> Finally, past the junction with 7th Avenue, and on the right of an island of trees at 59 Christopher Street, are steps leading down to what used to be a pub called **Lion's Head**. In the 1970s, Norman Mailer and his running mate Jimmy Breslin used the bar as a makeshift headquarters for his campaign to become Mayor of New York. Mailer's quite serious ambition was for New York City to secede and become America's 51st State.
>
> Walk another two blocks west along Christopher Street (taking care that you're still on it). After two blocks (and a dense clutch of hard core leather shops, hairdressers and massage parlours) turn left on to **Bedford Street** and walk south.

Bedford Street is only 24ft wide in some places and revered as the most beautiful in the Village; however, it's also one of the quirkiest. At the intersection with Barrow Street (next to a house with a full-grown iguana living in the basement window) you could turn right and try to find the unsignposted entrance (at 86 Barrow Street) to **Chumleys**, an original speakeasy (fairly touristy) with an escape route round the side. A block south at the intersection with Commerce Street is the distinctly new-looking oldest house in the Village, the clapboarded **Isaacs-Hendricks Residence**, and next to that the narrowest house, **75½ Bedford Street**, built in a

9½ft-wide alley in 1873 and lived in by John Barrymore, then Edna St Vincent Millay, and finally Cary Grant.

> *Turn left on to Commerce Street and walk a little way north, crossing 7th Avenue and continuing on to the intersection of Commerce Street and* **Bleecker Street**. *If you're still hungry the section of Bleecker between 6th and 7th Avenues has some fine Italian bakeries, pasticcerias and cafés.*

Zito's, at 259 Bleecker, has hot, crunchy bread which is so superior to most of the bread on offer in New York that Sinatra has sent to his hotel whenever he visits the city. Alternatively you can sit down to homemade soup in the **Bleecker Luncheonette**, on the corner of Bleecker and Carmine Streets, go for a coffee at **Rocco's Pastry Shop**, at No.243, eat famous pizzas in **John's Pizzeria** at No.278, or pick up an ice from **Casa Victoria** at No.271.

> *Walk a block down Bleecker Street and when you see John's Pizzeria turn left on to Jones Street. A block north up Jones Street takes you to 'The Slaughtered Lamb' an unconvincing 'English Pub' which sells Newcastle Brown and Guinness. Turn right here, on to West 4th Street (you'll notice a risqué clothes shop called Tic Tac Toe on the left) and walk two blocks east to 6th Avenue. The nearest subway for going home (the* **A** *and* **C** *trains) is a block south down 6th Avenue, opposite the Waverley Cinema and next to West 3rd Street. Anyone feeling adventurous, however, could walk four blocks north up 6th Avenue and take the PATH train from 9th Street to* **Hoboken** *in New Jersey.*

It costs a dollar and takes 13 minutes to get to Hoboken. Though it gets teased (affectionately) as Ho-Ho-Hoboken, the former shipbuilding city is currently enjoying a modest Renaissance as artists, bands and other independent spirits move in to convert its factories and townhouses into studios, galleries and clubs. Most New Yorkers know it as the birthplace of Frank Sinatra, and as the place where Elia Kazan, protected from the toughs by a fleet of bodyguards, shot *On the Waterfront* using real dockworkers as well as actors.

From the beautiful Erie Lackawana ferry terminal, (a grand verdigris palace of 1907), there's a magnificent view of the west side of Manhattan laid before you like a phantasmical pincushion; a scape which Cartier-Bresson snapped, encrusted in icicles, in 1947.

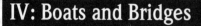

IV: Boats and Bridges

(Staten Island Ferry, Wall Street & Brooklyn Bridge)

Start: *Take the 1 or 9 to South Ferry*

Walking Time: *allow 4 hours. The Staten Island ferry takes an hour; so does the Stock Exchange tour.*
If you get tired, hitch a ride on **The Downtown Loop**, *a free shuttle between the World Trade Center and Staten Island Ferry terminal running every 10–15 minutes.*

Internet Events Information
www.downtownNY.com

Mammon, n. The god of the world's leading religion. His chief temple is in the holy city of New York.

Ambrose Bierce, The Devil's Dictionary, 1911

It's here at the nub-end of Manhattan, of course, that the city began. The Mohicans—Weckquaesgecks to the south and Reckgawawacks to the north—were in the area several thousand years before Manhattan was 'discovered' by Verrazano, who in 1524 sailed into the bay, claimed everything around him as the property of France, and sailed away never to be heard of again. Almost a century later the island was discovered a second time by Henry Hudson, who in 1609 sailed up the Hudson looking for a passage to India, claimed everything for the Dutch East India Company, introduced the Indians to alcohol and gunpowder, and went home to Europe. It was only in 1624 that the first settlers arrived. Twenty-three Dutch families and one engineer settled here, at the south end of Manhattan, calling the island New Amsterdam and laying it out in the image of the motherland with windmills, stoops, canals and traditional Dutch houses with crowstepped gables. The next year Peter Minuit bought Manhattan for $24 worth of baubles from Indians passing through the island on their way to somewhere else.

Today no relic of New Amsterdam and its colonists remains except the street plan of downtown Manhattan, an X-ray with roads and sidewalks marking pathways and canals, and skyscrapers towering in place of Dutch farmsteads. The spirit of the old Dutch colony, however, is the same, with business, speculation and commerce still very much the raison d'être. However, as some of the older financial institutions such as Morgan Stanley move out of Wall Street to premises which are cheaper and better equipped for computers, 1990s Wall Street is being colonized again. More and more businessmen actually inhabit the area, in Battery Park City (built on landfill from the World Trade Center in the 1980s), or actually on Wall Street in swanky condominiums being renovated for domestic use.

As you walk around you may agree with Ambrose Bierce that there is something satanic about Wall Street. Even on the sunniest days skyscrapers darken the narrow streets; city steam, smelling of bitumen, seeps from cicatrices in tarmac and stone work; bodies spew out of revolving doors and downwards into eight tunnels of subway. A Congestion Committee once calculated that if all the

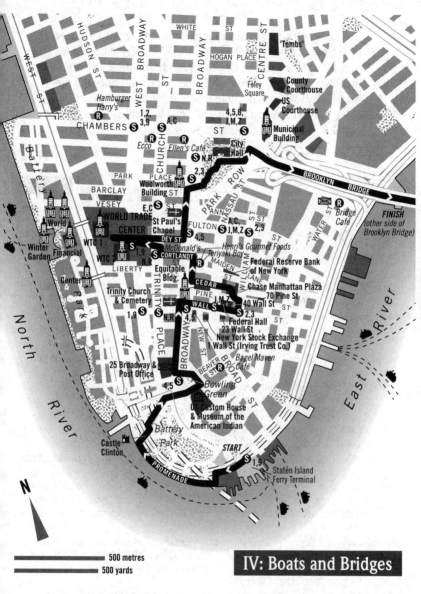

N

500 metres
500 yards

IV: Boats and Bridges

workers here left their offices at one time the streets would need six
levels of sidewalk. But Wall Street is also an area of sudden,
astonishing vistas and beautiful buildings. This walk takes you to the

best bits: to the Staten Island ferry for an immigrant's-eye view of the Statue of Liberty, to the top of the World Trade Center for a cocktail and a wondrous view, and finally and thrillingly across Brooklyn Bridge, the most handsome suspension bridge in the world. Downtown Manhattan is still above all a business centre—quiet on weekends, and at its energetic best on weekdays, when you can also visit the courthouses in Foley Square.

lunch/cafés

Bagel Maven Café, Beaver Street, between New and Broad Streets. Knishes from Brighton Beach: also borscht, pierogis, bagels and challah bread; french toast, burgers, fries in straightforward luncheonette—good for breakfast (*from $5*).

Hamburger Harry's, 157 Chambers St., near Greenwich St. Sixteen varieties of some of the best burgers in Manhattan, including the Mexican Ha-Ha made with guacamole and salsa verde. Also seafood (*from $10–15*).

Teriyaki Boy, 22 Maiden Lane. Japanese equivalent of McDonald's with soy bean soup for a dollar and combination teriyaki takeaways (*from $1*).

McDonald's, 160 Broadway, near Maiden Lane. This is the branch to choose: a classical pianist, dinner-jacketed doormen, espresso, cappuccino, fancy pastries, and bog standard Macs.

Henri's Gourmet Foods, 16 Maiden Lane. Big range of gourmet sandwiches: also salads, soups, cakes, and good coffee: a restroom in the back (*from $5*).

The Hors d'Œuverie at Windows on the World, 1 World Trade Center, 107th Floor. For the free view. Elaborate bar-food—beluga caviar, sushi, steak tartare, hamburgers, fish and chips 'in a silver basket' (*from $10*).

Ellen's Café, 270 Broadway, at Chambers St. The gamut of luncheonette fare—fountain drinks, potato skins, savoury muffins, fried fish, sundaes, pecan pie (*from $7*).

Chanterelle, 2 Harrison St., at Hudson St., ℂ 966 6960. Elegant, expensive, sleek French restaurant with excellent 3-course cut-price specials at lunch (*around $35*).

Ecco, 124 Chambers St., between West Broadway and Church St., ℂ 227 7074 (*reservations suggested*). Authentic north Italian food in Victorian saloon bar but pricey. Bouillabaisse with lobster, etc.; around $26 an entrée, cheaper for pasta (*from $30*).

Bridge Café, 279 Water St., near Dover St. Under the Manhattan side of the Brooklyn Bridge, and in tin-ceilinged, wood-framed building. Jolly at lunchtime when it fills with businessmen, tourists and civil servants eating straightforward but good fish, seafood, steaks, pasta (*from $20*).

The River Café, 1 Water St., Brooklyn. World-famous menu with classic view of lower Manhattan from the foot of the Brooklyn side of Brooklyn Bridge. (*ℂ 1 718 522 5200; lunch 12–2.30 Mon–Fri; supper 6–11 Mon–Thur; 7–11.30 Fri–Sat; set dinner $65.*)

Ferries to Staten Island leave every half-hour, 24 hours daily, from South Ferry terminal (© 806 6940). The fare for the round trip has risen, over the years, from a nickel to 50¢, which is still less than a cup of coffee, a packet of gum or the sleaziest peep show in Hell's Kitchen.

'It's free on the way over and you pay to come back,' says the man at the top of the escalator to whom, as to everyone else in Manhattan, Staten Island is a bit of a joke. As Brendan Behan put it, Staten Island is not exactly Monte Carlo, and apart from commuters, the intrepid few who set foot on New York's most suburban borough are Buddhists (visiting the Museum of Tibetan Art) and film buffs (who go to Todt Hill where Coppola filmed *The Godfather* and a tipsy Marlon Brando mooned members of the Mafia employed as extras on the cast). Meanwhile the average New Yorker would rather not take Staten Island too, thank you; and for visitors the point of going on the ferry is mainly the breathtaking view backwards of Manhattan.

While you're admiring the view you have to sympathize with Staten Islanders. Since 1948 the rest of New York has dumped so much garbage on the island that Staten Island's Fresh Kills landfill, circled by a dark cloud of seagulls, is now the biggest and smelliest in the world. Periodically, Staten Island's 400,000 inhabitants lobby for secession from New York City or even for a referendum on the issue—and fail. Finally in 1995 an arsonist set fire to the Manhattan side of the ferry terminal.

Ignoring these details, a ride on the ferry is one of the most romantic (and cheapest) things you can do in Manhattan. A reluctant Lauren Bacall was beguiled here by a millionaire manqué in *How To Marry A Millionaire*, and today, just as Brooklyn Bridge has its 'jumpers', the ferry is famous for its kissers—especially at night, when the boat creeks through eerie black waters in New York Bay and fog horns bellow distantly in the Atlantic. However, gangs of smoochers hog the deck in the daytime as well. In the mean time everyone else—office worker, tourist or commuter—gazes wistfully at the beautiful view. Before the Second World War even this was superior: there were no skyscraper boxes in Manhattan; the tops were jagged and the skyline resembled a floating alpine range, fenced in by a 4-mile wall of ships.

*After the ferry, turn left and wander west along **Admiral George Dewey Promenade**, a good place to view the Statue of Liberty without going to the time and expense of visiting it. To the left of the statue you see the **Verrazano-Narrows Suspension Bridge** built in 1964 and spanning the 4260ft between Staten Island and Brooklyn. To the right is **Ellis Island**, the enormous and grand-looking immigration station which from 1892 to 1954 processed 12 million newcomers to America, sometimes at the rate of 5000 a day. Paupers, prostitutes, polygamists, the varicose-*

veined, anarchists and anyone with a ticket paid for by someone else were amongst the 90 or so categories of people who could be sent home as undesirables. In fact only about two per cent were denied admission.

In the middle is the icon which saluted immigrants as they sailed into New York, the **Statue of Liberty**. *At the start of Kafka's comic novel* America *this salute is terrifying and an awed Karl Rossmann sees Liberty illuminated by a great shaft of light, wielding a sword rather than a torch. Kafka himself never visited America.*

In fact the portly matriarch, aka 'Liberty Enlightening the World', is a likeness of the sculptor's mother and only came to America by accident. Bartholdi originally designed her for a site on the Suez Canal where the statue, symbolizing 'Egypt Carrying Light to Asia', was going to double as a lighthouse (and second Pharos). However, Bartholdi's project never came off. Instead, when a group of French freedom fighters invited Bartholdi to design a centennial present identifying the French republic with the USA (thus furthering republican ambitions in France), Bartholdi offered them his 'Statue of Liberty'. A prototype was enlarged three times in the sculptor's studio in Paris (one version stands on a bridge over the Seine), and for the final stage the statue was constructed on the lines of a skyscraper out of a massive steel pylon made by Gustave Eiffel. Finally, in 1886 all 225 amply endowed tons were presented to the US Ambassador in Paris, dismantled, then transported to New York. During re-assembly on Liberty Island Congress ran out of funds for the project and San Francisco, Cleveland and St Louis all put in offers for the statue. Eventually though, New Yorkers were persuaded to stump up money themselves by a fund-raising campaign organized by newspaperman Joseph Pulitzer, with Emma Lazarus' sonnet as its remarkable and still rousing battle cry:

Not like the brazen giant of Greek fame,
With conquering limbs astride from land to land;
Here at our sea-washed, sunset gates shall stand
A mighty woman with a torch, whose flame
Is the imprisoned lightning, and her name
Mother of Exiles. From her beacon-head
Glows world-wide welcome; her mild eyes command
The air-bridged harbor that twice cities frame.
'Keep, ancient lands, your storied pomp!' cries she
With silent lips. 'Give me your tired, your poor,
Your huddled masses yearning to breathe free,
The wretched refuse of your teeming shore.
Send these, the homeless, tempest-tossed to me:
I lift my lamp beside the golden door!

The sonnet is carved on the base of the statue and not, as one imagines, inscribed on the tablet Liberty grasps in her left hand.

> *Well-signposted and about 300 yards west along the promenade past the seagulls and buskers is **Castle Clinton**, a sandy-coloured bunker where you can buy tickets for the boat to the Statue of Liberty (on Liberty Island) and the Museum of Immigration (renovated in 1990 on nearby Ellis Island) (open 8.30am-4.30pm daily; ferries leave from 9.15am daily, adm $6 adults; $5 senior citizens; $3 children 3–7, see p.178). However, unless you get here early or in the depths of winter, be warned. At the height of the season the trip can take 4 hours, and the boats can fill up altogether. Also, the authorities advise anyone suffering from crowd-phobia, heart trouble or varicose veins not to go to the Statue of Liberty. The elevator halfway up the statue is all right, but even if you suffer from none of the above, you may get queasy climbing 171 steps up a single-file staircase to the crown. Luckily the 42ft ladder to the torch was closed in 1916 when it was deemed too narrow and frightening for visitors.*

Reduced to a ticket office and lavatories, denuded of two storeys, a roof, doors and façade, Castle Clinton scarcely lives up to its name. Pathetic as it looks, few buildings have served so many purposes (though the one thing it never has been is a castle). In the beginning (before landfill) it was an anti-British fort surrounded by water; after that it was a theatre; then in 1842 (before Ellis Island) it was an immigration station and in 50 years it sifted 8 million immigrants. These days New Yorkers over a certain age remember it as home to the New York Aquarium. In 1950, when his plans to build a tunnel to Brooklyn were thwarted, New York's autocratic Parks Commissioner, Robert Moses, spitefully had its contents, electric eel, penguins and all, banished to Coney Island.

> *Walk through Castle Clinton to **Battery Park**, named after the battery of cannons which protected the island before the shoreline was extended.*

In the autumn, during the Jewish harvest holiday, a public sukkah or prayer hut strewn with Lawsonia fronds is set up in the middle of Battery Park. The plastic hut is decorated inside with tinsel and although anyone is welcome it is mostly frequented by orthodox businessmen who drop by to drink a free cup of Sprite with a biscuit, eat their lunch, to pray or even to sleep.

> *Walk through the middle of Battery Park to **Bowling Green** (a smaller egg-shaped park), where Broadway begins. As you get to Bowling Green, you'll see Cass Gilbert's **US Custom House** directly on the right and with banners outside advertising the Smithsonian's excellent **National Museum of the American Indian** inside (open 10am–5pm daily; adm free). This is well worth a visit.*

Above the swaggering beaux-arts entrance are sculptures of the four continents by Daniel Chester French, best known for the Lincoln Memorial in Washington. The allegory is fairly bombastic: Europe, clutching various icons of education, looks fuddy-duddy; Asia is slothful; Africa is asleep; America, stamping down an Aztec ruin and brandishing a sheath of Indian maize, is imperial and youthful. As you walk through the rotunda inside, look out also for the brilliant murals painted by Reginald Marsh in 1937. They depict the arrival of a passenger liner, and one on the right-hand side of the far end of the hall shows Marsh's favourite movie star, Greta Garbo, beseiged by reporters and flashbulbs while an unctuous publicity man liberates a pair of doves.

Behind the murals is the museum itself. Here you will find exquisitely displayed exhibits and videos celebrating Native America: Kapoo lip ornaments made of feathers, moccasin shoes, deer hoof rattles, Cherokee hats and drawings produced for sale to tourists by Cheyenne warriors in the 1880s after their defeat and subsequent imprisonment in the 1874 Red River War. Exhibits are mostly selected and donated by members of the tribes themselves: in the last five years many objects from the original collection (acquired early this century by piratical New Yorker George Heye)—human remains, funerary objects and tsantsa (shrunken heads)—have been returned to their original owners.

The Customs House stands on Manhattan's first colonized site, **Fort Amsterdam**—or James, Willem Hendrick, Anne, George, depending on whether the Brits or the Dutch were in power. The pentagonal fort, designed by an engineer from the East India Company, was a makeshift structure surrounded by a stumpy wooden fence. Nevertheless engravings sent back to Holland depicted it as a far more grandiose structure, 1600 by 2000ft and with hefty stone walls and fancy accoutrements.

Bowling Green in front of you is Manhattan's only circular park. It was laid out in 1732 when the English used it for bowling. The iron fence was put up in 1771 to stop people using it as a garbage dump and is intact except for the finials and the park's centrepiece, a gilded statue of George III sitting on a horse and dressed in a toga. These were melted down in 1776 and fired back at the English. In return the English knocked down a nearby statue by the same sculptor of William Pitt (Pitt had been cheeky enough to oppose the Stamp Act, which levied a tax on the Americans to finance the British army).

*If you are hungry now, you are close to the **Bagel Maven Café** on Beaver Street (on the east side of Bowling Green) between New and Broad Streets. The straightforward luncheonette serves knishes (or balls of strudel) filled with potato, kasha or cherry, imported from the famous Mrs Stahl's Knishes in Brighton Beach, Brooklyn. After breakfast walk to the north end of Bowling Green. Here you'll find two curious sculptures: the back side (not a pretty sight) of an enormous bronze bull (a tribute to the*

bulls of the Stock Exchange) and a colossal tree stump, donated by the
New York Road Runners Club who are going to carve it as soon as they
*have raised the money. On the left flank of the bull is **25 Broadway**.*

Don't be put off by a sinister man selling pieces of Berlin Wall, Jerusalem Earth, St John's wort and other thaumaturgical paraphernalia near the entrance. Inside is one of the most beautiful lobbies in the city, an echoey dome based on Raphael's Villa Madama in Rome (itself inspired by Nero's opulent Golden House). The building is now of all things a post office, but in the twenties and thirties it was Cunard's New York booking office. Above the counters skilfully painted murals of frigates, brigs, maps, porpoises and mermaids hark back to a long-lost world of glamorous travel for the upper crust.

*Now walk two blocks north up Broadway as far as **Trinity Church**, on*
the lefthand side of Broadway at the mouth of Wall Street.

Trinity is one of the wealthiest landowning ministries in the world. Dwarfed now by skyscrapers, its spire still casts a gothic shadow down Wall Street. Until 1892, Trinity was Manhattan's tallest building: its 264 ft brownstone tower could be seen 15 miles out to sea, and sightseers were encouraged to climb up for the view. The interior is no particular shakes, but there are concerts on Mondays at 12 and Thursdays at 1 (and tours on weekdays at 2). More interesting is Trinity's small **cemetery** and sometime drug-dealing spot, obscured from Broadway by a human wall of bankers having their shoes shined. 'Reader reflect how soon you'll quit this stage: you'll find but few attain to such an age...' is an alarming inscription near the entrance. It refers to William Bradford, who brought the printing press to New York, and printed the city's first dollar notes as well as its first Bible. Nearby are Alexander Hamilton, the first US Secretary to the Treasury (and the fellow on the $10 bill), and Robert Fulton, a painter who lived in France in a *ménage à trois* as 'Toot', with two Americans, 'Wifey' and 'Hub', and who invented among other things a submarine and a steam ferry linking Manhattan to Brooklyn.

From Trinity Church entrance, you can see the **Equitable Building**, a block north on 120 Broadway, between Pine and Cedar Streets. This colossus determined the shape of all New York's scrapers built between 1916 and 1962. Containing 1.4 million square feet of office space and 16,000 workers, the Equitable rises a sheer 40 storeys from the ground with no setbacks. It ate away light and air and led to calls for Zoning Laws, eventually passed in 1916, which restricted the bulk of skyscrapers by drawing up what was in essence a vertical grid plan for the city. When scrapers reached a certain height, depending on the size of their plot, they had to step back like pyramids from the street. Towers, however, could rise to an infinite height.

Diagonally across from Trinity at 1 Wall Street (on the right side of Wall Street as you walk down) is a skyscraper which is typical of the sort of building created by the 1916 Zoning laws, the **Irving Trust Company**, now owned by the Bank of New York. This truly sumptuous skyscraper was built in the midst of the Great Depression in 1932. The architect Ralph Walker pared the skyscraper to an elongated white limestone spire which soars so high that the top can't be seen from the bottom. What you do see is rippled like a curtain, with oversized entrances similar to the porches of a Gothic cathedral, and slim windows latticed like butterfly wings. Early in the afternoon the glass burns vermilion red. This happens when the lights are turned on in the lobby, a massive cathedral vault decorated fantastically for a bank with red and gold mosaics. At the top of the tower is a private dining room built on palatial proportions: three storeys high, with slender butterfly-veined windows stretching from top to bottom, a baronial marble fireplace, and a fish-scale ceiling made of mother of pearl. Sadly, though, doormen adamantly ensure that this amazing room is off-limits to visitors.

> *Walk down Wall Street to Broad Street. If you stand on the corner of both, you see a solid wall of banks including the Stock Exchange.*

Wall Street takes its name not from these more recent fortifications, but from an oak fence put up in 1653 by the Dutch governor Peter Stuyvesant to keep out the English. The original plan called for a palisade of sharpened tree trunks, but an Englishman, Thomas Baxter, supplied flimsy 13ft planks. These were plundered by residents to make firewood and lumber, and the fortifications soon became useless.

> *On the southeast corner of Broad Street, you can inspect pockmarks on the walls of 23 Wall Street, which is still owned by the **Morgan Guaranty Trust Company**.*

The pock-marks were made by flying debris from a horse-drawn wagon which exploded there in 1920, killing 38 and wounding a hundred. The perpetrator was never discovered, although Morgan Guaranty, a private bank for banks, was in some ways an obvious target... J. P. Morgan Jnr, at whom the bomb was directed, raised loans for the British during the First World War, while his father, the one with the enormous red nose, founded America's giant shipping and railway corporate monopolies, as well as US Steel, the country's first billion-dollar company. By 1929, a coterie that made up five per cent of the population were receiving a whopping one-third of all personal income. It was a turning point in Wall Street's history: after the crash of 1929, Roosevelt's New Deal reforms put a stop to the autonomy of private banks. Wall Street suffered such a fit of hysterical paranoia that at the Pecora Hearings into the crash a press agent had a midget sit on Morgan's lap in the witness stand.

> *Across the street from Morgan Guaranty, on the north side of Wall Street at 28 Wall Street, is **Federal Hall**, the old Custom House and Subtreasury (open Mon–Fri 9–5; adm free).*

The hall is two temples in one: the outside is a replica of the Parthenon, and the inside of the domed cockpit of the Pantheon. In the economic panic of 1873 this building was fortified with turrets on the roof, bullet-proof shutters, three Gatling machine guns and a stack of grenades. Before 1842, the original Federal Hall stood on the site: Washington was inaugurated on its steps in 1789, when New York was capital for a brief year before the Federal government moved to Philadelphia. Nowadays a somewhat spattered statue of Washington and a favourite with Manhattan pigeons commemorates the occasion. Inside is a small, dullish museum and free maps and information about Wall Street.

> *As you come down the steps of Federal Hall you'll see flags on the right side of Broad Street advertising the visitors' entrance to the* **New York Stock Exchange,** *visitors' entrance at 12 Broad Street, © 656 5168 (open Mon–Fri 9.15–4; adm free).*

An 1869 guide book called the Exchange the seat of 'all device and deception, ingenious invention and base fabrication'. Today the Exchange still has the same classical façade, a stage curtain from which Integrity, with winged ears, steps fearlessly out of the frieze; a few years ago, when polluted vapours began eating her away, the marble was secretively replaced with metal, so no one would know, as one critic put it, 'that any facet of the Stock Exchange was vulnerable'.

Today, the Exchange admits the public to a viewing balcony, from where they see a trading floor thickly littered in scraps of paper and a coffered ceiling almost completly obscured by an ugly black tangle of pipes connected to each of the 22 electronic trading posts. Meanwhile a mysterious voice spells out what is going on in words of one syllable, but the chaos is at first so hypnotic, then so bewildering that the conclusion—that the $3 trillion stock exchange is 'a public market: fair, orderly and regulated'—is less convincing. The description omits the crashes of 1929 and 1987, and the statistic that the average income of Wall Street's investment bankers has nevertheless increased over the last decade by 21 per cent. The Crash of 1929, when tickers could not keep up with the speed with which 16 million shares were traded in a few hours, is skimmed over as the product of 'reckless speculation on the margin'.

However, it is one of the great Wall Street myths that after the Crash the streets were littered with bodies hurled from skyscraper windows. Although two bankers with a joint bank account jumped hand in hand from the top of the Ritz, and the Spanish playwright Lorca described how he saw the crash 'amid suicides and groups of fainters', the suicide rate did not rise in 1929, and those who did kill themselves mostly used guns.

> *From the Stock Exchange, walk a block further east along Wall Street as far as William Street. On the way you pass on your left **40 Wall Street.***

In the race to build the world's tallest building in 1930, poor 40 Wall Street was briefly the highest until, just a few days later, it was cruelly dethroned by the Chrysler Building. So it seems a little unfair that just after the Second World War an aeroplane collided into this building rather than its rival. Finally, in 1996 a consortium with Donald Trump as figurehead bought up the 72-storey skyscraper and converted the whole lot into deluxe condominiums for rich Manhattanites.

> *At William Street turn left and walk a block north to Pine Street and* **Chase Manhattan Plaza**. *On the plaza itself, stranded in concrete, is Jean Dubuffet's witty black and white sculpture called Group of Four Trees.*

David Rockefeller turned the Chase Manhattan into the biggest bank in the world and a virtual right-arm of American foreign policy in developing nations from Chile, South Africa and Vietnam to Yugoslavia. The skyscraper (by Skidmore, Owings & Merrill) soars 813ft into the air. In the middle is a sunken garden created by Isamu Noguchi (*see* p.185) from meteoric basalt extracted from a riverbed near Kyoto. Below is a dystopian scene: office workers sitting at a grid of desks, and staring at Noguchi's dribbling fountain, whose fish, poisoned by coins and noxious fumes, have long since abandoned their pond for Elysian lakes.

The elevated plaza is a good spot for viewing nearby scrapers: to the south you can make out the verdigris pyramid of 40 Wall Street and to the east on Pine Street the lunatic Gothic spire of **70 Pine Street**, built in 1932 and one of the most beautiful Art Deco buildings in downtown (if you have time the lobby is well worth a visit).

> *Walk west, past the sunken garden, until you hit Nassau Street and its junction with Cedar Street. A block up to your right, on Liberty Street, is the* **Federal Reserve Bank of New York**, *a Florentine palazzo containing more gold than Fort Knox.*

You need to telephone a week in advance for a ticket to see the vaults which contain the gold reserves of 75 different nations worth $144 billion (© *720 6130*). Whenever an international transaction is made on the market, the Federal Bank acts it out by moving the gold a bar at a time from one compartment to another, at a cost of $1.70 an ingot. Five floors down, you see two workers performing this ritual: one who counts aloud and one who weighs, both wearing magnesium clogs in case they drop one of the 28lb bars on their toes. Upstairs is more distressing: defunct dollar bills are sucked into a vacuum cleaner at the rate of $40 million a day; deteriorated and counterfeit notes are shredded and used as stuffing, landfill or presents for visitors.

> *Now cross* **Nassau Street** *and walk a block west along Cedar Street to Broadway.*

In 1842 a cigar girl called Mary Rogers was brutally murdered at this junction. When her lacerated body was discovered the mystery became a cause célèbre and although it was never solved, Poe came up with a 'solution' in his short story 'The Mystery of Marie Roget', set in Paris as the sequel to *The Murders in the Rue Morgue*. Today Nassau is a cheery enough street, bustling with a jolly mixture of shops including Japanese fast food outlets, shoetricians, 'Milan' fashion houses, and nail and pantyhose shops with signs in their windows saying 'If you don't come in at least smile as you walk past' and 'We *always* have something special for you'.

> *As you reach Broadway, walk towards the **World Trade Center**, the unbeautiful twin towers which are the second tallest in the world, after the Sears Tower in Chicago, and one at least of which you will certainly make out ahead of you and a block to the east of Broadway.*

Avoid the observation deck in WTC 2 (*open daily Oct–Jul 9.30–9.30, Aug–Sept 9.30–11.30; adm $8 adults, $3 children 6–12, $3.50 senior citizens; www.wtc-top.com*). This is in the tower to your left and to get to the overpriced deck here you will have to wait in long boring queues and walk through a dreary Manhattan theme park at the top (complete with a subway cafeteria and a vibrating simulated helicopter ride). The *view* is what counts, and as long as you're not dressed in shorts or a sleeveless shirt, you can avoid the queues, security checks, admission fees and everything, by visiting WTC1 instead, at the top of which is **The Greatest Bar on Earth**. Up here, your ears imploding from the quarter-mile express ride up, you can get a cocktail for $8, or beer or wine by the glass (from a 50,000 long wine list); even fish and chips 'in a silver basket'. The view from the top of a two-dimensional Manhattan is basically the same as that from the observation deck on WTC2, except the waiters' uniforms may leave you wondering whether someone spiked your drink.

These days stuntmen such as Philippe Petit, the French acrobat who crossed a steel tightrope stretched from one tower to the other disguised as a construction worker, would not be able to infiltrate the centre so easily. After the terrorist bomb attack on February 26th 1993, security around the WTC is tight. A memorial on the plaza connecting WTC1 and WTC2 commemorates the six people who were killed in the bomb, and for the 50,000 people who work in the World Trade Center the memory of the blast 'tintulating every part of your body', as one put it, is still raw.

The building itself, by Minoru Yamasaki, has been much maligned over the years, and if the Center seems stuck in 1970s time warp, you can at least admire the sophisticated engineering that went into its construction. Instead of the steel cage conventionally used for skyscrapers, the entire weight of the building is borne by its outside walls: a fence of closely spaced aluminum piers which eliminates the need for interior columns. An unfortunate upshot of this is that each one of the WTC's 43,600 windows is only a foot wide and can't be opened.

When the Center was completed in 1982, at a cost of over $1 billion, 1.2 million cubic yards of muck had been removed from the site. The muck was dumped on the nearby wharves as landfill creating 23.5 acres of new land. This extended shoreline is now **Battery Park City**. Completed in the late 1980s, the complex of skyscraper offices and luxury condominiums has as its centrepiece Cesar Pelli's hideous **World Financial Center**: four office towers which sum up everything that's repellent about post-modern architecture, from the fast-food design and concept to the pretentious **Winter Garden**, an over-sized conservatory filled with palm trees and dark red marble.

> *Now return to Broadway, and walk north five or six blocks depending on where you rejoined. On the left, between Fulton and Ann Streets, you pass the English-looking St Paul's Chapel.*

The architect, Thomas McBean, was a pupil of James Gibbs, who designed London's St Martin's-in-the-Fields. Originally, St Paul's stood in wheat fields as well. Today it's the only pre-Revolutionary church in Manhattan, its pretty pink interior worth a look especially if you're passing during a lunchtime concert (*Mon at 12 noon or Thurs at 1*). In the 19th century St Paul's faced the famous Barnum's American Museum, which featured a bear chained to the roof, an anatomical freak show, a 'Feejee' mermaid assembled out of a fish tail and a monkey's torso, and the midgets General Tom Thumb, Commodore Nutt and Lavinia Warren.

> *Walk two blocks further north to 233 Broadway, between Park Place and Barclay Street, and straight through the revolving doors of the wonderful Woolworth Building.*

The lobby inside is the most delightful in New York—a green, gold and blue Ravenna mosaic which would remind one of a grotto if it didn't include mail chutes, barbers and Harry's Diner.

Under the cornices are gargoyles showing the men involved in the construction. One shows the architect Cass Gilbert, clutching a model of the building, another Frank Winfield Woolworth paying for his scraper with a saucer-sized nickel. (He coughed up $13.5 million for the building *in cash*.) Woolworth had started life as a salesmen on $8 a week; he opened the world's first five-and-dime store in Utica, New York in 1879, and by the time this skyscraper was finished he owned 59 stores in the city. With sales totalling $5 million annually, Woolworth was comfortably ensconced in 'Winfield,' a 62-room mansion in Long Island, with 14-carat gold ceilings and a suite of bedrooms where his wife used Marie Antoinette's dressing table and he slept in Napoleon's bed.

On completion the skyscraper (which was built according to the most sophisticated steel-framing techniques available) was briefly the tallest in the world. At the opening ceremony in 1913, President Wilson pressed a button in the White House and, to the strains of 'The Star Spangled Banner', it was illuminated by 80,000 lights. A charismatic radio preacher dubbed it the 'Cathedral of Commerce', a nickname which has stuck. Meanwhile the scraper really does soar, an effect Gilbert achieved by letting the tower rise sheer off Broadway for all its 792ft, and dressing the whole structure in a delicate Gothic tracery of 'tongues of flame'.

For years the Woolworth Building had an observation deck on the 58th floor with 'the most wondrous view in all the world'. This is now closed to the public; however it is possible to sneak a view by taking an elevator to the 47th floor—a part of the building colonized by lawyers' offices with names resembling Latin conjugations. Cross the lobby and take another elevator to the 54th floor, where there is a solitary lawyer's office and a spiral staircase. At the top of this is a set of miniature wooden steps leading to a window surrounded by gargoyles of frogs, bats and pelicans. From here, assuming no one discovers you, you have a dramatic view up Broadway (superior to the flattened views from the WTC) of northern Manhattan including the Empire State and the Chrysler buildings.

> *Not far from the Woolworth building is an amusing luncheonette serving fountain drinks and fried clams and potato called **Ellen's**, three blocks north at 270 Broadway, close to Chambers Street.*

Ellen Hart Storm was Miss Subways 1959, and her diner is plastered with photographs of Miss Subways past and present. (Look out for the demure Rosemary Wilson, of 1963: 'Ultimate ambition: Happy marriage and home in California: Recently mastered the art of making Argyll socks for a favorite beau'.)

> *Afterwards walk two blocks south again down Broadway and cross over to the street to City Hall Park and, in the middle, **City Hall**, designed by a Frenchman and a Scotsman (Mangin & McComb) in 1812. This is one of Manhattan's most winsome buildings (open Mon–Fri 10–2; adm free).*

Inside is a beautiful staircase, the Mayor's office, and on the 2nd floor the City Council which replaced the Board of Estimate, a committee made up of the Mayor and the borough presidents. This was the real fiscal power in New York until it was abolished in 1989 by the Supreme Court for violating the 'one person, one vote' principle. Back in 1812, City Hall stood at the city's northernmost edge, and the idea of New York expanding beyond this frontier was so absurd that the City Fathers saved $15,000 by facing the back in brownstone.

City Hall Park, meanwhile, contains '**a toilet of modern art**'—a public lavatory, which as you may have discovered already on your walk, is a rare commodity in New York. Even more delightfully, on Fridays all the year round and Tuesdays and Thursdays, April–December, there is a **farmers' market** in the park selling top quality produce (*see* **Shopping**, p.288).

Looking to the east side of City Hall Park you will see the white wedding-cake tower of **Municipal Building**, which more or less faces City Hall on the east side of Centre Street at the junction with Chambers Street. New Yorkers come here to get married and pay their parking fines. Stranger still, the building (by McKim, Mead & White) has influenced Stalinist architecture. Built in 1914, it was duplicated in the 1920s for Cleveland's Terminal Tower, then the tallest outside New York. This wowed the Soviets to the extent that they copied the design for Moscow University tower; and then reproduced it again for the 800ft-tall Palace of Culture in Warsaw. To complicate things further, the wedding cake on top of the Municipal Building is snitched from the very ancient Choragic Monument of Lysicrates in Athens. This first popped up in New York on top of St Paul's Chapel, but by the end of the 19th century had become so voguish that it mushroomed all over the city as a disguise for water towers.

> *From here you may walk directly to Brooklyn Bridge, or, if you have time and inclination, make a short detour to the **Foley Square Court-houses**, walking two blocks north along Centre Street on the east side of the park. For many New Yorkers trial-watching is a pastime.*

New York's federal and municipal courthouses are clustered here in **Foley Square**, their steps alive with cameras and journalists and their façades weirdly familiar—even if you've never visited Manhattan before—as the setting for a thousand *Kojak*-style police dramas. Nearest is Cass Gilbert's **US Courthouse**, 40 Centre Street, crowned by a golden pyramid, and backdrop for the trials of Leona Helmsley and Imelda Marcos. Next to the US Courthouse is the **County Courthouse**, 60 Centre Street, *Ⓒ 374 4780*, used for Sidney Lumet's *Twelve Angry Men*. These courts are open to the public (*9–5 Mon–Fri*), and if you would like to watch a case ask the doorman where to go. The most interesting courts for visiting are the criminal courts and prison known as the '**Tombs**', a gruesome-looking building that occupies the whole block between Hogan Place and White Street at 100 Centre Street. The macabre nickname actually refers to an Egyptian mausoleum which stood here in 1838. 'This dismal-fronted pile of bastard Egyptian', as Dickens called it, was sunk in a pit, and decorated with trapezoid-windows and lotus columns. It was here that Melville's existentialist anti-hero Bartleby the Scrivener stood with his face to the wall and said 'I prefer not to dine to-day', before he finally lay down on the floor with his knees huddled up against him and died.

In 1893 the Tombs was replaced by another prison, and in 1939 with the present building by Harvey Corbett, who built part of Rockefeller Center in the same year. Both are of white limestone, but the Tombs are terrifying. The gruff inscription 'Only the Just Man Enjoys Peace of Mind ', seems engineered to make you feel guilty, and there is a sinister green-coloured low-tide mark around the first two storeys. **Room 218**, inside, is used for the 24-hour **Night Courts** (*also open to the public*). Here arraignments go on round the clock to cope with the ever-increasing weight of arrests in the city, although sad to say most of the people who go up here have already been waiting for two days or more. Arrests have increased dramatically since former Police Commissioner Bill Bratton introduced new policing techniques which focused on improving the 'quality of life' on the streets by arresting petty criminals such as turnstile-jumpers and small-time marijuana dealers. The reason New York is nowadays one of the safest cities in the US is partly due to the fact that currently over 1.6 million criminals have been taken out of circulation to do time in New York jails.

> *Return to City Hall Park. The pedestrian entrance to **Brooklyn Bridge** is a narrow walkway with an iron fence on either side. It leads up to the bridge at the eastern edge of the park just past the point where Park Row joins Nassau Street. The walkway can be tricky to find at first; an easy way to spot it is to watch for a stream of pedestrians moving purposefully towards it and follow their example.*

Once you're on the walkway, the view backwards, framed by a cat's cradle of suspension cables, is New York's finest, especially as light falls. (The New York sunset is famous for its unnatural redness: with help from chemicals and fumes which spew out of New Jersey and filter out every colour except red, this special effect will sometimes transform Manhattan into a 'holy'-style vision of cloud-capped towers and glittering palaces.)

The walkway itself is much touted as a romantic spot, and John Travolta certainly danced across with gay abandon in *Saturday Night Fever*. However the way it shudders and rattles 12ft above the noisy roadway can also be quite nerve-racking. Venture here at rush hour, and you can expect to be rudely elbowed by gangs of burly secretaries jogging in sneakers.

The feat of engineering was the handiwork of John Augustus Roebling, who maintained that even if all the suspension cables broke at the same time, the bridge would merely sag. A keen student of Hegel, Roebling was a German immigrant who came to America in 1831 to live on a utopian farming community near Pittsburgh. Tragically he never even saw what he called the 'East River Bridge': while reconnoitring a site for the Brooklyn Tower, Roebling's foot was crushed against the pier by the Fulton ferry, which the bridge was putting out of business. Roebling's toes were amputated, but his foot became gangrenous, and a week before the bridge got planning permission, lockjaw set in and Roebling died of tetanus. More tragedies ensued. His son Colonel Washington Roebling took over, but was crippled three years later by an attack of the bends. (The divers' disease, caused by air decompression, was contracted by over a hundred men during the laying of foundations for the two granite towers. The human 'sandhogs' actually dug the foundations 75ft underwater, standing inside inverted boxes which were gradually filled with concrete.) Washington Roebling eventually retired to a sick-room in Brooklyn Heights, supervising the works from a telescope.

In the end the bridge took 14 years and 600 men to build, and as Roebling predicted, it became an icon for New York. The bridge inspired abstract painters John Marin and Joseph Stella, who both exhibited in the Armory Show; in 1930 Hart Crane wrote a sequence of poems to Brooklyn Bridge comparing it to a harp and beginning with an invocation exalting it above God.

But as usual in New York, where there is myth, there is also the publicity stunt. In 1884 P. T. Barnum led 24 elephants across the walkway to prove it was safe. Two years later in 1886 a Bowery boy called Steve Brodie launched a lifetime's career based on the hoo-haa generated by his 'jump' from the bridge. Sceptics insisted he merely swum into the middle of the river and surfaced just as a dummy hit the water from above. Despite this, Brodie swiftly gained celebrity status. He opened a saloon in the Bowery and then travelled the state, giving lectures in museums and touring with a show in which he plunged through a trap-door into a shower of rock-salt spray to rescue his 'Bowery goil', Blanche, 'a corkin' good looker' who was pushed off the Brooklyn Bridge by the blackguardly Thurlow Bleeckman. But the culmination of his illustrious career came many years later when Brodie got to star with Bugs Bunny in a cartoon in which he is 'twicked by the scwewy wabbit'.

On the Brooklyn side of the river, you can wander down for cocktails, brunch, lunch or supper at the **River Café** (*© 1 718 522 5200; brunch 11.30–2.30, Sun; lunch 12–2.30 Mon–Fri; supper 6–11 Mon–Thur; 7–11.30 Fri–Sat; set dinner around $65–70; for supper make reservations at least four days in advance*), famous for having Brooklyn's best view of Manhattan as well as a menu including such delights as squab, swordfish, pan-roasted lobster, and chocolate Brooklyn Bridge for pudding.

> To get to the restaurant, walk down Cadman Plaza West, which turns into Fulton Street, to the river. The restaurant is at 1 Water Street, at the foot of Fulton Street and Brooklyn Bridge.
>
> To get home, the steps to the right on the Brooklyn side of the bridge land you on Cadman Plaza West, and the **A** and **C** train subway stops—**High Street Brooklyn Bridge**—are directly in front of you across the patch of grass on Cadman Plaza West and Cranberry Street. (It's one stop to Manhattan where you can change to the **4**, the **2** or the **J** train.)

Museums

GUGGE

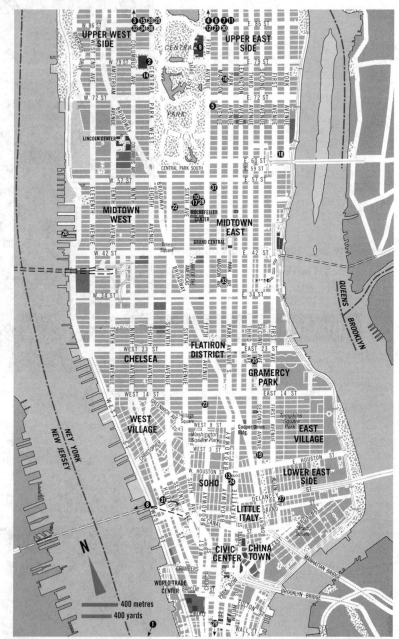

UPPER WEST SIDE

UPPER EAST SIDE

CENTRAL PARK

LINCOLN CENTER

MIDTOWN WEST

MIDTOWN EAST

Times Square

Grand Central

FLATIRON DISTRICT

CHELSEA

GRAMERCY PARK

WEST VILLAGE

EAST VILLAGE

Washington Square Park

Cooper Union Bldg.

Tompkins Square Park

SOHO

LOWER EAST SIDE

LITTLE ITALY

CIVIC CENTER

CHINA TOWN

WORLD TRADE CENTER

NEW JERSEY

NEW YORK

QUEENS

BROOKLYN

Manhattan Bridge

Brooklyn Bridge

N

400 metres
400 yards

New Yorkers love museums. On 'free' days (with the exception of the Frick Collection which has a policy of only admitting 200 people at a time) the big collections will almost always be crowded. Most museums charge admission (around $8), with concessions for students, senior citizens and children. Where there is 'suggested admission' (usually around $7 for adults) you can give as little or as much as you like as long as you give something. Museums are mostly closed on Mondays, and open late on Tuesdays or Thursdays when admission is sometimes free. Notable exceptions are the Museum of Modern Art, which is open late on Thursdays and Fridays and closed on Wednesdays, the Guggenheim which is open late on Fridays and Saturdays and closed on Tuesdays, and the American Museum of Natural History which is open daily and late on Fridays and Saturdays.

Fortunately for the visitor, nearly all the museums are lined up in one place along a riviera on 5th Avenue, between 70th and 105th Streets, known as 'Museum Mile'. (On the first Tuesday of June the stretch is closed to traffic, and ten of the museums are open free.)

The museums below start with the heavyweight and finish up with smaller, idiosyncratic museums which are scattered all over the city and include some institutions which are only partly museum but so charming, quirky or specialized they deserve to qualify anyway (the North Wind Undersea Museum, the Socrates Sculpture Park, the Police Museum, the Poe Cottage and the Isamu Noguchi Garden

Museum). Where a more detailed description of a museum has been provided in one of the Walks in this book there is a reference.

The Big Museums and Collections

Ellis Island Immigration Museum

Ellis Island, © 363 7620 or 363 3200. Open daily 9–5; adm free but the ferry ride there costs $7, seniors $5, ages 3–17 $3, under 3 free. Transport by the Circle Line–Statue of Liberty Ferry (© 269 5755) which leaves every half-hour from Battery Park, ticket sales from Castle Clinton, Battery Park.

Four out of every ten Americans alive have ancestors who came to America via Ellis Island. Between 1892 and 1954 the station received over 12 million immigrants—the grandparents and great-grandparents of nearly half the US population. The museum inside Ellis Island immigration station opened in 1990 and despite renovations is still quite eerie, especially the cavernous Registry Room which has been restored (poignantly with no exhibits) exactly as it was at its peak in 1907 when 1.3 million immigrants passed through at a rate of 12,000 a day (the station was designed to cope with half that number). In the same year New York's most reforming mayor, Fiorello LaGuardia, came to work at the station as an interpreter of Croatian, Italian and German, and experienced at first hand the harsh processing in which human beings were sorted, diagnosed, rejected and occasionally sent back—or accepted, deloused and renamed. The renovated building now contains thirty other galleries off the main hall, some inside original interview rooms where verbal questioning was followed by a physical examination. These now contain photographs, artefacts, voice recordings and temporary exhibitions. The museum cost in the region of $150 million, some of which was raised from a Wall of Honor inscribed with ancestors' names at $100 a throw (*see* **Walk IV**).

American Museum of Natural History and Hayden Planetarium

Central Park West at West 79th St., © 769 5100, IMAX © 769 5034, www.amnh.org. Open Sun–Thurs 10–5.45, and Fri–Sat 10–8.45. Suggested contribution $8, students and seniors $6, children $4.50; separate admission to the IMAX Theater and Planetarium (opening in 2000) with discount combination tickets available.

New York's enthralling shrine to natural history, at its theatrical best at night, after the youngsters have gone. Inside are 34 million exhibits, many displayed in fascinating dioramas in which stuffed and fake animals are frozen in spookily lifelike poses in front of painted land and seascapes. Highlights include a 10-ton steel and fibreglass blue whale, suspended over the Hall of Ocean Life, and the entertaining 4th floor Dinosaur Halls, one of the largest collections of its kind in the world. This was smartly renovated at a cost of $12m from 1992–6, and contains 120 specimens and brilliantly animated videos. There is also entrance through the museum to the **Planetarium**, which is being massively renovated from 1997 onwards into a Center for Earth and Space, due to open by the year 2000. If you get there before 2000, the Imax films in the IMAX Theater are excellent, especially *Cosmic Voyage* which ambitiously recreates the birth of the cosmos and the Big Bang. There are laser light shows as well, set to Pink Floyd and the Beatles (*see* **Walk II**).

The Cloisters

Fort Tryon Park, © 923 3700. Closed Mon. Open Tues–Sun 9.30–5.15 March–Oct; 9.30–4.45 Nov–Feb. Suggested adm $8, students and seniors $4; all tickets include same-day admission to the Metropolitan Museum of Art.

Home to the Metropolitan Museum's medieval art collection, in a building which is Manhattan's weirdest *trompe l'œil*: a mocked-up medieval monastery at the far northwestern tip of Manhattan. The turret you see from afar is a 1938 replica of St Michel de Cuxa in France; the rest of the building is more authentic, incorporating four genu[w]ine Gothic and Romanesque French and Spanish cloisters. These were assembled before the First World War by the eccentric George Grey Barnard, who spent years trawling the French countryside for medieval artefacts. Frequently he stumbled on priceless works of art mouldering away in barns, or used as garden ornaments (one find was a Romanesque torso of Christ used as a scarecrow). In 1925 John D. Rockefeller Jr bought the collection, and land in New Jersey on the other side of the Hudson River, so the view from the Cloisters would never be spoilt.

The collection is in roughly chronological order, starting with Romanesque and finishing with Late-Gothic. Upstaging everything else are the 16th-century **Unicorn Tapestries** which were salvaged from the La Rochefoucauld estate in Verteuil (where they were used to keep frost off vegetables), and reluctantly donated by Rockefeller in 1938. They alone make the laborious slog to Washington Heights worthwhile. The museum grounds are attractive, and include a herb garden which destroys all suspension of disbelief with the creepy sound of medieval chants and monks' voices booming from invisible loudspeakers.

Cooper-Hewitt Museum

2 East 91st St., on 5th Ave., © 860 6898. Closed Mon. Open Tues 10–9, Wed–Sat 10–5, Sun noon–5; adm $3, students and seniors $1.50, children free.

The Smithsonian's collection of decorative arts (including the largest collection of architectural drawings in the world), housed in style in Andrew Carnegie's 64-room Georgian mansion on 5th Avenue. A panoply of '*objets*' includes textiles, wallpaper, jewellery and, more intriguingly, pornography, especially seeing as the Hewitts who assembled them at the turn of the century were granddaughters of Peter Cooper (the sturdy industrialist who founded the Cooper Union School of Science and Architecture). Only a fraction of the collection is on show at one time, but revolving exhibitions are always excellent and the museum shop is the best for books about the decorative arts (also hand-made toys).

Frick Collection

1 East 70th St., at 5th Ave., © 288 0700. Open Tues–Sat 10–6, Sun 1–6; adm $5, students and seniors $3, under 10s not admitted.

An astonishing collection of European Old Masters (two Rembrandt self-portraits, *The Polish Rider*, two Goyas, two El Grecos, two Van Dykes, three Vermeers; also, Whistler, Ingres, Duccio, Bellini, Holbein, Turner, Velásquez, Titian, and David) (*see* **Walk II**).

Guggenheim Museum

1071 5th Ave., at 88th St., © 423 3500, www.guggenheim.lehman.cuny. edu/gugg. Closed Tues. Open Sun–Wed 10–6, Fri–Sat 10–8; adm $8, students and seniors $5, Fri 6–8 'pay what you wish'.

Frank Lloyd Wright's uppity white shell, defying everything else on 5th Avenue not least its own exhibits. These are vengefully hung at an angle to the floor on the outside wall of a spiralling ramp, with the upshot that the viewer can never get more than a few inches away from a painting, and never see it straight.

The collection began years before the Guggenheim was built with Old Masters, which copper and silver mine magnate Solomon Guggenheim bought in a desultory fashion to beautify his rooms in the Plaza Hotel. The 'revolution' came in 1927, when he commissioned a portrait from bizarre artist Baroness Hilla Rebay von Ehrenwiesen. Soon after, Rebay became Guggenheim's mistress and art advisor; Rebay transmitted to Guggenheim her passion for 'cosmic non-objective' art (as opposed to figurative art, which was 'nicht cosmic') while Guggenheim coaxed her with gifts: paintings by the likes of Kandinsky, Klee, Chagall, Arp, Moholy-Hagy and Rebay's lover, Rudolf 'Bubbles' Bauer. By 1939 Rebay had been presented with enough of these to furnish a Museum of Non-Objective Painting in an automobile showroom with walls, windows and sofas upholstered in blue-grey flannel at 24 East 54th Street. The museum had about three visitors a day, including the messy baroness, carrying her lap-dog and latest copy of *Modern Screen Romance*, and Rudolf Bauer, who arrived together each morning to inspect the employees (usually 'non-objective' artists whose work Rebay was apt to 'improve' with triangles or dots). Four years later, in 1943, the baroness persuaded Guggenheim that Frank Lloyd Wright (then 74) should design a new museum, the Solomon R. Guggenheim Museum of Non-Objective Painting. What with squabbles between the trustees and New York City planning authorities, and tiffs between Rebay, Guggenheim's son, and Lloyd Wright himself, it took 16 years to build. By the time it was completed in 1969 both Solomon Guggenheim and Lloyd Wright were dead.

Between 1990 and 1992 the Guggenheim was given a $60m facelift and a 10-storey tower, based on early designs by Lloyd Wright. This is used to show selections from Rebay's original collection (the many 'Bubbles' Bauer paintings remain in storage) and a mostly post-impressionist collection donated by art dealer Justin Thannhauser in the 60s. Although the walls here are at least straight and paintings from both collections include works by Cézanne, Degas, van Gogh, Picasso, Chagall, Klee, Miro and Kandinsky, a lot are surprisingly underwhelming. The main body of the museum is used for temporary exhibitions by contemporary artists (best for 3-dimensional works, like Claes Oldenburg's shuttlecock). For all its architectural conceitedness, a stride down the ramp is an entertaining antidote to establishment museums. The Dean & Deluca café is sophisticated if overpriced, ditto the poky museum shop.

International Center of Photography

7 *1130 5th Ave., at 94th St., ℂ 860 1777, www.icp.org/chim. Closed Mon. Open Tues 11–8, Wed–Sun 11–6; adm $4, students and seniors $2.50, 'pay what you wish' Tues evenings.*

Fascinating exhibitions of famed photographers and groups like Magnum—and the grandest lavatory in the city—all housed in an elegant 5th Avenue townhouse.

Liberty Science Center

8 *Liberty State Park, 251 Phillip St., Jersey City, New Jersey, ℂ 1 (201) 200 1000. Open Tues–Sun 9.30–5.30; adm $9, students and seniors $8, children $6.*

As the price of admission suggests, America's smartest, newest and most up-to-date science museum: imaginative exhibitions, the largest IMAX theatre in the country, and an observation tower for stupendous views. Accessible via the PATH train from 33rd, 24th, 14th, 9th, Grove and Christopher Streets or via a ferry from the World Financial Center across the Hudson (call ☎ 1 800 533 3779 for transport and other details).

Metropolitan Museum of Art

5th Ave., at 82nd St., ☎ 879 5500 or recordings on ☎ 535 7710, internet on www.metmuseum.org. Closed Mon. Open Tues–Thurs and Sun 9.30–5.15, Fri–Sat 9.30–8.45; suggested adm $7, seniors and students $3.50, under 12s free.

The biggest of them all. The sheer scope of the collection can be overwhelming, so whichever section you visit, make sure that at some point you find your way to the **sculpture garden** on the roof. This has fine views of Central Park, as well as a small bar serving drinks and a friendly man in the elevator who has developed his own Beaufort Scale for sunsets (access to the roof garden is via 20th Century Art). Highlights elsewhere include the amazing **Temple of Dendur** in a brilliantly theatrical gallery designed by Roche and Dinkeloo; the Garden Room in the **American Wing** (American decorative arts and crafts surrounded by trees and ponds); **Primitive Art** (spanning 3000 years, Africa and the Americas); and finally an underrated (because small and haphazard) collection of paintings from 1940 to the present day in the beautiful **20th Century Art** galleries, which includes works by Pollock, Clyfford Still (according to himself, the first and only Abstract Expressionist), Rothko, Barnet Newman, Rosenquist (pop art), Chuck Close (American photo-realism), Lipchitz ('Fabulous but what a name', as one visitor was overheard saying to her friend), Philip Guston (abstract figuration), and two contemporary British painters, John Walker and Sean Scully.

In 1908 The Met was the first museum to introduce air-conditioning, five years after it was invented. Nowadays the elegance and modernness of the museum will come as a delightful shock to anyone used to European mouldiness; throughout the Met, Victorian kleptomania is wonderfully contrasted with large, airy, uncluttered rooms. As a result New Yorkers are able use the Met somewhat like a club: they drop in for lectures, concerts and rendezvous, or just to eat in the restaurant and do their present-buying in the Museum Shop, practically an institution in itself.

Museum of Modern Art (MoMA)

11 West 53rd St., between 5th and 6th Aves., ☎ 708 9400/9480, www.moma.org. Closed Wed. Open Sat–Tues 11–6, Thurs–Fri 12–8.30; adm $8.50, seniors and students $5.50, under 16s free, and 'pay what you wish' Thurs–Fri 5.30–8.30. Gallery talks Sat–Tues 1pm and 3pm, Thurs–Fri 3pm, 6pm and 7pm.

20th-century painting, design and sculpture from the Post-Impressionists to now, cleanly laid out on four floors, and due to expand on to 54th Street and 6th Avenue in 1998. Outstanding examples of American abstract expressionism on the third floor begin with an astonishing drawing (*Summation*) by the Armenian artist Arshile Gorky, executed shortly before he hanged himself at the age of 44. The suicide was a tragic end to a life which had tragic beginnings, and the culmination of two years of catastrophe in which time Gorky had a car crash and broke his painting arm, was diagnosed with throat cancer, was left by his wife, and finally watched his studio burn down, destroying the vast body of his work... Next door are some excellent Pollocks, including *One*, and works by his wife Lee Krasner. The floor continues with the best of de Kooning (including *Woman, I*), Barnett Newman's colour-field paintings (*Onement, III*), Rothko, Ad Reinhardt, Franz Kline and Robert Rauschenberg and Cy Twombly. The second floor below takes the visitor from Post-impressionism to Surrealism, via staggering examples of Bonnard (*The Breakfast Room*), Picasso (*Les Demoiselles d'Avignon*) and four brilliant panels by Kandinsky commissioned for a New York apartment in 1914. Despite its avant-garde origins, the museum probably did not relish the DaDa-styled sabotage performed on it in 1988 by Monty Cantsin, the Hungarian founder of 'Neoism', in which Cantsin spattered the walls and incidentally Picasso's *Interior with a Girl Drawing* (worth $4million) with six vials of his own blood in the shape of an X, then read out a manifesto denouncing gentrification on the Lower East Side.

MoMA also includes sections on Architecture and Design on the fourth floor, a video room and film theatre in the basement for showing the museum's collection of over 13,000 films and 4 million stills, a sculpture garden, and photography, drawing and print galleries which tend to get neglected. There's a posey restaurant called Sette on the third floor (not the best value in the world) and a cheaper café on the ground floor being refurbished in 1997, but featuring Meccano seats at the time of going to press. As a rule the 'fashionable' night to visit MoMA is on a 'pay what you wish' Thursday evening, when an arty crowd wearing funny-looking shoes cuts a dash through the museum. Whether they're actually interested in the art on show is another question: for nearly two months in 1961 over 100,000 visitors failed to notice that a painting by Matisse was hanging upside down.

Before going home, visit MoMA's **Design Store**, opposite the main museum. If consumer art ever had an apotheosis, this is it: even if you don't have enough money for a Suprematist tea cup or a Bauhaus coffee pot, you can probably afford the Italian-designed lavatory brush.

Museum of the City of New York

 1220 5th Ave., at 103rd St., ℭ 534 1672. Closed Mon and Tues. Open Wed–Sat 12–6, Sun and holidays 1–5; suggested adm $5, students, seniors , children $4.

Considering the material, fairly dull exhibitions describing the history of the city, with whole galleries devoted to dolls' houses and fire engines. The museum hosts worthwhile weekend walking tours, and will no doubt sharpen up after a six-storey wing is added in 1997.

National Academy of Design

 1083 5th Ave., at 89th St., ℭ 369 4880. Closed Mon and Tues. Open Wed–Sun 12–5, Fri 12–8; adm $3.50, students and seniors $2; free Fri 5–8.

Blessed with the knack of putting on imaginative temporary exhibitions. In the past these have included Fantasy Furniture (including a 'queer'-looking sleigh or Siège d'Amour used by Nazi-sympathizer Edward VII for visiting bordellos in Paris), Recent American Drawings, Edward Lear, and London Transport graphic designer, E. McKnight Kauffer.

New Museum of Contemporary Art

 583 Broadway, between Houston and Prince Sts., ℭ 219 1355. Closed Mon and Tues. Open Wed–Sun 12–6, Sat 12–8.; adm $4, students, seniors and artists $3; free Sat 6–8.

Exhibitions, performance pieces and a crowd-stopping window installation celebrating the good, the bad and the ugly in contemporary art. The museum's ventures into the weird and wonderful in experimental art are predictably hit-and-miss: ranging from the site-specific and time-based to sight-based and time-specific.

New York Historical Society

 2 West 77th St., at Central Park West, ☎ 873 3400. Closed Mon and Tues. Open Wed–Sun 12–5; adm $5, seniors and children $3.

Audubon watercolours, Tiffany lamps and works by early American painters, including a self-portrait and a series of nutty end-of-the-world architectural fantasies by Thomas Cole called 'The Course of Empire'. The museum building itself is especially handsome.

The Studio Museum in Harlem

144 West 125th St., ☎ 864 4500. Open Wed–Fri 10–5, weekends 1–6; adm $5, seniors and students $3, under 12s $1.

Paintings, sculpture and photographs by contemporary black artists, and exhibitions on black culture (African-Amercian, African, Caribbean and Black America and the African Dispora). The studio has an artist-in-residence and opened 'The Listening Sky', an excellent new sculpture garden in 1996.

Whitney Museum of American Art

945 Madison Ave., at 75th St., ☎ 570 3676, www.echonyc.com/~whitney. Open Wed 11–6, Thurs 1–8, Fri–Sun 11–6; adm $8, students and seniors $6; free Thurs 6–8.

More than 10,000 20th-century American paintings and sculptures, in one of New York's more sinister buildings: a grim granite carcass with an eye cut into the front and over-hanging brows, designed by Marcel Breuer in 1966 ('Our building does not have any use for windows'). According to Ada Huxtable, for a time the museum was the 'most disliked building in New York'.

Gertrude Vanderbilt Whitney—the heiress, amateur sculptor and aspiring West Village Bohemian—originally founded the museum in 1929 after the Metropolitan Museum ungraciously turned down her collection of American realist painters (assembled from 1905 onwards and including works by Edward Hopper, Reginald Marsh, Stuart Davis, John Sloan and Thomas Hart Benton). Paradoxically, as America was staggering through the Depression, this school of painting (which Gertrude Whitney housed in a townhouse in Greenwich Village decorated with stars and stripes and signs of the zodiac) came to stand for a newfound faith in America and its cultural virility, and a spirited rejection of European smuggery.

The Whitney carries on in the same spirit at least, with a massive biennial in every odd-numbered year devoted to contemporary American art filling each floor of the building, and a rich permanent collection of 20th-century American artists, from early homespun abstract figuration to contemporary. The collection, selections from which will be shown on the renovated 5th floor from autumn 1997 onwards, is especially strong on Marsden Hartley, de Kooning, Ad Reinhardt, Jasper Johns, Claes Oldenburg and Alexander Calder. (As well as many of his sculptures, a case in the museum contains Calder's 'Circus' of animals and performers made of tin, lead, paperclips, rags, springs and clockwork movements, put together in Paris in the 1920s. A video next to it shows Calder-the-Ringmaster giving one of his laconic 'performances', sometimes considered the first example of performance art, in which horses are propelled by egg beaters, riders by springs, and a lion made of wire is brutally shot to the ground by Calder himself.)

Temporary exhibitions at the Whitney in 1997 include solos on Keith Haring, Richard Deakin and Frank Lloyd Wright. In 1999, instead of the usual biennial, the Whitney will be staging a massive **Century Show** of works from the permanent collection—not to be missed if you are visiting Manhattan that year.

Small, Quirky or Specialist Museums

Abigail Adams Smith Museum, 421 East 61st St., between York and 1st Aves, ✆ 838 6878. *Open Tues 11–9, Tues–Sun 11–4; adm $3, seniors and students $2, under 13s free.* 18th-century carriage-house, guarded by the robust Colonial Dames of America, and doughtily holding its own in the midst of Midtown's skyscrapers. **18**

American Craft Museum, 40 West 53rd St., between 5th and 6th Aves, ✆ 956 3535. *Open Wed–Sun 10–6, Thurs 10–8; adm $5, seniors and students $2.50, under 12s free.* Craft elevated to Art: bright, well-meaning museum showing crafts from 1900 to the present day (pottery, puppet-making, patchwork, textiles, furniture, etc.). **17**

American Museum of the Moving Image (AMMI)

> *35th Ave at 36th St., Astoria, Queens, ✆ 1 (718) 784 0077. Open Tues–Fri 12–5, Sat–Sun 11–6; adm $7, students, seniors and children $4, all adm includes screenings.*

A complete history of the 'art form that defined America', sadly fuzzily defined here, especially compared to the MoMI in London. The most important exhibits are shown in two screening rooms; and the esoteric programmes here make a trip well worthwhile (call ahead for details, some screenings include seminars with top screenwriters and directors). The museum itself features mostly interactive exhibits (add your own sound effects, make your own commercial etc., all excellent for children) and a collection of fanzines.

AMMI stands on part of the vast Kaufman–Astoria Studios, a stamping ground in the 1920s for the great D. W. Griffith, Rudolph Valentino, Louise Brooks, handsome William Powell and finally the Marx brothers who made *Animal Crackers* and *Cocoanuts* on this site. The studios were requisitioned in the war for making propaganda films, then abandoned for many years until 1976 when the entire compound was completely renovated in an attempt to revive New York's film industry. Since then *The Cotton Club*, *Radio Days* and that all-time flop *Ishtar* have all been made in Astoria, which nowadays is the largest film studios on the East Coast. Unfortunately visitors to the museum have absolutely no access whatsoever.

Anthology Film Archives, 32 2nd Ave, ✆ 505 5181. *Adm $7, students and seniors $5.* Large and extraordinary archive for avant-garde and experimental 'art films' from America and Europe. Programmes excellent and sometimes outré beyond wildest dreams (think 'fatalistically, brilliantly pessimistic', 'seminal' and 'torch singer'). **19**

Black Fashion Museum, 155 West 126th St., ✆ 666 1320. *Open weekdays 12–8 by appointment only; adm free.* Work by contemporary black fashion designers, as well as clothes from the 19th century worn and made by black slaves. Though the collection includes 5000 items, less than a score seem to be on display at any one time. **20**

El Museo del Barrio, 1230 5th Ave., at 104th St., ℂ 831 7272. *Open Wed–Sun 11–5; suggested adm $4, students $2.* Contemporary Puerto Rican and Latin American art in a museum which started in a Barrio classroom. Spirited exhibitions of work by local artists, plus a collection of *santos de Palo* carved votive figures on permanent display. **21**

Equitable Center Gallery, 787 7th Ave., at 51st St., ℂ 544 4818. *Open Mon–Fri 11–6, Sat 12–5; adm free.* Big lobby including Roy Lichtenstein's 68-foot *Mural with Blue Brush*, a small gallery (often with exhibitions about New York City) and also a branch of the wonderful Brooklyn Museum shop. A block away at 1290 6th Avenue between 51st and 52nd Streets, and also owned by the Equitable, are Thomas Hart Benton's fascinating *America Today* murals, painted on linen panels in egg tempera for the New School in Greenwich Village (Benton got members of his family and students to pose for scenes with themes such as American industry and popular culture; Jackson Pollock, his student, assisted). **22**

Forbes Magazine Galleries, 62 5th Ave., at W. 12th St.,ℂ 206 5548. *Open Tues–Wed and Fri–Sat 10–4; adm free.* Malcolm Forbes' impish collection of 300 Fabergé eggs, plus an army of 12,000 toy soldiers and 500 boats. **23**

Garibaldi Meucci Museum, 420 Tompkins Ave., Staten Island, ℂ 1 (718) 442 1608. *Open Tues–Sun 1–5; suggested donation $3.* Relics, including 17 candles made by Garibaldi while he lived in exile on Staten Island with his friend Anotonio Meucci and worked as a candlemaker.

Guggenheim Museum, SoHo, 575 Broadway at Prince St., ℂ 423 3500. *Closed Mondays and Tuesdays. Open Wed–Sun 11–6 and Sat 11–8; adm $6, students and seniors $4.* Downtown branch of the Guggenheim (*see* above) on three floors, showing selections from the uptown permanent collection (in 1997, Max Beckmann) and work by less established artists in new media—video installations etc. The deluxe tea 'salon' in the basement seems to have had the most impact on media sensibilities. **24**

Hispanic Society of America, Broadway at 155th St., ℂ 926 2234. *Open Tues–Sat 10–4.30, Sun 1–4; adm free.* One of the city's neglected museums: an opulent Spanish Renaissance courtyard in Harlem. Inside there's exquisite lustre-ware, majolica and carved panelling in a gallery with paintings by Goya, Velásquez, Zurbaran and El Greco. 'Some of them look of doubtful origin,' Simone de Beauvoir wrote snobbishly in 1947. 'Americans, no doubt, are too avid for Old Masters to be over-particular.' **25**

Intrepid Sea Air Space Museum, Intrepid Square, Pier 86, West 46th St. and 12th Ave., ℂ 245 0072 information line. *Open May–Sept, Mon–Sat 10–5, Sun 10–6; Oct–April, Wed–Sun 10–5; adm $10, seniors and 12–17yr olds $7.50, 6–11 $5.* Historical exhibition of America's naval achievements in sea, air and space technology. Many exhibits are housed in the aircraft carrier USS *Intrepid* (used in the Second World War and the Vietnam War), surrounded by other historic vessels including a submarine and a destroyer. Restaurant and café on premises. **26**

Isamu Noguchi Garden Museum, 32–37 Vernon Blvd., Long Island City, Queens, ℂ 1 (718) 721 1932. *Closed Nov–March. Open April–Oct, Wed–Sat 11–6. On weekends a bus to the museum leaves Manhattan at 30 minutes past the hour from the Asia Society, Park Avenue, fare $5 (call museum for schedule). Suggested contribution $4, students and* *seniors $2.* Sculpture gardens in Isamu Noguchi's old studio, originally a lamp factory, and well worth a special expedition. Noguchi (1904–88) was born in LA, and trained under Gutzon Borglum, who sculpted Mount Rushmore, and who had such a low opinion of his young apprentice's work that he made the young sculptor work for him as an artist's model. Despite this, Noguchi turned out to be one of the most intrepid artists of his generation, producing work for architectural sites in Manhattan, as well as designs for furniture, the stage, and playground equipment. Inside the studio are two floors of galleries devoted to Noguchi's work; outside is one of the huge, bleak sculpture gardens for which the sculptor is most famous. According to Noguchi, gardens were a way of including the impermanent, the intangible and the functional in sculpture. While you're here, have a look at the **Socrates Sculpture Park**, on the other side of Vernon Boulevard *(see below)*.

Jacques Marchais Museum of Tibetan Art, 338 Lighthouse Ave., Staten Island, *℃* 1 (718) 987 3478. *Open April–Nov Wed–Sun 1–5; adm $3, students and senior citizens $2.50.* In the Himalayas of Staten Island, a lavish Buddhist Temple and the largest collection of Tibetan art in the West. Jacques Marchais was the pseudonym of Jacqueline Klauber, a rich art dealer who changed her name to compel the respect of the New York art world, succeeded, and then started this extraordinary collection of all things Tibetan.

Louis Armstrong House & Archives, Rosenthal Library, Queens College, Queens, *℃* 1 (718) 997 3670. *Open Mon–Fri, 10–5, appointments recommended; adm free.* Letters, photographs, drawings and mementoes of the great Louis Armstrong.

Lower East Side Tenement Museum, 90 Orchard St., between Broome and Delancey Sts, *℃* 431 0233. *Open Tues–Sun 11–5. Adm $7, students and seniors $6. Tours of tenement apartments leave Tues–Fri at 1, 2 and 3pm, Sat–Sun 11–4.15, every 45 minutes.* Lively and illuminating museum in the middle of the Orchard Street market devoted to tenements and immigrant cultures, filled with photographs of the Lower East Side, and including an excellent tour of the oldest tenement house, across the street, and hour-long walking tours. **㉗**

Museum of TV and Radio, 23 West 52nd St., between 5th and 6th Aves, *℃* 621 6600 and recordings *℃* 621 6800, *iwww.mtr.org. Open Tues–Sun 12–6, Thus 12–8, Fri 12–9; adm $6, students and seniors $4, under 13s $3.* Guilt-free television. Not really a museum, but a brilliant library archive of over 60,000 television and radio shows which visitors request by computer, then watch on private consoles. (The two most popular are an hour of vintage tv commercials and the Beatles' live debut on television.) There are also four video theatres which the museum uses for retrospectives (Denis Potter, the Three Stooges, Watergate, etc). **㉘**

National Museum of the American Indian, 1 Bowling Green, between State and Whitehall Sts., *℃* 668 6624, *www.si.edu/nmai. Open daily 10–5; adm free.* Exquisitely displayed exhibits and videos celebrating Native America, its people, religions, literature and art. This is intelligently done (mostly by Native Americans) and well worth a visit. Also it's free *(see* pp.163–4) **㉙**

New York Academy of Medicine, 1216 5th Ave at 103rd Str. *Open Mon–Fri 9–5; adm free.* Four thousand cookery books, including a rare manuscript on roast boar, in a library which is otherwise the best in America for research into history of medicine. **㉚**

New York City Fire Museum, 278 Spring St., between Varick and Hudson Sts, © 691 1303. *Open Tues–Sun 10–4; suggested contribution $4, students and seniors $2, under 12s $1.* Fire apparatus, in all its incarnations. **(31)**

New York Hall of Science, Flushing Meadows Park, 47–01 111th St at 48th Ave., Flushing Meadows, Corona Park, Queens, © 1 (718) 699 0005, *www.nyhallsci.org. Open Wed–Sun 10–5; adm $4.50, seniors and children $3; free Wed–Thurs 2–5.* This delightful museum is housed in an eccentric left-over from the 1964 World's Fair: a massive cement brain protected by an undulating concrete wall of cobalt blue stained-glass, with two rockets and a launcher in its car park (other amazing kitsch excesses from the Fair such as the Unisphere are well within walking distance—*see* Queens Museum of Art, below). Inside, the hall is arranged like a laboratory and includes such fascinating exhibits as anti-gravitational mirrors, magnified microbes, robotic insects, live germs and Watt's steam engine. Children love it, especially the demonstrations of Brownian motion and how-to-dissect a cow's eye. The Technology Gallery has free access to the Internet and a 16-screen video wall linked to astronomical data bases around the world; a massive $80m renovation is planned for the future, including a planetarium and new laboratories.

New York Transit Museum, Boerum Place, at Schermerhorn St., Brooklyn, © 1 (718) 243 5839. *Open Tues, Thurs, Fri 10–4, Wed 10–6, Sat–Sun 12–5.; adm $3, children and seniors $1.50.* Ancient trains and carriages housed underground in an enormous abandoned subway station in Brooklyn.

North Wind Undersea Museum, 610 City Island Ave., Bronx, © 1 (718) 885 0701. *Open Mon–Fri 10–5; adm $3, children $2. Transport: 6 to Pelham Bay Park, then BX21 bus to City Island.* A room constructed out of 9ft wide gaping jaw, belonging to a grey whale, with exhibits including walrus' tusks, sharks' teeth and a 100-year-old tug boat. Round the back in a tank is a Turtle Rescue Area. Sadly the seals (which the institute trained on behalf of the NYPD to retrieve weapons and drugs from under the water and to undo seat belts and haul people to the surface) have been moved to the New York Aquarium in Brooklyn. It's a good hour's trek to get to this extraordinary and incongruous enclave, well depicted as a gangster's hideaway in E. L. Doctorow's *Billy Bathgate*. More street than island, City Island is nowadays home to a community of fishermen and boatbuilders (who originally made their living evaporating sea water to make salt). Dainty clapboard houses, American flags, nostalgia, fish restaurants. **(32)**

Pierpont Morgan Library, 33 East 36th St., at Madison Ave., © 685 0610. *Closed Mon. Open Tues–Fri 10.30–5, Sat 10.30–6, Sun 12–6; contribution $5, students and seniors $3.* Sumptuous library and Italianate palazzo used for recondite but interesting exhibitions ('Orientalism' and '18th-century prints of Venice') and a swanky glass-roofed café. **(33)**

(Edgar Allan) Poe Cottage, Kingsbridge Rd and Grand Concourse, Bronx, © 1 (718) 881 8900. *Open Sat 10–4, Sun 1–5; adm $2.* Impossible, incongruous relic from those long-lost days when the Bronx was a rural hinterland. Edgar Allen Poe moved into this cottage in 1846, hoping the country air would restore the health of Virginia Clemm, his first cousin and wife (Poe married her when she was 13). However, Virginia Clemm died of tuberculosis within the year. Poe stayed on and wrote 'Ulalume' and the eulogy 'Annabel Lee', but only two years later he died as well, in bizarre circumstances in Baltimore (apparently he was drugged by a political gang during an election, and dragged from one polling station to another to place his vote)... In 1913 the cottage was moved to the other side of the Bronx's Concourse. It's one of the more obscure tourist destinations in New York, with a curator who describes his job as a perfect situation for a misanthrope. **(34)**

New York City Police Museum, 235 E. 20th St., between 2nd and 3rd Aves, ✆ 477 9753. *Open by appointment only, Mon–Fri 9–2; adm free.* By appointment only, and the quirkiest museum in Manhattan. Exhibits range from the usual police memorabilia (police hats from all over the world) to enthralling explanations of counterfeiting, ballistics, and the spurious Bertillon Phrenological Identification Method, used for 30 years to detect criminal tendencies by measuring the shape of the head. Fascinating histories of New York's organized crime networks and display cases of 'recently acquired contraband weapons' including daggers disguised as a fountain pens, umbrella swords, and silk-stocking blackjacks. **(35)**

Queens County Farm Museum, 73–50 Little Neck Parkway, Floral Park, Queens, ✆ 1 (718) 347 3276. *Open Mon–Fri 9–5, Sat–Sun 10–5; adm free.* Farm museum: guided tours of a 224-year-old farmhouse for New York urbanites, exhibitions of farm crops and animals and, in October, the world's largest Apple Cobbler.

Queens Museum of Art, New York City Building, Flushing Meadows, Corona Park, Queens, ✆ 1 (718) 592 9700. *Open Wed–Fri 10–5; Sat–Sun 12–5; suggested donation $3, students and seniors $3, children free.* Another underrated museum, set next to the imponderable Unisphere and other ruins of the 1964 World's Fair. The main extraordinary exhibit, dating from the 1964 World's Fair, is the 18,000 sq ft **New York Panorama**, a diorama of the city's 895,000 buildings which is constantly updated. This is the world's largest architectural model; you can walk across it or watch it change from night to day every 15 minutes through binoculars ($1 a go). The museum has recently been refurbished at a cost of $15 million, and now includes a fine art gallery and a smart memorabilia-packed exhibition on the World's Fair incuding an original 'Futurama' car from the General Motors Pavilion.

Schomburg Center for Research in Black Culture, New York Public Library, 515 Malcolm X Boulevard, ✆ 491 2200. *Open Mon–Wed 12–8, Thurs–Sat 10–6, Sun 1–5; adm free.* Excellent collection of photographs, maps, paintings, books and artefacts relating to Black and African culture, in a sleekly designed research library with a 30 seat video room, art gallery and theatre. **(36)**

Socrates Sculpture Park, Broadway at Vernon Blvd, Long Island City, Queens, ✆ 1 (718) 956 1819. *Open daily, 10–sunset.* Four and a half acres of giant sculptures—weather vanes and oversized coloured buoys—set in industrial wasteland on the edge of the East River. Stalking the park and using it as a kind of outdoor laboratory are the sculptors; shadowy figures wielding chainsaws, welding torches, rivets and canisters of propane gas.

Sony Wonder Technology Lab, Sony Building, 550 Madison Ave., between 55th and 56th Sts., ✆ 883 8830. *Open Tues–Sat 10–6, Sun 12–6; adm free.* More a publicity gimmick than a museum, an intoxicating network of interactive workstations, where visitors (mostly adolescents in a frenzy of over-stimulation) can edit a Billy Joel rock video, design their own computer game, direct a video adventure or operate a sonogram. **(37)**

Food and Drink

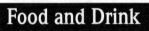

A sallow waiter brings me beans and pork...
Outside there's fury in the firmament.
Ice-cream, of course, will follow; and I'm content.
O Babylon! O Carthage! O New York!

Siegfried Sassoon, 'Storm on Fifth Avenue'

In Manhattan consumption is conspicuous. Everywhere you go, you see New Yorkers eating; as they walk down the sidewalk, in elevators, as they run to catch a bus. Dining out is cheaper and better than eating at home, and you can do it round the clock.

This may be why Manhattanites seldom cook at home, and why Manhattan dinner parties sometimes revolve around home deliveries (even though unwrapping one of these can be as complex as cooking). Fridges in New York apartments can be distressing—a thorough inspection will reveal such disappointments as miso paste, jam, camera film, lemons, flour, saltines, old bagels, artificial sweetener, cold grapes and vitamins, year-old muesli, and endless plastic bottles: steak sauce, ketchup, relish and Thousand Island dressing. Turn in desperation to the freezer, and you'll find a packet of half-finished frozen cigarettes, diet ice cream, an empty vodka bottle, a phial of something like urine and a glacier of ice.

In fact Manhattanites are so fanatical about restaurant food that many are happy to eat out most nights of the week. Manhattanites eat at speed, pushing food around the plate until it's mixed into a mulch, then munching it down in a frenzy, with the upshot that most of the meal is taken up with talking, and most of the talk is about the food. Meals, chefs, dining rooms and patrons are discussed with the relish of a hypochondriac describing his illness. Crazes for new cuisines (from Greek and Belgian to Korean and Vietnamese) sweep the city with viral speed. Meanwhile restaurant critics happily devote whole essays to single restaurants and blow-by-blow accounts of their fascinating encounters with butter knives and banquettes.

The 9th Avenue Food Festival

Every May nearly a million New Yorkers visit Food Valhalla at the 9th Avenue International Food Festival, where an astonishing number of ethnic food-sellers from all over the city as well as 9th Avenue (nicknamed Paddy's Market) set out stalls along the length of the avenue.

Ground Rules on Choosing a Restaurant

How to choose the right restaurant? This is an imponderable, in Manhattan. On the whole it's a good idea (if you have time) to ask a New Yorker—almost any New Yorker given that the subject fascinates everyone. Another instant guide will be the reviews displayed in restaurant windows—especially Eric Asimov's dependable *New York Times' Under $25 Cheap Eats* (also published in book form at $10.95 by HarperCollins).

A few last words of advice:

- *avoid restaurants or bars named after famous painters ('Gauguin' etc.) or any other kind of 'theme-u-rants' (inexplicably popular and overpriced)*
- *be wary of menus expounding philosophy*
- *keep away from restaurants with curtains*
- *avoid dishes with 'accents' of chervil or whatever*
- *give a wide berth to restaurants or bars with names ending in 's' (e.g. 'Puddleducks', 'Pookies', 'Bubbas' or 'Clowns').*

Smoking

As far as New York City is concerned, smokers are scum. Under the law passed in April 1995, smoking is limited to restaurants seating less than 35 people. Don't panic too much, because in most restaurants there is at least a smoking bar. However, remember that you can *only* smoke in the bar areas of larger restaurants if the bar is at least 6ft away from dining tables. An upshot of the new laws is that one visit to the clouded confines of a 35-person 'smoking restaurant'—packed with a clientele chain-smoking with all the desperation of the condemned—should be enough to turn you off the habit forever. For detailed listings of smoking restaurants see *The Smoker's Guide to Dining*, touchingly subtitled *Lighten Up New York* by Michael Leo, also available over the Internet: *www.lighten-up.com.*

Breakfast

The best and cheapest meal in Manhattan: whether you're ordering from a fancy hotel or a cheap diner, portions come in big sizes and with little distinction between sweet and savoury—French toast is doused in maple syrup, sweet pancakes arrive on the same plate as bacon. Ordering can be a complicated business: waiters cannot handle even the tiniest indecision, and you should get straight to the point with a 'I'll have a...', or better still 'Gimme a...'.

Eggs come 'any style', and you must specify which:

sunny side up	fried on one side only	*over*	fried on both sides
over-hard	fried so the yolk is hard	*over-easy*	fried on both sides, but quickly so the yolk is runny

Most diners don't have egg cups, and if you ask for a boiled egg you will get it in a bowl. Toast and sandwiches are as complicated as eggs, and you must identify which kind of **bread** you want:

wholewheat	brown bread with grains
rye	black rye bread
light rye	brown rye bread
white	white bread, which like brown bread is usually mixed with honey or sugar
pumpernickel	German rye bread, from the German '*pumpe*', to break wind
challah	Jewish braided egg bread pronounced 'halla'
sour bread	made with vinegar and delicious

Sometimes orders get cryptic, viz:

whisky down	egg fried on both sides on a slice of dark rye bread
Adam and Eve on a raft and wreck 'em	scrambled eggs on toast
a corn muffin 'high and dry'	toasted with no butter
wadder	all restaurants serve customers iced water as a matter of course, but if you want more remember to ask for wadder or you will get blank looks
budder	(*see* above)
'wait on them'	'please accept our apologies as you may have to wait a little longer for your order to arrive'
grape jelly	a purple glue-like substance tasting of bubblegum which accompanies toast
Krispy Kremes	doughnut brand made in the American south which are neither crispy nor creamy, but very tasty
policeman's heaven	a table spread with every possible kind of doughnut: the scent of doughnuts has been proved in scientific studies to be an aphrodisiac, especially in combination with pumpkin pie and liquorice
pancakes	thick, sweet and perfectly round
corn/bran muffins	sponge H-bombs filled with blueberries and raisins or nuts and usually tasting of nothing
English muffin	unsweetened, like a crumpet
hushpuppies	potato croquettes
hash browns	fried potatoes with onions
egg cream	not egg nog nor eggs with cream, but a delicious froth of iced milk, a squirt of chocolate or vanilla syrup and a blast of seltzer in a tall glass
OJ	orange juice
regular coffee	can mean anything: usually white coffee with sugar, sometimes black coffee with no sugar
light coffee	white, and it comes with a packet of 'half and half' —a mixture of milk and cream. If you sit around long enough, most restaurants refill your cup free.
tea	comes iced (and often heavily sweetened) or as a do-it-yourself mug of boiling water with a bag of Lipton's and a lemon
the check/tab	the bill

Brunch and Bargain Lunch

On weekends, New Yorkers who stay in town will meet friends or read the papers over **brunch**—a lavish midday meal combining breakfast, lunch and alcohol. In midweek New Yorkers will as often as not eat their meals on the run, so a three-course **gourmet lunch** in an expensive restaurant is always a spectacular bargain. Some of the choicest, most inaccessible restaurants in Manhattan do a prix fixe lunch for $15–30. These include **Gramercy Tavern** bar and the **Mark Hotel** (who both do a set lunch for $19.97, rising a penny a year), **Chanterelle**, **Grand Central Oyster Bar** (with a counter bar serving oysters, clam chowder for $3, etc.), **Petrossian** (around $22), **Le Bernadin**, the elegant **Gotham Bar and Grill**, **Daniel's** and **Dawat** ($15 for the best Indian in the city), **Jo Jo** (run by New York ultra chef Jean-Georges Vongerichten), the ever-fashionable **Union Square Café** and **Montrachet** in TriBeCa. Even more cheap are the $5 lunch specials in **Little India**—a row of thirty or so Indian restaurants on 6th Street and 1st Avenue.

If you've lost your appetite because of a big breakfast, you can do as the New Yorkers do and grab a hot-dog, a *gyro* (spit-roasted meat in a soggy pitta bread envelope), a *hero* (a sandwich with French bread), or a carton of frozen yoghurt. Best of all and astoundingly good value is a salad-in-a-box from one of the many delis in Manhattan. The **deli salad bars** are cherished by Manhattan office workers and were invented originally in the 1970s by Korean entrepreneurs (who presently own around 3500 groceries, delis and supermarkets in New York). Inside you'll find hot and cold counter-bars filled not just with salad but an astonishing range of delicacies, from dim sum to chicken cacciatore. Thrillingly, everything on display, from dull-looking mounds of iceberg lettuce to fat and juicy hot and sour tiger prawns, is sold by weight and weight alone: this is something to enjoy and Manhattan at its egalitarian best.

Brief Glossary of Unfamiliar Terms

adobo	Filipino chicken/pork/octopus stew	*bagel*	chewy doughnut-shaped bread, plain or with cinnamon and raisins, poppy or sesame seeds (Jewish)
à la mode	with ice cream		
Anisakis simplex	a worm parasite living in cod and salmon caught off the Pacific coast, which can cause salmonella-like symptoms when eaten raw by humans, e.g. in sushi	*batido*	milkshake with tropical fruit (Latin American)
		bialy	onion-roll (Jewish)
		bigos	sliced up kielbasa or sausage with sauerkraut
bacalao	dried, salted cod (Caribbean/Portuguese)	*biscuit*	hot bread-roll
		blintz	pancake filled with cheese or fruit

broiled	grilled
burrito	rolled up flour tortilla with a filling (Mexican)
Caesar's salad	cos lettuce with anchovy paste, olives and lemon
café con leche	espresso with warm milk (Latin American)
caldo verde	Brazilian chicken soup, green thanks to collard greens and kale
chips	crisps
club sandwich	skyscraper-high sandwich with two fillings, three slices of bread and a cocktail stick holding the whole thing together
collard greens	boiled spiced greens (Afro American)
cuchifrutos	fried pork-parts (Puerto Rican)
empanada	meat or vegetable pasty (Latin American)
feijoada	Brazilian national dish of black beans and meats
frijoles	refried beans (Latin American)
gefilte fish	white fish balls (Jewish)
gravlax	salmon cured in sugar, salt and dill (Scand)
grits	crushed maize served with butter
gumbo	thick tomato soup often made with shellfish (Cajun-Southern)
halo–halo	Filipino drink made of preserved fruit, sweet beans, evaporated milk and ice
hero	baguette sandwich, invented in New York, same as a 'sub' (marine)
home fries	giant-sized chips—potatoes cut into the size of fingers and thumbs, cooked with onions and pepper (American)
jello	viscid jelly
jerk	hot barbecued chicken or pork (Jamaican)
kasha	buckwheat crushed oats served with gravy (E. European/Jewish)
kielbasa	spicy pork sausage (Pol)
kirbies	not something you wear in your hair, but a gherkin
knish	savoury dough envelope filled with cheese or potato (Jewish)
kugel	sweet potato pudding (Jewish)
lox	smoked salmon, best eaten with cream cheese on a bagel (Jewish)
mammia	The Finns' favourite pudding: rye, malt, molasses and orange peel
manicotti	ravioli stuffed with cheese
matzoh brei	egg pancakes scrambled with pieces of broken matzoh (Jewish)
mauby	Jamaican drink made of bark
mahi mahi	Hawaiian fish, very tasty
mole poblano	savoury sauce of bitter chocolate, chilli and spices, served with meat or *enchiladas* (Mexican)
mondongo	tripe soup (Colombian/Dominican)
plantain	green, banana-like fruit, fried and served as a side-dish (Latin American)
polenta	a savoury porridge made of maize (Italian)
red snapper	carnivorous fish, delicious grilled
reuben	sandwich of corned beef, melted Swiss cheese and *sauerkraut*
scrod	young cod or haddock

seafood	all kinds of fish, not just shellfish	*tabouli*	cracked wheat salad (Middle Eastern)
seltzer	fizzy or soda water	*tatami room*	private dining room where Japanese food is eaten on mats with shoes off
shashlik	skewered meat (Russian)		
shrimp	prawns		
soda	soft drinks		
soft-shell crabs	delicious, recently moulted blue crabs which you eat whole	*teriyaki*	marinade for meat, poultry and fish (Japanese)
spanakopita	spinach pie (Greek)	*zakuski*	Russian appetizers, hot and cold
squash	a kind of marrow	*zucchini*	courgettes
svart	black soup made of goose and pigs' blood (Swedish)		

Supper

Below is a select list of good restaurants. Bear in mind that as one restaurant gets popular, so menu prices go up and rivals will close down. Always phone ahead to doublecheck prices, existence and opening times. Reservations are also advisable, and if you go to a top-notch restaurant, you may need to reserve a few days or weeks in advance. Some restaurants are closed on Sundays and even Mondays.

In the smartest restaurants make sure you have a jacket and tie if you are a man, and at least a gesture to establishment tastes (a scarf or brooch) if you are female. If you turn up wearing shorts you may be turfed away. Remember, your New York compatriots who look so scruffy by day will nearly always dress to the symphonic nines when going 'round the corner' to their favourite neighbourhood restaurant. In fancy restaurants, **waiters** divide into three types: the *cringing and pandering*, who tell you their name and interrupt to ask if everything is all right; the *haughty and despising*, who make customers feel guilty for ever stepping into the restaurant in the first place; and finally the *kindly, informative and sagacious*, sometimes so kindly and informative that they'll draw up a seat and deliver a passionate lecture on corruption in the highest echelons of Manhattan politics. Remember, after all this, to ask for the 'check' when you want the bill.

Cute Prices

There are presently more than 15,000 restaurants in New York serving practically every dish under the sun; eating out in them is one of the supreme pleasures of being in Manhattan. Restaurants are roughly half the price and double the quality of their European equivalents; and at lunchtime many of Manhattan's most exclusive eateries offer a prix-fixe menu for an incredible $20–30 (*see* p.193). In July, in 'Restaurant Week', even more of the posh restaurants go democratic, offering a standard prix fixe lunch at around $20–25 a head.

The **price ranges** below, used throughout the chapter, are for an evening meal, excluding drinks, service (15–20%) and sales tax (8¼%). Tipping is a matter of course in America, (*see* p.50) and the easiest way to calculate the right amount is to double the sales tax, giving an instant 16½%. You may add or subtract from the resulting figure, depending on service. Waiters, captains, wine stewards, busboys and bartenders usually pool their tips, and unless you especially want to it's not necessary to separate out the tip. In some restaurants and night clubs the *maître d'* may expect up to $10 for showing you to your table; however, as a rule sucking up to *maître d's* with a tip is considered over the top.

luxury	over $65*	*inexpensive*	under $20
expensive	$40–$65	*cheap*	under $10
moderate	$20–$40		

*Prices are relative and based on the average cost of an entrée plus first course or pudding, and exclude sales tax (8¼%), tips or alcohol. A **$** sign indicates that a restaurant offers a bargain lunch, or is particularly good value in general.

credit cards

AE, American Express; **D/DC**, Diner's Club; **MC**, Mastercard; **V**, Visa; **DIS**, Discover Card.

Lower Manhattan and TriBeCa   *map A*

luxury

Chanterelle ($), 2 Harrison St., near Hudson St., ✆ 966 6960; *French (AE, D, MC, V; reservations requested)*. Elegant, very elegant, French cuisine and though equivalently priced at around $73 for supper, there's an excellent cut-price three-course lunch for around $35. The menu changes once a fortnight, but is big on raw fish lovingly handled by a chef who trained in marine biology. Guests eat amongst the biggest flower arrangements in Manhattan.

expensive

Capsouto Frères, 451 Washington St., at Watts St., ✆ 966 4900; *French (AE, D, MC, V; closed Mon lunch)*. Cheaper and better value than most in the 'expensive' bracket: in the meat-packing district inside a splendid 1891 landmark warehouse restored by three brothers. American-French menu, including grilled quails with raspberry butter, veal kidneys and calves' liver; best for steaks and beef fillet.

The Restaurant at Windows on the World, 1 World Trade Center, 107th Floor, ✆ 524 7000; *Continental (AE, D, MC, V; lunch Mon–Fri 11.30–2, buffet lunch Sat and Sun 12–3, Sun brunch 12–4, bar open Mon–Sat 4–1am)*. The highest restaurant in the US: after a $25 million refurbishment now divided into three with waiters in Art Deco uniforms. Sunday brunch/breakfast is excellent value: $8 for smoked salmon omelette or a continental breakfast plus a free view of Manhattan. Supper is a *prix fixe* of $77 for a seven-course meal, with fine wines from a list of 800. The cheaper bar food is a mish-mash encompassing fish and chips 'in a silver basket'. Smokers are banished to The Skybox—'a raised area with moveable glass panels'.

1	Chanterelle	12	Bubby's
2	Capsouto Frères	13	The Sporting Club
3	The Restaurant at Windows on the World	14	Mandarin Court
4	Nobu	15	Golden Unicorn
5	TrBeCa Grill	16	20 Mott Street
6	Layla	17	Wong Kee
7	Duane Park Café	18	Sweet 'n' Tart Café
8	Odeon	19	Nom Wah Tea Parlour
9	El Teddy's	20	New Vietnam
10	Bridge Café		
11	Riverrun Café		

Map A

Nobu, 105 Hudson St., at Franklin St., ℭ 219 0500, 🖃 219 1441; *'New' Japanese (MC, V, D, AE; around $55).* Owned by Robert De Niro and Drew Nieporent, and named after Nobu Matsuhisa, the chef. The interior includes a see-through plastic screen, a free-standing wall of black pebbles, a floor lacquered with cherry blossom, and celebrity eaters. The cooking: ethereal 'New' Japanese, with Mexican and Italian 'accents'—'squid pasta' (ribbons of squid cut up and disguised as tagliatelle), and crème caramel made with green tea.

TriBeCa Grill, 375 Greenwich St., at Franklin St., ℭ 941 3900; *American (V, D, AE, MC; Sun brunch).* De Niro's first venture in the restaurant business, and predictably fashionable: in a loft, with paintings by De Niro's father and a private movie-screening room upstairs. Food: 'lightly grilled bistro'—pan-seared snapper with warm vinaigrette, sausage cheese bread, peanut 'whipped' potatoes plus curve-enhancing puddings—banana tart with milk chocolate malt ice-cream or almond strudel with stir-fried pineapple and coconut brittle ice-cream.

Layla, 211 West Broadway at Franklin Street, ✆ 431 0700; *Moroccan* (*MC, V, D, AE*).
6 The third De Niro restaurant and slightly cheaper: slick Moroccan food, and belly dancing three times a week.

moderate

Duane Park Café, 157 Duane St., between West Broadway and Hudson St., ✆ 732 5555;
7 *American* (*AE, D, MC, V; reservations suggested, closed Sun; $34*). Fashionable but reliable American cuisine in tranquil surroundings: duck, skate, steak; sweetbreads with polenta, fancy pasta: the sort of cooking where you count on a coulis with every course.

Odeon, 145 West Broadway, at Thomas St., ✆ 233 0507; *American* (*AE, D, MC, V; reservations suggested*). Hot stuff when it opened in 1980, still trendy decades later.
8 Best for meat dishes—leg of lamb with sautéed artichokes, or grilled chicken with mash. A jolly bar-cum-brasserie stays open for burgers, mussels and *frites* until 2am.

El Teddy's, 210 West Broadway, between Franklin and White Sts., ✆ 941 7070. *Mexican*
9 (*MC, D,V, AE*). Mexican kitsch: neon fish tanks, plastic mosaics, Christmas decorations, stained glass and a Statue of Liberty. All quite 'wacky', with strong Margheritas and inventive Mexican cooking.

Bridge Café, 279 Water St., near Dover St., ✆ 227 3344. *American* (*AE, D, V, D*). Food
10 no great shakes, but in a good location, under the Brooklyn Bridge, in an old and lovely tin-ceiled, wood-framed building. Cheaper at lunchtime when it fills with businessmen and civil servants from Wall Street and the Civic Center. Swordfish, pasta, buffalo steak, soft shell crab and 30 per cent off wine on Tuesdays.

Riverrun Café, 176 Franklin St., between Hudson and Greenwich Sts., ✆ 966 3894.
11 *Continental* (*MC, D, AE, V*). Cheaper than anything else in this category: pub-like, lively and small, with comfortable food: meat loaf, chicken potpie and seafood.

inexpensive

Bubby's, 120 Hudson St, at N. Moore, ✆ 219 0666; *Continental* (*MC, V, D, AE*).
12 Cheapish, jolly corner café, best for breakfast and lunch. The owners can be faxed on ✆ 219 0666 for a copy of their newsletter.

The Sporting Club, 99 Hudson St., at Franklin St., ✆ 219 0900; *American* (*MC, V, D,*
13 *AE*). Five televisions, screening British football as well as American, two pool tables and unmemorable food in large helpings.

SoHo and East SoHo   *map B*

expensive

E&O, 100 West Houston St., between La Guardia Place and Thompson St., ✆ 254 7000;
1 *Vietnamese* (*AE, MC, V, D; reservations suggested*). Colonial hotel-style joint with palm trees and terraces, owned by Nell Campbell (from eighties nightclub Nell's) and Lynn Waggonack (from Odeon (*see* above) and Café Luxembourg (*see* below). Trendy Vietnamese bistro-cooking.

Downtown/DT, 376 West Broadway at Broome St., ✆ 343 0999; *Northern Italian* (*MC,*
2 *V, D, AE*). Swell branch of Cipriani's in Venice with rooftop dining in the summer (another branch is in the Sherry-Netherland Hotel on 5th Avenue and 59th St.).

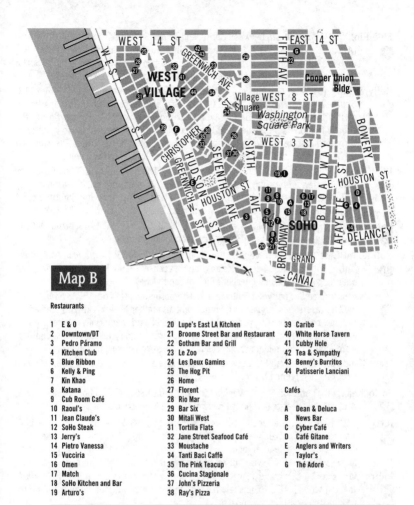

Map B

moderate

Pedro Páramo, 12 Vandam Street, between 6th Ave and Varick St., © 647 1111; *Mexican*
3 (*MC, V*). Family-run, one of the nicest cheap neighbourhood restaurants.
Authentic Mexican cooking: crispy deep-fried taquitos, homemade tortillas, fried
chicken with cactus hearts and a powerful *ceviche*, fish marinated in lime.

Kitchen Club, 30 Prince St., between Mulberry and Mott Sts., © 274 0025; *Continental*
4 (*cash only; closed Mon*). More room than restaurant, this is run by a
Japanese/Dutch couple offering an idiosyncratic mixture of Japanese home
cooking and continental. Candlelit, scented with incense and dinkily furnished.

Blue Ribbon, 97 Sullivan St., between Spring and Prince Streets, ✆ 274 0404; *American*
5 (*MC, AE, V; Tues–Sun 4pm–4am*) & **Blue Ribbon Sushi**, 119 Sullivan St.,
✆ 343 0404; *sushi* (*MC, AE, V*). Like Match, open until 4am, and typically SoHo:
noisy and busy. Good eclectic menu especially for raw and cooked fish.

Kelly & Ping ($), 127 Greene St., between Prince and Houston Sts., ✆ 228 1212;
6 *Southeast Asian* (*MC, AE, V, D*). Quirky Asian noodle parlour plus exotic grocery,
owned by ex-model, Braiden Kelly, and ex-model-booker, Lee Ping, who run the
equally fashionable Kin Khao and Katana (*see* below). Queues of SoHo types form
early for lunch served from a canteen: soba noodle soups, noodle salads, steamed
fish in ginger, lemongrass chicken; supper is more formal and candlelit.

Kin Khao, 171 Spring St., between West Broadway and Thompson Sts., ✆ 966 3939; *Thai*
7 (*MC, V, AE; supper only, reservations suggested*). Designer-noodle. Trendy, tiny
and only open for supper, with exotic decor and atmospheric low lighting: good
sticky Thai rice and hot and sour prawn salad.

Katana, 179 Prince St., between Thompson and Sullivan Sts., ✆ 677 1943; *sushi* (*MC, V,*
8 *AE*). Kelly & Ping's third SoHo venture (*see* above): a sushi boite.

Cub Room Café ($), 183 Prince St., at Sullivan St., ✆ 777 0030; *American* (*AE, lunch*
9 *only*). Attached to the fashionable and expensive Cub Room restaurant, but
offering good and much cheaper lunch or sandwiches.

Raoul's, 180 Prince St., between Sullivan and Thompson Sts., ✆ 966 3518; *French* (*AE,*
10 *MC, V; reservation suggested*). French, but also rather New York, with pressed tin
ceilings, posters, booths, paper tablecloths, blackboard menu, jolly waiters. You'll
enjoy yourself even if you're not usually endeared to noisy restaurants: straightforward food including lamb chops, sea-bass with crevettes, snapper and sole.

Jean Claude's, 169 Sullivan St., between Houston and Prince Sts., ✆ 475 9232; *French*
11 (*AE, MC, V*). French bistro.

SoHo Steak, 90 Thompson St., between Spring and Prince Sts., ✆ 226 0602; *French* (*AE,*
12 *MC, V*). BSE-free steaks cooked by Jean Claude (*see* above).

Jerry's, 101 Prince St., between Mercer & Greene Sts., ✆ 966 9464, 🖷 219 9179;
13 *American* (*MC, V, AE; reservations suggested*). 'Hip' diner-style restaurant with
chrome and red leather booths, best for brunch, and serving 'diner-gourmet'
food—grilled chicken with tangerine marinade, lime chicken with mixed greens.

Pietro Vanessa, 23 Cleveland Place, between Spring and Kenmare Sts., ✆ 226 9764;
14 *Italian* (*MC, V, AE*). Exquisitely named, with a pretty outdoor garden, and pretty
good prices—pasta, veal, gnocchi.

Vucciria, 422 West Broadway, between Prince and Spring Sts., ✆ 941 5811; *Italian* (*MC,*
15 *V, D, AE*). Not varuca—*Vucciria*: pasta from Sicily, in a romantic dining room.

Omen, 113 Thompson St., between Prince and Spring Sts., ✆ 925 8923; *Japanese* (*AE;*
16 *reservations suggested*). Elegant Japanese restaurant with branches in Kyoto,
serving sake martinis. The scary-sounding 'Omen' is a bowl of Japanese noodles.

Match, 160 Mercer St., between W. Houston and Prince St., ✆ 343 0020, 🖷 343 0241;
17 *American* (*MC, V, AE*). Extreme chic, with noisy crowds, loud bands, banquette
seating and sleek interior décor. Open until 4am, it includes a downstairs smoking
lounge with disc jockey. Food is a 'Fusion'—a hodge-podge including Szechuan
steak *au poivre*, sushi, potato chive dumplings, tuna burgers and grilled oysters.

SoHo Kitchen and Bar, 103 Greene St., between Prince and Spring Sts., ✆ 925 1866; (18) *American (AE, D, MC, V; reservations suggested)*. With 400 wines by the glass and 50 beers, the bar is more inspiring than the menu: soups, burgers, homemade pizza and fruit salad—perfectly tasty but noisy and crowded.

inexpensive

Arturo's, 106 West Houston St., at Thompson St., ✆ 677 3820; *Pizzeria (AM, D, MC)*. (19) Popular and loud, with a jazz band after 8pm, and crusty coal-oven-baked pizzas (between $10 and $16 a go)—rivalling John's Pizzeria in Greenwich Village.

Lupe's East LA Kitchen, 110 6th Ave., between Wells and Broome Sts., ✆ 966 1326; (20) *Mexican (no credit cards)*. The best kind of neighbourhood storefront, with basic decor and scrumptious tortillas. Cheap as well, around $7 an entrée.

Broome Street Bar and Restaurant, 363 West Broadway, near Broome St., ✆ 925 2086; (21) *American (AE, D, MC, V)*. Noisy, hectic, cheap SoHo stalwart; burgers, chilli dogs and beer in saloon-style bar.

Cafés

Dean & Deluca, 121 Prince St., at Broadway; or 560 Broadway, between Prince and Spring Sts. Manhattan's handsomest food shop, more a gallery of food than an emporium. The smaller branch on Prince Street has a sit-down café. (A)

News Bar, 366 West Broadway, near Broome St. Espresso shop, selling pastries and sandwiches, with stools on castors and 400 newspapers and magazines to read. (B)

Cyber Café, 273 Lafayette St., at Prince St. The shape of things to come: breakfast, lunch and supper to keep customers going in front of the screens. (C)

Café Gitane, 242 Mott St., between Houston and Prince Sts. Light bistro: cous-cous, smoked salmon and good French coffee. (D)

Lower East Side and East Village   *map C*

moderate

Jules, 65 St Mark's Place, between 1st and 2nd Aves., ✆ 477 5560; *French (DIS)*. Jolly (1) East Village bistro attempt: smoky and noisy with jazz and loud East Village professional types: pricey food including beef carpaccio with shaved parmesan, mussels, hot and sour shrimps and crème caramel.

Café Tabac, 232 East 9th St., between 2nd and 3rd Aves., ✆ 674 7972, ✆ 388 9703; (2) *American (AE, MC, V; reservations suggested; women only on Sun)*. Packed out and catering to 'models, writers, big names, artists'. With a bar, DJ, pinball machine and upstairs pool room (the latter for an élite only). Bistro food.

Casanis, 54 East 1st St., between 1st and 2nd Sts., ✆ 777 1589; *French (AE)*. Tiny and (3) attractive, with basic (but not cheap) bistro food: moules, snails and duck, etc.

Sammy's Famous Roumanian Jewish Steakhouse, 157 Chrystie St., near Delancey St., (4) ✆ 673 0330; *Continental/Roumanian-Jewish (AE, V, D, MC; reservations suggested, supper only)*. Sublimely non-kosher Roumanian-Jewish, *not* for the easily intimidated. Massive portions—potato pancakes, beef sausages, sliced brains, vodka frozen in a block of ice, chopped liver and make-your-own egg creams. The menu comes with a dictionary, to be avoided if the concept of 'herb stuffing in an intestinal casing' (kishka) or 'chicken skin fried in rendered chicken fat' disturbs.

Lucky Cheng's, 24 1st Avenue, between 1st and 2nd Sts., ℂ 473 0516, ✆ 473 0481; (5) *Asian* (*MC, V, AE, D, DIS*). The theme is drag: drag queens for waitresses, drag make-overs on weekends, a drag if you don't like that sort of thing.

Roettelle A.G., 126 East 7th St., between 1st Ave., and Ave. A, ℂ 674 4140; (6) *German/Swiss/Italian/French* (*AE, D, MC, V; reservations suggested*). Foods from the Common Market in tiny 4-roomed eatery, with a garden in the back big enough for one table and lit with fairy lights. If you don't reserve, someone will get there before: *rösti*, sauerkraut, polenta and *linzer torte*.

O.G., 507 East 6th St., between Aves. A and B, ℂ 477 4649; *Asian* (*V, MC; supper only*). (7) Imaginative fusion of Chinese, Japanese, Indonesian and Thai cuisines: good prices, high noise level.

Miracle Grill, 112 1st Ave., between 6th and 7th Sts., ℂ 254 2353; *Texan-Mexican* (*MC*, (8) *AE, V*). Small, tasty, pricy Tex-Mex, with a garden with peach trees. Spicy fajitas, Yucatan chicken and delicious vanilla-bean flan for pudding.

Circa, 103 2nd Ave., at 6th St., ℂ 777 4120, ✆ 677 0405; *Mediterranean* (*MC, V, D*, (9) *AE*). Desperately trendy, thanks mainly to the interior, a lounge with gold-painted walls and plushly upholstered booths: pizzas, risottos, steaks, frites.

NoHo Star, 330 Lafayette St., near Bleecker St., ℂ 925 0070; *Chinese/American* (*AE*, (10) *MC, V, D*). Laidback Chinese/American fusion which means complicated chicken, crabcakes and salads: popular and busy, especially at brunchtime.

La Paella, 214 East 9th St., between 2nd and 3rd Aves., ℂ 598 4321 (*MC,V; open till* (11) *midnight weekdays, 1am weekends*). Small, happy, noisy, smoky: good tapas and five kinds of paella (voted best in Manhattan) including one with squid ink. Portions are big and orders works out cheaper the more people per party.

Time Café, 380 Lafayette St., at Great Jones, ℂ 533 7000; *organic* (*AE, MC, V; reserva-* (12) *tions suggested*). Mortality-conscious people eating food that's nutritious as well as delicious in an airy dining room. Runs a jazz club in the evenings.

Acme Bar & Grill, 9 Great Jones St., between Broadway and Lafayette, ℂ 420 1934; (13) *Cajun* (*MC, V, D, DIS*). Cajun, with endorphin-releasing hot sauces.

inexpensive

Dok Suni's, 119 1st Ave., at 7th St., ℂ 477 9506; *Korean* (*cash only, open 4pm–11pm*). (14) Fashionable Korean cooking in trendified East Village joint.

Veselka, 144 2nd Ave., and 9th St., ℂ 228 9682; *Polish-Ukrainian* (*no credit cards*). A (15) big mural outside the East European diner and news-stand says 'We serve soup to nuts' but eaters inside are well-behaved East Villagers. Authentic soups: red Ukrainian borscht and also blintzes, kielbasa, *pirogis* (Polish dumplings), buck-wheat pancakes and 'mother's milk' vanilla shakes.

El Sombrero, 108 Stanton St., between Ludlow and Houston Sts., ℂ 254 4188; *Mexican* (16) (*no credit cards*). Nicknamed 'The Hat', it looks a bit shabby, which to many an East Villager is the ultimate in chic. Potent frozen margheritas.

Ludlow Street Café, 165 Ludlow St., between Stanton and East Houston Sts., ℂ 353 (17) 0536; *Cajun* (*no credit cards, supper only, brunch on Sunday*). Good for brunch, with a bar, live music, East Village sophisticates and cajun food.

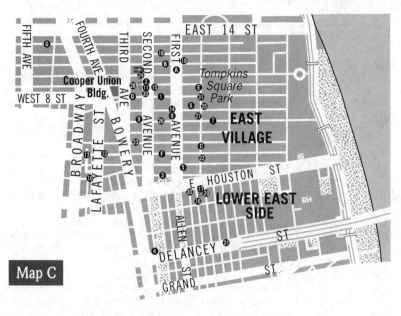

Map C

Restaurants

1 Jules
2 Café Tabac
3 Casanis
4 Sammy's Famous Roumanian Jewish Steakhouse
5 Lucky Cheng's
6 Roettelle A.G.
7 O.G.
8 Miracle Grill
9 Circa
10 NoHo Star
11 La Paella
12 Time Café
13 Acme Bar & Grill
14 Dok Suni's
15 Veselka

16 El Sombrero
17 Ludlow Street Café
18 Angelica Kitchen
19 KK's
20 Katz's Delicatessen
21 Ratner's
22 Two Boots
23 Cucina di Pesce
24 2nd Avenue Deli
25 Odessa
26 6th Street Little India
27 Leshko Coffee Shop
28 Cloisters Café
29 Pink Pony Café
30 Tsampa
31 Stingy Lulu's

Cafés

A Di Roberti's Pastry SHop
B Veniero's
C Limbo
D @Café
E alt.coffee
F The Internet Café
G Cyberfelds

Angelica Kitchen, 300 East 12th St., between 1st and 2nd Aves., ✆ 228 2929; *vegan-vegetarian-macrobiotic etc.* (*no credit cards*). Radically self-accepting clientele and macrobiotic menus based on equinox and solstice. A tasty alternative to laxatives, this is one of the best vegetarians in Manhattan.

KK's ($), 192–4 1st Ave., between 11th and 12th Sts., ✆ 777 4433; *Polish 'Cooking like Mama Made it'* (*no credit cards*). A family business, KK's has the pleasantest garden in New York, a deck lit by fairy lights, shaded by honey locust trees and in August festooned with spinning caterpillars. Very cheap, laid-back and best for brunch on a hot sunny day: borscht, challah French toast, cheese blintzes, excellent grilled swordfish or stuffed breast of veal.

Katz's Delicatessen, 205 East Houston St., near Orchard St., ✆ 254 2246 (*cash only*).
(20) Filmic Lower East Side cafeteria: pastrami and corned beef piled high with a pickle and Dr Brown's celery soda—not worth having an orgasm over, perhaps, but atmospheric (*see* **Walk III**, p.147).

Ratner's, 138 Delancey St., between Norfolk and Suffolk Sts., ✆ 677 5588; *Jewish* (*no*
(21) *credit cards*). Nice for brunch on a Sunday: poppyseed rolls, potato pancakes, lox and eggs and matzo brei. Interior plus quintessential waitresses cover an eclectic range of styles from 1930s to the 70s.

Two Boots, 37 Ave. A, between 2nd and 3rd Sts., ✆ 505 5450; *Cajun/Italian* (*DIS*).
(22) Cuisine chain based on the premise that Louisiana and Italy have the same geographical shapes. Apparently the mixture isn't an oddity in New Orleans, and at the friendly and unpretentious Two Boots the violently spiced combination (including creole popcorn) is surprisingly good.

Cucina di Pesce, 87 East 4th St., between 2nd and 3rd Aves., ✆ 260 6800; *Italian*
(23) *seafood* (*no credit cards*). Good value but crowded; you'll have to wait patiently or try **Frutti di Mare** the annexe opposite at 84 East 4th St. Baked clams, trout, tuna, salmon, first-class pasta, free mussels at the bar.

2nd Avenue Deli, 156 2nd Ave., at East 10th St., ✆ 677 0606; *Jewish* (*AE*). Classic deli
(24) with queues on weekends: *kasha*, knishes, chopped liver, boiled beef flank, strudel, and *kugel*, (noodle pudding). Superior to Katz's (*see* above).

Odessa, 117 Ave. A, between 7th and 8th Sts., ✆ 473 8916; *Ukrainian* (*no credit cards*).
(25) The biggest meal in New York and one of the cheapest: blintzes and pastries, patronized by ancient chess-playing Ukrainians and recent East Villagers.

6th Street Little India ($), 6th St. between 1st and 2nd Aves. About thirty mostly Bengali
(26) restaurants on one block, serving Indian food at staggeringly good prices (lunches from $5). **Panna**, **Windows on India** and **Sonali** are three of the best. Bring your own beer, unless going to one of the more upmarket establishments with a licence, like **Mitali** or **Haveli**.

Leshko Coffee Shop, 111 Ave. A, and 6th St., ✆ 473 9208; *Eastern European* (*no credit*
(27) *cards*). Good for watching the to-ing and fro-ing on Tompkins Square. Fried egg sandwiches (the cheapest in Manhattan) and open 24 hours.

Cloisters Café, 238 East 9th St., between 2nd and 3rd Aves., ✆ 777 9128; *American* (*no*
(28) *credit cards*). Pleasant cobble-stoned garden and fish pond, and a vulgar stained-glass interior; good for brunch or tea.

cheap

Pink Pony Café, 176 Ludlow St., between Houston and Stanton Sts., ✆ 529 3959; *health*
(29) *food* (*cash only; open until 4am weekends*). Holier-than-wow late night café, with faux-naif new-age décor, health drinks, snacks, and poetry magazines.

Tsampa, 212 East 9th St., between 2nd and 3rd Aves., ✆ 614 3226; *Tibetan* (*no credit*
(30) *cards*). Blindingly cheap Tibetan bistro serving superior potato curry.

Stingy Lulu's, 129 St Mark's Place, at Ave. A, ✆ 995 5191; *American* (*no credit cards,*
(31) *open until 6am*). Friendly ersatz fifties diner, with kitsch decor, and serving basic American food: burgers, meatloaf, chops, chicken and flapjacks.

Cafés

Di Roberti's Pastry Shop, 176 1st Ave., between 10th and 11th Sts. Delightful, family-run Italian pâtisserie with Art Nouveau tiled interior.　**(A)**

Veniero's, 342 East 11th St., between 1st and 2nd Aves. Bigger and brassier than its rival Di Roberti's, but the same range of delicious Italian pâtisserie.　**(B)**

Limbo, 47 Ave. A, between 3rd and 4th Sts. Snacks, sandwiches and cappuccinos in pudding basins: a nice atmosphere with coolly oblivious waiters.　**(C)**

Cybercafés

@Café, 12 St Mark's Place, near 3rd Ave., at *www.fly.net*. Work at the web on 18 terminals for $5/hour. Some computers have video links with other cybercafés; there's a bar and food, a limited but worldwide range of spring rolls, Irish stew and German sausage.　**(D)**

alt.coffee, 139 Ave. A, between St Mark's Place and 9th St, *www.flotsam.com*. Six computers at $10/hour.　**(E)**

The Internet Café, 82 East 3rd St., between 1st and 2nd Aves., at *www.bigmagic.com*. More terrible terminals.　**(F)**

Cyberfelds, 20 East 13th St., between 5th Ave and University Place, ✆ 647 8830 (*open daily, noon–midnight*).　**(G)**

Chinatown, Little Italy and the Civic Center　　*map A*

moderate

Mandarin Court, 61 Mott St., between Bayard and Canal Sts., ✆ 608 3838; *Hong Kong* **(14)** (*no credit cards, dim sum 8am–3pm*). Small, calm, sleekly done-up and catering to an elegant Hong Kong/American crowd: dim sum carts until 3pm, some of the best in Chinatown, and fine Hong Kong-Cantonese main courses.

Golden Unicorn, 2nd Floor, 18 East Broadway, at Catherine St., ✆ 941 0911; *Cantonese* **(15)** (*AE, MC, V*). Lavish, popular and chaotic, this caters to 400 diners on two floors: freshly cooked dim sum, best for a large group.

20 Mott Street, 20 Mott St., between Park Row and Pell St., ✆ 964 0380, 🖷 571 7697; **(16)** *Cantonese (MC, V, AE, DIS)*. Perfect for Sunday brunch: the best dim sum in Chinatown, trundled round between 8am and 3pm. Seafood good as well; specialities include braised shark's fin and conch baked in its shell.

cheap

Wong Kee, 113 Mott St., near Hester St., ✆ 966 1160; *Chinese (no credit cards; reserva-* **(17)** *tions requested*). One of the best in Chinatown: service at breakneck speed, fresh noodles, duck and pork; all cheaper than eating at home.

Sweet 'n' Tart Café, 76 Mott St., between Canal and Bayard Sts., ✆ 334 8088; *Chinese* **(18)** (*cash only; no alcohol; open 8am–midnight*). Specialising in '*tong shui*' ('sweet soup') dishes—health foods which balance yin and yang to cure a panoply of ailments. Ingredients include lotus seeds, gelatin and ginkgo nuts, good for you but also delicious.

Nom Wah Tea Parlor, 13 Doyers St., ✆ 962 8650 (*no credit cards; open daily 9am–8pm*). Dim sum made on the premises, steamed buns, Chinese pastries and chrysanthemum tea in Chinatown's oldest tea house/café. Busy and grotty.
⑲

New Vietnam, 11–13 Doyers St., near Chatham Square, ✆ 893 0725 (*no credit cards*). Dubbed the nouvelle cuisine of Asia, Vietnamese food is remarkably light and delicate. This is one of the oldest Vietnamese restaurants in town: spartan inside, with a comprehensive menu, including Vietnamese spring rolls or *cha gio*, wrapped in rice paper, filled with fish or pork with lemongrass and noodles and dipped in a tasty anchovy sauce called *nuoc mam.*
⑳

West Village   *map B*

expensive

Gotham Bar and Grill ($), 12 East 12th St., near 5th Ave., ✆ 620 4020; *Northern Italian* (*AE, D, MC, V; reservations requested*). Patronized by an elegant Manhattan élite but offering even more elegant food: quail salad with *shiitake* mushrooms, butternut squash risotto, rabbit ravioli, skate wings, warm chocolate cake. The Gotham also offers one of the best deals in Manhattan—a bargain set lunch for $19.97. Come when you're fed up with burgers.
㉒

moderate

Le Zoo, 314 West 11th St., at Greenwich Ave., ✆ 620 0393; *French* (*MC, V, AE; supper only; closed Mon*). Magnificent French cooking, but so small and fashionable it's hard to get a table—roast monkfish with lime sauce, sweetbreads in a salad.
㉓

Les Deux Gamins, 170 Waverly Place, at Grove St., ✆ 807 7047, 🖷 627 9087; *French bistro* (*AE; breakfast, lunch and dinner; open from 7am*). Chi chi bistro food, appealing to model types and their oglers, and best for continental breakfast or bacon and eggs with a mound of tedious frisée.
㉔

The Hog Pit, 22 9th Avenue, at 13th St., ✆ 604 0092; *Southern* (*AE, MC, D*). Barbecued meat and steak for rich tonkies.
㉕

Home, 20 Cornelia St., between Bleecker and West 4th Sts., ✆ 243 9579; *American nostalgic* (*AE; breakfast, lunch and supper*). This is small and attractive, and excellent for breakfast or brunch—delicious American home-cooking: pork chops crusted with cumin, sausages and apple crumb pie for pudding. Try to get a seat in the tiny back garden, and don't tell anyone the farmhouse-kitchen style restaurant is charmingly homely, as 'homely' in America means 'ugly'.
㉖

Florent, 69 Gansevoort St., between Greenwich and Washington Sts., ✆ 989 5779; *French bistro* (*no credit cards; reservations suggested; open 24 hours*). Tarted-up diner—fashionable because situated in the glamorously squalid 'meat-packing district' (think existentialism/Francis Bacon), and functioning as a breakfast station for exhausted club-goers in the small hours. The food is stuff like black pudding, steak, frites, and French toast. In the summer the whole place is just too cool for its own good with air-conditioning that's chillier than a refrigerated lorry.
㉗

Rio Mar, 1 9th Ave., near Little West 12th St., ✆ 243 9015; *Spanish* (*AE*). Spanish joint on two floors, with sodden customers, flamenco music and *paella*, octopus and custard flan for pudding, all washed down with a jug of Sangria.
㉘

Bar Six, 502 6th Avenue, between 12th and 13th Sts., ✆ 645 2439, 📠 691 1392;
(29) *French-Morrocan (MC, V, AE)*. Elegant brasserie and a magnet for anyone with a passion for merguez (spicy Moroccan sausages). Traditional Moroccan cooking plus French bouillabaisse, etc.

Mitali West, 296 Bleecker St., between Barrow and Grove Sts., ✆ 989 1367; *Indian (AE,*
(30) *V, MC)*. Reliable Northern Indian cooking.

Tortilla Flats, 767 Washington St., near West 12th St., ✆ 243 1053, 📠 627 1251;
(31) *Tex/Mex (AE)*. Cheap and unremittingly 'fun', with bingo on Mon and Tues, Vegas night on Wednesday and a Happy 'Hour' 1am–4am. Tex-Mex cuisine from natural ingredients, including tofu *enchiladas*, quesadillas, in large portions.

Jane Street Seafood Café, 31 8th Ave., at Jane St., ✆ 242 0003; *Seafood (AE, MC, D, V,*
(32) *DIS; reservations suggested)*. Staunchly unpretentious New England seafood, on the pricey side. Best for sole—grilled and fried, also clam and lobster.

inexpensive

Moustache, 90 Bedford Street, between Grove and Barrow Sts., ✆ 229 2200; *Middle*
(33) *Eastern (cash only)*. Small café serving 'Foul'—a blend of fava beans, parsley and garlic in pita bread—plus other cheap Middle Eastern fare: spicy merguez sandwiches, 'pitza', and 'loomi', a kind of iced citrus tea.

Tanti Baci Caffè ($), 163 West 10th St., at 7th Ave., ✆ 647 9651; *Italian (MC, V, AE; no*
(34) *alcohol licence)*. The nicest Italian restaurant in the Village. Perfectly cooked pasta, gnocchi and salad, in basement smoking restaurant. Bring your own bottle.

The Pink Teacup, 42 Grove St., between Bleecker and Bedford Sts., ✆ 807 6755;
(35) *Southern Soul Food (cash only; no alcohol licence)*. Much-loved minuscule Village institution serving memorable sausage patties, macaroni cheese, smothered pork chops, salmon croquettes, sweet potato pie, cornbread and pig's feet.

Cucina Stagionale, 275 Bleecker St., between 6th and 7th Aves., ✆ 924 2707; *Italian (no*
(36) *credit cards; bring your own wine)*. Italian cooking 'like Mama made it' and sometimes just as erratic: imaginative range of pastas, fish dishes and pastas, all decently priced. Be prepared for queues, or come for lunch.

John's Pizzeria, 278 Bleecker St., between 6th and 7th Aves., ✆ 243 1680 *(no credit*
(37) *cards)*. Queues for Manhattan's most famous pizzas, cooked in a coal oven in more varieties than Heinz. The owner, Pete Castelotti, flaunts a pizza medallion encrusted with sapphires and devoted fans include Joe Pesci, Danny De Vito and Woody Allen (who asked him to act in three of his films).

Ray's Pizza, 456 6th Ave., at 11th St., ✆ 243 2253 *(no credit cards)*. Pizza slices swim-
(38) ming in oil, delicious and *very* cheap.

Caribe, 117 Perry St., at Greenwich St., ✆ 255 9191; *Caribbean (MC, V)*. Powerful cock-
(39) tails in tropical rain-forest setting, rowdy but good-natured patrons, cheap prices and good Caribbean food—conch salad, frogs' legs, jerk chicken.

White Horse Tavern, 567 Hudson St., at 11th St., ✆ 989 3956; *Saloon (no credit*
(40) *cards)*. Hard-boiled eggs, cheeseburgers, fries, watery beer, honouring Dylan Thomas who famously drank himself to death here.

Cubby Hole, 281 West 12th St., at West 4th St; ✆ 243 9041; *Lesbian cuisine*. All very
(41) Bloomsbury.

Tea & Sympathy, 108 Greenwich Ave., between 12th and 13th Sts., ✆ 807 8329; *British*
42 (*cash only*). Themed cockney tea rooms: roast beef, scotch eggs, shepherd's pie, apple crumble: all of it mysteriously appealing to somebody.

cheap

Benny's Burritos, 113 Greenwich Ave., at Jane St., ✆ 727 0584, 🖨 242 3163; *Cal-Mex*
43 (*no credit cards; late night meals Mon–Sun and brunch weekends*). Cheap, popular and crowded—burritos, enchiladas and tortillas in store-front dining room.

Patisserie Lanciani, 271 West 4th St., between Perry and West 11th Sts., ✆ 979 0739
44 (*AE*). Pastries, brioches and tarts; cappuccino, espresso and homemade lemonade.

Tea Rooms

Anglers & Writers, 420 Hudson St, at St Luke's Place. This is quite strange: coffee and/or afternoon tea (*from 4pm–7pm*) in a book-filled tea room specializing in thirties fiction and fly-fishing guides. Stews, pies, puddings, English tea.   **E**

Taylor's, 523 Hudson St., between West 10th and Charles Sts. Quaint tea rooms: monkey bread, zebra bread, muffins for muggins.   **F**

Thé Adoré, 17 East 13th St., between 5th Ave. and University Place (*closed Sat and Sun in the summer*). Tea rooms with pastries downstairs, sandwiches and soups upstairs.   **G**

Union Square, Gramercy Park & Flatiron District   *map D*

luxury

Gramercy Tavern ($), 42 East 20th St., between Park Avenue South and Broadway,
1 ✆ 477 0777; *American* (*MC, V, D, AE; reservations required*). Run by Danny Meyer (responsible for the Union Square Café, *see* below) for the chattering classes: bustling, jolly, impossible to get into, and well on the road to permanent respectability. The excellent bar menu (*available noon–11pm*) does *not* require reservations and is drastically cheaper. At the full price sit-down supper, you're guaranteed fine wines, classy service and a chance to try such exotica as roast rabbit, sea urchin ragoût, butterflied quail with polenta or chicken with truffles.

expensive

Union Square Café ($), 21 East 16th St., near Broadway, ✆ 243 4020; *Northern*
2 *Californian* (*AE, D, MC, V; reservations required*). Still a Manhattan favourite: elegant, civilized, with an innovative menu and laidback atmosphere. Food at the bar is cheaper and you won't need reservations. Supper includes: brown rice pancakes covered with caviar and sour cream, baked lobster, and exceptional ice-creams and tarts. For when you want to feel proud of the US of A.

An American Place, 2 Park Ave., at 32nd St., ✆ 684 2122; *American* (*AE, D, MC, V;*
3 *reservations suggested*). New American cooking at a pinnacle of sophistication in informal dining room: warm oysters in buttered sauce, New Orleans blackened fish, roast boneless quails, and the rude-sounding Banana Betty for pudding.

Mesa Grill, 102 5th Ave., between 15th and 16th Sts., ✆ 807 7400, 🖨 989 0034; *south-*
4 *western* (*AE, V, MC; reservations suggested*). Hot in both senses, with a

fashionable crowd and the best SW cooking in Manhattan: red snapper in a blue tortilla, steaks and roasted seafood.

Follonico ($), 6 West 24th St., at 5th Ave., ✆ 691 6359; *Italian* (*MC, V, D, AE; reservations suggested*). Clean Italian trattoria cooking: excellent pasta and squid, expensive at supper and a bargain at lunch.
5

Bolo, 23 East 22nd St., near 5th Avenue, ✆ 228 2200; *Spanish* (*AE, MC, V; reservations suggested*). Run by the Mesa Grill chef (*see* above): 'absolutely fabulous' nouveau Spanish dishes—pine nuts, black and gold rice, hard-to-get reservations.
6

Periyali, 35 West 20th St., between 5th and 6th Aves., ✆ 463 7890; *Greek* (*MC, V, D, AE*). 'Sophisticated Greek cuisine', the ultimate cooking oxymoron—octopus marinated in red wine, filo and baklava in elegant dining room with friendly staff.
7

moderate

The Coffee Shop, 29 Union Square West, at 16th St., ✆ 243 7969; *Brazilian* (*MC, V, D, AE; breakfast, lunch and dinner*). Trendy Brazilian diner, good paella, excellent sandwiches, sugar cane juice drinks and *feijoada* on Saturdays.
8

Café Beulah, 39 East 19th St., between Broadway and Park Avenue, ✆ 777 9700; *Creole* (*MC, V, D, AE; supper only*). Elegant Southern and Creole cuisine: crab cakes, gumbo and food that's good for the soul.
9

inexpensive

Yama, 122 East 17th St., between Lexington and 3rd Aves., ✆ 475 0969; *sushi* (*MC, AE, V*). Superior basement sushi bar: excellent value, ultra-fresh, crowded to capacity at lunchtimes: top quality yellowtail, flying fish roe and seaweed hijiki.
10

Edo, 9 East 17th Street, off Union Square, ✆ 989 2938; *Japanese* (*MC, V, D, AE*). Lunch from $7 in stylish Japanese sushi bar: *sukiyaki, negimaki futomaki.*
11

Zen Palate, 34 Union Square, at East 16th St., and various locations in Manhattan, ✆ 614 9291, 🖷 614 9401; *New Age Asian vegetarian* (*MC, V, D, AE; bring your own alcohol; reservations suggested*). Excellent, fast, cheap, Asian vegetarian diner, part of a chain and featuring healthy clientele and tofu tasting better than meat: Japanese/Chinese/Thai noodles, pasta and vegetables, lots of soup, home-made soy pasta, also spookily convincing soy imitations of sausage, salami and pâté.
12

Old Town Bar, 45 East 18th St., between Broadway and Park Avenue South, ✆ 529 6732; *Saloon* (*MC, V, AE*). 1890s saloon with avuncular regulars who enjoy their lunchtime beers. Good bar food with perfect hot dogs, burgers and fries.
13

Picnic, 52 Irving Place, near East 14th Street; *gourmet take-out* (*MC, AE, V*). The tastiest home-made take-away food in Manhattan, in an elegant space designed by architect Chris Bundy, and including ring-dings: chocolate cake rolled up with butter cream and dipped in chocolate, based on the mass-produced kiddies' cakes which were popular in the 60s and 70s, but homemade and better.
14

cheap

Curry in a Hurry, 130 East 29th St., at Lexington Ave., ✆ 889 1159, 🖷 685 6385; *Indian* (*MC, V, D, DIS*). The nicest-named restaurant in Manhattan—if you have time to savour it, good quality.
15

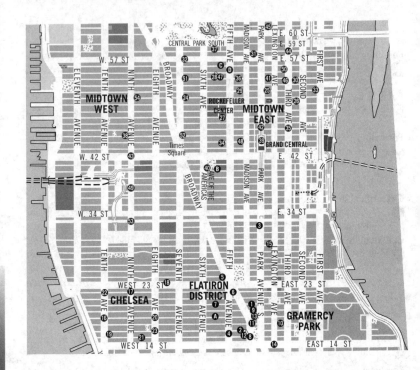

Restaurants

1 Gramercy Tavern
2 Union Square Café
3 An American Place
4 Mesa Grill
5 Follonico
6 Bolo
7 Periyali
8 The Coffee Shop
9 Café Beulah
10 Yama
11 Edo
12 Zen Palate
13 Old Town Bar
14 Picnic
15 Curry in a Hurry
16 La Luncheonette
17 Luma
18 Blu
19 Frank's Restaurant
20 Eighteenth & Eighth
21 El Cid
22 Empire Diner

23 Mary Ann's
24 Le Bernadin
25 The Four Seasons
26 Lutèce
27 The Rainbow Room
28 La Caravelle
29 La Grenouille
30 Vong
31 57/57
32 Russian Tea Room
33 Le Périgord
34 44
35 Sparks Steak House
36 Bice
37 Nirvana on Rooftop
38 Jezebel
39 Grand Central Oyster Bar
40 Bryant Park Grill & Café
41 Brasserie
42 Hatsuhana
43 Chez Josephine
44 Dawat

45 Mme Romaine de Lyon
46 Lipstick Café
47 Lyn's Café
48 Mezze
49 Manganaro's Hero-Boy
50 P.J. Clarke's
51 Carnegie Delicatessen & Restaurant
52 Cabana Carioca
53 Cheyenne Diner
54 Afghan Kebab House

Cafés

A Book-Friends' Café
B Focaccia Fiorentina
C Felissimo
D Takashimaya Tea Box

Map D

Cafés

Book-Friends Café, 16 West 18th St, between 5th and 6th Aves. Tea in book-lined salon for Manhattan *bas bleus*. **Ⓐ**

Chelsea *map D*

moderate

La Luncheonette, 130 10th Ave., at 18th St., ℭ 675 0342; *French (MC, V)*. Small bistro, **⑯** with partly visible kitchen, serving unbelievably delicious French 'home-cooking': veal sweetbreads vinaigrette, pan-fried trout with lemongrass and wild mushroom, swordfish, lobster gratinée.

Luma, 200 9th Ave., between 22nd and 23rd Sts., ℭ 633 8033; *organic American (MC, V, AE, D; supper only; reservations suggested)*. Preservative-free, organic cooking **⑰** with Thai twist, in minimalist surroundings. Fashionable and healthy.

Blu, 254 West 23rd St., between 7th and 8th Aves., ℭ 989 6300; *eclectic American (MC, V, D, AE, DIS)*. Bustling with happy eaters, and best for supper in the garden or **⑱** brunch (with jazz band) on Sunday. Exotic 'eclectic' menu.

Frank's Restaurant, 85 10th Ave., between 15th and 16th Sts., ℭ 243 1349; *Italian-American steakhouse (AE, V, D, MC, DIS; reservations recommended; closed* **⑲** *Sun)*. Legendary steakhouse in the meat district: *filet mignon*, shell steak, also sweetbreads, tripe and pasta, key-lime tart, pecan pies and cheesecake.

Eighteenth & Eighth, 159 8th Ave., at 18th St., ℭ 242 5000; *American (AE, D, V)*. **⑳** Small, quirkily decorated corner café serving excellent Middle American family cooking: roast lamb, chicken and pork, meatloaf, etc.

inexpensive

El Cid, 322 West 15th St., between 8th and 9th Aves., ℭ 929 9332; *Spanish (D, AE)*. **㉑** Down-to-earth Castilian tapas bar, small and cheery with good Sangria.

Empire Diner, 210 10th Ave., at West 22nd St., ℭ 243 2736; *(AE, MC, V, DIS, D; open* **㉒** *24 hours)*. Shrine to the classic 1930s diner, gleaming with stainless steel and a piano—omelettes, sandwiches, brownies and burgers, pricey but good at 4 am.

Mary Ann's, 116 8th Ave., at 16th St., ℭ 633 0877; *Mexican (no credit cards)*. Cheap, **㉓** reliable Mexican mini-chain; crowded in the evenings, very satisfactory for lunch.

Midtown *map D*

luxury

Le Bernadin ($), 155 West 51st St., between 6th and 7th Aves., ℭ 489 1515; *French* **㉔** *seafood (AE, D, MC, V; reservations requested)*. The best fish restaurant in Manhattan and, for many Manhattanites, the best restaurant, period. Understated fancy seafood: baked sea urchins in butter, black bass, yellow-tail snapper, halibut in warmed vinaigrette, oysters, Little Neck clams. Splendid puddings, including chestnut soufflé and mille-feuille of green apples and raisins. The 'bargain' *prix fixe* lunch is $42 and if you like seafood worth the expense.

The Four Seasons, 99 East 52nd St., between Park and Lexington Aves., ✆ 688 6525; (25) *American (AE, D, MC, V; reservations requested)*. Definitive Manhattan eatery, designed in the 1970s by Philip Johnson, and including a mural by Picasso. A $42 *prix fixe* three-course supper in the Grill is good value. In the Pool Room there's staples like calves' liver and tuna, and a still hallowed pudding trolley.

Lutèce, 249 East 50th St., near 2nd Ave., ✆ 752 2225; *French (AE, D; reservations are* (26) *requested)*. The 'institution that never changes' has a new chef and owner and is currently going through a wobbly phase. Although some say it's getting ever more under-whelming, the restaurant still has its champions. Whatever, you'll find an elegant brownstone and a wide variety of Alsatian delicacies: foie gras en brioche, snails *à l'alsacienne*, sole, soufflé, salmon and bass *en croûte*. Cheaper at lunchtime; with a *prix fixe* supper at around $60.

The Rainbow Room, 30 Rockefeller Plaza, near 5th Ave. and 48th St., ✆ 632 5100; (27) *American (AE, D, MC, V; reservations requested)*. Manhattan's most loveable and camp restaurant, 65 floors up in Rockefeller Center. The flamboyant Art Moderne dining room includes a revolving dance floor, 10-piece band, and breathtaking views. The food—lobster thermidor, glazed salmon, quail and foie gras terrine, roast guinea-fowl, and caviar samplers—is over the top and unmemorable, but what you eat is secondary. If you haven't money to burn the adjoining Rainbow Promenade cocktail room has equally good views, amusing waiters and much cheaper food including burgers and sandwiches (*see* p.105).

La Caravelle, 33 West 55th St., between 5th and 6th Aves., ✆ 586 4252; *French with a* (28) *Japanese edge (AE, D, MC, V; reservations requested)*. Decades ago number one in Manhattan, and now with a Japanese chef it has managed a comeback: ultra-elegant service and a menu including pike quenelles, scallops and fluke.

La Grenouille, 3 East 52nd St., between 5th and Madison Aves., ✆ 752 1495; *French* (29) *(AE, D, MC, V; reservations requested)*. Gallic opulence teetering on snobbish-ness in one of the handsomest interiors in Manhattan: frogs' legs, quails, ducklings, sweetbreads amidst banquettes of flowers.

expensive

Vong, 200 East 54th St., between 2nd and 3rd Aves., ✆ 486 9592, ✉ 980 3735. (30) *Thai/French (MC, V, D, AE; reservations requested)*. A favourite with trendy Manhattanites: flash, high-decibel, and created by 'superchef' Jean-Georges Vongerichten. Innovative Thai/French food in elegant dining room with garden. Appetizers such as sautéed foie gras with ginger and mango or raw tuna in rice paper. For entrées rabbit curry, black bass with stir-fried cabbage, water chestnuts and chillis, cod with curried artichoke, beef in ginger broth, and so on.

57/57, 57 East 57th St., between Madison and Park Aves., ✆ 758 5757; *new American* (31) *(MC, D, V, AE; reservations suggested)*. Ferociously smart dining room in the Four Seasons Hotel, with grandiose interior by I. M. Pei and expensive 'New American' health cuisine, cooked by a female chef, elegantly presented and so deli-cate that it makes little impact on palates damaged by years of indulgence.

Russian Tea Room, 150 West 57th St., near 7th Ave., ✆ 265 0947; *contemporary* (32) *Russian (AE, D, MC, V; reservations requested)*. Under new ownership and completely renovated, the celebs' restaurant supposedly has a more 'contempo-rary' Russian menu. Vodka, blinis, caviar etc.

Le Périgord, 405 East 52nd St., near 1st Ave., ✆ 755 6244; *French* (*AE, D, MC, V; reservations requested*). Old-fashioned and charmingly French: cold and hot hors-d'œuvres and for entrées sturgeon with beurre blanc, pigeon with shallots and garlic confits, veal bourguignon.

(33)

44, Royalton Hotel, 44 West 44th St, at 5th Ave., ✆ 944 8844; *American* (*MC, V, AE, D*). Popular with the journalists and overpriced, but good for simple food like sandwiches and snacks in amusing post-modern hotel lobby (*see* p.102).

(34)

Sparks Steak House, 210 East 46th St., near 3rd Ave., ✆ 687 4855 (*AE, D, MC, V; reservations requested*). The place where mafia mobster Paul Castellano was rubbed out: fine cuts, extra-thick veal chops, seafood and steaks cooked to order; expensive, big portions.

(35)

Bice, 7 East 54th St., between 5th and Madison Aves., ✆ 684 0215; *Northern Italian* (*AE, D, MC, V*). This has a nice atmosphere: it's elegant and enduringly popular with a straightforward Northern Italian menu: pasta made on the premises, risotto, sautéed calves' liver, chicken with herb butter. All satisfyingly predictable.

(36)

Nirvana on Rooftop, 30 Central Park South, between 5th and 6th Aves., ✆ 486 5700; *Indian* (*AE, D, MC, V; reservations suggested*). Unfashionable because touristy. Panoramic views of Manhattan and unimaginative Indian cooking.

(37)

moderate

Jezebel, 630 9th Ave., at West 45th St., ✆ 582 1045; *Southern and soul food* (*AE; reservations suggested*). This is entertaining, decadently decorated Louisiana-style with jolly waitresses, and excellent soul food: deep-fried porgies (a kind of fish), salmon with black-eyed peas and macaroni, spare ribs, grits, fried chicken, the best corn bread in Manhattan, sweet-potato pie for pudding.

(38)

Grand Central Oyster Bar and Restaurant ($), Grand Central Terminal, ✆ 490 6650; *Fish* (*AE, D, MC, V; open to 9.30pm weekdays, closed weekends; reservations only necessary for the main dining room*). One of Manhattan's wondrous establishments: in the bowels of Grand Central Station serving 20 varieties of oysters, one at a time or by the dozen. Service is brisk but jolly, fish pricey and sometimes overcooked; fortunately the atmosphere makes up for everything. Best and less touristy for lunch, with a counter bar to the right as you walk in which is seriously cheap (*see* **Walk I**, p.111).

(39)

Bryant Park Grill & Café, 25 West 40th St., between 5th and 6th Aves., ✆ 840 6500; *American* (*MC, V, D, AE*). This is attractive especially in summer when brunch or supper is served on the roof of a cricket pavilion cum B&Q conservatory. Over-complicated food that's not so bad—black and blue yellowfin tuna carpaccio, etc.

(40)

Brasserie, 100 E. 54th St., between Lexington and Park Aves., ✆ 751 4840; *American-French* (*AE, D, MC, V; reservations suggested; open 24 hours*). Likeable, old-world, Manhattanesque restaurant in the Seagram Building: bustling, open 24 hours with stoical waiters, but closed for renovations in 1997.

(41)

Hatsuhana, 237 Park Ave., on 46th St., ✆ 661 3400; 17 East 48th St., between 5th and Madison Aves., ✆ 355 3345; *Japanese* (*AE, D, MC, V; reservations requested*). Superior, expensive sushi—some say the best in New York—frantic at lunchtime.

(42)

Chez Josephine, 414 West 42nd St., near 9th Ave., ✆ 594 1925; *French* (*AE, MC, V; reservations suggested*). Effervescent theatreland French bistro run by Josephine Baker's son. Dark, tedious jazz club atmosphere.
(43)

Dawat ($), 210 East 58th St., near 3rd Ave., ✆ 355 7555, 🖬 355 1735; *Northern Indian* (*AE, D, MC, V; reservations suggested*). With its own tandoor and much-liked in Manhattan: reliably good Indian cooking and imaginative menu developed by actress and cookery writer Madhur Jaffrey. With a popular $13–15 set lunch.
(44)

Mme Romaine de Lyon, 132 East 61st St., between Lexington and Park Aves., ✆ 759 5200 (*AE, D*). 560 omelettes.
(45)

inexpensive

Lipstick Café, 885 3rd Ave., at East 54th St., ✆ 486 8664; *American* (*AE, V, D; breakfast and lunch Mon–Fri*). Excellent value: deluxe sandwiches, soups, salads at civilized prices by Jean-Georges Vongerichten, chef at fashionable Vong (*see* above).
(46)

Lyn's Café, 28 West 55th St., between 5th and 6th Aves; *American* (*AE*). Happy café around the corner from MoMA serving decently priced club sandwiches, 'French' onion soup and fries in charitable portions.
(47)

Mezze, 10 East 44th St., between 5th and Madison Aves., ✆ 697 6644; *American* (*AE*). Bearable prices for a good lunch or breakfast in stylish surroundings.
(48)

Manganaro's Hero-Boy, 492 9th Ave., between 37th and 38th Sts., ✆ 947 7325; *Italian* (*no credit cards*). The owners claim to have coined the term 'hero'. You can order the submarine-style sandwiches up to 6ft-long here, but for daintier appetites the standard-sized prosciutto and provolone heroes are scrumptious with strong mustard and washed down with a bottle of Italian beer.
(49)

P. J. Clarke's, 915 3rd Ave., at 55th St., ✆ 759 1650 (*AE, D; reservations suggested*). Recreated as Nat's Bar for Billy Wilder's *The Lost Weekend*. With good urinals.
(50)

Carnegie Delicatessen & Restaurant, 854 7th Ave., near West 54th St., ✆ 757 2245 (*no credit cards*). Touristy, pricey, and very entertaining (*see* **Walk II**, p.120).
(51)

Cabana Carioca, 123 West 45th St., near 7th Ave., ✆ 581 8088; *Brazilian* (*AE, D, MC, V; reservations suggested*). Enormous, on three levels, popular and crowded; huge steaks, big pork chops topped with fried eggs, cod, clams, piles of fried potatoes and *feijoada*, a celebratory stew of black beans, blood sausage and pork.
(52)

cheap

Cheyenne Diner, 411 9th Ave., at 33rd St., ✆ 465 8750; *diner* (*MC, V, AE, D; open 24 hours*). Authentic diner-in-aluminum-trailer, quality burgers and omelettes.
(53)

Afghan Kebab House, 764 9th Ave., between 51st and 52nd Sts., ✆ 307 1629 (*cash only; closed Sun*). Kebabs that actually taste good, in divey dining room on 9th Avenue, and very, very cheap.
(54)

Cafés and Japanese Tea Rooms

Focaccia Fiorentina, outside the New York Public Library, 5th Ave., between 40th and 42nd Sts. Twenty kinds of focaccia sandwiches, eaten outside at tables.
(B)

Felissimo, 10 West 56th St., between 5th and 6th Aves, *www.felissimo.com*. Breakfast, lunch and elegant afternoon haiku tea on the 4th floor of the stylish Japanese department store: thirty kinds of tea ranging from wuyi oolong to proletarian chai. Afternoon tea with miniature scones from around $18, pastas, puddings and sandwiches as well (*see* **Walk II**, p.134). **(C)**

Takashimaya Tea Box, basement, 693 5th Ave., between 54th and 55th Sts. More Asian elegance: 40 kinds of tea in Midtown's second Japanese-owned department store: dainty cucumber on rice or sandwiches, with Japanese wasabi seasonings. **(D)**

Upper East Side   *map E*

luxury

Daniel ($), 20 East 76th St., between Madison and 5th Aves., ✆ 288 0033, 🖷 737 0612; *French* (*MC, V, D, AE; reservations necessary*). Run by ex Le Cirque masterchef, and about the best gourmet French in Manhattan, making up for uninspiring surroundings. *Prix fixe* lunch is good value at around $33; in the evening there are three *prix fixe* suppers ranging from $65–95. **(1)**

Parioli Romanissimo, 24 East 81st St., off 5th Ave., ✆ 288 2391; *Italian* (*MC, DIS, V, D; reservations requested*). Pleasingly stuffy, staggeringly priced and reliably good; also quiet, family-run and inside an elegant Upper East Side townhouse. Delicately cooked pasta, sausage, veal, deep sea scallops, dover sole and scampi; a huge and comprehensive cheeseboard and floating islands for pudding. **(2)**

expensive

Rosa Mexicano, 1063 1st Ave., at East 58th St., ✆ 753 7407, 🖷 421 4091; *Mexican* (*AE, D, MC, V; reservations suggested*). One of the best and most ancient Mexicans in Manhattan: unerringly good and not too expensive—authentic mole sauce or chicken wrapped in paper and steamed in beer. **(3)**

Jo Jo ($), 160 East 64th St., between Lexington and 3rd Aves., ✆ 223 5656; *French* (*MC, V, D, AE; reservations suggested*). Run by Jean-Georges 'Vong' Vongerichten, good fun and less expensive than you would expect for inventive brasserie food: squab, lobster, chicken in liquid coriander, steamed red snapper; all good value at lunch, with a $25 *prix fixe* three-course special. **(4)**

moderate

The Mark ($), 25 East 77th St., at Madison Ave., ✆ 879 1864; *French.* Excellent $19.97 set lunch in sleek but jolly hotel dining room, also English afternoon teas. Around the corner from the Whitney. **(5)**

The Kiosk, 1007 Lexington Ave., between 72nd and 73rd Sts., ✆ 535 6000; *American* (*MC, V, D, AE*). Designer-concept, newspapered walls, an eat-to-be-seen restaurant. **(6)**

Paola's, 347 East 85th St., between 1st and 2nd Aves., ✆ 794 1890; *Northern Italian* (*AE; reservations suggested; supper only*). Assuming you get a table and your hearing's at its prime, you should enjoy this: small, cramped and noisy but serving pasta a cut above the rest. **(7)**

Sofia Fabulous Pizza, 1022 Madison Ave., at 79th St., ✆ 734 2676; *Italian* (*MC, V, AE*). Pizza cooked in wood-fired ovens, reasonably priced with a candlelit sit-down roof area popular with Upper East Side yoofs. Avoid overpriced pastas. **(8)**

Island, 1305 Madison Ave., between 92nd and 93rd Sts., ℂ 996 1200; *eclectic* (*AE, D, MC, V; reservations suggested*). Smart food from everywhere (pasta, grilled goat's cheese salad, fish and crème brûlée). Eclectic menu, hectic atmosphere, youthful diners.

⑨

Fu's, 1395 2nd Ave., between 72nd and 73rd Sts., ℂ 517 9670; *Chinese* (*AE, D, MC, V; reservations suggested*). Delicately cooked Peking duck, shredded beef and dumplings, none of it greasy, in welcoming dining room. The Grand Marnier shrimp special which sounds revolting is quite nice.

⑩

inexpensive

Mocca Hungarian Restaurant, 1588 2nd Ave., near 83rd St., 734 6470; *Hungarian* (*no credit cards; reservations suggested*). Cheese pancakes, wiener schnitzel, *kolbasz*, chicken paprika and poppy-seed strudel. Good value and big portions.

⑪

Istanbul Kebap, 303 East 80th St., between 1st and 2nd Aves., ℂ 517 6880; *Turkish* (*no credit cards*). Minuscule café, friendly and cheap, serving the best of Turkish cuisine: stuffed vine leaves, kebabs, *piyaz* (Turkish white beans), honey puddings.

⑫

John's Pizza, 408 East 64th St., near York Ave., ℂ 935 2895 (*no credit cards*). Uptown annexe to the downtown John's (*see* below, West Village), just as good but politer and more quiet.

⑬

Chef Ho's Hunan House, 1720 3rd Ave., between 89th and 90th Sts., ℂ 348 9444; *Chinese* (*AE, MC, V*). Steak with oyster sauce, dim sum, and cheap at lunch.

⑭

cheap

Papaya King, East 59th St., on 3rd Ave., and East 86th St., and 3rd Ave., ℂ 753 2014 (*no credit cards*). Papaya juice, frankfurters, luminous green relish. Delicious.

⑮

Upper West Side   *map E*

expensive

Café Luxembourg, 200 West 70th St., near Amsterdam Ave., ℂ 873 7411, 🖷 721 6854; *American/French* (*AE, D, MC, V; reservations suggested*). One of the snazziest brasseries on the Upper West Side with Manhattan sophisticates in attendance. Food good and not bad value (around $35–45 a head).

⑯

Café des Artistes, 1 West 67th St., near Central Park West, ℂ 877 3500 (*AE, D, MC, V; reservations requested*). Famous for having a mock Tudor exterior, tasteful murals inside, and lunching ladies. Expensive but reliably good.

⑰

Tavern on the Green, Central Park West, at 67th St., ℂ 873 3200. *American* (*AE, D, MC, V; reservations requested*). Supremely vulgar—chandeliers, rhinestone 'rococo ceiling' and 350,000 lightbulbs. The cooking—roasted lobster with caramelized fennel, etc—flamboyant and forgettable.

⑱

moderate

Monsoon, 435 Amsterdam Ave., at 81st St., ℂ 665 2700; *Vietnamese*. One of the best Vietnamese in Manhattan. Crowded, popular and serving remarkably delicate summer rolls, noodle rolls and rice.

⑲

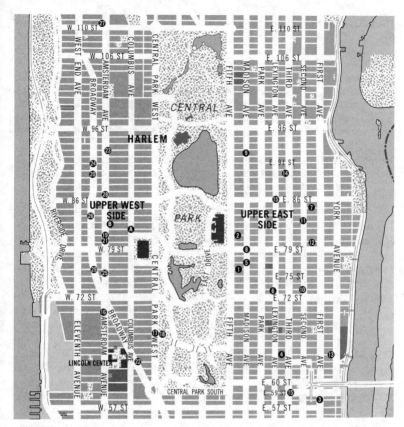

Restaurants

1	Daniel	
2	Parioli Romanissmo	
3	Rosa Mexicano	
4	JoJo	
5	The Mark	
6	The Kiosk	
7	Paola's	
8	Sofia Fabulous Pizza	
9	Island	
10	Fu's	
11	Mocca Hungarian Restaurant	
12	Istanbul Kebap	
13	John's Pizza	
14	Chef Ho's Hunan House	
15	Papaya King	
16	Café Luxembourg	
17	Café des Artistes	
18	Tavern on the Green	
19	Monsoon	
20	Docks Oyster Bar & Seafood Grill	
21	Sarabeth's Kitchen	
22	Josephina	
23	Gabriela's	
24	Mary Ann's	
25	Mingala West	
26	Ollie's Noodle Shop	
27	V & T Restaurant	
28	Popover Café	
29	Gray's Papaya	

Cafés

A Columbus Bakery
B Café Lalo

Map E

Docks Oyster Bar & Seafood Grill, 2427 Broadway, between 89th and 90th Sts., ✆ 724
20 5588; *seafood* (*MC, V, D, AE, DIS; reservations recommended*). Jolly neighbourhood restaurant, tiled in black and white, with energetic seafood eaters and clattering plates.

Sarabeth's Kitchen, 423 Amsterdam Ave., between 80th and 81st Sts., ✆ 496 6280 (*AE,*
21 *DIS, MC, D, V*). Sunday brunch institution, frequented by polite Manhattan. The prissy décor and twee menu ('Goldie Lox eggs' and 'Papa Bear and Mama Bear oatmeal') make you long for some anarchic spirit to stumble in off the street and vomit over everything. But the food is excellent: club sandwiches, scrambled eggs with smoked salmon and toast etc.

Josephina, 1900 Broadway, at 63rd St., ✆ 799 1000, ✆ 799 1082; *American* (*MC, V, D,*
22 *AE*). High quality dairy-free health food in such big portions that plates are double normal size. Crowded, fashionable with New Yorkers, especially for brunch.

inexpensive

Gabriela's ($), 685 Amsterdam Ave., at 93rd St., ✆ 961 0574; *Mexican* (*AE, MC, V*).
23 Authentic, very delicate Mexican food, handmade tortillas with cactus salads, very hot sauces in friendly, family-run restaurant with nice atmosphere.

Mary Ann's, 2454 Broadway, at 91st St., ✆ 877 0132; *Mexican* (*no credit cards*).
24 Branch of the excellent value Mary Ann's in Chelsea (*see* above).

Mingala West ($), 325 Amsterdam Ave., between 75th and 76th Sts., ✆ 873 0787;
25 *Burmese* (*MC, V, D, DIS, AE*). Rangoon Night Market Noodles with tender strips of duck and scallions, and a thousand-layered butter pancake with a chicken curry. Excellent, dependable value with a $5 lunch special.

Ollie's Noodle Shop, 2315 Broadway, at 84th St, ✆ 362 3111, ✆ 362 3097; *Chinese*
26 *American* (*AE, MC, V*). Cheap Chinese and American dumplings and noodle soup in quality fast food chain.

V&T Restaurant, 1024 Amsterdam Ave., between 110th and 111th Sts., ✆ 663 1708;
27 *pizza* (*no credit cards*). Morningside Heights' mecca for perfectly cooked pizza.

Popover Café; 551 Amsterdam Ave., between 86th and 87th Sts., ✆ 595 8555 (*no credit*
28 *cards*). Popovers are hot parcels of happiness: unsweetened buttery pastry smeared with 'strawberry butter'. Also sandwich extravaganzas—scrambled eggs (forced down a cappuccino jet and steamed) and mind-boggling puddings.

cheap

Gray's Papaya, 2090 Broadway, at West 76th St., ✆ 799 0243 (*no credit cards; open 24*
29 *hours*). Frothy batter-coloured papaya juice (an aphrodisiac); shiny, visceral frankfurters supposed to be 'tastier than filet mignon'.

Cafés

Columbus Bakery, 484 Columbus Ave., between 82nd and 83rd Sts. Good smelling bakery/café, with comfortable seating area and first class breads including succulent sour-dough rolls called '*chapeaux*'. **A**

Café Lalo, 201 West 83rd St., at Amsterdam Ave (*open until 2am weekdays, 4am weekends*). Pastries and desserts only, in conservatory on 83rd Street. Somewhere to linger over coffee, tiramisu or Snicker's Bar cheesecake. **B**

East and Central Harlem

moderate

Sylvia's, 328 Lenox Ave., between 126th and 127th Sts., *C* 996 0660; *soul food* (*AE*). Breakfast, lunch and supper by Harlem's self-proclaiming Queen of soul food: eggs any style, sausage patties, grits, pork chitterlings, smothered chicken, collard greens, candied yams, home fries, black-eyed beans, sweet-potato pie and Sylvia's World Famous, Talked About, Bar-B-Cue Ribs Special. Touristy but good.

cheap

Jamaican Hot Pot Restaurant, 2260 Adam Clayton Boulevard/7th Ave., at 133rd St., *C* 491 5270; *Jamaican* (*no credit cards*). Pot roasts, curried goat stews and oxtails served with corn bread, collard greens and fried plaintains or macaroni and cheese, from lunch until late.

Floridita, 3219 Broadway and 129th St., *C* 662 0090; *Puerto Rican* (*no credit cards, no reservations*). Puerto Rican family-run chain, best for *mofongo*, a broth of plantains and fried pork.

Wilson's Bakery and Restaurant, 1980 Amsterdam Ave., at 158th St., *C* 923 9821. The best soul food breakfasts in Manhattan.

Brooklyn

luxury

The River Café, 1 Water St., under the Brooklyn Bridge, *C* (718) 522 5200; *American* (*AE, V, D, MC; reservations requested*), *see* **Walk IV**, p.174.

Bars

New York has millions of bars. There are five main categories: the cheery neighbourhood bar (in the West and East Villages, Chelsea and Midtown), the gay and lesbian bar (in the East and West Villages and Chelsea), the rowdy Upper East and West Side bar (preppy singles), chi-chi designer cocktail bars (in Midtown and the West and East Villages and sometimes very snobby) and 'brewpubs' offering authentic 'microbrews' made in copper kettles on the premises (everywhere). (A microbrew is a small brewery that serves its own beer on site, and has a statutory limit to its distribution.) They are exempt from certain regulations in exchange for limiting their distribution.

In most Manhattan bars, it's usual to tip the barman a dollar a round.

Spirits and soft drinks come with ice, which Americans eat. There are thousands of different brands of beer in America. 'Dark' beer is stronger than 'light' beer. Mexican and Canadian beers are as popular as American beers. Amongst the American-made beers there are brands with such eye-catching names as 'Wanker Light Beer', available in most liquor shops in Manhattan.

Below is a brief list of bars. As well as the cheerful dives and designer-trendy, remember that many of New York's smartest restaurants and hotels—Windows on the World, Beekman Tower, the Rainbow Room, the Four Seasons or the Waldorf-Astoria—have good-humoured cocktail bars where you can strike an attitude without breaking the bank. Liquor laws dating back to the 1920s allow bars to stay open until 4am, and most do until at least 1 or 2am. At 4 they must close and 'air out' the premises, and can only re-open again at 8am or noon on Sundays.

Lower Manhattan and TrBeCa

pub

North Star Pub, 93 South St., at Fulton St. British pub selling appropriately revolting food and 70 single malt whiskies.

champagne

The Bubble Lounge, 228 West Broadway, between White and Franklin Sts. Champagne, in 18 varieties, in sofa-filled sitting rooms.

SoHo

chi-chi cocktails:

Pravda, 281 Lafayette St., between Prince and Houston Sts, © 226 4944. Celebrity 'theme-u-rant', appealing to household names from Sharon Stone to Salman Rushdie. Plush leather furniture, booths and red paint give the place Russianness, with blinis and Beluga caviar and 73 vodkas, malt whisky and flavoured martinis to dull the nerve-endings. Run by Brian and Keith McNally, Londoners responsible for several other concept eateries in Manhattan, including 44, Indochine and Odeon.

Temple Bar, 332 Lafayette, between Houston and Bleecker Sts. Classy SoHo bar kitted out with 1920s cruise liner remnants, famous for martinis and romantically dark.

Lucky Strike, 59 Grand St., between Wooster St. and West Broadway. Typically SoHo, and appealing to nicotine types, with a DJ from 10.30 onwards.

Wax Bar, 114 Mercer St., between Spring and Broome Sts. Fashionable with models and the English.

saloon

Fanelli, 94 Prince St., at Mercer St. Old-fashioned SoHo dive with good pub food.

Lower East Side and East Village

designer trendy

Tenth Street Lounge, 212 East 10th St., between 1st and 2nd Aves (*open 5pm–3am*). Designer-scary, with metal front and steel garage door entrance. Elegant and comfy inside, with leather sofas, candles, and elegant waitresses.

Global 33, 93 2nd Ave., between 5th and 6th Sts. Cocktails and food from all over the world, including Pimm's.

The Beauty Bar, 231 East 14th St., between 2nd and 3rd Aves. Converted hairdressers, with original barber's chairs and mirrors.

B Bar, 40 East 4th St., near the Bowery, © 475 2220 for food reservations (*open 11.30am–4am*). Brunch and supper also, in abandoned petrol station with pretentious crowd and large walled garden.

neighbourhood

The Holiday Inn, St Mark's Place, between 1st and 2nd Aves. The most fashionable bar in the world with a kindly Ukrainian management. Best in the week.

Sophie's, East 5th St., between Aves. A and B. Elegant East Village dive: crowded on weekends, with die-hard regulars on weekday lunchtimes. Beer and vodka.

Blanche's, Ave. A, between 7th and 8th Sts. Authentic drinker's bar lit with baldness-revealing lights.

Blue & Gold, 79 East 7th St. Ukrainian bar known as the 'Loser's Bar' because of its clientele: a bolthole from the more fashionable bars.

Joe's Bar, East 5th St., between Aves. A and B. More easy-going than most, with a pool table and country music jukebox.

The Horseshoe Bar aka Vazac's aka 7B, 108 Ave. B, at East 7th St. Horseshoe-shaped bar used for *Crocodile Dundee* and *The Victim*, attracting students to its pinball machine.

gay

The Bar, 68 2nd Ave., at East 4th St (*happy hour 4–8pm*). 'Spartan' gay bar for young men from the neighbourhood. Straights are welcome.

Tunnel Bar, 116 1st Ave., at East 7th St (*open 2pm–4am*). Small gay neighbourhood bar, with pool and billiards, and all-day porno films Tuesdays and Thursdays.

pubs

McSorley's Old Ale House, 15 East 7th St., between 2nd and 3rd Aves (*open until 1am*). One of the oldest in the city with Irish barmen and ancient furnishings. It became internationally famous in the 1970s when the owner went (unsuccessfully) all the way to the Supreme Court to keep women out.

Telephone Bar & Grill, 149 2nd Ave., between 9th and 10th Sts. Cider, shepherd's pie and fish and chips wrapped in fake newspaper in East Village's English pub effort. With a friendly atmosphere.

Sapphire Lounge, 249 Eldridge St., off Houston St. (*open 7pm–2.30 Mon–Tues and until 4am Wed–Sat*). Different DJ every night.

bOb, 245 Eldridge St., off Houston St. After fines for unlicenced dancing imposed in 1996, more bar that club, with sofa areas for the fashionable clientele.

Save the Robots, 25 Ave. B at 2nd St, ℂ 995 0968 (*open daily 10pm–8am except Sun*). East Village bar-scene upstairs with a decadent dance floor below.

chi-chi cocktails

Max Fish, 157 Ludlow St., between Hudson and Stanton Sts (*open 5.30pm–4am4*). Featuring 'bohemian' art exhibitions and a yellow pool table.

West Village

honky-tonk

Hogs & Heifers, 859 Washington Ave., at West 13th St. Exuberant mix of celebrities, trannies, Hell's Angels and biker barmaids in the meat-packing district.

speakeasy

Chumley's, 86 Bedford St., between Barrow and Grove Sts. Still unmarked, with two entrances on Barrow and Grove Streets. Headquarters of the US Chess Federation.

bowling

Bowlmor Lanes, 110 University Place, at 12th St. (*Mon–Thurs 10am–1am, Fri–Sat 10am–4am*). Convivial bar and grill in one of the city's last bowling alleys.

mainly gay

Marie's Crisis Café, 59 Grove St., at 7th Ave. Gay piano bar with enthusiastic singing clientele, popular with tourists and natives alike.

Keller's, 384 West St., at Christopher and Varick Sts. Oldest gay bar in the West Village, mostly black crowd.

Crazy Nanny's, 21 7th Avenue South at Leroy St. Lesbian, with free pizza on Mondays.

Uncle Charlie's, 56 Greenwich Ave., between Perry St., and 7th Ave. Gay video bar with mixed bunch of students, Wall Street execs, and Madison Avenue advertising men. Women also allowed.

Chelsea and Flatiron District

pub

Old Town, 18th St., between Park Ave. South and Broadway. Lovable pub.

hardcore

The Spike, 120 11th Ave., at West 20th St. Hardcore denim and leather bar near the Eagle's Nest in Chelsea. Wednesday is Bikers and Blue Jeans night.

Rawhide, 212 8th Ave., at West 21st St. Leather, Western and S&M in a friendly neighbourhood gay bar with an *8am* happy hour.

topless

Billy's Topless, 729 6th Ave., at 23rd St. Topless sleaze for men.

chi-chi cocktails

Flowers, 21 West 17th St., between 5th and 6th Aves. Drinking lounge and roof garden above a French bistro.

brewpub

Zip City Brewery, 3 West 18th St., at 5th Ave. Homemade beers, malty smells and hamburgers.

Midtown

views of Manhattan

Beekman Tower, 3 Mitchell Place, between 1st Ave. and 49th St. Swish piano bar at the top of beautiful Art Deco skyscraper.

Rainbow Promenade, 30 Rockefeller Plaza, between 49th and 50th Sts, 65th floor. If you can't afford the restaurant, come here for cocktails.

Top of the Sixes, 666 5th Ave., 39th floor. Extremely touristy but boasting another view. Drinks on the pricey side but with free *hors-d'œuvre*, a meal in themselves.

Top of the Park, Gulf and Western Plaza, Columbus Circle. A thrilling Midtown view—this time of Central Park.

old-fashioned

Algonquin Hotel, 59 West 44th St. Still just as fuddy-duddy.

Sir Harry's, at the Waldorf Astoria, 301 Park Ave., at 50th St. Soothingly dark, expensive, but compensate with huge bowls of luxury nuts. Elias the barman is 'Sir Harry'.

Rudy's, 627 9th Ave., between 44th and 45th Sts (*open until 4am*). Entertaining neighbourhood bar, with pitchers of beer and free hot dogs.

elegant

The Monkey Bar, at the Hotel Elysée, 60 East 54th St., between Madison and Park Aves. Dark, noisy and fashionable with media-types and publishers, an 18th-century coffeehouse-style interior, with drinkers sitting at refectory tables.

Whisky Bar at the Paramount Hotel, 235 West 46th St., between 8th Ave. and Broadway. Dark and elegant except for waitresses dressed in Max Wall leggings.

Morgans Bar, in the cellars of Morgans Hotel, 337 Madison Ave., between 37th and 38th Sts. Still trendy, decorated with antiques and leather furniture, and featuring a chicly invisible 'bar without a bar' with no bartenders, no back bar, waiters appearing as if from nowhere from behind a dark curtain.

Upper West Side

chi-chi cocktails

Shark Bar, 307 Amsterdam Ave., between 74th and 75th Sts. Sports people and moderately priced Southern cooking in swanky split-level bar.

Upper East Side

executive

Swell's, 1429 York Ave., at 76th St. Upper East Side young people—striped shirts, pictures of racehorses, and backgammon.

Elaine's, 1703 2nd Ave, between 88th and 89th Sts. Celebrity restaurant, where drinks are better than the cooking.

singles

Jim McMullen, 1341 3rd Ave., between 76th and 77th Sts. Football players and a sexual undertow.

Where To Stay

Finding a place to stay is a headache. With a permanent shortage of space in Manhattan, prices are inflated and sometimes astronomical. If you don't mind a little discomfort and have a friend in New York, ask if you can stay on their floor. In the summer especially it's possible to find short sublets listed in *Time Out New York* or the *Village Voice* (available at news-stands in the West End of London), but the best way is always by word of mouth.

Hotels in the city range from a stratosphere of luxury—$7000 a night for a penthouse in the Four Seasons, for example—to semi-residential dumps filled with muttering old men. Even if you don't mind slumming it, it's worth taking into account the location of the hotel and, just as important in New York, noise levels. Whatever you do, don't expect anywhere to be charmingly spartan, elegantly faded or appealingly shabby—just expect it to be spartan, faded, shabby, and sometimes miserable as well. In general, hotels along 5th Avenue or on the Upper East Side are the most expensive, and hotels on the quieter east side of Midtown are the best value. The west side of Midtown has a handful of designer hotels but is mostly full of unbeautiful cheapo hotels, the sort frequented by package groups and conventions. Since Disney arrived on the scene in 1996 most of the sex shops in Times Square have been closed down and safety in the area has greatly improved. Nevertheless peep shows, prostitutes and their tricks are still a feature of life on 8th Avenue; and the area around Penn Station in particular can be unsavoury at night. Hotels in unusual areas like Gramercy Square, the Flatiron District, the Upper West Side, the far north end of the Upper East Side, Chelsea, SoHo and the West Village are good value and quieter than west Midtown. Most gay hotels accept straights as well, and are often superior to anything in similar price brackets. Youth hostels, mostly on the far reaches of the Upper West Side and in Harlem, are cheaper than anywhere else but are a slog to get to. B&Bs are a pleasant alternative, with the bonus that if you choose to stay in a hosted apartment you will get an insight into the weird and, yes, wonderful ways of New Yorkers *au naturel*.

When to Book

Hotels get *fully* booked during those seasons when it's nicest to be in New York (April, May, June, Sept, Oct, and Christmas). The rest of the year businessmen and conventions swarm around Manhattan like starlings. It's *vital* to book as far in advance as possible: in peak seasons *at least* two months before you go. You can book by fax and e-mail. Some hotels exact a penalty if you cancel at short notice.

Hidden Taxes, Tips, Extra Beds and Discounts

All hotels add a 13¼ per cent **tax** on to the price they quote to customers and in brochures. This tax includes city and sales taxes, but does *not* include another $2 per person per night 'occupancy tax'.

Other hidden extras include **tipping**, **mini-bars** and **telephones**. When bell-hops and doormen eagerly offer to help you with your bags or fetch you a taxi, in their mind's eye they are picturing a tip. Food eaten from mini bars will have to be paid for, and bear in mind that, however hungry you are, the prices for mini-bar food will make you choke. Telephone calls from bedrooms cost an average of $1 within New York City (four times the price of a call from a public phone box) and this usually includes (1) 800 'toll-free' numbers. Most hotels have public phone-booths in their lobbies which visitors as well as guests may use. An added advantage of these is that they are nearly always pleasant, quiet and upholstered in velvet.

Reservation agencies claim to be able to save up to 60% on normal rates (more like 25%) and can book rooms of varying quality at quite short notice.

Take Time to Travel ✆ (1 800) 522 9991 or ✆ (212) 840 8686, ✉ (212) 221 8686. A
    New York based agency offering lower rates for hotels from budget to luxury.
Hotel Reservations Network, 8140 Walnut Hill Lane, Suite 1010, Texas 75231, ✆ 1
    800 964 6835/96 HOTEL, ✉ (214) 361 7299. Guarantees to find a (non-discounted) room even when the city is 'sold out'.
The New York Tourist Bureau's Hotel Hotline, ✆ and ✉ (212) 924 7935, *www.hotel
    discount.com*. Discount deals at peak season, arranged by the all-powerful New York Convention and Visitors Bureau.

Most hotels accept the major **credit cards**, a few demand an American Express card as a guarantee. Before you book, ask about **weekend packages**, when many hotels reduce rates by as much as 40 per cent, or **weekly rates** (giving one night in seven for free). Children under 12 and sometimes under 16 usually stay for free in a bed moved into a double room. If you're travelling in a party of three, or sometimes even four, no one will mind if you fill a double room with an extra bed or two (at a cost of around $25 per night).

Checking In

You can expect to get into your room at 3pm and kicked out at noon the day you leave. Most hotels will let you store your baggage with them at no charge for the rest of the day.

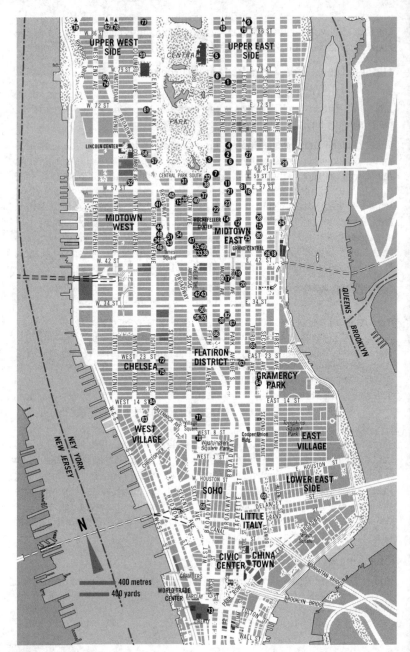

1	Hotel Carlyle	30	The Roger Williams	59	Excelsior
2	The Lowell	31	Ritz-Carlton	60	Broadway American
3	The Pierre	32	The Plaza	61	Olcott
4	Plaza Athénée	33	The Royalton	62	Malibu Studio Hotel
5	The Stanhope	34	The Paramount	63	Gramercy Park
6	The Regency	35	The Algonquin	64	Hotel 17
7	Sherry Netherland	36	The Mansfield	65	Carlton Arms
8	The Mark	37	The Shoreham	66	The Gershwin
9	The Franklin	38	The Wyndham	67	Howard Johnson
10	Hotel Wales	39	Gorham	68	SoHo Grand
11	Four Seasons	40	Warwick	69	Off-SoHo Suites Hotel
12	Waldorf-Astoria	41	Ameritania	70	Washington Square Hotel
13	Rihga Royal	42	The Metro	71	The Larchmont
14	New York Palace	43	Comfort Inn Murray Hill	72	Chelsea
15	The Box Tree	44	Days Hotel	73	Millennium Hilton
16	Fitzpatrick Manhattan	45	Wellington Hotel	74	Banana Bungalow
17	Morgans	46	Milford Plaza	75	Chelsea International Hostel
18	UN Plaza-Park Hyatt	47	Wentworth	76	International House of New York
19	Doral Tuscany	48	Hotel Edison	77	International Student Center
20	Shelburne Murray Hill	49	Hotel Iroquois	78	New York International American
21	Drake Swissotel	50	Best Western Manhattan		Youth Hostel
22	Omni Berkshire Palace	51	Remington	79	YMHA de Hirsch Residence
23	Hotel Elysée	52	Westpark Hotel	80	YMCA Vanderbilt Avenue
24	Beekman Tower Hotel	53	Broadway B&B Inn	81	Allerton House
25	The Roger Smith	54	Portland Square Hotel	82	Martha Washington
26	Crowne Plaza	55	Herald Square	83	Incentra Village House
27	Barbizon Hotel	56	Wolcott	84	Chelsea Pines Inn
28	The Pickwick Arms	57	Mayflower		
29	59th Street Bridge Apartments	58	Radisson Hotel Empire		

The prices below are for double rooms, excluding 13¼ per cent city and state sales tax and $2 occupancy tax. For single rooms, deduct 10–15 per cent. For prices from 1998 onwards, add 5–10 per cent. All hotels have private baths and air-conditioning, unless otherwise stated. If you need extra information, ring the **Hotel Association of New York City**, 437 Madison Avenue, NY 10022, ✆ 1 (212) 754 6700.

★★★★★	*luxury*	over $340
★★★★	*expensive*	$280–340
★★★	*moderate*	$170–280
★★	*inexpensive*	$120–170
★	*budget*	below $120
$		exceptionally good value within this price bracket

Upper East Side

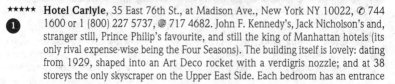

★★★★★ **Hotel Carlyle**, 35 East 76th St., at Madison Ave., New York NY 10022, ✆ 744 1600 or 1 (800) 227 5737, ✆ 717 4682. John F. Kennedy's, Jack Nicholson's and, stranger still, Prince Philip's favourite, and still the king of Manhattan hotels (its only rival expense-wise being the Four Seasons). The building itself is lovely: dating from 1929, shaped into an Art Deco rocket with a verdigris nozzle; and at 38 storeys the only skyscraper on the Upper East Side. Each bedroom has an entrance hall, jacuzzi, and dainty European furnishings. Within the hotel is a lavish fitness centre and the Café Carlyle, famous for jazz pianist Bobby Short, who has worked there for over a quarter of a century. Next door is the less expensive, slightly jollier Bemelmans' Bar with whimsical murals by ex-waiter and the author of the 'Madeleine' children's books, Ludwig Bemelmans. Tea in the Turkish Palace Gallery is also good (*singles from $285, doubles from $310, suites $500–1600 one of which includes a second bedroom plus grand piano*).

***** **The Lowell**, 28 East 63rd St., between Park and Madison Avenues, New York NY
② 10021, ✆ 1 (212) 838 1400 or 1 (800) 345 3457, @ 319 4230. The classiest townhouse hotel in Manhattan. Discreet, grand, luxurious, with only 60-odd bedrooms, all elegantly furnished. The hotel includes a library, a fitness centre and one suite (used by Madonna) with a private gym. Other rooms include wood-burning fires and small kitchens. Tea and breakfast are served in the quiet Pembroke Room, supper in the Post House Restaurant (*singles $295–365, doubles from $315, suites from $515*).

***** **The Pierre**, 5th Ave., at 61st St., New York NY 10021, ✆ 1 (212) 838 8000 or
③ 1 (800) 332 3442, @ 940 8109. Salvador Dali's favourite hotel, the Art Deco skyscraper was built in 1929, with an icing sugar tower, and views directly on to Central Park from gargantuan bedrooms and bathrooms. In 1972, a few weeks after the premiere of the Sidney Lumet film *The Anderson Tapes* depicting the simultaneous robbery of a whole New York apartment house by a huge gang of convicts, the Pierre was robbed in exactly the same way. Good staff and elegant rooms; the Rotunda tea-room is one of the nicest in Manhattan (*singles from $285, doubles from $325*).

**** **Plaza Athénée**, 37 East 64th St., between Madison and Park Aves., New York NY
④ 10021, ✆ 1 (212) 734 9100, @ 772 0958. Opulent, frightening French-style hotel, with three security guards in the lobby. Each of the 200 rooms has a marble fireplace, 'oil painting', pantry, two-burner stove and trouser press. Guests are treated to fresh flowers and slippers by the bedside. The hotel's French restaurant Le Regence is one of the best in Manhattan, and this is where Princess Diana used to stay (*$275–390 for a luxury double or $2300 for a penthouse suite with two bedrooms, solarium and rooftop terrace; ask about summer discounts*).

**** **The Stanhope**, 995 5th Ave., at 81st St., New York NY 10028, ✆ 1 (212) 288
⑤ 5800 or 1 (800) 828 1123, @ 517 0088. Snooty enough for ties and jackets to be required at all times, and featuring Second Empire chandeliers and sofas. In a choice location overlooking the Metropolitan Museum with an outdoor café and terrace, friendly staff and limousine service to the Lincoln Center and the Theater District (*doubles from $275*).

**** **The Regency**, 540 Park Ave., near East 60th St., New York NY 10021, ✆ 1 (212)
⑥ 759 4100 or 1 (800) 23LOEWS, @ 826 5674. Slightly anonymous, modern hotel dignified with French antiques. Rooms are big, service good, and there's a lively bar downstairs, popular with bourbon-swigging ladies (*doubles from $285*).

**** **Sherry Netherland**, 781 5th Ave., at 59th St., New York NY 10022, ✆ 1 (212)
⑦ 355 2800 or 1 (800) 247 4377, @ 319 4306. One of two Art Deco châteaux looking on to Central Park by Schultze & Weaver, who designed the Pierre next

door as well as the Waldorf-Astoria. An atmosphere of antiquated swank—high standards, friendly staff, room service from Cipriani's. Some guests are residential (*doubles from $270*).

★★★ **The Mark ($)**, 25 East 77th St., near Madison Ave., New York NY 10021, ✆ 1 ⑧ (212) 744 4300 or 1 (800) 223 6800, @ 744 4586. Snappy, elegant, charming and surprisingly jolly, this is one of Manhattan's nicest smart hotels. It's neatly situated in a sleek part of the Upper East Side on Madison Avenue, around the corner from the Whitney Museum and Bemelmans' Bar in the Carlyle. Rooms are large and tasteful, each with a pantry (many with dishwashers and microwaves). All bathrooms have heated towel rails and whirlpools; some suites have French doors opening on to terraces with lovely views down Madison Avenue. Guests have access to a fully equipped gym including steam and sauna room. Downstairs in the lobby, bar and restaurant there's an atmosphere of bustling activity. The restaurant has a three course prix fixe lunch for $19.97 (rising a penny a year); and nothing is too much trouble for the good-humoured staff. (*Ask beforehand about the good low season and weekend rates; standard rates are for doubles from $355–2400, all rooms including continental breakfast, with children under 16 staying free*).

★★★ **The Franklin ($)**, 164 East 87th St., off Lexington Avenue, New York NY 10128, ⑨ ✆ 1 (212) 369 1000, @ 369 8000. Small, designery, and owned by the Gotham chain (*see* **The Mansfield**, p.236), this is in a German/Hungarian part of the Upper East Side, close to the Metropolitan and the other massive museums along Museum Mile but a bus ride away from Midtown. Prices are good for spruce rooms lavishly done up in black granite, cherrywood and steel, plus free breakfast, evening dessert buffet, parking and CD and video library (*standards from $145 and $189–209*).

★★★ **Hotel Wales**, 1295 Madison Ave., at 92nd St., New York NY 10028, ✆ 1 (212) ⑩ 876 6000, @ 860 7000. Built in 1900, and quaintly Edwardian, with a lobby filled with flowers and free afternoon tea and music recitals in the twee Pied Piper Room. Dainty rooms and old-fashioned bathrooms, some rooms overlooking the Central Park reservoir, in a genteel part of Carnegie Hill, next to Sarabeth's restaurant and Museum Mile. (It takes about ten minutes by subway to get to Midtown Manhattan and there are reasonably fast buses running down 5th Avenue.) Dependable value overall and good room service (*standard from $170, suites from $225 and penthouses from $270*).

Midtown East

★★★★★ **Four Seasons**, 57 East 57th Street, between Park and Madison Avenues, New ⑪ York NY 10022, ✆ 1 (212) 758 5700, @ 758 5711. This opened in 1993: 52 storeys high, and now the tallest, most expensive hotel in Manhattan, and on close inspection already slightly dog-eared. The theatrical post-modern interior is by I. M. Pei, the architect responsible for recent additions to the Louvre and New York's less impressive Jacob Javits Center. The 370 suites are each the size of an average Manhattan apartment, with walk-in dressing rooms, laser multi CDs, exceptional views, contemporary prints, private balconies and alarming-sounding baths which fill in 60 seconds. The hotel includes a fitness centre, a bar and the 57/57 restaurant serving healthy American grill. If you're passing by, the cavernous lobby is worth a look, 33ft high with an onyx ceiling, Magny limestone-clad columns and amber panelling (*singles $440–625, doubles $490–675, suites $825–7000, with discount weekend rates with doubles from $385 and extra beds from $50; pets welcome*).

★★★★★ **The Waldorf-Astoria**, 301 Park Ave., between E.49th and 50th Sts, New York
12 NY 10022, ✆ 1 (212) 355 3000 or 1 (800) 924 3673, ✆ 872 7272. Occupying a whole city block with 1692 rooms and its own underground railway spur, the handsome Waldorf was the swishest hotel of thirties New York. Now it's owned by the Hilton, slightly impersonal and with unimaginative suites. The labyrinth of lobbies downstairs is worth a walk through if you're not staying (*singles $255–375, doubles from $335, suites from $550*), (*see* **Walk I**, p.109).

★★★★★ **The Rihga Royal**, 151 West 54th Street, between 6th and 7th Aves., New York
13 NY 10019, ✆ 1 (212) 307 5000 or 1 (800) 937 5454, ✆ 765 6530. Big, vulgar and showy, with 500 suites of varying enormousness and cost, in a newly built 54 story faux Art Deco skyscraper attracting businessmen, flashy tourists and royalty (from Emperor Akihito to Oasis). Comfortable rooms and spectacular views over Central Park make the Rihga a good option if nothing else is available. The Japanese owners are lavish with mod cons, offering guests such mixed delights as a complimentary limousine to Wall Street, a complimentary daily paper (remember to ask for it), ice-makers in every room, exhaustive business and fitness facilities and a weather forecast for the next day beside each bedside (*one-bedroom suites from $350, two bedroom suites from $700, Grand Royal Suites from $2500*).

★★★★ **New York Palace**, 455 Madison Ave., at 50th St., New York NY 10022, ✆ 1
14 (212) 888 7000 or 1 (800) 697 2522, ✆ 303 6000. Recently refurbished, this is at first glance one of the prettiest hotels in Manhattan, a group of six brownstone palazzos designed in 1884 by McKim, Mead & White (*see* pp.77–8) but incorporating a galumphing 20th century skyscraper behind. The intention of the original owner Henry Villard was to fill a conspicuous spot on Madison Avenue as ostentatiously as possible. However, Villard (a publisher of the *New York Evening Post*), went bankrupt during building works and was bought out by his own lawyer. As a hotel, the Palace is in a good location, around the corner from the Rockefeller Center. Bedrooms are comfortable, luxurious, exquisitely dull: guests have access to a gym with a rollerblade training machine, and for everyone Stanford White's disgustingly opulent Gold Room is an amusingly glittery place to stop for cocktails or tea (*singles and doubles from $275, suites $450–1200*).

★★★ **The Box Tree ($)**, 250 East 49th St., between 2nd and 3rd Ave, New York NY
15 10017, ✆ 1 (212) 758 8320, ✆ 308 3899. Loveable and eccentric 18th century townhouse hotel with 13 minuscule rooms, each quirkily decorated in a different style (Egyptian, British Empire, Chinese, Japanese and so on), each with working fireplace, marble bathroom, antique beds and a clutter of curious ornaments. Rates include breakfast and on weekends prices go up instead of down but include a discount voucher for $100 off supper in the excellent Box Tree Restaurant (*doubles from $190 Sun–Thurs, $290 Fri–Sat, penthouses from $230, no roll-away beds as rooms are too small*).

★★★ **Fitzpatrick Manhattan**, 687 Lexington Ave., between 56th and 57th Sts., New
16 York NY 10022, ✆ 1 (212) 355 0100 or 1 (800) 367 7701, ✆ 308 5166, email *fitzusa@aol.com*. This friendly, resolutely Irish hotel is small, green all over and

reasonably lavish as well, with sophisticated business facilities (including modems), coffee machines and free access to a fitness club down the road. With only 92 rooms, it's an unpretentious place to stay, not exactly chic or immaculate, but warm, cheery, well situated near Bloomingdale's and with delightfully down-to-earth staff. The Irish-staffed bar and restaurant downstairs does an all-day Irish breakfast including black pudding, porridge and soda bread (*doubles from $245–60 and $295–360 for suites, but investigate significantly cheaper weekend, family, corporate and summertime deals*).

★★★
(17) **Morgans**, 237 Madison Ave., at 38th St., New York NY 10016, ✆ 1 (212) 686 0300, 1 (800) 334 3408, ✉ 779 8352. Opened in 1984 by disco entrepreneurs Ian Schrager and the late Steve Rubell (responsible for Studio 54), and the first in Schrager's mini hotel chain which includes the Royalton and Paramount hotels in New York, the Delano in Miami and the Mondrian in Los Angeles. Renovated in 1996, Morgans is quieter than its progeny and just as endearingly ridiculous, with its bar 'with no bar-tenders', beds with suede headboards, and 'unconventional air-plane-like sinks and hospital fixtures' in bath and restrooms. If you can swallow all this, it's a comfortable, amusing place to stay, in a nice part of Midtown, with newspapers delivered to the door, Mapplethorpe photographs, fresh flowers, free breakfasts, and computers available on request. The swish penthouse on the 19th floor has its own greenhouse, kitchen, 'multimedia room' and two terraces (*singles $195–225, doubles $220–250, one bedroom apartments from $325; ask about weekend discounts*).

★★★
(18) **UN Plaza-Park Hyatt**, 28th floor, 1 United Nations Plaza, New York NY 10017, ✆ 1 (212) 355 3400 or 1 (800) 228 9000, ✉ 702 5051. Flash glass skyscraper by Kevin LaRoche, opposite the United Nations, with a clientele of elegant businessmen, overseas visitors, diplomats and their well-behaved families. Service in the Japanese-owned hotel is unbeatable, views spectacular, lobbies refreshingly unpretentious, and rooms unusually spacious with discreet but elegant furnishings. All of which easily makes up for the fact that the windows and bathroom fittings were designed for dwarfs. There's a health club with a wonderful rooftop pool and sauna, and many free services including papers, fresh fruit and transport to Wall Street and west Midtown (*singles and doubles from $210, suites from $375*).

★★★
(19) **Doral Tuscany**, 120 East 39th Street, between Lexington & Park Aves., New York NY 10016, ✆ 1 (212) 686 1600 or 1 (800) 223 6725, ✉ 779 0148. First class Midtown hotel set among the quiet brownstones of Murray Hill; large rooms with private halls plus TV in the bathrooms (*singles $194–249, doubles $194–249, suites $350*).

★★★
(20) **Shelburne Murray Hill**, 303 Lexington Ave., between 37th and 38th Sts., New York NY 10016, ✆ 1 (212) 689 5200, ✉ 779 7068. All rooms are suites with kitchens . In genteel Murray Hill with a restaurant and sauna centre. Hairdryers, video players and secretarial services on request (*studio suites from $135, one bedroom suites from $170, two bedroom suites from $335*).

★★★
(21) **Drake Swissotel**, 440 Park Ave., at 56th St., New York NY 10022, ✆ 1 (212) 421 0900 or 1 (800) 372 5369, ✉ 371 4190. Jet-setty Swiss-owned hotel with spacious, dull 'European' rooms. Every mod con is provided, and the hotel is proud of its lively cocktail bar and good gourmet dining room, the Restaurant Lafayette (*doubles from $270*).

★★★ **22**   **The Omni Berkshire Place**, 21 East 52nd St., near 5th Ave., New York NY 10022, ☎ 1 (212) 753 5800 or ☎ 1 (800) THE-OMNI, 🖷 754 5018. Greatly improved after a $50m renovation in 1995, a huge European-style hotel with comfortable, big rooms plus a new health club and fitness centre (*from $265*).

★★★ **23**   **The Hotel Elysée ($)**, 60 East 54th St., between Madison and Park Aves., New York NY 10022, ☎ 1 (212) 753 1066, 🖷 980 9278. A lovely gem—elegant, civilised and tucked away on a block around the corner from the Seagram Building and Park Avenue with intelligent, humorous staff. Guests have access to a large newspaper-filled library and clubroom, a corner of which serves free breakfasts, coffee and biscuits all day long, and *hors-d'oeuvres* with unlimited wine in the evenings. Rooms are well-proportioned and elegantly furnished with antiques, chests of drawers and walk-in wardrobes, huge beds and lavish bathrooms. Marlon Brando, Vladimir Horowitz and Jessica Tandy stayed in this clubbable hotel and Tennessee Williams died here. Downstairs is the fashionable Monkey Bar, famous since the 1930s (*99 rooms, singles $245, deluxe doubles $265, suites—including fireplace, terrace, kitchen and solarium—$295–$375, piano suite $775*).

★★★ **24**   **Beekman Tower Hotel**, 3 Mitchell Place, at East 49th St. and 1st Ave., New York NY 10017, ☎ 1 (212) 355 7300, 🖷 753 9366. On the far east side of Midtown near the UN, an all-suite hotel with fully equipped kitchens. The newly renovated Art Deco **Top of the Tower** cocktail bar has breathtaking views (*suites from $200*).

★★★ **25**   **The Roger Smith ($)**, 501 Lexington Ave., between East 47th and 48th Sts., New York NY 10017, ☎ 1 (212) 755 1400 or 1 (800) 445 0277, 🖷 319 9130. In an excellent location for walking in Midtown, with lots of character. The lobby and bar are decorated with contemporary paintings and sculptures, some by the owner, James Knowles. Staff are relaxed and rates include breakfast, fridge and coffee machine in most rooms and use of the 2000 volume video library. Downstairs is Lily's, a restaurant and bar (*singles from $210, doubles from $225*).

★★★ **26**   **Crowne Plaza**, 304 East 42nd St., between 1st and 2nd Ave, New York NY 10017, ☎ 1 (212) 986 8800, 🖷 986 1750. Convivial and well placed in Tudor City, an unnaturally quiet enclave close enough to Midtown. Big rooms (since a recent renovation) with wonderful views, marble bathrooms, and telephones. Nice staff, plus an excellent restaurant and bar and small fitness centre (*from $200*).

★★ **27**   **Barbizon Hotel**, 140 East 63rd St., on Lexington Ave., New York NY 10017, ☎ 1 (212) 838 5700 or 1 (800) 223 1020, 🖷 888 4271. Originally the buttoned-up women-only hotel dubbed the Amazon in Sylvia Plath's *The Bell Jar* (in real life Grace Kelly and Candice Bergen were guests). Now it caters to both sexes. In 1996 its 310 dowdy rooms were straightforwardly smartened up for $40 million. Now there's a health club and indoor pool; rooms are tasteful but still quite small and dowdy. In a lively part of the Upper East Side, close to Midtown (*singles $105–170, doubles $105–190*).

★ **28**   **The Pickwick Arms ($)**, 230 East 51st St., between 3rd and 2nd Aves., New York NY 10022, ☎ 1 (212) 355 0300 or 1 (800) PICKWICK, 🖷 755 5029. The best deal in Manhattan, especially for anyone new to the city: the location is good, rooms are clean, comfortable and quiet, staff are humorous as well as helpful. There's a garden on the roof, a coffee shop and an Italian restaurant. Only a few rooms lack private bathrooms and all have telephones, cable TV and room service. Reports of the hotel over the last decade are unanimously excellent (*singles from $85, doubles $105, but singles with shared baths from as low as $45*).

★ 29 59th Street Bridge Apartments ($), 351 East 60th St., at York Avenue, New York NY 10022, ✆ 1 (212) 754 9388, ✉ 754 9593, toll free ✆ (888) 754 9389, e-mail *THE59STAPT@aol.com*. Exceptional value and a good alternative to conventional hotels. Studio apartments ($89–150) include full kitchens, air conditioning, television, Internet, fitness club membership (with access to a pool, sauna and racquetball courts) and room service. There's an Italian restaurant on the premises, a private garden, café and garage, all in a safe if dull location, close to Bloomingdale's, Barney's, the Roosevelt Island cable car and the Guggenheim and Museum Mile.

★ 30 The Roger Williams, 131 Madison Ave., at 31st St., New York NY, ✆ 1 (212) 448 7000, ✉ 448 7007. Large 209-room hotel in Murray Hill, had a designer-facelift along the lines of the Shoreham Hotel (*see* below) (*rooms $165–195*).

Midtown West

★★★★★ 31 The Ritz-Carlton, 112 Central Park South., at 6th Ave, New York NY 10019, ✆ 1 (212) 757 1900 or 1 (800) 241 3333, ✉ 757 9620. Swanky but welcoming, the smallish hotel improved in spirit after a $20m refurbishment in 1993. From the 8th floor up front rooms have spectacular views over the undulating treetops of Central Park. Rates include two phone lines, limousine to Wall Street, shoe shine and use of business and fitness centres. Rooms are decorated in a conventional furnishings and the hotel includes Fantoni's, a small north Italian restaurant well recommended in Zagat's (*doubles from $400, but ask about special rates*).

★★★★ 32 The Plaza, 768 5th Ave., at 59th St., New York NY 10019, ✆ 1 (212) 750 3000 or 1 (800) 228 3000, ✉ 759 3167. Home to Frank Lloyd Wright and Marlene Dietrich, a dapper, white Edwardian château on Central Park (by Henry Hardenburgh who also did the Dakota). Faced with financial ruin in the 1990s, Donald Trump reluctantly sold it, but the inside is still quintessentially Ivana, big on flowers and flounces, and with bedrooms varying wildly in size and slippery marble-ized bathrooms (*singles and doubles $235–505, suites $395–1500*).

★★★★ 33 The Royalton, 44 West 44th St., near 5th Ave., New York NY 10036, ✆ 1 (212) 869 4400 or 1 (800) 635 9013, ✉ 869 8965. Quintessentially 1980s, featuring such favourites as furniture in dust sheets, conical steel basins, slate bathrooms, red roses and staff dressed in black. Designed by Philippe Starck ('crazy genius and terribly lucid' as his Eric Cantona-style CV has it) in 1988, and still lavish. Guests may call upon the services of an in-house personal trainer; all rooms have round bathtubs, stocked fridges, and 40 have working fireplaces (*singles $265–330, doubles $295–360, suites $425: remember to ask about cheaper weekend rates*).

★★★ 34 The Paramount ($), 235 West 46th St., at 8th Ave, New York NY 10021, ✆ 1 (212) 764 5500 or 1 (800) 225 7474, ✉ 354 5237. Ian Schrager's third Manhattan venture, designed like the Royalton by Frenchman Philippe Starck on a scraggy part of 46th Street just off Times Square. The entrance is manned by bouncers in Jean-Paul Gaultier outfits, and looks like a funeral parlour, with red roses stuck in individual holes in the door. Inside, inspiration for the enormous lobby seems to have come from *Roger Rabbit* or else the sets on *You've Been Framed*, with 1930s black telephones, skew-whiff staircase, and celluloid orange, violet and green colours and lighting. Sleeping quarters are an excellent deal and a lot cheaper than Morgans or the Royalton (or equivalent designer hotels) possibly because the Paramount is bigger and less successful than either with 610 (very small) bedrooms. One redeeming aspect is the small branch of Dean & Deluca, the SoHo gourmet delicatessen (*single double beds from $155, doubles from $210, weekend packages including buffet breakfast from $185, suites from $375*).

★★★
(35) **The Algonquin**, 59 West 44th St., between 5th and 6th Aves., New York NY 10036, ✆ 1 (212) 840 6800 or 1 (800) 548 0345, @ 944 1419. Small, restored, 165-room, old-fashioned hotel, now under Japanese management, well-maintained and still charming, especially the lobby with its atmosphere of plump businessmen to-ing and fro-ing between meetings. Guests get a free breakfast buffet and, for a fee, use of laptop computers and cellular phones, but the best feature of the hotel is its location: near the New York Yacht Club on 44th Street, and a few steps away from 5th Avenue and MoMA. The Rose Room restaurant is terrible (*singles from $220, doubles from $240, suites from $400*), (*see* p.102).

★★★
(36) **The Mansfield ($)**, 12 West 44th St., near 5th Ave., New York NY 10036, ✆ 1 (212) 944 6050, @ 764 4477. Attractive boutique hotel suitable for honeymooners in a good location next door to the more famous Royalton and Algonquin across the street. Suites very elegantly done up in the style of chic 1920s hotel, with glass-engraved French doors separating bedrooms from sitting rooms furnished with velvet sofas, window seats, wooden blinds and writing desks. A downstairs lobby includes two dimly lit sitting rooms (with harpist), where guests are served free breakfast (mostly cakes), evening dessert-buffet and all-day coffee and tea. Staff are friendly and helpful, but even they are mystified by the hotel's motto: 'The infinitely little have a pride infinitely great' (*standard from $195, suites from $245, penthouses from $270*).

★★★
(37) **The Shoreham ($)**, 33 West 55th St., off 5th Ave., New York NY 10019, ✆ 247 64700, @ 765 9741. In the same small chain as the Mansfield (*see* above): a very deluxe designer hotel with pristine bedrooms including roses, in-room safes, Irish linen sheets and beds lit from back with perforated steel mesh headboards. A sleek but not intimidating lobby, with an undulating ceiling ending in a large opaque glass square of blue light and 1930s murals by Winold Reiss. A free breakfast buffet (cakes again) in the lobby and a first-class gourmet French restaurant, La Caravelle. Two blocks away from MoMA and Rockefeller Center (*standard from $245, suites from $295, penthouses from $375*).

★★★
(38) **The Wyndham**, 42 West 58th St., near 5th Ave., New York NY 10019, ✆ 1 (212) 753 3500 or 1 (800) 257 1111, @ 754 5638. To my mind, the nicest hotel in Manhattan: a 1950s relic with *no* mod cons, and bedrooms with curtains, wallpaper, bed linen, headboards and cushions all in the same extravagant chintz, plus 1950s Louis Quatorze dolls house furniture. Almost non-existent service, eccentricity everywhere, cheap phone calls from bedrooms and an excellent value old-fashioned hotel restaurant. In a prime location, around the corner from the

Plaza Hotel. Don't expect any kind of modern luxuries—this is the sort of hotel you grow to love (*singles from $125–$140, doubles from $140–$155*).

★★★
(39) **Gorham**, 136 West 55th St., between 6th and 7th Aves., New York NY 10019, ✆ 1 (212) 245 1800 or 1 (800) 735 0710, @ 582 8332. Old-fashioned, well looked after and in a good spot on West 55th Street. Rooms are olde worlde and comfy, with microwaves, fridges, VCR, voice mail and espresso machines on request (*singles and doubles $235, suites from $275*).

★★★
(40) **Warwick**, 65 West 54th St., nr 6th Ave., New York NY 10019, ✆ 1 (212) 247 2700, @ 957 8915. Well-kept with exceptionally large rooms, with a suite on the top floor once owned by Cary Grant and nowadays used for weddings (*singles from $220, doubles from $245*).

★★
(41) **The Ameritania ($)**, 1701 Broadway, at 54th St., New York NY 10019, ✆ 1 (212) 247 5000, @ 247 3313. Decent and reliable budget hotel in a central spot off Broadway and within walking distance of 5th Avenue, Central Park and Times Square. Don't be too put off by the horrid sci-fi lobby and disorganized front desk. Rooms are modern, neutral and large, with every convenience, including TVs, air-conditioning and hairdryers. Guests are mostly Europeans, and the hotel has 24-hour room service plus its own 24-hour bagel café downstairs (*singles $119–139, doubles $129–139, suites $149–179*).

★★
(42) **Metro**, 45 West 35th St., between 5th and 6th Avenues, New York NY 10001, ✆ 1 (212) 947 2500 or 1 (800) 356 3870, @ 279 1310. Straightforward well-run hotel in the Garment District near Macy's. Pleasant, newly done-up rooms with a wood decked roof terrace on the 14th floor looking on to the Empire State Building. Exercise room, restaurant, and free breakfast buffet in the library (*170 rooms, singles $125–140, doubles $125–150*).

★★
(43) **Comfort Inn Murray Hill ($)**, 42 West 35th St., between 5th and 6th Aves., New York NY 10001, ✆ 1 (212) 947 0200 or 1 (800) 228 5150, @ 594 3047. Sullen staff in clean hotel with well-polished lobby: good value for its location (near the Empire State) and free breakfast (*coffee, Danish pastries plus newspapers*) (*singles from $99, doubles from $114*).

★★
(44) **Days Hotel**, 790 8th Ave., between 48th and 49th Sts., New York NY 10019, ✆ 1 (212) 581 7000 or 1 (800) 572 6232, @ 974 0291. OK hotel chain, decently priced, with a rooftop outdoor pool (*singles $110–130, doubles £140–187*).

★★
(45) **Wellington Hotel**, 871 7th Ave., at 55th St., New York NY 10019, ✆ 1 (212) 247 3900 or 1 (800) 652 1212, @ 581 1719. Big and basic and not too welcoming, but recently the rooms and lobby were redecorated. Full of tour groups, but central and good value if travelling in a group—some of the family rooms include two bathrooms and kitchenettes (*singles or doubles from $165*).

★★
(46) **Milford Plaza**, 270 West 45th St., at 8th Ave., New York NY 10036, ✆ 1 (212) 869 3600 or 1 (800) 221 2690, @ 944 8357. Even more basic and bigger, with chaos reigning in the lobby and uninspiring, impersonal rooms. A cheapish option if you can't find anything else (*from $120–190*).

★
(47) **Wentworth**, 59 West 46th St., near 6th Ave., New York NY 10036, ✆ 1 (212) 719 2300 or ✆ 1 (800) 848 0020, @ 768 3477. Old Art Deco hotel, now tackily

refurbished, but good value. Rooms are rudimentary but clean, and the hotel is in a good position with its own garden. All rooms with private baths, thank goodness (*doubles from $139, two doubles from $105, suites from $130*).

★ **48** **Hotel Edison**, 228 West 47th St., near 8th Ave., New York NY 10036, ✆ 1 (212) 840 5000 or 1 (800) 637 7070, ✉ 596 8650. Enormous 1000-room hotel with a splendid renovated Art Deco lobby and matter-of-fact bedrooms with most conveniences including hairdryers on request. In touristy Times Square, with a brilliant Polish diner and English-style bar (*singles from $105, doubles from $115, suites from $108*).

★ **49** **Hotel Iroquois**, 49 West 44th St., between 5th and 6th Aves., New York NY 10036, ✆ 1 (212) 840 3080 or 1 (800) 332 7220, ✉ 398 1754. Small family-run hotel in swish location next to the Algonquin. Dreggy at first glance, but although the rooms need renovating they are clean and comfortable (*singles from $125, doubles from $150*).

★ **50** **Best Western Manhattan**, 17 West 32nd Street, near 5th Ave., New York NY 10001, ✆ 736 1600, reservations 1 (800) 567 7720, ✉ 563 4007. Newly done-up and slightly naff, with 'themed' rooms, but cheap, friendly and in a useful location, next to the Empire State. Coffee makers in all rooms, a gym on the ground floor and free morning papers (*singles from $119, doubles from $129, cheap rates for families or groups of three or more*).

★ **51** **Remington**, 129 West 46th St., near Broadway, New York NY 10036, ✆ 1 (212) 221 2600, ✉ 764 7481. Budget prices in this basic hotel in Times Square. Rooms are real value if you're travelling in a party of three or more (*singles and doubles with shared baths from $70, singles with from $85, doubles from $149, triples and quads from $95*).

★ **52** **Westpark Hotel ($)**, 308 West 58th St., near Columbus Circle, New York NY 10019, ✆ 1 (212) 246 6440 or ✆ 1 (800) 248 6440, ✉ 246 3131. Exceptionally good deal in this bracket: modest public areas but rooms are tastefully decorated and welcoming. Rooms with a view of Central Park cost more (*singles from $95, doubles from $110*).

★ **53** **Broadway B&B Inn ($)**, 254 West 46th St., between Broadway and 8th Ave., New York NY 10036, ✆ 1 (800) 826 6300, ✉ 768 2807. Near the Paramount Hotel, on an unexciting block off Times Square. Good value, clean, modern and cheap, with breakfast included (*doubles from $85*).

★ **54** **Portland Square Hotel**, 132 West 47th St., between 6th and 7th Aves., New York NY 10036, ✆ 382 0600 or ✆ 1 (800) 388 8988, ✉ 382 0684. Dingy but cheap, in Times Square (*singles with shared bath from $50–99, doubles from $79*).

★ **55** **Herald Square ($)**, 19 West 31st St., off 5th Ave., New York NY 10001, ✆ 279 4017 or 1 (800) 727 1888, ✉ 643 9208. Basic and small, recently renovated and in a convenient location for getting around. Exceptionally good rates (*singles from $75 with shared bath, doubles from $95, discounts for students*).

★ **56** **Wolcott ($)**, 4 West 31st St., between Broadway & 5th Ave., New York NY 10001, ✆ 268 2900, ✉ 563 0096. Dependable good value in a good, safe, lively part of the Garment District with friendly management. Rooms not huge, but straightforward and comfortable, and the hotel has a nice lobby (*singles from $70, doubles from $100, suites $115–160, limited no. rooms with shared bath $65*).

Upper West Side

★★
(57)
Mayflower ($), 15 Central Park West, at 61st St., New York NY 10023, ✆ 265 0060, 1 (800) 223 4164, ✉ 265 0227. This is brilliant value for money, on Central Park, with spectacular views and close to the Lincoln Center, with 365 large old-fashioned, high ceilinged, tastefully chintzy rooms—many with pantries and walk-in closets. Free newspapers and horribly early morning coffee (6–7am), a good restaurant and a fitness room. Robert De Niro, Joe Pesci, Mickey Rourke, Alec Baldwin and Pavarotti have all stayed in this tranquil and smart hotel (*singles from $155, doubles from $170, suites from $205–85*).

★★
(58)
Radisson Hotel Empire, 44 West 63rd St., nr Broadway, New York NY 10023, ✆ 1 (212) 265 7400 or (1 800) 333 3333, ✉ 245 3382. Well-maintained and ostentatious, with a grand mahogany-panelled lobby hung with velvet drapes and pictures of Shakespearean actors. Opposite the Lincoln Center, and with a bar, restaurant and jazz club, a self-service laundry, free daily newspapers, and videos and CD players in every room. Luxurious alternative to similarly priced hotels in less salubrious locations (*singles and doubles from $148, suites from $250*).

★
(59)
Excelsior ($), 45 West 81st St., between Columbus Ave. and Central Park West, New York NY 10024, ✆ 362 9200 or ✆ 1 (800) 368 4575, ✉ 721 2994. Fuddy duddy and peeling, with elegant Art Deco details and guests who come back time after time. In a choice and quiet position, overlooking the Natural History Museum, close to Central Park and shops and restaurants on Columbus Avenue. Always heavily booked in November, as it overlooks the Natural History Museum park where (the night before Thanksgiving) cartoon characters are inflated for the Macy's Parade next day (*singles from $65, doubles from $149, suites from $99*).

★
(60)
Broadway American, 2178 Broadway, near 77th St., New York NY 10024, ✆ 362 1100, ✉ 787 9521. Cheap if you don't mind sharing bathrooms and in a reasonably lively part of the Upper West Side. Rooms quasi Art Deco and quite big: shared kitchen and laundry on each floor and a 24-hour restaurant (*singles from $45 and doubles from $65 with shared bathroom; or singles from $79 and doubles from $89 with private bathroom*).

★
(61)
Olcott, 27 West 72nd St., off Central Park West, New York NY 10023, ✆ 877 4200, ✉ 580 0511. Dull but decent, next to Manhattan's most illustrious apartment building and the spot where John Lennon was shot by Mark Chapman on 8 December 1980 (*singles from $85, doubles from $95, suites from $115*).

★
(62)
Malibu Studio Hotel, 2688 Broadway, at 103rd St., New York NY 10025, ✆ 222 2954, ✉ 678 6842. *Very* cheap and cheerful, with a lavender lobby stencilled with palm trees... Rooms are matter-of-fact: no telephones but a message-taking service, and only one-third with private baths. Near Columbia University, an express subway-ride away from Midtown (*singles with shared bath from $35, doubles with shared bath from $50; no credit cards*).

★★
(63)
Gramercy Park ($), 2 Lexington Ave., at 21st St., New York NY, ✆ 1 (212) 475 4320, ✆ 505 0535. One of the nicest. Like a fusty English gentleman's club and popular with Europeans, the Gramercy is the best medium-priced hotel in Manhattan: away from the noise, but within walking distance of Midtown and Villages. Gramercy Square is quiet and Bloomsbury-esque, round the corner from fashionable shops and restaurants sprouting up around the Flatiron Building. Old-fashioned, elegantly faded rooms and staff who keep themselves to themselves but are friendly. Guests have access to Gramercy Park, the private park facing the hotel (*singles $125–135, doubles from $135, suites from $160*).

★
(64)
Hotel 17, 225 East 17th St., between 2nd and 3rd Aves., New York NY 10003, ✆ 475 2845, ✆ 677 8178. Just seedy enough to appeal to fashion types (ever since Madonna was photographed here in her knickers for *Details* magazine). To stay in, it's passable and in a quiet location close to the East Village. Unless you're intending to see Manhattan through a haze of clubs and narcotics, the dim lights, nylon sheets and 'characters' may get depressing (*singles from $65, doubles $85–90, cheaper weekly rates work out at about $40 a night; no credit cards*).

★
(65)
Carlton Arms, 160 East 25th St., near 3rd Ave., New York NY 10010, ✆ 1 (212) 679 0680 or 684 8337. Not for those who savour their creature comforts, a 'wacky' hostel-style hotel (*see* the Gershwin below) which trades on appealing to a 'European artist crowd'. Translated, this means quasi Lichtenstein murals and shared baths. In a good location, with a basin in every room, friendly, helpful management (*singles from $44–53, doubles from $57–65, cheapest rooms have shared baths; ask about discounts for students and Europeans*).

★
(66)
The Gershwin, 7 East 27th St., between 5th & Madison Aves., New York NY 10016, ✆ 545 8000, ✆ 684 5546. Mostly a hostel but incorporating 70 private rooms, this is for 'young persons' and about as bohemian as a youth club gets, with hastily painted alternative décor in the bedrooms (a gold curlicue here, a silver swirl there), German tourists and few facilities. The cheapest private rooms have no phone or TV, but are very clean with decent bathrooms. Downstairs there's a neurasthenic art gallery and an institutional café; on the roof an astroturfed terrace used for parties. Staff are so stressed out that the atmosphere in the lobby is like the youth hostel version of *Fawlty Towers*: you might have to wait around until 5pm only to find you've failed to get a bed, and if anyone's sent a telephone message or fax, you can wait forever (*from $22 per person in dormitories, $70–82 for 1–3 people in private rooms*).

★
(67)
Howard Johnson, 429 Park Avenue South, between 29th and 30th Sts., New York NY 10016, ✆ 532 4860 or 1 (800) 258 4290, ✆ 545 9727. Part of a hotel chain but friendly and revamped with new, improved décor and a breakfast bar and cocktail lounge (*singles from $89, doubles from $95, suites from $135–215*).

SoHo

★★★
(68)
SoHo Grand ($), 310 West Broadway, nr. Broome St., New York NY 10013, ✆ 965 3000, 1 (800) 965 3000, ✆ 965 3141. Chic but tasteful, this is excellently

placed in SoHo, a few minutes' walk away from the most interesting parts of down-town: SoHo itself, Canal Street and Chinatown. The big lobby inside is industrial-designer, with metal staircases, velvet sofas upholstered in William Morris, and a cocktail bar serving cheap bar food. Bedrooms are elegant, with linen sheets and white-tiled bathrooms (*367 rooms, singles from $209, doubles from $229–369*).

★
(69) **Off-SoHo Suites Hotel ($)**, 11 Rivington St., between Christie St. and the Bowery, New York NY 10002, ✆ 353 0860 or 1 (800) OFF SOHO or 800 633 7646, @ 979 9801. This has real charm and is an alternative to what the owners dub New York's 'over-priced, under-sized hotel rooms'. Instead the Off-SoHo is divided into suites for up to four people, each with a large kitchen and bathroom, plus TV and phone in each bedroom. You may have to share the bathroom and kitchen with another couple, but barring strange encounters with briefs, this is preferable to the 'shared baths' in budget hotels. The Off-SoHo suites, from the kitchens to bathrooms, are clean beyond clean with neutral furnishings and lovely staff. A downstairs café will send up ultra cheap food from 7am onwards. There's also a small gym and self-service laundry. Although the hotel is close to the sleekest parts of SoHo, it's also around the corner from a flophouse on the Bowery: be a little wary at night, until you get to know the area (*economy suites for two from $89, deluxe suites for four from $149*).

West Village

★
(70) **Washington Square Hotel**, 103 Waverly Place, New York NY 10011, ✆ 1 (212) 777 9515 or 1 (800) 222 0418, @ 979 8373. Refurbished, but the bedrooms are still dumps. Worthwhile not just for the price and iffy continental breakfast, but also for the excellent, safe location (*singles from $60, doubles from $89, quads $128*).

★
(71) **The Larchmont ($)**, 27 West 11th St, between 5th and 6th Aves., New York NY 10011, ✆ 989 9333, @ 989 9496. Small, pristine, outstanding value: in the heart of the West Village, with nicely decorated rooms, all with telephones, TVs and basins. Shared bathrooms and kitchens on each floor (*singles from $60–70, doubles from $85–90 including complimentary continental breakfast*).

Chelsea

★★
(72) **Chelsea**, 222 West 23rd St., between 7th and 8th Aves., New York NY 10011, ✆ & @ 1 (212) 243 3700. Mark Twain, Sarah Bernhardt, Jackson Pollock, Vladimir Nabokov, Virgil Thompson and Sid Vicious all made the Chelsea their New York headquarters, and the famously fleabitten hotel, with its sixties relics, ramshackle furnishings and semi-permanent residents still has atmosphere. As art galleries and restaurants drift into Chelsea from SoHo, the area itself is becoming ever more gentrified. Rooms on the expensive side and varying wildly: ask for one that's large, renovated and with a private bathroom (*singles from $135–65, doubles from $150–250, studios from $165, suites from $225*).

Wall Street/TriBeCa

★★★ **Millennium Hilton**, 56 Church St., between Fulton and Dey Sts, New York NY
73 10047, ✆ 693 2001, 1 (800) 835 2220, ✉ 737 0538. Antiseptic skyscraper hotel
close to the World Trade Center catering mostly to businessmen. Its most pleasant
feature is a glass-roofed swimming pool with views of New York Harbor (*singles
$195–245, doubles $220–270, suites from $475, very good weekend rates*).

Alternative Accommodation

Students and Hostels

★ **Banana Bungalow**, 250 West 77th St., at Broadway, New York NY 10024,
74 ✆ 769 2441 or 1 (800) 6HOSTEL, ✉ 877 5733. Cheapest in New York, for international (non-American) travellers only, with two week maximum stays. Small
dormitories, no telephones or air-conditioning but in a fairly lively location on the
Upper West Side (*$15–18 a person in 6-bed dorms inc. linen and lockers*).

★ **Chelsea International Hostel ($)**, 511 West 20th St., between 7th and 8th
75 Aves., New York NY 10011, ✆ 243 4922 or 647 0010, ✉ 727 7289. Very small
and one of the best deals not just for the price, garden dining area and free breakfast, but for its excellent downtown location (*from $20 in 4–6 people dorms, or
$45 for a two-person room with private bath*).

★ **International House of New York**, 500 Riverside Drive, at West 122nd St.,
76 New York NY 10027, ✆ 1 (212) 316 8400, ✉ 316 8415. Open from June–mid-
August. Full-time student-only hostel on Riverside Park with a civilized sitting
room and subsidized canteen (*singles with shared bath from $25, doubles or
suites with private baths from $85*).

★ **International Student Center**, 38 West 88th St., between Columbus Ave. and
77 Central Park West, New York NY 10024, ✆ 1 (212) 787 7706, ✉ 580 9283.
Dormitories, very cheap and a nice location close to Central Park and the Natural
History Museum location (*from $25*).

★ **New York International American Youth Hostel**, 891 Amsterdam Ave, at
78 103rd St., New York NY 10025, ✆ 932 2300, ✉ 932 2574. Clean, pleasant and
very cheap with beds (including some family rooms) for visitors of all ages. Not
exactly in the centre of New York but it is accessible, and includes a library,
meeting room, chapel, garden and espresso bar with jukebox (*singles from $22 in
10–12 people dorms, $25 in 4 people dorms, $75 for suites for 1–4 people, $3
extra for non members of AYH*).

★ **YMHA de Hirsch Residence at the 92nd St.**, 1395 Lexington Ave., at 92nd St.,
79 New York NY 10128, ✆ 415 5650 or 1 (800) 858 4692, ✉ 415 5578. Very comfortable, with two desks per room and kitchen and dining rooms on each floor, on
the expensive but dull Upper East Side (*$210 per week in shared rooms*).

★ **YMCA Vanderbilt Avenue**, 224 East 47th St., between 2nd and 3rd Aves., New
80 York NY 10017, ✆ 756 9600, ✉ 752 0210. Lavishly done-up with two pools and
a restaurant, in the centre of town. Small rooms, all non-smoking. Only the executive suites have baths (*singles from $46, doubles from $57, suites from $95*).

As a rule safety for women depends more on the area you're staying in than the hotel, though if you're skint a women-only hotel might turn out cheaper. (Even smart hotels can be problematic for women—managements, assuming that anyone who hangs about in a lobby is a call-girl, will collar the most innocently single lady.)

★ **(81)** **Allerton House**, 130 East 57th St., at Lexington Ave, New York NY 10022, ✆ 1 (212) 753 8841. Old-fashioned, on a classy block, with smallish rooms (*singles from $60*).

★ **(82)** **Martha Washington**, 30 East 30th St., between Park and Madison Aves., New York NY 10016, ✆ 1 (212) 689 1900, ✆ 689 0023. Dour and spartan but cheap (*singles without bath from $45, or with baths from $59, but ask about weekly rates*).

Gay and Lesbian

★ **Aaah Bed & Breakfast**, PO Box 2093, New York, NY 10108, ✆ 246 4000, ✆ 765 4229. Reservation service for stays in private homes. Specify the neighbourhood you want to stay in (*$60–150*).

★ **(83)** **Incentra Village House ($)**, 32 8th Ave., between 12th and Jane Sts., New York NY 10014, ✆ 206 0007, ✆ 604 0625. Good value, excellently-maintained 12 room hotel in quaint part of the West Village with a front parlour and attractively decorated quirky rooms including antiques, working fireplaces and galley kitchens. Minimum stay two nights at weekends; straight guests are welcome (*from $99*).

★ **(84)** **Chelsea Pines Inn ($)**, 317 West 14th St., nr 8th Ave., New York NY 10014, ✆ 929 1023, ✆ 645 9497. Not all rooms have private bathrooms but all have basins and fridges and rates include breakfast. Well-run, friendly and in a good location close to the West Village as well as Chelsea. Also welcomes straight guests (*from $55, doubles only*).

Bed and Breakfast

Although you can stay in a good hotel for similar rates, you'll have a more interesting time in a B&B. On the minus side, some B&B's are out in the boroughs, and travelling in and out of Manhattan is a bore. Most of the agencies ask for at least a 25% deposit; hosted apartments often include continental breakfast.

As You Like It B&B, ✆ (1 212) 695 3404.

Bed & Breakfast (& Books), 35 West 92nd St., Apt. 2C, New York NY 10025, ✆ & ✆ (1 212) 865 8740, but call in office hours. Literary hosts and hostesses from $75 for a single and $85 for a double.

Bed and Breakfast Network of New York, 134 West 32nd St., Suite 602, New York NY 10001, ✆ (1 212) 645 8134 or 1 (800) 900 8134. A list of 200 residences, mostly in Manhattan: hosted doubles from $80–90, unhosted apartments for $90–300.

City Lights Bed and Breakfast Ltd., Box 20355, Cherokee Station, New York NY 10028, ☎ (1 212) 737 7049, ✆ 535 2755. Minimum 2-night stay; hosted doubles from $85, unhosted 1–4 apartments from $95–250.

Manhattan B&B, ☎ (1 212) 977 3512, 1 (800) 747 0868, B&B from $60, also private apartments.

New World Bed and Breakfast, 150 5th Ave., Suite 711, New York NY 10011, ☎ (1 212) 675 5600, ✆ 675 6366. Call during office hours; hosted doubles from about $80, unhosted studios from $70.

Urban Ventures ($), 38 West 32nd St., Suite 1412, NY 10001, ☎ (1 212) 594 5650, ✆ 947 9320. Over 600 Bed & Breakfasts most of which are in Manhattan and personally checked out by the organisers. 'Comfort Range' rooms from $55, 'Budget Range', mostly with shared bath, from $34 and whole apartments from a bottom range of $60 a night.

Home Exchange

Ask for very precise details.

Vacation Exchange Club, ☎ (602) 972 2186. Part of a worldwide network listing people with homes to exchange (*fee $24.70*).

Renting and Sublets

Thousands of sublets are advertised in the *Village Voice*, and quite a few in *Time Out New York*, both available at some news-stands in Central London.

Apartments International, 67 Chiltern St., London W1M 1HS, UK, ☎ (0171) 935 3551, ✆ 935 5351. Swish but pricey apartments on the Upper East Side from £450 a week.

The Manhattan Hotel Alternative, ☎ (1 212) 206 9237. Private brownstone apartments for rent.

Internet sublets

Sublets are just beginning to be advertised on the net. Try:

Rent Online: *www.aptsforrent.com*
Rent Net: *http://rent.net*
Manhattan Apartment Guide: *www.aptguides.com*

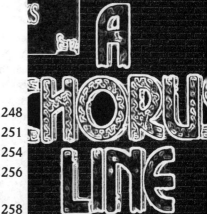

Arts, Entertainment and Nightlife

New York is like a disco, but without the music.

Elaine Stritch, *Observer*,17 Feb 1980

The city's cinemas, galleries, off-Broadway theatres, jazz, rock and nightclubs seethe with activity—as for dance, New York is without comparison. Fashions breeze in at such a speed that keeping abreast with what's new requires some stamina. New Yorkers are blessed with a seemingly endless choice of venues, which perhaps explains why, in his secret heart of hearts, even the most energetic Manhattanite prefers to spend the evening slumped on a sofa watching telly. With so much going on, however, it would be a shame to follow this unedifying example.

To get a good overview of what's happening, get hold of some of the local magazines and newspapers. Friday's Metropolitan and Sunday's Arts & Leisure sections in the *New York Times* have reviews, selected listings and week-ahead surveys; the free weekly *Village Voice* and the $2 English interloper *Time Out* have comprehensive listings (especially good for films and the week's free–$2.50 events).

1	CO Encore Worldwide	27	Coney Island High	53	Sidney Janis
2	Angelika Film Center	28	Brownies	54	Robert Miller
3	Angelika 57	29	Manny's Car Wash	55	PaceWildenstein
4	Anthology Film Archives	30	The Mercury Lounge	56	Leo Castelli
5	Cinema Village	31	Pyramid	57	The New York Earth Room
6	Film Forum	32	Tramps	58	Max Protetch
7	The Kitchen	33	Wetlands	59	Paolo Baldacci Gallery
8	The Knitting Factory	34	Arthur's Tavern	60	Greene/Naftali Gallery
9	Millennium Film Workshop	35	Blue Note	61	Dia Center for the Arts
10	The Paris	36	Bradley's	62	Clocktower Gallery
11	Quad Cinema	37	Fat Tuesday's	63	City Center
12	Bryant Park	38	57/57	64	The Bowling Club
13	A Different Light	39	Five Spot	65	Cake
14	Lincoln Center	40	Iridium Room	66	Don Hill's
15	Carnegie Hall	41	Michael's Pub	67	Club CyberSex at Downtime
16	Merkin Concert Hall	42	Village Vanguard	68	Life
17	Town Hall	43	Nuyorican Poets Café	69	Mother
18	St Thomas Church	44	S.O.B.		(Clit Club, Click and Drag)
19	Beacon Theater	45	Atlantic Theater Company	70	Nell's
20	Irving Plaza	46	La MaMa ETC	71	Robots
21	Madison Square Garden	47	Public Theater	72	Roseland
22	Palladium	48	The Duplex	73	Roxy
23	Radio City Music Hall	49	Café Carlyle	74	Sound Factory Bar
24	The Bottom Line	50	Catch A Rising Star	75	Tatou
25	Continental Club	51	André Emmerich		
26	CBGB	52	Gagosian		

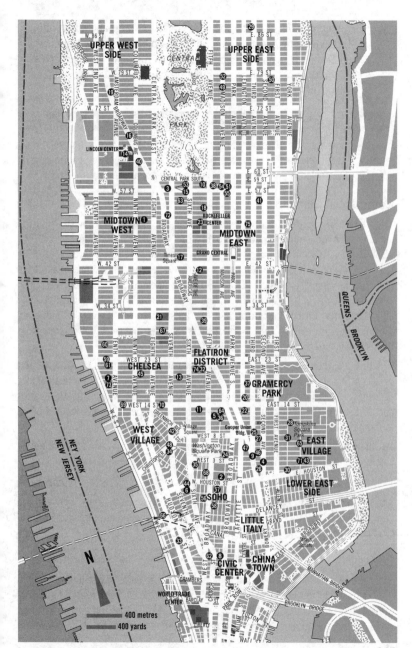

The monthly *New Yorker* includes concise listings and entertaining film reviews by Anthony Lane. Both the monthly *Paper Magazine* and *Details* are good on current trends in nightclubs and as well as in film, theatre and dance, and the free *Sound Views* fanzine has listings on the 'subterranean music scene'.

Movies

Even the most inert New Yorker will stir him or herself to go to the movies. Almost without exception New Yorkers are passionate about films, so passionate that when they really like a film they launch into a round of applause at the end.

Commercial Cinemas

The **CO** or **Cineplex Odeon** chain is the cheapest (around $8.50–9, with the excellent **Three Dollar Encore Worldwide** on 50th St and 8th Ave, ✆ 246 1583 or 505 CINE # 610, showing fairly recent films on seven screens for $3 a ticket). Cinemas around Times Square are the rowdiest (worth visiting for audience participation alone); the **Ziegfeld** has the biggest screen (in a theatre on West 54th Street and 6th Avenue, ✆ 765 7600, and home originally to the Ziegfeld Follies); and the **Sony Lincoln Square** has the most screens (twelve, including an astounding 8-storey-high Imax screen showing a strange selection of films from flights to Mars to concerts by the Rolling Stones—*see* p.124).

In late 1997 the new Times Square **AMC Multiplex** will open on 42nd Street, between 7th and 8th Avenues. Owned by the Kansas company, American Multi-Cinemas, this will be the largest in the USA, and to make way for its 26 theatres and 17 escalators, an entire theatre—the old Empire Theater—will be lifted off its foundations and rolled on steel rods 72 feet down 42nd Street.

For listings of commercial films consult *Time Out* or the *New York Post* movie clock, or phone ✆ 777 FILM for listings by telephone.

cheap seats

The seven screen **CO Encore Worldwide** on 340 West 50th Street, between 8th and 9th Aves, ✆ 246 1583 or 505 CINE # 610, shows recent films for $3 a go. Otherwise *see* 'Free Tickets and Screenings', p.250. ❶

Revivals

Sadly the Manhattan repertory house of past years has more or less died a death (a few years back you could spend a whole day in one of these watching quirky double bills of 'American classics' on prints speckled in dust and curly hairs, and revelling in the general atmosphere of nostalgia, communal loneliness and trampled popcorn). These days 'Revival' or 'Art Houses' show a more esoteric range of programmes including foreign films, profoundly serious films (the sort that bores a mass audience to tears), beautifully photographed 'coffee and cake' films, cult movies or erudite retrospectives focusing on a particular director or actor (ones you've never heard of). These programmes are intelligent as well as original and easily become an addiction. For listings and reviews on these, the best places to look are *Time Out* and the *Village Voice*.

Angelika Film Center, 18 West Houston Street, at the corner of Mercer St., ✆ 995 2000. Six screens showing art-house and revival films, plus a coffee-and-cake counter managed by the gourmet food shop Dean and Deluca.

Angelika 57, 225 West 57th St., at 7th Ave., ✆ 586 1900. Large, recently restored 556–seat theatre, showing revivals/art-house movies.

Anthology Film Archives, 32 2nd Ave., at 2nd St., ✆ 505 5181. Large and extraordinary archive for the preservation of independent film and video (including avant-garde and experimental 'art films') from America and Europe. Programmes are sometimes delightfully outré (think 'seminal Polish documentaries').

Cinema Village, 22 East 12th St., near 5th Ave., ✆ 924 3363. The programme is a spirited mix of recent movies like *Withnail and I* and *Diva*, and classics by Bertolucci, Truffaut and Fellini.

Film Forum, 209 West Houston St., near Varick St., ✆ 727 8110, *www.filmforum.com*. Three screens: FF1 for independent American and foreign films; FF2 for repertorial profiles of film-makers (from Fellini to Mizoguchi); and FF3 for extended runs of films that had successes in the first two theatres. A concession stand sells cappuccino, brownies, espresso and popcorn.

The Kitchen, 512 West 19th St., at 10th and 11th Aves. Screening room for experimental art-videos.

The Knitting Factory, 74 Leonard St., between Broadway and Church Sts, ✆ 219 3055. **Loud Music Silent Film**—silent movies accompanied by live modern music, usually on Sundays.

Millennium Film Workshop, 66 East 4th St., at 3rd Ave., ✆ 673 0090. Howard Gutenlan's always innovative avant-garde arts centre, formed in the 1960s. The centre organizes screenings of experimental works, workshops on film-making and access to film-making equipment for film-makers.

The Paris, West 58th St., at 5th Ave., ✆ 688 2013. Swish auditorium next to the Plaza showing mainstream films from abroad.

Quad Cinema, 34 West 13th St., between 5th and 6th Aves, ✆ 255 8800. Four small screens, showing foreign films and American independents.

Screening Room, 54 Varick St., ✆ 334 2100. Recent revivals: Hartley, Tarantino, Jarmusch, etc.

Symphony Space, 2537 Broadway at West 95th St., ✆ 864 5400. One night a week devoted to films by an eclectic range of directors (Kenneth Anger, Gus Van Sant).

Festivals and Public Screenings

At the end of September there is the prestigious **New York Film Festival** at Alice Tully Hall in Lincoln Center, which premieres more than 25 new American and European films. To be sure of getting tickets apply about five weeks in advance (call ℮ 877 1800 ext 489 for details); however, it is possible to get returns on the day of the performance. Other film festivals include an **Underground Film Festival** held in the downtown art houses in March/April, a **Gay and Lesbian Film Festival** in July in the West Village and a **Black Film Festival** in Harlem in August.

Also in March and April, the **Museum of Modern Art** has a festival devoted to **New Directors/New Films**, and throughout the rest of the year the museum also has at least 25 screenings a week (free with general admission) of films from its fascinating archives. The Donnell branch of the **New York Public Library** has a continuous programme of films, which they show free, and the **Museum of TV and Radio** has a unique collection of over 30,000 television and radio programmes, also free. Finally from June until September there are **free screenings in Bryant Park** of American classics projected on to an enormous outdoor screen.

Free Screenings and/or Public Collections

Check the advertisements in the film pages of *Time Out* for details of **free** advance screening passes for two (*see* 'Cheap Seats', above).

American Museum of the Moving Image, 35th Ave., at 36th St., Astoria, Queens, ℮ 1 (718) 784 0077 (*see* **Museums**, pX).

Bryant Park, 42nd St., between 5th and 6th Aves, ℮ 512 5700. Free outdoor screenings **(12)** of popular classics (e.g. *Casablanca*) June–Sept, on Mondays at 8.30pm.

Donnell Branch of the New York Public Library, 20 West 53rd St., between 5th and 6th Aves., ℮ 621 0618. Free screenings from a large archive.

Metropolitan Museum of Art, 5th Ave., at 82nd St., ℮ 535 7710. Documentaries in the Uris Center Auditorium relating to current exhibitions in the museum (*see* **Museums**, pX).

Museum of Modern Art, 11 West 53rd St., between 5th and 6th Aves., ℮ 708 9480. Twenty-five free screenings a week from their extensive archives.

Museum of TV & Radio, 25 West 52nd St., between 5th and 6th Aves. A wonderful archive of 30,000 programmes (*see* pX).

Walter Reade Theater, Lincoln Center, 70 Lincoln Center Plaza, Broadway and 65th St., ℮ 875 5610. Custom built in 1991 as part of the Lincoln Center, with a huge screen, superb sound quality and perfect sightlines: varied programmes, and host to the New York Film Festival in September.

A Different Light, 151 West 19th St., between 6th and 7th Aves, ℮ 989 4850. Gay and **(13)** lesbian bookstore and café with occasional free Sunday evening screenings of American 'classics'.

New York pulls all the big names, of course, and standards are outstanding. Critics complain that the repertoire veers from conservative mainstream to the wildly adventurous, with nothing in between; but if you scrutinize programmes carefully, there is something for more or less everyone. The best places to look are the Sunday *New York Times* Arts & Leisure section, *7 Days Magazine* and *New York Magazine*. The two most important venues are Carnegie Hall and the Lincoln Center, which has four separate auditoriums (two for opera and two for concerts).

discount tickets

Half-price tickets for a huge variety of music venues are available from the **Bryant Park Music & Dance Half-Price Ticket Booth**, 42nd St., at 6th Ave., ✆ 382 2323. Opening times vary, but 12 noon–2pm is a safe bet. **New York Philharmonic Audience Services**, Avery Fisher Hall, 132 West 65th St., at Broadway, ✆ 875 5030 offers half-price tickets after 6pm, but phone ahead to ask about availability. Otherwise *see* 'Ticket Agencies', below.

Concert Halls

Lincoln Center

62nd to 66th Streets, between Amsterdam and Columbus Aves, ✆ 875 5400 for programmes and information. You can get 25–50% discounts on the day of performance from the Duffy Square TKTS Ticket Booth (at West 47th St and Broadway) or the TKTS booth in the mezzanine of Two World Trade Center between Church, Vesey, West and Liberty Sts (call ✆ 221 0013 for more information). 'Rush' tickets for students can be purchased from the venue itself (ring ahead to ask about availability).

The classical music side of the Center comprises:

Avery Fisher Hall, ✆ 875 5030; tickets available from Centercharge on ✆ 721 6500. When it first opened in 1962 the acoustics were such a disaster that the then Philharmonic Hall turned to electronics moghul Avery Fisher, who renovated it and added oak panelling. Since then the hall has been home to the 150-year-old New York Philharmonic and its principal conductor, Kurt Maser. In the summer there is the popular six-week **Mostly Mozart Festival**, in which every seat is reduced to the same low price. During the season (Sept–May) the public can attend rehearsals at massively cut rates at 9.45 on Thursday mornings (phone ahead to check).

Alice Tully Hall, ✆ 875 5050; tickets c/o Centercharge, ✆ 771 6500. Recitals, string quartets, *lieder* and chamber music. Considered acoustically perfect.

Metropolitan Opera House, ✆ 362 6000 and free web site newsletter and programme information, *www.met–opera.org*. Home to the Metropolitan grand-opera machine and (in the spring) the American Ballet, this is the most lavish Lincoln Center auditorium—the one with the garish red and gold décor, clinking Austrian crystal chandeliers which disappear into the ceiling as performances start, and two large Chagall murals. Top international stars fill the line-up and the New York upper-crust puts in a glittery appearance, but productions tend to be old-fashioned and reductions are scarce. Supertitles for foreign language operas.

New York State Theater, ✆ 870 5570; tickets from TicketMaster ✆ 307 4100. Home to the New York City Opera and the New York City Ballet. The Met's more proletarian neighbour, this has cheaper seats and a policy of employing American performers only. Unfamiliar ballet and opera works (including a 1990 run of Schoenberg's *Moses und Aaron* which even the composer doubted could be staged), musical comedies and old favourites like *La Bohème* and *Swan Lake*. Supertitles for foreign language operas.

Carnegie Hall

154 West 57th St., at 7th Ave., ✆ 247 7800 (tickets can also be purchased online at www.carnegiehall.org). Cheap seats in the front half of the top balcony can be good value—the only problem being the steep rake of the auditorium, which can bring on mild vertigo. Tours on Tuesdays and Thursdays (✆ 247 7800 for information).

One of the top three concert halls in the world, although apparently its acoustics have never been quite as good as the Boston Symphony Hall and the Vienna Musikverein. Now a centenarian, in its time Carnegie Hall has hosted everyone (including Isaac Stern, Sir Thomas Beecham, Arnold Toscanini, Itzhak Perlman, Pinchas Zukerman, Leornard Bernstein, Jack Benny, even the Beatles).

After refurbishment in 1986 fibre screens and chemical coatings were added to improve the spoilt accoustics. There's no resident orchestra, but the Boston, Chicago and Philadelphia Symphonies, and the Vienna Philharmonic put in regular appearances. Any performances coded with coloured blobs distinguish those occasions when the main auditorium or smaller Weill Recital Hall are hired out by amateurs for 'vanity recitals'.

Other Big Concert Halls

Merkin Concert Hall, Abraham Goodman House, 129 West 67th St., at Broadway and Amsterdam Ave., ✆ 362 8719. Small, as unbeautiful as it sounds, and more intimate than the big halls—often used for professional debuts and chamber music. Meaty, inventive programmes.

Town Hall, 123 West 43rd St., at 6th Ave. and Broadway, ✆ 840 2824. Wide-ranging programme, including New Music, World Beat, New Jazz and Afro-pop as well as intrepid Classical. Some people say the acoustics here are as good as Carnegie Hall.

Brooklyn Academy of Music (BAM), 30 Lafayette St., Brooklyn, ✆ 1 (718) 636 4100; call TicketMaster ✆ 307 4100 for tickets. Four auditoriums, including the 2085-

seat Opera House, and space for the Brooklyn Symphony, new music and dance as well. Currently the BAM is one of the few New York institutions supporting alternative and avant-garde composers (John Cage, Lou Harrison, Steve Reich and Philip Glass). It commissions new work from contemporary composers, puts on lesser-known productions in conjunction with the Metropolitan Opera and every autumn mounts the blockbuster Next Wave Festival of American and foreign contemporary work.

Smaller Venues

Cathedral of St John the Divine, 1047 Amsterdam Ave., at 112th St., ✆ 662 2133. All kinds of free lunchtime and evening concerts, often by distinguished touring groups from abroad. Concerts take place in St John's cavernous vault, two football fields long, a century old and still unfinished. A dramatic setting if ever there was one.

The Damrosch Park Guggenheim Bandshell, southwest corner of Lincoln Center, ✆ 870 1630. Free outdoor concerts in the summer, including the excellent Serious Fun (contemporary and avant-garde) and Classical Jazz Festivals.

The Donnell Library, 20 West 53rd St., off 5th Ave., ✆ 621 0618. All kinds of concerts for free in a branch of the New York Public Library. There are also concerts in other libraries throughout the city (see listings in the Voice).

Frick Collection, 1 East 70th St., on 5th Ave., ✆ 288 0700. Splendid occasional afternoon concerts by top performers which are kept deadly secret. If you ring the number above you may be able to extract some dates. Tickets are free.

The Juilliard School, Michael Paul Hall, Lincoln Center, ✆ 769 3300. Free or fantastically low admission to recitals, master-classes and full-blown operas put on by students and faculty members. Standards can be outstanding.

Metropolitan Museum of Art, Grace Rainey Rogers Auditorium, 5th Ave. and 82nd St., ✆ 570 3949. Particularly good on string quartets, chamber music and early music. First-class performers like the Lindsay and Guarini Quartets are imported from abroad, so tickets can be pricey. In the evenings various performers are stationed all round the hall—on galleries in the main hall, in the Temple of Dendur and the Spanish Patio.

Museum of Modern Art Summergarden, 11 West 53rd St., between 5th and 6th Aves, ✆ 708 9480. Late-summer concerts outdoors in the elegant sculpture garden with a highbrow selection of 20th-century composers.

92nd Street Y Kaufmann Concert Hall, 1395 Lexington Ave., at 92nd St., ✆ 415 5440. The Y has its own symphony orchestra and a varied programme. Also recitals by visiting string quartets and top soloists (Dietrich Fischer-Dieskau and Elly Ameling), and poetry readings by contemporary writers.

St Thomas Church, 1 West 53rd St., at 5th Ave., ✆ 757 7013. Lunchtime concerts and choral music in Manhattan's most beautiful church.

Summer Parks Concerts, ✆ 362 6000. Starting in June, a big programme of free music events takes place in parks throughout the five boroughs, including productions and concerts by the Metropolitan Opera and the New York Philharmonic in

Central Park, halted temporarily in 1997 for the renovation of the Great Lawn. Thousands of people gather with beers and picnics as the sun sets. Arrive as early as possible to get tickets, served on a first-come basis. The Metropolitan Opera stages two productions each summer; the Philharmonic's programme is more varied.

Symphony Space, Broadway at 95th St., ✆ 864 1414. From gospel to HMS Petticoat.

ticket agencies

Bryant Park Music and Dance Half-Price Ticket Booth, 42nd St., at 6th Ave., ✆ 382 2323. Try to get to the booths by lunchtime on the day of the performance.

Centercharge, ✆ 874 6770. Tickets by telephone for Avery Fisher Hall and Alice Tully Hall in the Lincoln Center.

TicketMaster, ✆ 307 4100. Tickets for New York City Opera and BAM, $3.50 surcharge.

CarnegieCharge, ✆ 247 7800. Tickets for Carnegie Hall, with a $4 surcharge.

Rock, Disco, Punk

Venues range from massive 55,000-seat stadiums to seedy caverns in the East Village or New Jersey, with bands with names like Total Annihilation String-Vest and My Papa is a Curry. The latter are easy enough to get into. For details see *Time Out* for everything, or for a selection the entertaining listings in the *New Yorker* or *New York Magazine*. If you want to go to one of the big cheeses (Shea Stadium to see the Rolling Stones) you need to act quickly: consult the listings in *Time Out* or the *Village Voice*, then try ticket agencies or phone **Ticketmaster**, ✆ 307 7171, *www.livetonight.com*, with your credit card number at the ready, or try the Ticketmaster stands in Tower Records, HMV and Bloomingdales.

The Big Venues

Apollo Theater, 253 West 125th St., between Adam Clayton Powell Jr and Frederick Douglas Boulevards, ✆ 749 5838. Legendary Harlem theatre where performers as diverse as Ella Fitzgerald, James Brown, the Jackson Five, and Frankie Lyman and the Teenagers were baptized by fire. Revamped and restored in 1978, the Apollo closed again in the eighties; it was brought back to life by the Wednesday Amateur Nights organized by the octogenarian Ralph Bellamy, who managed them back in the thirties. Tickets range between $5 and $30, and between $5 and $40 for the Supershow on the last Wednesday of the year, when previous winners are brought together in one performance.

Beacon Theater, 2124 Broadway, at West 75th St., ✆ 496 7070. Biggest venue on the Upper West Side for mainstream and offbeat rock groups (the likes of Bob Dylan, Bryan Ferry and Chris Isaak in the olden days).

Irving Plaza, 17 Irving Place, at 15th St., ✆ 777 6817, *www.irvingplaza.com*. Elegant old theatre, with chandeliers and balcony all the way round: R&B, pop, country, funk, blues, hip-hop, techno, even comedy, and well-heeled bands such as Suzanne Vega, Bob Mould, Tragically Hip and Pulp.

Madison Square Garden, 8th Ave., between West 31st and West 33rd Sts, ✆ 465 6741.

21 Stadium hovering over Penn Station with room for 20,000. Various pop extravaganzas as well as boxing, basketball, wrestling.

Meadowlands, East Rutherford, New Jersey, ✆ 1 (201) 935 3900. Another 20,000-seat arena, including the Giants Stadium next door, for big crowds.

Palladium, 126 East 14th St., between 3rd and 4th Aves., ✆ 473 7171. Vast disco hall,

22 with mainly mainstream gigs, from the Gypsy Kings to Neil Simon. An old Academy of Dance, it was converted in 1985 by the Japanese designers Arata Isozaki and Eiko Ishioko; inside is a double staircase, a suspended glass-block disco floor lit by 2400 glass lights, and frescoes by Keith Haring, Kenny Scharf and Francesco Clemente.

Radio City Music Hall, 1260 6th Ave., at 50th St., ✆ 247 4777. The most elegant of the

23 rock venues: an Art Deco palace for firmly established stars (in the past, Madonna, Billy Joel, and the Grateful Dead). From late November the Rockettes (Radio City's can-can girls) swing their legs for a two-month extravaganza of camp—the 'Magnificent Christmas Spectacular' (adm $20–45).

Shea Stadium, 126th St., at Roosevelt Ave., Flushing, Queens, ✆ 1 (718) 507 8499. The biggest of all, with seating for 55,000, where the Beatles played in 1965 and the Stones in 1989. Pope John Paul II appeared here in 1979.

A Random List of Smaller Venues

Academy, 234 West 43rd St., between 7th and 8th Aves., ✆ 840 9500. Large and anonymous converted theatre, red velvet seats and alternative rock bands.

The Bottom Line, 15 West 4th St., near Mercer St., ✆ 228 6300. Established West Village

24 venue, not as wild and crazy as its East Village counterparts, with folk music as well as rock and a mixed bag of up-and-coming bands including Acoustic Alchemy, Filigree Curtains and Steeleye Span. Bruce Springsteen, Stevie Wonder and Suzanne Vega all catapulted to fame from here.

Brownies, 169 Ave. A, between 10th and 11th Sts., ✆ 420 8392. A grab-bag of known

28 and aspiring bands: Skeleton Key, Ultra Bidet and Wisdom Tooth.

The Cooler, 416 West 14th St., between 9th Ave and Washington St., ✆ 645 5189; avant garde and alternative music in a lavender-coloured basement in the meat-packing district; the Sun Ra Arkestra plays here every Wednesday.

Continental Club, 25 3rd Ave., at St Mark's Place, ✆ 529 6924. Excellent East Village

25 rock club and bastion, featuring four bands a night—in the past the Blue Jays, Mumbo Gumbo, Dashboard Mary and Christy Rose. No cover or minimum at the bar; $5 entrance fee on weekends.

CBGB, 315 Bowery, at Bleecker St., ✆ 982 4052. In the 1970s, the birthplace of New

26 York punk and the Talking Heads. At the end of a long dark corridor, new violent rock bands: the Sic F*cks, Lunachicks, Unsane, Educated Monkeys, Breeze Block and Osgood Slaughter. CBGB stands for country, bluegrass and blues, though no one alive can remember hearing them here. Between $5 and $10 entrance a night.

CB's 313 Gallery, 313 Bowery, at Bleecker St., ✆ 677 0455. A more tranquil offshoot of CBGB's with folk, acoustic and experimental music seven nights a week for a $5 entrance fee.

Coney Island High, 15 St Mark's Place, between 2nd and 3rd Aves., ✆ 674 7959, ㉗ *www.coneyhigh.com*. Jungle on Monday nights, videos, pinball, DJs, 'sleaze' in the Detention Lodge upstairs, hardcore and rock including the Red Aunts, Funkface and Clowns for Progress.

Knitting Factory, 74 Leonard St., between Broadway and Church St., ✆ 219 3006, *www.knittingfactory.com*. Experimental jazz, rock, folk, performance pieces and poetry readings in friendly neighbourhood bar, café and performance space: from Philip Glass to Lou Reed and Yo La Tengo.

Manny's Car Wash, 1558 3rd Ave., at E. 87th St., ✆ 369 2583. Chicago blues bar: small, ㉙ with standing room only; bands including Robert Golden, plus jams on Sunday, and free entrance for women on Mondays.

Maxwell's, Washington and 11th Sts., Hoboken, New Jersey, ✆ 1 201 798 4064. Quirky alternative rock bands and indie rock in influential but friendly New Jersey club.

The Mercury Lounge, 217 East Houston St., at Avenue A, ✆ 260 4700, entrance around ㉚ $10. Well-respected and very East Village: pop, art rock and indie rock bands (Dave Alvin and Me'shell N'degeocello); also bands from the neighbourhood: Brilliantine, Dogwater and Moxy Fruvous.

Pyramid, 101 Ave. A, between 6th and 7th Sts, ✆ 420 1590. Ratty East Village mainstay ㉛ for punk, drag, 'industrial music' and heavy rock with an interior including a bar, cellar and a small dance floor. As well as gigs, the club hosts a drag night on Sundays, and sometimes performance art.

Tramps, 51 West 21st St., near 5th Ave., ✆ 727 7788, or information on ✆ 544 1666. ㉜ Hugely varied programme, from the Mekons, 'the sole remaining legacy of UK punk' and ex-Animals singer Eric Burdon, 'the soul remaining legacy of UK garage' to New Orleans Blues (Snooks Eaglin) and Irish folk (the Wolftones).

Wetlands, 161 Hudson St., at Laight St., ✆ 966 4225. 'Eco-saloon' with booze-free rock, ㉝ reggae and psychedelic blues, plus gigs to benefit the environment.

Jazz and Blues

Since the forties, when they clustered around Harlem and the speakeasies of 52nd Street ('The Street'), most of the jazz clubs have drifted down to the Greenwich Village. Most are stereotypically small, dingy basement rooms, with cramped bars, so-so food and doleful aficionados. In general, there are two or three sets a night starting at 9 or 10pm and finishing at 2 or 3am. All clubs demand a cover charge of $10–20 and also a minimum charge for food or drink (about the price of two vodkas), except the piano bars (where drinks are expensive to make up for it) and Arthur's (*see* below). Often you can sit at the bar for less, and weekdays and brunches at weekends are normally a better deal as well. Otherwise in the summer there is free open-air jazz in Central and Riverside Parks, and remarkably good buskers in subways such as Times Square and Grand Central.

The best deal is the 10-day **Greenwich Village Jazz Festival** which takes place in early September, when a $15 pass gets you into Village clubs for free or at massively reduced cover charges (℃ 242 1785). Also, in June there is a **New York Women's Jazz Festival** with free entrance to many performances (℃ 505 5660).

Consult club advertisements in the *Voice* and reviews and listings in *Downbeat*, the city's jazz monthly and *Hot House,* a monthly give-away which you can pick up in the clubs themselves. There are also listings in the *New Yorker* and telephone listings on ℃ 1 (718) 465 7500.

Telephone listings: Jazzline, ℃ 479 7888.

Arthur's Tavern, 57 Grove St., near 7th Ave. and Sheridan Square, ℃ 675 6879. Good
34 value with entrance for the price of a drink. A youngish crowd, dim lights.

Birdland, 2745 Broadway, at 105th St., ℃ 749 2228. Reincarnation of the elegant forties and fifties 'Charlie Parker' supper club: Mark Morganelli and the All-Stars, Peggy Stern and Freddie Bryant.

Blue Note, 131 West 3rd St., between Macdougal St. and 6th Aves, ℃ 475 8592. Looks
35 like a garage conversion, but still pulls the big names—Ray Brown, Dave Brubeck and the Duke Ellington Orchestra. For one of these, the cover charge can be astronomical ($20–60). The club packs in all types, including Bruce Lee lookalikes.

Bradley's, 70 University Place, between 11th and 12th Sts, ℃ 228 6440. Low-lit piano bar
36 with wood-panelling, now 20 years old. Traditional jazz, mostly duos or trios, with a low cover charge. Good for brunch.

Fat Tuesday's, 190 3rd Ave., between 17th and 18th Sts, ℃ 533 7902. A literal transla-
37 tion of 'Mardi Gras', Fat Tuesday's is easy-going compared to some of the downtown clubs; a wide range of jazz artists but pricey covers (from $17.50–25).

Fez, in the Time Café, 380 Lafayette St., at Great Jones St., ℃ 533 7000. Café/restaurant with a 1970s-style stage attracting big audiences for 'Mingus Big Band Workshop' on Thurs nights in honour of the late great Charles Mingus. Better food than most.

57/57, 57 East 57th St., near 5th Ave., ℃ 758 5757. Elegant piano and bass room in the
38 Four Seasons Hotel, with lively martini bar.

Five Spot, 4 West 31st St., at 5th Ave., ℃ 631 0100. Sleek jazz and elegant dining in turn-
39 of-the-century hotel ballroom restored in 1993: these days featuring melodious bop and blues and jazz fusion.

Greene Street Café, 101 Greene St., ℃ 925 2415. Cavernous two-storey club/restaurant in SoHo, with seating on two levels and sleek clientele. Good food, piano on weekdays and trios on weekends.

Iridium Room, 44 West 63rd St., near Columbus Ave., ℃ 582 2121. Restaurant with an
40 upstairs bar and a downstairs club with 'surreal' décor: 'living legend' Les Paul, inventor of the electric guitar, on Mondays, and the rest of the week gutsy contemporary jazz. Jazz brunches at the weekends include unlimited free cocktails from 11.30am to 4pm.

Knickerbocker's, 33 University Place, at 9th St., ℃ 228 8490. Quality piano and bass duos in elegantly panelled restaurant and bar, open until 3am.

The Knitting Factory, 74 Leonard St., between Broadway and Church St., ℃ 219 3055. East Village outpost with a wildly eclectic range of programmes, usually experimental.

Michael's Pub, 211 East 55th St., between 2nd and 3rd Aves, ✆ 758 2272. Flash Upper
(41) East Side club famous for Woody Allen's appearances on Monday nights.

Smalls, 183 West 10th St, ✆ 929 7565. Up-and-coming jazz players in small but robust
West Village jazz club.

Sweet Basil, 88 7th Ave., between Bleecker and Grove Sts, ✆ 242 1785. High-calibre
mainstream jazz, in the requisite tin-ceilinged, wood-panelled room. Firmly on the
tourist circuit.

Tramps, 45 West 21st St., between 5th and 6th Aves, ✆ 727 2288. Mostly blues but programmes can be more excitingly varied.

Village Vanguard, 178 7th Ave. South, at Perry St., ✆ 255 4037. Six decades old and still
(42) going strong, Max Gordon's poky cellar in the West Village. Performers in the past
included Mingus, Davis and Monk and the basement has been used for hundreds
of recordings. Now the 17-piece Vanguard jazz orchestra plays Monday nights,
with a programme of mainstream and avant-garde jazz the rest of the week
including Pharoah Sanders, Kenny Barron and Ray Drummond, and imports from
Europe like Pierre Michelot and Christian Escoudet. No food.

Zinno, 126 West 13th St., ✆ 924 5182. Easy-going restaurant and chamber jazz club, with
the emphasis mostly on the high quality pasta.

Country, Folk, World and Spoken Word

New York isn't exactly the folk and country centre of the world, but they are well
represented. Poetry has had a come-back and is currently re-invigorating the folk
scene. Reggae and Afro-Caribbean are also strong, and salsa sounds, a mash of Latin
and African rhythms and American jazz, are all-pervasive in New York: on the
streets, in clubs and over the radio.

Centerfold Coffee House, Church of St Paul and St Andrew, 263 West 86th St., at
Broadway, ✆ 866 4454. Folk, jazz, bluegrass.

Les Poulets, 16 West 22nd St., at 5th Ave, ✆ 229 2000. Big name salsa and freestyle performers including Hector Tricoche, and Willie Cortes and Sweet Sensation.
Dancing all night and free admission for women on Thursdays. Popular and
crowded on weekends.

Nuyorican Poets Café, 236 East 3rd St., between Aves B and C, ✆ 505 8183. Set up in
(43) the 1970s as a venue for Puerto Rican poets, this re-opened in 1990 after the late
Miguelo Pinero, a former member and playwright, became internationally famous.
Now a wide variety of poets perform on their own or accompanied by music; no
food.

Rodeo Bar, 375 3rd Ave., at 27th St., ✆ 683 6500. Country music seven nights a week.

S.O.B. (Sounds of Brazil), 204 Varick St., at Houston St., ✆ 243 4940. Convivial supper
(44) club with Brazilian food and audience that likes to dance. Mostly Brazilian music,
also salsa, Haitian compas, calypso, reggae, Trinidad-carnival, zydeco.

The Spiral, 244 East Houston St., at Ave. A, ✆ 353 1740. Rock and country—Cowboy
Dick, the Smokestack Bros and the Rough Riders.

Wetlands, 161 Hudson St., near Vestry St., ✆ 966 4225. Popular blues and country club, in the style of the Lone Star, with organic food. British blues band Noel Redding, Latin R&B from Los Angeles in the form of the Wildcards, funk-rockers Bootsy and his Rubber Band, reggae and Irish folk.

Zinc Bar, 90 West Houston St., between La Guardia Place and Thompson St., ✆ 477 8337. Brazilian sounds and flamenco.

Theatre and Performance Art

Seats on Broadway are hideously expensive and tyrannized by apparently indestructible musicals (*Grease*, *Phantom of the Opera*, now in its 9th year, and *Les Misérables*), some of which the British can take responsibility for. In amongst the dross are good, sometimes excellent, productions. To find them, skim through the *New Yorker*, the On Stage column in the Friday Weekend section in the *New York Times*, or the *TheaterWeek*, a weekly magazine which lists every production.

The most interesting productions are staged on the fringe. Here prices are cheaper, writers grapple with real life as well as whimsy, and shows are less commercial. Standards vary, but you will always be able to dig out something exciting or shocking, or outstanding. 'Off-Broadway' theatre productions (seating audiences of 300) are professionally staged, and lean towards contemporary political and social dramas, often by American authors. 'Off-off-Broadway' productions are the cheapest, most experimental and weird. The best reviews for these can be found in *Time Out* or the *Village Voice*.

The TKTS booth in Times Square at 47th Street and Broadway (✆ 221 0013) sells half-price tickets for Broadway and off-Broadway productions on the day of the performance (between 3 and 8 for an evening performance, between 10 and 2 for matinées, although queues for both start forming in the morning). 'Twofer' coupons, from shops, hotels and restaurants, and the Visitors and Conventions Bureau on Columbus Circle, entitle you to two tickets for the price of one and also to book ahead. Students with ID can get standby 'rush' tickets half an hour before the performance (phone the theatre for details). At most of the agencies listed below you'll be charged full price plus a $2 surcharge, but you can pay over the telephone.

ticket agencies

Ticket Central, ✆ 279 4200, specialising in Off- and Off-off-Broadway.

Telecharge, ✆ 239 6200.

Ticketmaster, ✆ 307 7171.

Ticketron, ✆ 1 (800) SOLD OUT.

TKTS, West 47th St., and Broadway, half-price tickets on the day of the performance (*see* above).

Experimental Theatres and Repertory Companies

Atlantic Theater Company, 336 West 20th St., at 9th Ave., ✆ 947 8844. Presenting plays by the brilliant and technically tyrannical David Mamet, and new unknown writers in the company. **(45)**

Circle in the Square Downtown, 159 Bleecker St., between Thompson and Sullivan Sts, ✆ 254 6330. One of the oldest Off-Broadway theatres, consistently imaginative.

Circle Repertory, 99 7th Avenue South, at Sheridan Square, ✆ 924 7100. New American writers including Lanford Wilson, who was a member of the company for several years. *Burn This* and *As Is* moved from here to Broadway.

Jean Cocteau Repertory, 330 Bowery at Bond St., ✆ 677 0060. Mix of new plays in metre and classics including Genet, Sophocles, Sartre etc.

The Kitchen, 512 West 19th St., ✆ 255 5793. *The* place for performance art.

La MaMa ETC, 74a East 4th St., between Bowery and 2nd Ave., ✆ 475 7710. Bastion of Off-off-Broadway experimental theatre, founded in 1961 by Ellen Stewart and based in the East Village and launch-pad for writers like Lanford Wilson, Sam Shephard and Harvey Fierstein. For the most part, productions are of a high standard, and they cover a range: avant-garde, experimental, foreign playwrights and companies (*Crime and Punishment* improvised in Polish), and performance art. **(46)**

Nuyorican Poets' Café, 236 East 3rd St., between Aves B and C, ✆ 505 8183. Plays as well, including Greek tragedy with a 'contemporary twist'.

P.S. 122, 150 1st Ave., at East 9th St., ✆ 477 2588. A whole range of exciting events taking in performance art, new music, improvisation and comedy (including Eddie Izzard) with inspiring work by John O'Keefe and a marathon festival in February.

Public Theater, 425 Lafayette St., ✆ 598 7150, *www.publictheater.org*. Productions by Joseph Papp's New York Shakespeare Company. Papp was the man who fought for the Central Park Shakespeare festival against all the odds (*see* below) and his work at the Public is nearly always controversial, spanning Yiddish theatre, Afro-American playwrights, and new or lesser-known plays such as Chikamatsu's *Gonza the Lancer.* **(47)**

Ridiculous Theater Company, 1 Sheridan Square, ✆ 691 2271. Farce, parody, lampoons and revivals, including a production of *Turds in Hell* by the late Charles Ludlam, who founded the company in the sixties.

Shakespeare Festival in Central Park, Delacorte Theater, Central Park at West 79th St., ✆ 598 8500. Two Shakespeare productions per summer in Central Park's outdoor theatre between June and September. Names like Meryl Streep, Kevin Kline and Michelle Pfeiffer draw big crowds and you should get to the queue (with a picnic) by the late morning. Tickets are free and limited to two per person.

Sullivan Street Theater, 181 Sullivan St., between Houston and Bleecker Sts, ✆ 674 3838. New York's equivalent of London's *Mouse-Trap*, the endearing fifties musical *The Fantasticks* has run here for nearly four decades since 1960 and is currently the longest-running show in American theatre history.

Writers Theater, 145 West 46th St., ✆ 869 9770. Platform for new writers, who are given the opportunity to work with established directors and develop their plays in front of an audience, with an audience discussion afterwards.

Comedy and Cabaret

In the seventies the cult TV show 'Saturday Night Live' spawned a clutch of new clubs, giving New York comedy a much-needed boost. Now clubs range from dingy 'rooms' to full-blown theatres; standards plummet from outstanding to bomb. Check listings in *New York Magazine* and the ads in the *Voice* or *Time Out.*

Piano bars and cabarets are also a mixed bag; paradise for some, hell for others. In the downtown piano bars, audiences are jollied into boistrous singalongs round a piano or silly dances during the choruses. Those who don't join in will be ostracized in a crowded room with no escape. Uptown cabarets and piano bars on the other hand are more staid affairs, in plush drawing rooms with jazz on the piano and Cole Porter songs. The only required audience participation here is to sip cocktails.

Café Carlyle, Madison Ave., at East 76th St., ✆ 744 1600. Bobby Short, the entertaining (49) aristocrat of New York cabaret, plays Gershwin and Cole Porter to assorted glitterati. The cover charge is $35 and you should dress swish.

Catch a Rising Star, 1487 1st Ave., between 77th and 78th Sts, ✆ 794 1906. Packed but (50) comfortable: the club which launched a thousand comedians, including Robin Williams.

ComedySportz, Telephone Bar and Grill, 149 2nd Ave., between 9th and 10th Sts., ✆ 875 7428. 'Who's Line is it Anyway' competitive charades on Wednesday nights at the Telephone Bar.

The Comic Strip, 1568 2nd Ave., between 81st and 82nd Sts, ✆ 861 0386. Bare room with a sharp audience and an open mike: anyone can get up and have a go, sometimes with disastrous consequences. About 15 comedians a night including, occasionally, Eddie Murphy, who got his first break here.

The Duplex, 61 Christopher St., at 7th Avenue South, ✆ 255 5438. West Village cabaret (48) and piano bar (New York's oldest) with a kindly audience composed of gays and tourists. Established comedians and an open-mike spot for foolhardy amateurs.

Gotham Comedy CLub, 34 West 22nd St., between 5th and 6th Aves., ✆ 367 9000. A rich assortment, with a new talent showcase on Wednesdays and 'Stand Up & Queer' gay and lesbian comedy on Tuesdays.

Luna Lounge, 171 Ludlow St., between Houston and Stanton Sts., ✆ 260 2323. Free alternative comedy on Monday nights: Michael Portnoy, Marc Maron and David Wain.

The Original Improvisation, 433 West 34th St., between 9th and 10th Aves., ✆ 279 3446. Over a quarter of a century old with a very funny amateur night on the first Sunday of each month.

Stand-Up New York, 236 West 78th St., ✆ 595 0850. Upper West Side comedy club with a stage and an amateur contest at midnight. Brave souls are jeered off, survivors win money.

Surf Reality, 172 Allen St., between Stanton and Rivington Sts., ✆ 673 4182. Satirical comedy club, with Faceboyz, the best open-mike in town.

Art Galleries

There's supposed to be around 90,000 artists and 500 art galleries in New York. Don't be diffident about sauntering into the most exclusive gallery: inside you can see work rivalling exhibitions in the Guggenheim or Whitney museums, and all for free (including the *New York Earth Room*, a room full of earth in SoHo). To find out what's going on get a copy the *Art Now Gallery Guide*, a monthly guide (with useless maps), available free in galleries and bookstores. Also look at any reviews in the *New York Times* and the magazines *Artscribe*, *Arts Magazine* and *Artnews*.

Practically all the maverick East Village galleries which titillated the New York art world in the eighties have closed down, or moved out. These days some of the liveliest art is shown in **Chelsea**, at pioneering galleries like Greene-Naftali or the publicly funded DIA Arts Center, who have quickly drawn Upper East Side and SoHo galleries into the area. Conceptual art and process painting do not have as vice-like a grip over the art galleries as they do in England, and in general there is a greater willingness in New York to show work that challenges.

With the exception of SoHo, the city's art galleries divide into two camps: those on the Upper East Side and 57th Street, showing well-known and respectable artists (Julian Schnabel, Robert Rauschenberg and Louise Nevelson); and those in SoHo, showing slightly more provocative works (Cindy Sherman, Stephen Westfall and Eric Fischl). At opposite ends of the spectrum are the galleries on Madison Avenue in the Upper East Side (the stuffiest of all); and 'Alternative Spaces' established in the seventies: not-for-profit, co-operatively run institutions which show a mix of conceptual art, installations, performance art, the unsaleably shocking, the way-out or the political.

Remember that the galleries each represent a 'stable' of artists whose work is often available for viewing in a back room. *Galleries are mostly closed on Mondays and open 12–5 Tuesday–Saturday; nearly all close in July and August.*

Upper East Side and 57th Street

ACA, 41 East 57th St., near 5th Ave. Specializes in 20th-century Americans: good for lesser-known work by Georgia O'Keeffe, Reginald Marsh, the Ashcan School, the Stieglitz group and Judy Chicago.

André Emmerich, 41 East 57th St., between Madison and Park Aves. Contemporary American, especially the colour-field school: Morris Louis, Lawrence Poons, Kenneth Noland, and also some British work: Hockney prints and photographs and Anthony Caro sculptures.

Gagosian, 980 Madison Ave., at 76th St. The first one-man Damian Hirst show in New York, shown here in 1996 to media swoons over 'Damian'. Normally a broader selection of contemporary and modern art, in quite a large space: paintings by Francesco Clemente, David Salle and Andy Warhol.

Marion Goodman, 24 West 57th St., between 5th and 6th Aves. Emphasis on the European and Latin American avant-garde—Anselm Kiefer, Christian Boltanski, Gabriel Orozco and Gerhard Richter.

Sidney Janis, 110 West 57th St., between 6th and 7th Aves. Museum-like gallery with heavyweight shows of 20th-century and contemporary art: Mondrian, Giacometti, Saul Steinberg and Jackson Pollock (who showed here at the height of his success).
53

M. Knoedler & Co. Inc., 19 East 70th St., between 5th and Madison Aves. Specializes in American Abstract Expressionists, also Frank Stella, Alexander Calder and Howard Hodgkin.

Robert Miller, 41 East 57th St., at Madison Ave. Grand, tall-ceilinged gallery showing slick and exciting contemporary work, Robert Mapplethorpe, Yayoi Kusama, Louise Bourgeois and Basquiat.
54

PaceWildenstein, 32 East 57th St., between Park and Madison Aves. Glossily commercial, with a branch in Los Angeles, and a brace of 20th-century untouchables including Picasso, Rauschenberg and Rothko. Also prints, small Impressionist works and an exquisite collection of African art.
55

SoHo

Mary Boone, 416 West Broadway, between Spring and Prince Sts. A prime mover in the eighties, Boone specializes in neo-expressionist contemporary art and introduced New York to the likes of Francesco Clemente, Julian Schnabel and David Salle, all of whom eventually left her for smarter venues.

Leo Castelli, 420 West Broadway, between Spring and Prince Sts. The Jupiter of the New York art world since the sixties, when he battled for Andy Warhol and Roy Lichtenstein. Now representing Jasper Johns and Bruce Nauman, with a graphics annex up the road at 578 Broadway.
56

The New York Earth Room, 141 Wooster St, between Prince and W. Houston Sts. Open 12–6 Wed–Sun. As it says: a room full of earth on Wooster Street, by installation artist Walter De Maria.
57

Exit Art: The First World, 548 Broadway, between Prince and Spring Sts. 'Sound installations'.

O. K. Harris, 383 West Broadway, between Broome and Spring Sts. Solo shows of 'significant artwork with no prejudice as to the style or materials employed' in a spectacular gallery space owned by Ivan Karp ex art and film critic for the *Village Voice* and director of the Leo Castelli Gallery.

Phyllis Kind, 136 Green St. Figurative American art, contemporary Russian art and the Chicago School of 'Hairy Who' artists.

Max Protetch, 560 Broadway, at Spring St. Contemporary architectural drawings and models (Louis Kahn, Aldo Rossi and Frank Lloyd Wright), as well as architecturally inspired sculpture.
58

Thread Waxing Space, 476 Broadway, between Broome and Grand Sts. Art and films for the club-going fraternity.

John Weber, 142 Greene St., between Houston and Prince Sts. Conceptual and Minimal art, young to established artists including Sol LeWitt.

Williamsburg, Brooklyn

Supposedly the East Village of the nineties, though so far not explosive.

Momenta, 72 Berry St., between North 9th and 10th Sts. Alternative group shows by neighbourhood artists including Jennifer Bolande and Bill Schuck.

Chelsea

Paolo Baldacci Gallery, 521 West 23rd St., between 10th and 11th Aves. Italian and
59 international contemporary painting, sculpture and photography, here from East 57th St, and including work by Nan Goldin, James Hyde and Medrie MacPhee.

Greene/Naftali Gallery, 8th floor, 526 West 26th St., between 10th and 11th Aves. A
60 big space with freight elevators taking you to the top floor of a warehouse. Showing an impressive selection of contemporary and 20th-century art—including Fiona Rae and Louise Bourgeois—with an emphasis on women.

Dia Center for the Arts, 548 West 22nd St., between 10th and 11th Aves, with an exhi-
61 bition site at *www.diacenter.org/*. Sponsors ambitious environmental projects and long-term installations, like Walter De Maria's *The New York Earth Room* at 141 Wooster, and the same artist's *The Broken Kilometer*, at 393 West Broadway. The big centre on 22nd Street is worth a visit for installations including Juan Munoz' *A Place Called Abroad* which takes up the whole 4th floor. A rooftop (including a restaurant) has deck projects by Dan Graham. Closed July and September.

Pat Hearn 530 West 22nd St., between 10th and 11th Aves. Pop abstract, mixed media and conceptual art.

Annina Nosei, 530 West 22nd St., between 10th and 11th Aves. Originally based in SoHo and showing painting and conceptual art.

Alternative Spaces and Not-for-profit Galleries

Angelo Orensatz Foundation, 172 Norfolk St., near East Houston St., ✆ 529 7194. Occasional/unconventional performance art and contemporary dance pieces in synagogue on the Lower East Side. Call for details.

Alternative Museum, 594 Broadway, neqar Prince St., suite 402. Run by artists for unknowns.

Artists Space, 38 Greene St., between Grand and Broome Sts. Cockpit for new artists like Cindy Sherman, David Salle and Jonathan Borofsky. Instant stimulation exhibitions, video art and installations.

Clocktower Gallery, 108 Leonard St. and Broadway, open noon–6pm, Wed–Sun.
62 Installations, conceptual and contemporary art in a clocktower which incidentally has one of the best views of Manhattan.

The Drawing Center, 35 Wooster St., between Broome and Greene Sts. Anything on paper including architectural drawings and musical scores.

P.S.1, 46–01 21st St., Long Island City. Enterprising exhibitions of contemporary work and the chance to see resident artists at work in a school in Queens.

Dance

New York is the dance capital of the world. Jerome Robbins, Twyla Tharp, Gerald Arpino, Martha Graham, Alvin Ailey, Arthur Mitchell, Eliot Feld, Trisha Brown, Susan Jaffe, Paul Taylor and Merce Cunningham are all permanent residents in New York. Dance Valhalla is to be found in the Lincoln Center, the base for New York's two main companies—the New York City Ballet (in the process of moving to a new auditorium in Times Square) and the American Ballet Theater (ABT).

During the seasons (September to January and April to June), you can see almost any kind of dance in New York: classical, ballet-based modern dance, experimental performance dance, swing, tap, be-bop, hop. For the best listings consult *The New Yorker*, the *Sunday New York Times* or *New York Magazine*.

The Established Companies

New York City Ballet (NYCB), New York State Theater, Lincoln Center, ✆ 870 5570 (*see* also 'Classical Music', above). Founded by George Balanchine, and now directed by Pater Martins, the quality of the dancing is still innovative and first-class. Usually there are tickets left over on the day of the performance, and some returns.

American Ballet Theater (ABT), Metropolitan Opera House, Lincoln Center, ✆ 362 6000 (*see* also 'Classical Music', above). After Baryshnikov's resignation, the debt-plagued ABT has gone through 3 artistic directors in almost as many years and is now under ex-dancer Kevin McKenzie. Exceptional dancing, from corps to stars, although the company only performs from May until July at the Met. Repertoire ranges from 19th-century classical to modern, and tickets from $21 to a staggering $145. Cheaper deals on the day of the performance.

Brooklyn Academy of Music (BAM), 30 Lafayette Ave., Brooklyn, ✆ 1 (718) 636 4100. One of the most important platforms for contemporary dance in the city. Three theatres, including the handsome 19th-century Opera House, used for dance premieres and encompassing mainstream and way-out. The Next Wave Festival in the autumn celebrates the international and American avant-garde.

Other Venues

Aaron Davies Hall, City College, West 135th St., at Convent Ave., ✆ 690 4100. Big venue for the classical Dance Theater of Harlem which always has a stimulating mix of works in repertory (✆ 690 2800 for venues).

City Center, 131 West 55th St., between 6th and 7th Aves, ✆ 581 7907. Based under a Moorish dome and a paradise for classical and modern dance. Companies come and go from September until June: the Joffrey Ballet (under Gerald Arpino); the Alvin Ailey American Dance Theater (modern, jazz and blues); the Dance Theater of Harlem; and the companies of Merce Cunningham, Paul Taylor and Trisha Brown.

Dance Theater Workshop (DTW), Bessie Schomberg Theater, 219 West 19th St., between 7th and 8th Aves, ✆ 619 6500. Highly respected and championing unknown avant-garde works in a poky theatre.

Joyce Theater, 175 8th Ave., at 19th St., ✆ 242 0800. Contemporary and classical dance in a converted movie palace, with eight or nine top-class touring companies per season. The Eliot Feld company, performing Feld's own works, is in permanent residence.

The Kitchen, 512 West 19th St., between 10th and 11th Aves, ✆ 255 5793. Sometimes bizarre and sometimes innovative.

P.S. 122, 122 150 1st Ave., at 9th St., ✆ 477 5288. Post-modern dance, often combined with performance art, in a converted school gymnasium.

St Mark's-in-the-Bowery Dancespace Project, 2nd Ave., and East 10th St., ✆ 674 8112. Experimental contemporary dance from Sept to June as well as poetry readings (by Allen Ginsberg up until his death in 1997) in Manhattan's second oldest church.

Nightclubs, Strip Clubs, Ballrooms, Lounges and Cigar Bars

You need to be brave or stupid to get into a New York Club. Bouncers require at least a gesture to fashion (for both sexes anything with holes in it should suffice). The other option is to tag along with people who cut a dash and hope you will blend in. In 1996, 24.3 million people visited Manhattan's 300 or so clubs. As a rule it's easier to get in if you arrive early, if you're a woman, or if you look like one. Sometimes, if you arrive before 10.30, you'll get in free.

Once inside, you'll be inundated with cards inviting you to other clubs at discount prices. With these, you can start circulating, and if the bouncers take a shine to you they may let you in free. Some clubs don't have alcohol licences. In those that do it's a good idea not to drink anyway as prices are high even for tap water. Some clubgoers conceal hipflasks in their clothing, but clubs are live with security guards who will spy out such offenders. Arrive in a voluminous coat and you'll have to pay to have it stored in the cloakroom.

Clubs here, like everywhere else, have the reproductive abilities of aphids. Recently though, many are going through a beleaguered phase as community groups and city regulators try to crack down on noise, drugs and crime. Raids, licence violations and permit checks have hit club owners badly, and many gay or hard-core clubs have been heavily fined or shut down. **Lounge and cigar bars**, where men and women puff away on cigars (what next, pipes?) are still popular.

Before you venture out, consult magazines and papers like *Time Out*, *Paper Magazine*, *Project X* and *Details*, also gay papers like *Homo Xtra* and *Next*. The most exciting clubs won't be listed, so ask around. Otherwise you might find out the hard way that somewhere that calls itself a 'club' is really only a bistro decorated with chequered tablecloths; and that a 'bowling alley' or 'café' is dark and sweaty and full of people dancing to jungle; whereas something called a 'lounge bar' may include chain-mail curtains and involve a lot of cryptic posing.

Finally, 'House' music, played in most clubs, has diversified in the 1990s but still includes 'handbag' house, happy and upbeat and danced to around a handbag. The fashionable night to go out is still Thursday (New Yorkers like to prove that they can dance all night, and still get themselves to work the next morning).

@Café's Urban Reality/Snow Peas, 12 St Mark's Place, near 3rd Ave., *www.fly.net*, ✆ 726 1898. Acid, trance, progressive house and techno soundtracks attended by New Japanese in East Village Internet cafés.

Baby Doll Lounge, 34 White St., at Church St., ✆ 226 4870. Go-Go bar: female exotic dancers, heavy metal music.

The Bowling Club, Bowlmor Lanes, 110 University Place, between 12th and 13th Sts., ✆ 255 8158. From 10pm onwards, bowling at the Bowlmor Lanes with fluorescent balls and shoes, and underground house, jungle and techno music by DJ Kazimir. $10 entry and shoe rental.

Buddha Bar, 150 Varick St., at Vandam St., ✆ 255 4433. Hip-hop on Mondays and fashion models in a lounge decorated with plaster-cast buddhas.

Cake, 99 Ave B between 6th and 7th Sts, ✆ 388 2570. Famous for its retro music and outlandishness (including a 'sleazefest' competition for the 'hairiest hole') this re-opened as a straight bar in 1997 after it was shut down for disorderliness.

Coney Island High, 15 St Mark's Place, between 2nd and 3rd Aves., ✆ 674 7959, information on Konkrete Jungle at *www.interport.net/-mixedbag*. Rockabilly, R&B, swing, soul and mambo on the dance floor for '50s throwbacks on Saturdays and '70s 'grooves' on Tuesdays. Jungle music, at 'Konkrete Jungle', on Mondays.

Den of Thieves, 145 Houston St., between 1st and 2nd Aves., ✆ 477 5005. Small bar/club on the Lower East Side playing an arbitrary mix of music including jungle, hip-hop, 'trip-hop', goth, soul, reggae etc. Electronic music on Sundays.

Don Hill's, 511 Greenwich St., at Spring St., ✆ 334 1390. K-Tel music, a tame looking crowd, and a gay bent on Fridays and once a month queer party. Closed Mon.

Club CyberSex at Downtime, 251 West 30th St., between 7th and 8th Aves., ✆ 695 2747. Live 'psychedelic' bands, punk and 'cyber' music, and CyberSex go-go dancers. If all this means anything to you, you'll no doubt enjoy yourself. 'Fantasy art exhibitions' and a free glass of wine on Thursdays.

Expo, including 'Café Con Leche', 124 West 43rd St., between Broadway and 6th Ave., ✆ 819 0377. Raunchy lesbians, go-go boys, drag queens and kings, heterosexuals and Latin disco and merengue soundtracks; open until 6am.

Flamingo East, including the 999999's, 219 2nd Ave., between 13th and 14th Sts., ✆ 533 2860. Pleasantly dark 'neo-lounge' of clothes designers.

Life, 158 Bleecker St., at Thompson St., ✆ 420 1999. Ultra-fashionable ironic 80s-style disco club with a VIP lounge, tongue-in-cheek posing and Kenny Kenny on the door.

Limelight, 47 West 30th St., at 6th Ave., ℗ 807 7850. Opened in 1984 in a church, much to the horror of New York's Episcopal community, and closed by police on narcotics-related disorderly premises charges in 1996. Due to re-open in late 1997.

Liquid Sky, 241 Lafayette St., at Prince St., ℗ 343 0532. For information on raves within and around Manhattan.

Ludlow Bar, 165 Ludlow St., between Houston and Rivington Sts., ℗ 353 0536. With-it bar for Lower East Side poseurs, bands every night.

Meow Mix, 269 Houston St., at Suffolk St., ℗ 254 1434. Lesbian club popular with East Village types and a hostess who performs a breakdance solo on Sundays at 2am.

Mother: including 'Clit Club' and 'Click and Drag', 432 West 14th St., at Washington
69 St., ℗ 366 5680, info 529 3300 or at *www.echonyc.com/-interjackie.html*. Lesbian club popular with heterosexuals, in the meat-packing district. Kitsch disco on Mondays, 'Clit Club' on Fridays with dancing girls on podiums and a strictly enforced 'high femme' or 'sleek male drag' dress code. 'Click and Drag' is a cyber-fetish night devoted to the technological cult of *anime* or Japanese sci-fi animation, and including CD Roms, and go-go, fetish and *anime* performances.

Nell's, 246 West 14th St., betwen 7th and 8th Aves, ℗ 675 1567. Sitting-room with chan-
70 deliers, velvet sofas and wood-panelling, in a former Edwardian gentlemen's club. Now more than a decade old and indestructible, the lounge club is less frantic than its rivals, with hip-hop (Mondays), reggae and house, and a Sunday jazz and funk evening with live bands and food that's an institution in itself.

Organic Grooves, locations vary. Floating Friday night club with unlikely locations, from community spaces decked out in baco-foil to cafés, shops or, more conventional, disco parlours. Dub-funk, trip-hop and live musicians.

Palladium, 126 East 14th St., between 3rd and 4th Aves., ℗ 473 7171. Superannuated eighties club now concentrating on hip-hop with the radio station Hot 97 pre-senting a night of hip-hop 'madness' on Fridays ($20), DJ Junioe Vasquez on Saturdays.

Pyramid, 101 Ave A, between 6th and 7th Sts. Live jungle on Tuesday nights.

Robots, 25 Ave B at 3rd St., ℗ 995 0968, open Wed–Thurs 10pm–7am, Fri–Sat 10pm–
71 noon. Apocalyptic opening hours, a bar and dance floor dedicated to brutal house and acid-style trance music, luckily so dark the pallid faces and staring eyes are hard to make out.

Roseland, 239 West 52nd St., near Broadway, ℗ 247 0200. Ballroom-dancing heaven
72 with sambas, waltzes and fox-trots for 9½ hours from 2pm on Thursdays and Sundays, in fifties relic ballroom. A Wall of Fame dating from 1923 is inscribed with the names of more than 600 couples who met and married at the Roseland. At other times the ballroom is used for discos and rock bands like Yo La Tengo, Pavement and Jamiroquai.

Roxy, 515 West 18th St., at 10th Ave., ℗ 645 5156. Decadently renovated in 1996, the
73 club which began as roller-disco for gays and became wildly fashionable in the early nineties. Popularity has smoothed away its edges and nowadays it includes a cigar bar, martini lounge, Alan Sanctuary's Saturday party and feverish disco-dancing to the usual mix of house, reggae and hip-hop.

SFB Sound Factory Bar, 12 West 21st St., between 5th and 6th Aves., ✆ 206 7770. An
(74) excellent (computerized) lighting and sound system, a juice bar and impressive
dancers. Good variety of music, with Latino salsa and merengue combined with
hip-hop and R&B for a mainly black clientele plus 'banjee boys' (Puerto Rican
homeboys) and a 'voguing' crowd for Mr Frankie Knuckles, DJ, on Fridays.

Social Toilet at the Q Bar, 188 Ave A, at 12th St., ✆ 777 6254. Dark passageways and
twirling jockstraps in colourful East Village gay club.

Tatou, 151 East 50th St., between 3rd and Lexington Aves., ✆ 753 1444. Elegant supper
(75) club for sleek types turning into a disco from 11pm onwards, with a cigar bar
upstairs.

Twilo, 530 West 27th St., between 10th and 11th Aves., ✆ 268 1600. Formerly known as
Sound Factory, and these days playing deep and progressive house. Occasional art
shows, a temporary gym catering to Chelsea 'gym queens', and a monthly 'tea
dance' to 'handbag' house.

Tunnel, 220 12th Ave., at 27th St., ✆ 695 4682. Latin and African bands in the week;
house and Garage soundtracks on the weekends.

Vinyl, 157 Hudson St., between Laight and Hubert Sts., ✆ 343 1379. Hot, loud and
sweaty; open Fridays until 7am, Saturdays until 10am, and promoted and hosted
by E-Man. Dancing, drag queens, sofas in the lounge and a Sunday morning party
starting at 6am and culminating in 'mega-reggae' in the evening.

Webster Hall, 125 East 11th St., between 3rd and 4th Aves., ✆ 353 1600, reservations
for Havana Lounge ✆ 606 4202. Commerical club on four floors, with a maze of
stairs and corridors, go-go dancers, a massive dance floor with easy-to-dance-to
music (and a mainstrain salsa night on Sundays), plus a cigar lounge on the
balcony. As dead as tank tops, but fun.

A Guide for the Musically Clueless

ambient	cerebral muzac for the 90s with no repetitive beats, described by Brian Eno as 'thinking music'.
banjee boys	Puerto Rican boys from the neighbourhood.
bluegrass	songs and dances from the Appalachians, played fast.
breakbeat	another word for drum and bass (*see* below), incorporating futuristic electronic music via complex technology.
cyber	futuristic fusion of thrash (*see* below) and punk incorporating electronic world wide web sounds.
dark cyber	electronic and mean.
drum and bass	ragga sound shattered by house, classic jazz formations and techno beats; emanating from the dance halls of Jamaica.
dub	ragga-influenced dance hall sound.
funk	a style of urban black music dating from the 50s, dominated by bass guitar, a languorous, syncopated beat and incorporating African rhythms ('ethno-funk'), the blues, and early rock, roll and jazz.

funky	Either very good or really bad, meaning 'excellent' or 'stinking'. (originally US dialect used to describe the 'smell' of sex). In music: urban, earthy or melodiously compelling; dominated by bass guitar.
future jazz	a fusion of trip-hop, dub and drum and bass (*see* above and below).
garage	fast, highly-produced form of house originating in a club called the Paradise Garage.
gig	for musicians: a playing date or one-night engagement.
home-boy	someone from the neighbourhood who's cool and safe to hang out with.
house	diversifying in the 90s from 'handbag' house (dancing round a handbag) to 'progressive' house, 'hard' house, 'tribal' house, 'Hi' house, 'under ground' house, 'doll' house, 'detached' house and 'deep' house, the subtleties of which are too microscopic to go into.
illbient	muzac that gives you a headache.
jungle	a mutant hybrid created in England from drum and bass (*see* above) and characterized by shattering beats and, increasingly, dreamy ambient chords and funky jazz samples. The holistic philosophy of 'Junglism' tries to promote 'multi-racial unity and respect for ourselves, each other and the earth'.
polyrhythmic future funk	could mean anything.
psychedelic	funk on drugs, hence 'funkadelic'.
riff	improvised passage, usually performed solo.
soul	music expressing the essence of black America.
techno	style of urban black music from Detroit, characterized by sounds which are as harsh as the industrial landscape. European techno is considered a hybrid and is comparatively more multicultural and dance-orientated.
thrash	sexual abuse of a guitar; the antithesis of 'mellow' or melodious music.
trance	a less frenetic form of acid house music.
tribal	people who remain true to their origins, in music meaning 'earthy'.
trip-hop	slowed down hip-hop with a 'mellow' vibe.
vibe	an aura set off by music or generally by people getting together and having a good time.

Shopping

A man without a smiling face must not open a shop.

Chinese proverb

You can buy practically anything in Manhattan, including heated toilet seats. Like nowhere else in the world, shops here fuse the theatrical, the slick and the tongue-in-cheek. Barnes & Noble bookstores, for example, are mock-libraries, open until midnight and furnished with sofas and armchairs. Antique and household goods shops like ABC sell furniture from premises as cluttered as real homes—and which sometimes actually *are* homes. Record and clothes shops, like Dance Tracks in the East Village or Diesel on Lexington Avenue, have in-house DJs and dancing cashiers. Department stores like Barneys have the world's most surreally dressed windows including, one Christmas, a real Jungian psychoanalyst and his authentic analysee. In Manhattan, even the shop-o-phobe can gratify him or herself—at F A O Schwarz, where pre-gift-wrapped toys are sold from a 'quick pick' desk, or at most department stores, where 'personal shoppers' are paid to buy clothes, Christmas and birthday presents on their client's behalf.

Most of the big department stores, electronics and clothes shops are clustered around **Midtown** on 5th Avenue and 57th Street, though the area also includes the enjoyable retail mayhem of the **Garment District**. The **Upper East Side** has the world's most expensive antiques and art galleries. On weekends shoppers tend to decamp to the Upper West Side, Chinatown, the Flatiron District and the East and West Villages. The **Upper West Side** has natty clothes shops, gourmet delis, expensive crafts and flea markets, and second-hand books on the sidewalks. The **East Village**, where shops stay open late into the night, has alternative fashion designers, junk shops, book shops, record shops, delis and kitsch and offbeat novelties. The **Flatiron District** has elegant household goods, sportwear and furniture shops. **SoHo** has art galleries, delis, furniture and toy shops and quantities of sleek fashion designers. The best places for bargains and discounts are **Chinatown**, the **Lower East Side** and **8th Avenue**; the best flea and flower markets are in **Chelsea** and **Canal Street**; and the two best places for food are the **Lower East Side** and **9th Avenue**. The **West Village** has gourmet delis, vintage clothes, antiques, books, pets plus shops specifically for gays, from gay insurance brokers to gay opticians. Finally, the best second-hand clothes store is the Domsey Warehouse in **Williamsburg** in Brooklyn.

One thing to get used to is the 8¼ per cent **sales tax**; it's not shown on the price displayed on shelves, but whacked on to everything at the till. This can come as a shock to British visitors who are used to having their sales taxes (which are actually double those in the US) worked into the shelf price already.

Providing you know what to buy, Manhattan can be staggeringly cheap. Artists' supplies, at Pearl Paint for example, are half the price of similar goods in London. Computers, electronics, cameras and hi-fi are half price, but remember *videos and televisions won't be compatible*. Cosmetics, like Revlon, Clinique and Max Factor, are half or two thirds the price of anything in London. And clothes, for example Levis, Nike, Oshkosh and Adidas are between 25 and 50% cheaper in New York.

Sizes

Cuts tend to be more generous in America, so if you're a size 12 in the UK you will shrink to a size 10 (US: size 8) in New York.

Women's clothes

UK	8	10	12	14	16	18	
US	6	8	10	12	14	16	
Eu	38	40	42	44	46	48	

Men's shoes

UK	6	7	8	9	10	11	12
US	8	9	10	11	12	13	14
Eu	39	40	41	42	43	44	45

Women's shoes

UK	4	5	6	7	8
US	5	6	7	8	9
Eu	37	38	39	40	41

Remember: tights are pantyhose, waistcoats are vests, vests are undershirts, dressing gowns are robes and trousers are pants, but panties are knickers.

Weights and Measures

The US uses imperial weights and measures—inches, yards, miles, ounces and pounds (body weight is measured in pounds and not stones). American gallons/quarts/pints are five-sixths the size of Imperial gallons/quarts/pints. In cookery, a 'cup' of liquid is half a US pint, and an Imperial pint is 2½ US cups.

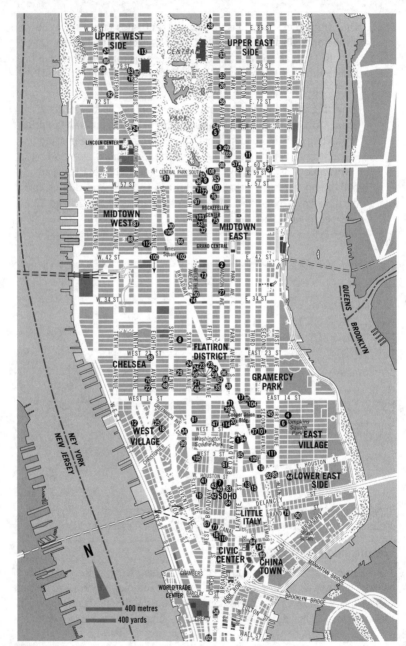

1	Astor Wines and Spirits	
2	Park Avenue Liquor Shop	
3	Sherry-Lehmann Inc.	
4	20th Century Design	
5	American Hurrah	
6	Atomic Passion	
7	Backpages	
8	Chelsea Antiques Building	
9	Bergdorf Goodman	
10	Irreplaceable Artefacts of North America	
11	Tender Buttons	
12	Kelter/Malcé	
13	Lost City Arts	
14	Sinotique	
15	Cheap Paint	
16	Pearl Paint	
17	Utrecht	
18	Angel Feet	
19	The Aveda Institute	
20	Body Shop	
21	Carapan	
22	The Service Station	
23	Academy Book Store	
24	Barnes & Noble	
25	The Biography Bookshop	
26	Books & Co.	
27	The Complete Traveler Bookstore	
28	Cooper Hewitt Museum Shop	
29	A Different Light Bookstore	
30	Drama Bookstore	
31	Forbidden Planet	
32	Gotham Book Mart	
33	New York Bound	
34	Oscar Wilde Bookshop	
35	Revolution Books	
36	Rizzoli's	
37	St Mark's Bookshop	
38	Union Square Book Stall	
39	Strand Book Store	
40	Anna Sui	
41	Betsey Johnson	
42	Morgane Le Fay	
43	Todd Oldham	
44	The Dress	
45	Steven Alan	
46	Emporio Armani	
47	Patricia Field	
48/49	Barney's	
50	Macy's, Herald Square	
51	Bloomingdale's	
52	Chanel	
53	Diesel	
54	Gianni Versace	
55	Issey Miyake	
56	Polo/Ralph Lauren	
57	The Original Levi's Store	
58	Century 21	
59	Daffy's	
60	Syms	
61	Blades	
62	Paragon Sports	
63	Alice Underground	
64	Canal Jean Co.	
65	Screaming Mimi's	
66	47th Avenue Photo	
67	Uncle Uncle's	
68	Barney's	
69	Barney's Madison Avenue	
70	Earth General	
71	Felissimo	
72	Henri Bendel	
73	Lord & Taylor	
74	Macy's	
75	Saks Fifth Avenue	
76	Takashimaya	
77	Canal Street Casbah	
78	1S 44 Greenflea Market	
79	Orchard Street	
80	Greenmarkets	
81	Balducci's	
82	Citarella Fish Bar	
83	Dean & Deluca	
84	Kamman Supermarket	
85	Russ & Daughters	
86	Zabar's	
87	Amy's Bread	
88	Bruno the King of Ravioli	
89	The Hong Kong Egg Cake Lady	
90	Kossar's Bialys	
91	Petrossian	
92	Yonah Schimmel	
93	Frank E. Campbell	
94	Astor Place Hair Designers	
95	Peppe and Bill at the Plaza Hotel	
96	ABC Carpet and Home	
97	MoMA Design Store	
98	Williams-Sonoma	
99	Pink Pussycat Boutique	
100	8th Avenue	
101	Gem Spa	
102	Hotalings Foreign News Depot	
103	Studio Optics	
104	Kiehl's	
105	Bleecker Bob's Golden Oldies	
106	Virgin Megastore	
107	NikeTown	
108	F.A.O Schwartz	
109	Bowery Restaurant District	
110	Canal Rubber/Canal Surplus	
111	Little Rickie	
112	Luther Music Corp.	
113	Maxilla & Mandible	
114	Star Magic	

Alcohol

Liquor stores sell wine but not beer and are closed on Sundays and forbidden to sell cigarettes by law. The cheapest places for beer (which *is* sold on a Sunday) are food emporiums or bodegas.

Astor Wines & Spirits, 12 Astor Place at Lafayette St. Practically a department store of wines and spirits, often at generous discounts. **1**

Park Avenue Liquor Shop, 292 Madison Ave., between 40th and 41st Sts. Specializes in Californian wines. **2**

Sherry-Lehmann Inc., 679 Madison Ave., at 61st St. Smartest wine merchant in the city with a large range of whisky. **3**

Antiques

Between East 70th and East 90th Streets, Madison Avenue has hundreds of antiques shops specializing in objects verging on the priceless. Prices are slightly more realistic down in the West Village, along the stretch of Bleecker and Hudson Streets north of Christopher Street. Some of the best bargains can be had from the row of furniture warehouses on 4th Avenue between 10th Street and Union Square: they have auctions once a week or once a month. Even better finds crop up in junk shops, flea markets (see 'Flea Markets', below) or along sidewalks in the Lower East Side.

20th Century Design, 151 Ave. A, between 10th and 11th Sts. Specializes in 1970s ④ plastic furniture.

American Hurrah, 766 Madison Ave., at 66th St. Americana including quilts. ⑤

Atomic Passion, 430 East 9th St., between 1st Ave. and Ave. A. 1950s kitsch. ⑥

Backpages, 125 Greene St., between Prince and Houston Sts. Wurlitzer jukeboxes, Coca-Cola vending machines, and advertising memorabilia. ⑦

Chelsea Antiques Building, 110 West 25th St., between 6th and 7th Aves. Twelve ⑧ floors of classy antiques with 150 stalls.

Ilene Chazanof, ✆ 254 5564 or 737 9668. Open by appointment only. A loft stuffed with all kinds of oddities, especially jewellery.

Irreplaceable Artefacts of North America, 14 2nd Ave., near East Houston St. ⑩ Architectural salvage—fireplaces, doors, cast-iron staircases, gargoyles, bars—on 12 floors.

Irving Barber Shop Antiques, 210 East 21st St. Crockery, cutlery and jewellery.

Kelter/Malcé, 74 Jane St., between Greenwich and Washington Sts., ✆ 989 6760, by ⑫ appointment. Done up like an elegant home, except everything is for sale: early folk art, Native American tapestries, antique quilts.

Lost City Arts, 275 Lafayette St., between Houston and Prince Sts, with a warehouse ⑬ at 257 West 10th St., and a gallery at 339 Bleecker St. Architectural antiques and American urban ephemera in a cavernous warehouse—urinals, juke boxes, street lamps, mail boxes, gas pumps, barber's chairs, shop signs, etc. Fascinating, but not cheap.

Sinotique, 19A Mott St, near Bayard St. Asian pottery from BC to 18th century. ⑭

Art Supplies

Cheap Paint, 11 Prince St., near Elizabeth St. Limited to paint and brushes, with dis- ⑮ counts on oils, acrylics and watercolours.

Pearl Paint, 308 Canal St., off Broadway. Largest discount art store in Manhattan, on ⑯ four floors, half the price of Europe.

Utrecht, 111 4th Avenue, near 13th St. Good range of cut-price art supplies, including ⑰ portable drafting boards.

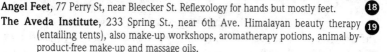

Beauty Therapy, Alternative Therapy & Spas

Angel Feet, 77 Perry St, near Bleecker St. Reflexology for hands but mostly feet. ⑱

The Aveda Institute, 233 Spring St., near 6th Ave. Himalayan beauty therapy ⑲ (entailing tents), also make-up workshops, aromatherapy potions, animal by-product-free make-up and massage oils.

Body Shop, 759 Broadway, between 9th and 10th Sts. Branch of the English chain. ⑳

Carapan, 4 West 16th St., off 5th Ave. Mexican spa with candlelit massage and aro- ㉑ matherapy rooms.

The Service Station, 137 8th Ave., at 16th St. Tanning, massage, electrolysis, waxing ㉒ and a mainly male clientele.

hypnosis and psychotherapy

The Hypnosis Clinic, 133 East 73rd St. Become a valid human being.

The New York Psychotherapy Group, ✆ 673 0884. Have an ego massage.

manicure parlours

New Yorkers frequently have manicures, which are wonderfully cheap here. The treatment usually includes a hand massage, wax, silk or porcelain tips, and 'sculpturing'; the whole experience is very soothing. The business is more or less monopolized by Koreans and there are parlours all over New York, the cheapest on 14th Street or in Chinatown, where you can get the complete works, including a body massage and rub-down, for under $20.

Shalom Finger Nails, 791 Lexington Ave., between 61st and 62nd Sts. Silk and linen weap pedicures and manicures from $15, also therapy for nail-biters.

Books

New York has thousands of bookshops, from the encyclopaedic to recherché; browsing though them is addictive, and a bookshop tour can last several days.

Peddling any sort of literature is legal, as it ought to be. You can stumble on excellent finds on sidewalks in the areas around the Cooper Union and Astor Place, and Columbia University up on Broadway in the 90s.

Academy Book Store, 10 West 18th St., off 5th Ave. Good selection of second-hand ㉓ academic and art books; also second-hand classical and jazz CDs and records.

A Photographer's Place, 133 Mercer St., near Prince St. Photographic books and prints.

Barnes & Noble, 2289 Broadway at West 82nd St., and several other locations in ㉔ Manhattan, including 105 5th Ave at 18th St, 1972 Broadway at West 67th St and 674 6th Avenue at 21st St. Open 10am–10pm. New books, many reduced, at Manhattan's biggest bookseller. The superstore on Broadway and 82nd Street includes a café frequented by single women looking for men who can at least read. The Barnes & Noble on 18th Street at 105 5th Avenue specializes in text books, and includes a section on books about New York in the thirties and an annexe where you shop with supermarket trolleys for remaindered books.

The Biography Bookshop, 400 Bleecker St., at 11th St. The only specialist bookshop **25** like this in the city.

Books & Co., 939 Madison Ave., at East 75th St. Choice and highbrow selection of **26** new fiction and non-fiction, and staff who go out of their way to help.

The Complete Traveler Bookstore, 199 Madison Ave., at East 35th St. Thousands **27** of travel books and maps about the globe.

Cooper Hewitt Museum Shop, 2 East 91st St., at 5th Ave. Excellent selection of dec- **28** orative arts books—also handmade toys.

A Different Light Bookstore, 151 West 19th St., between 6th and 7th Aves. **29** America's largest alternative bookstore, open from 10am to midnight, and mostly gay and lesbian literature.

Drama Bookstore, 723 7th Ave., at West 48th St. Established in the twenties and **30** with a comprehensive range of scripts and biographies.

Forbidden Planet, 821 Broadway, corner East 12th St. Two floors of books, maga- **31** zines and comics devoted to science fiction, run by an Englishman and featuring a duffel-coat-affecting clientele.

Gotham Book Mart, 41 West 47th St., near 6th Ave. Has nearly half a million books. **32** Frances Steloff, the late owner, started the Gotham in the twenties. Nowadays the Gotham has a particularly good poetry department, an art gallery and a whole area devoted to signed books by writer and illustrator, Edward Gorey (*see* p.103).

New York Bound, Associated Press Building, lobby of 50, Rockefeller Plaza. **33** Fascinating and complete range of books about New York, from extremely rare and out-of-print to recently published guides.

Oscar Wilde Bookshop, 15 Christopher St., near 6th Ave. World's first gay bookshop. **34**

Revolution Books, 13 East 16th St., between Union Square and 5th Ave. The eastern **35** seaboard's largest Marxist and radical literature bookshop.

Rizzoli's, 31 West 57th St., between 5th and 6th Aves. Haute couture books (espe- **36** cially on art, architecture and fiction); permanent classical muzac and elegant interiors. Lovely calendars.

St Mark's Bookshop, 13 St Mark's Place, off 3rd Avenue. 'Alternative' books on every **37** thinkable minority subject. Vendors flog coffee-table books and Rizzoli art books for big reductions on the sidewalk outside.

Union Square Book Stall, west side of Union Square, between 15th and 16th Sts. **38** Small stand of second-hand books on Union Square next to the postcard man and fruit and vegetable market. Mainstream and good.

Strand Book Store, 828 Broadway, at East 12th St; also at 95 Fulton Street (call **39** ℅ 473 1452 for free telephone book search, or email on *strand@strandbooks.com*). Eight-mile long emporium (probably the largest in the US) of two million second-hand books, most reduced by 50 per cent. The store specializes in reviewers' copies, unproofed trade paperbacks, proof copies and hardbacks: the quantities can be overwhelming at first, but staff are always knowledgeable.

Urban Center Books, Villard Houses, 457 Madison Ave., between 50th and 51st Sts. The Municipal Arts Society's excellent selection of books dealing with urban design and architecture.

Botánicas

Otto Chicas Rendon, 56 and 60 East 116th St., and 177 East 115th St. Of the many *botánicas*, or religious shops devoted to *Santería* scattered all over Hispanic Manhattan, Rendon's is the oldest and best. Based in Spanish Harlem and selling thousands of charms, incense, aerosols, evil eyes, statuettes and all kinds of paraphernalia, some dedicated to *Santería*.

Saint Jacques Majeure & Sainte Viergo, 1248 Flatbush Ave at 26th St., Brooklyn. Haitian religious paraphernalia, from Voodoo to Christian.

Clothes

New York's mainstream clothes shops are quite boring. To find anything more exciting you'll have to go to top class designers or 'vintage' shops (mostly involving secondhand, 'reconditioned' and pastiche clothes from the 1940s–1970s). For designer clothes, New York divides into four demesnes: SoHo; Madison Avenue and 57th Street; 5th Avenue; the East Village. In **SoHo** shops are expensive but fascinating: fashions range from the impossible but elegant to the implausible but zany. Shoppers here are the sleekest in Manhattan and constitute a display in themselves. The area including **Madison Avenue and 57th Street** is undiluted designer-land, from large department stores like Barney's and Bloomingdales to 'flagships' for the world's top designers: Armani, Nicole Miller, Prada, Lauren, St Laurent, Sonia Rykiel, Versace and Kenzo, all much visited by the surface-conscious. **Fifth Avenue** has magnificently overdressed shoppers, Persian carpet discount stores and a clutch of department stores including Bergdorf Goodman, Saks and Dior. The **East Village** is a mecca for club, retro, spike, underwear and leather, with smaller stores showing new young designers and recent fashion school graduates.

designer clothes

SoHo

Anna Sui, 113 Greene St., near Prince St. New York's most sought-after fashion designer: club clothes inspired by Biba and Barbie dolls and updated to incorporate the latest trends in techno and hip-hop. Fans include Madonna; prices are comparatively low. **(40)**

APC, 131 Mercer St., between Prince and Spring Sts. Understated French casual in store designed by jobbing artist Julian Schnabel.

A/X, 568 Broadway, near Prince St. For the decal-conscious dresser: Armani branch selling a more mainstream Gap-style range of the designer's clothes at high street prices.

Betsey Johnson, 130 Thompson St., between Houston and Prince Sts (and three other branches on the Upper West and East Sides). Established in the 1960s, a mix of weird, funny and skin-tight (in 1996, transparent chiffon baby-doll dresses), alongside more conventional designs. **(41)**

Big Drop, 174 Prince St., near Thompson St. Entertaining range of new designers from the zany to the tiresome.

Commes des Garçons, 116 Wooster St., between Spring and Prince Sts. Elegantly constructed, Japanese-designed clothes in sleek shop by Japanese architect Rei Kawakubo. Nearby, on 103 Grand Street, similar minimalist fashion is offered by **Yohji Yamamoto**.

J. Morgan Puett, 140 Wooster St., near Prince St. Underwired puff balls of gauze, hessian and tulle.

Keiko New York, 62 Greene St., between Broome and Spring Sts. Expensive Art Deco swimming costumes.

Liquid Sky, 241 Lafayette St., at Prince St. Hip-hop, trip-hop and rave clubwear.

Miu Miu, 100 Prince St., between Mercer and Greene Sts. Fashions by Milan's queen of handbags, Miuccia Prada.

Morgane Le Fay, 151 Spring St., between Wooster and West Broadway. One of the **42** best: gowns, capes and skirts in jersey, wool and flannel (and matching outfits for mothers and daughters), quirkily conceived and elegantly styled.

Nicole Miller, 134 Prince St., between Greene and Wooster Sts. Understated elegance for slender figures only, 'dinky' accessories.

Todd Oldham, 123 Wooster St., near Prince St. Tongue-in-cheek designs by Dallas- **43** born designer who uses drag queens to catwalk his designs: new wave ballgowns, shoes and accessories for shoppers with bravado.

Steven Alan, 60 Wooster St., between Broome and Spring Sts. New designers, including Daryl K, Pixie Yates and Built by Wendy.

Lower East Side & East Village

Daryl K, 208 East 6th St., between 2nd and 3rd Aves. Raunchy sixties and seventies chic: bustiers and quilted mini-dresses etc.

The Dress, 159 Ludlow St., near Stanton St. Sixties kitsch by Mary Adams; garish hats, **44** organza party clothes.

TG170, 170 Ludlow St., between Stanton and East Houston Sts. Young, mostly zany designers, including Cake and Girly.

Steven Alan, 330 East 11th St., between 1st and 2nd Aves. New and outlandish **45** Manhattan designers: Cake, Pixie Yeats etc.

Union Square/Ladies Mile

Emporio Armani, 110 5th Ave., at 16th St. Offshoot of the main store on Madison **46** Avenue, this is the 'diffusion' line: 'younger' styles, jeans, slightly less earth-shatteringly expensive price tags.

Paul Smith, 108 5th Ave., between 15th and 16th Sts. Popular with the Japanese: well-cut retro suits, ties and socks by English designer, Paul Smith.

West Village

Patricia Field, 10 East 8th St., between University Place and 5th Ave. Designer dyke **47** clubwear by Patricia Field, New York's aspiring Vivenne Westwood: glitter, boas and wigs.

The Fat Sheep Cheap Trading Post, 19 Christopher St., near Greenwich Ave. Native American Indian clotheswear and masks.

Chelsea

Barney's, 106 7th Ave., between 16th and 17th Sts (*see* 'Department Stores', below). **48** Six floors of interesting clothes taking in the lesser-known designers (at the Co-op on level 2) as well as big names: Issey Miyake, Gaultier, John Galliano, Ally Capellino, Gianni Versace, Matsuda and Montana. Also antiques, jewellery, hairdressing, a small Conran design shop and smart café.

Fizt & Fitz, 641 6th Ave., at West 20th St. Reasonably priced flamboyance by Biba-founder Barbara Hulanicki.

Midtown

Macy's, Herald Square, 34th St. and 6th Ave. (*see* 'Dept Stores'). Giorgio Armani, **50** Anna Klein, Claude Montana, Calvin Klein, etc. The New Signatures department is a platform for young designers including Gemma Khang and Michael Leva.

Upper East Side

Since 1993, when Barney's opened a store on Madison Avenue at vast, potentially bankrupting expense, the Upper East Side has enjoyed a new lease of life with fashion houses like Diesel, Calvin Klein, Valentino, Moschino, Piaget and Prada all opening shops in the area, most of which are worth a visit for the flower arrangements alone.

Barneys, 660 Madison Ave, at East 61st St. Largest fashion store built in Manhattan **49** since the Depression—costing $100 million, it opened in 1993 with nine floors and 230,000 square foot of space. Clothes for women and men, cleanly laid out in soothingly stylish surroundings.

BCBG, 700 Madison Ave., at East 63rd St. Not the vaccination but designs by fashion idol Max Azria.

Bergdorf Goodman, 754 5th Ave., at 57th St. (*see* 'Department Stores', below). For **9** Donna Karan, Gaultier, Angela Cummings, Azzedine Alaïa, Geoffrey Beene, Manolo Blahnik and jewellery by Barry Kieselstein-Cord. Across the street Bergdorf Goodman for men has Turnbull & Asser shirts and ties and Italian designers Romeo Gigli and Valentino.

Bloomingdale's, 1000 3rd Ave., at 59th St. (*see* 'Department Stores', below). Special **51** rooms set aside for Ralph Lauren, Missoni, Sonia Rykiel and Yves St Laurent. On the fourth floor are more unusual designs.

Brooks Bros, 346 Madison Ave., at East 44th St. Shrine of the striped shirt, now owned by Marks & Spencer.

Calvin Klein, 654 Madison Ave., at East 60th St. The whole caboodle: from tedious knickers and unisex scents to accessories and furnishings, in large and naked space, by the British minimalist architect John Pawson.

Chanel, 5 East 57th St., off 5th Ave. Elegantly presented vulgarity in a boutique mod- **52** elled on Coco Chanel's Paris atelier, including a hairdressing salon. Make-up, handbags and brass buttons, from $4000 a twinset.

Charivari 57 and Charivari 72, 18 West 57th St., between 5th and 6th Aves. Sometimes staid, sometimes off-beat, mostly expensive 'avant-garde' clothes by Japanese and European designers, on four floors with video screens in Japanese designed interior. The Charivari on 72nd St and Columbus Avenue on the Upper West Side sells casual clothes and sportswear. **Charivari Workshop** at 441 Columbus Avenue at 81st St., concentrates on minimalist Japanese designers like Yamamoto and Miyake.

Diesel, 770 Lexington Ave., at 60th St. Tongue in cheek Italian retro-chic, involving ⟨53⟩ zips, 1950s to 70s derived sports styles and ski-hats with perspex inserts. New shop in Midtown with fluorescent tumble-dryers in the windows, café, terrapinarium, glass floors, music lounge and dancing cashiers: all very hip.

Emanuel Ungaro, 792 Madison Ave., between 67th and 66th Sts. Unyouthful cuts, flowery fabrics.

Gianni Versace Uomo & Donna, 816 and 817 Madison Ave., at 68th and 69th Sts. ⟨54⟩ Flamboyant denim jackets and skirts for ageing rockers.

Giorgio Armani, 815 Madison Ave., at 66th St. Catastrophically expensive.

Gucci, 683 5th Ave., at 54th St. Stirrups, red-and-green stripes and other vulgarities, with a dash of irony, by American designer Tom Ford. Special customers Bill Cosby and Whitney Houston have access to a private room.

Issey Miyake, 992 Madison Ave., at 77th St. Sculpturally constructed hessian tents, ⟨55⟩ useful for hiding unsightly droops.

Joseph Tricot, 804 Madison Ave., near 65th St. Trendy but expensive knitwear from London.

Missoni, 836 Madison Ave., at 69th St. Italian-designed jacquard jerseys, socks and coats in ditchwater colours.

OMO Norma Kamali, 11 West 56th St., between 5th and 6th Aves. Class cut linens, silks and plaids. Good for coats, also underwear and the most elegant swimming costumes in Manhattan.

Polo/Ralph Lauren, 867 Madison Ave., at 72nd St. Elegant couture for both sexes, ⟨56⟩ plus free alterations and made-to-measure suits for American preppies in deluxe Upper East Side mansion, renovated by Lauren for $14 million. Antiques, gilt bedsteads and trunks amongst the clothes, and furniture and decorative accessories on the top floors. More casual designs (cheaper) sold opposite at **Polo Sport**, 888 Madison Ave.

The Original Levi's Store, 750 Lexington Ave., near 60th St. Purchases limited to six ⟨57⟩ per customer, such is demand, although in practice the store turns a Nelson's eye. The average price of a pair of jeans here is around $50.

Romeo Gigli & Spazio, 21 East 69th St., at 5th Ave. Italian exuberance and a suitably extravagant interior.

Tse Cashmere, 827 Madison Ave., at East 69th St. The highest quality cashmere, cut into understated suits, dresses and cardigans.

Yves St Laurent Rive Gauche, 855 Madison Ave., at 71st St. Devilish evening dresses, dreary day clothes.

discount labels

The towns of **Secaucus, Paramus** and **Woodbury Common** (about half an hour away from Port Authority by train) have factory outlet malls, with staggering discounts on some of the biggest fashion designers in America. For the latest designer discounts and sample sale bargains call the Sales and Bargain hotline on ✆ 540 0123 (at $2 a minute and 75¢ a minute from then on) or consult the excellent Sales and Bargains page in *New York Magazine*.

Camberwick Greene, 377 Broome St., between Mott and Mulberry Sts. Nearly-new designer clothes and samples by top designers at top discounts (as much as 80%).

Century 21 Department Store, 22 Cortlandt St., off Broadway. Arrive early for fantastic bargains, with big discounts on last season's Prada, Ungaro, Thierry Mugler, Genny, Gaultier Junior, Gigli, Calvin Klein Sport, Versace and Perry Ellis (especially good for men). Also lingerie, luggage, kitchenware, cheap cosmetics and household goods. Clothes can't be tried on and must be returned within 12 days. **58**

Daffy's, 111 5th Ave., at 18th St. Three floors of reduced clothing, from run-of-the-mill casual to designer. **59**

Dollarbills, 99 East 42nd St., between Lexington and Vanderbilt Aves. Especially good for designer coats.

Syms, 42 Trinity Pace, at Rector St., also 400 Park Avenue at 54th St. Seven floors of designer clothes, discounted by 50 per cent, especially good for men's and women's shirts and suits. **60**

sportswear

Blades, 659 Broadway, between Bleecker and Bond Sts. Roller blades, skateboards and snowboards, for hire as well as for sale. **61**

King of Skates, 383 Canal St., between West Broadway and Thompson St. Roller blades from $19.99.

Paragon Sports, 867 Broadway, near East 17th St. The best in Manhattan: sportswear of every kind including ultra-cheap trainers and tracksuits etc. **62**

Scuba Network, 175 5th Ave, at 22nd St. Scuba gear and holidays.

(*see* also NikeTown in 'Shoes', p.294)

second-hand clothes & shoes

Allan & Suzi, 416 Amsterdam Ave., at 80th St. Celebrity cast-offs, mostly designer.

Alice Underground, 380 Columbus Ave, between 78th and 79th Sts; also in SoHo at 481 Broadway near Broome St. All the leather and suede is good quality. **63**

Andy's Chee-Pees, 691 Broadway, between 4th and 5th Sts. Grimy but full of bargains.

Antique Boutique, 712–714 Broadway, between Washington Place and West 4th St. Enormous, with over 30,000 garments. Best for leather jackets, winter coats, tight satin trousers and other clubbers' staples.

Arkle & Sparkle and Smylobylon, 216 and 222 Lafayette St., between Broome and Spring Sts. Expensive fashion 'classics' from 1960–1979 in fur-lined boutique.

Canal Jean Co., 504 Broadway, between Spring and Broome Sts. Legendary warehouse selling cheap new Levis, also second-hand clothes, wigs, Converse shoes and designer underwear (Ralph Lauren etc.) at knock-down prices. **(64)**

Domsey Warehouse, South 9th St., between Kent and Wyeth Aves, Williamsburg, internet: www.domsey.com. This is a find: a modest trek on the J train to Marcy Avenue in Williamsburg, but worth it for four floors of clothes: jackets, dresses and coats for $8, shirts for $4 and vests for $2; or you can buy by the pound. In amongst a good deal of rubbish are silk dresses and cashmere coats.

Fan Club, 22 West 19th St., between 5th and 6th Aves. Celebrity cast-offs, including glamorous frocks worn by Madonna.

Harriet Love, 126 Prince St., between Wooster and Greene Sts. Pastiche vintage clothes, at predictably high prices. Re-created styles, including jewellery and crocodile handbags, mostly from the forties and fifties.

Housing Works Thrift Shop, 143 17th St., near 7th Ave. In fashion-conscious Chelsea, with the odd brilliant bargain.

Love Saves the Day, 119 2nd Ave., at East 7th St. Where Rosanna Arquette bought her jacket in *Desperately Seeking Susan*. A lot of Elvis-paraphernalia.

The 1909 Company, 63 Thompson St., near Broome St, internet: *The1909Co@aol.com*. Elisa Casas' expensive but exquisite vintage clothing and reproductions: 1920s ribbon dresses, purses and shoes etc.

Panache, 525 Hudson St., between West 10th and Charles Sts. Expensive and pristine twenties and thirties clothes.

Resurrection, 123 East 7th St., between 1st Ave and Ave A. Second-hand seventies shoes.

Rue St Denis, 376 Amsterdam Ave, near West 78th St. 1950s–70s women's clothes, in perfect condition.

Screaming Mimi's, 382 Lafayette St., at Great Jones St. 'Re-conditioned' shoes, clothes and accessories from the sixties, clean but expensive. **(65)**

Computers, Electronics, Cameras and Hi-Fi

You can get computers and hi-fi more cheaply in America than in Europe. If you buy out of state (in New Jersey for example) you can also avoid paying the New York sales tax. To get an idea of prices, ask for advice in one of the smarter electronics shops and scrutinize the *New York Times*' Science supplement on Tuesdays for advertisements by out of state dealers. Then head off to one of the cheap places listed below, the cheapest of which is **Uncle Uncle's** on Canal Street. If you're buying electrical equipment to take to Britain or Australia, check the equipment can take a 240-volt adapter. **American televisions and videos don't work in Britain and most of Europe**.

Argo Electronics, 396 Canal St., between West Broadway and Thompson St. Bizarre range of secondhand and back of a lorry electronics: keyboards, discmans, health-o-meters, cauterizers, army survival camouflage wear. Also motorized bicycles from $600. Whether any of it works is another matter.

47th St Photo, 115 West 45th St., between 6th and 7th Aves and 67 West 47th St., ⑥⑥ between 5th and 6th Aves. Chaos reigns, but bargains in both branches are incredible (ask for the best price and make sure you know comparative prices in other discount shops).

Uncle Uncle's, 343 Canal St., near West Broadway, ✆ 226 4010. Even cheaper than ⑥⑦ 47th St. Photo, and even more chaotic. Audio equipment and answerphones.

Willoughby's, 110 West 32nd St., between 6th and 7th Aves. Supposedly the world's largest camera and video store.

Department Stores

A&S, Herald Square, 899 6th Ave., at West 33rd St. An import to Manhattan from Brooklyn. Prices are good and the place is unpretentious, although some of the women's clothes are seriously afflicted by designer epaulettes.

Barney's, 106 7th Ave., between 17th and 18th Sts. Manhattan's sleekest department ⑥⑧ store. It began in 1923 as a discount suit store, and nowadays is expanding with branches in Tokyo, Massachusetts, the World Trade Center and uptown on Madison Avenue. The Chelsea store is the original Barney's, at its most enter-taining on the first Monday of each month when the window dressers—looking as fashionable as catwalk models—assemble next month's display. **CO/OP** inside is a store within a store, slightly cheaper, with the latest in women's fashions; the men's designer clothes department is the best in the city; and in the warehouse sale in September prices are reduced by 50 per cent. Designers include Beene, Lagerfeld, Calvin Klein and Fendi. In the rest of the shop there's silver, china, antiques, children's clothes, an elegant café and garden.

Barney's Madison Avenue, 660 Madison Ave., at 61st St. When it opened in 1993 ⑥⑨ this was the largest built in Manhattan since 1933. Window displays are as amusing as Chelsea's; the supposedly snooty staff are polite and helpful. Mad.61, the fancy basement restaurant, has a good counter menu, from veal stew to pizza.

Bergdorf Goodman, 754 5th Ave., at 58th St. Established on 5th Avenue in 1928, ⑨ elegant and tasteful, with chandeliers, a fountain, and classy fashions, jew-ellery, antiques and accessories, tailored to people to whom life is bowl of pot pourri. The shop includes two cafés; a branch for men is directly opposite.

Bloomingdale's, 1000 3rd Ave., at East 59th St. Established in 1886, it became ⑤① famous with tourists in the 1960s and 70s. Inside you'll find showbiz, chaos, scent-sprayers, aggressive shoppers. The shuffling can be tiresome or amusing, depending on your mood and the weather. Some parts of the 10-floor store are quite dog-eared, but with excellent children's, linen, food and kitchenware depart-ments, plus five restaurants and the whole of the fourth floor devoted to 'adventurous' fashion.

Felissimo, 10 West 56th Street, between 5th and 6th Aves. Extremely elegant ⑦① Japanese-owned design store based in beautiful McKim, Mead & White townhouse off 5th Avenue. 'Eco-sensitive products' on four floors from hair ornaments and sculpture to the iceberg lettuce of design—aromatherapy candles. All beautifully wrapped, with a small, tranquil tearoom on the fourth floor serving 27 kinds of tea with scones and sandwiches. Worth a visit for the birdsong-playing elevator alone.

Henri Bendel, 712 5th Ave., between 55th and 56th Sts. Tormentingly elegant **72** clothes, shoes, 'tabletop ware' and sophisticated windows: housed in two of 5th Avenue's swankiest mansions, and featuring small boutiques instead of rambling departments. Smaller and classier than Saks or Bergdorf Goodman.

Lord & Taylor, 424 5th Ave., between 38th and 39th Sts. Endearingly old-fashioned, **73** with in-store restaurants, a massive perfume hall and ten floors of mostly American designed fashions.

Macy's, Herald Square, 151 West 34th St., between Broadway and 7th Ave. Less glit- **74** tery than Bloomingdales, though not necessarily cheaper. Established in 1858, the 'largest department store in the world' was Manhattan's biggest bargain basement. Founded by a Quaker, it dealt in cash-only, undercutting all the other big stores in New York. Nowadays it's more up-market and just as enormous, covering two million square feet and nine floors with everything you need if only you could find it. The Cellar has good food and kitchenware departments, there's a Metropolitan Museum of Art shop, and between Thanksgiving and Christmas the toy floor— scene for the 1947 film *Miracle on 34th Street*—should be avoided.

Saks Fifth Avenue, 611 5th Ave., between 49th and 50th Sts. Opposite Rockefeller **75** Center and the most archetypical of 5th Avenue stores: with cupcake celebrities, clothes, furnishings and childrens' departments, all in the best possible taste, plus Penhaligon's and an elegant 8th floor restaurant and café with views.

Takashimaya, 693 5th Ave., between East 54th and 55th Sts. Sleek Manhattan **76** branch of the sleek Japanese design store, 'commingling' as the copywriters have it 'Eastern and Western aesthetics': objects on sale include designer accessories for the home, beauty products, luggage, flowers, even artefacts 'scoured from the top flea markets in Paris'. The store's 4500 square foot contemporary art gallery closed down in 1996. By contrast, the Tea Box café in the basement wowed New Yorkers with Japanese flavoured cucumber sandwiches and 40 kinds of tea, from lapsang souchong to lemongrass.

discount department stores

Fulton, Nassau and Chambers Streets, off Broadway. Discount electronics and hi-fi, and odd-lot surplus stores.

Job Lot Trading, 80 Nassau St., near Broadway. Massive discounts on cosmetics, toiletries, chocolate and kitchenware.

National Wholesale Liquidators, 612 Broadway, between Bleecker and Houston Sts. Even more massive discounts on cosmetics, toiletries, chocolate and kitchenware.

Ecologically Sound

Earth General, 147 8th Ave., near 17th St. 2000 eco-products.

Fabrics and Trimmings

Garment District, between 34th and 40th Sts, and 5th and 7th Avenues. Hundreds of shops supplying trimmings, buttons, ribbons and hat-dummies to the fashion designers in the vicinity. Two of the best are **Gordon's Button Company** at 222

West 38th St., (over half a century old and selling antique as well as new buttons), and **Sheru Enterprises**, 49–53 West 38th St., between 5th and 6th Aves (*see* **Walk I**, p.96).

Tender Buttons, 143 East 62nd St., between 3rd and Lexington Aves. A knephobic's nightmare: millions of buttons in every shape and size, some of which can be made into cuff-links.

A. A. Feather Co., 16 West 36th St., between 5th and 6th Aves., 8th floor. Feathers.

Art Max Fabrics, 250 West 40th St, at 7th Ave. Three floors of fabrics, especially good for bridal wear.

Flea Markets and Auctions

New York has only a few established flea markets, perhaps because everywhere you go someone is trying to flog something; even on Park Avenue mysterious men will brush past muttering 'Sheets from Macy's, sheets from Macy's, ten dollar!' As well as the proper flea markets there are 'floating' illegal flea markets—in the East Village (outside the Cooper Union on Astor Place, or down Avenue A) and Chelsea—a range of bric-a-brac, clothes and bicycles with locks still on them.

For the dedicated junk collector, Manhattan's sidewalks and rubbish bins can be fruitful hunting grounds. New Yorkers move and get so bored with their clutter so quickly that they regularly dump it on sidewalks (the Upper East Side has the best quality cast-offs of all). Finally, in the spring and summer there are block fairs in neighbourhoods all over the city, which often have stalls selling all kinds of junk.

Annex Antiques Fair and Flea Market, 6th Ave., between 24th and 27th Sts. This is huge and wonderful: millions of bits and bobs on at least three city blocks: jewellery, Americana, second-hand clothes and bicycles. If you stand your ground, prices can be excellent (open Sat–Sun 9–5; most crowded on Sunday mornings).

Canal Street Casbah, near Greene and Wooster Sts. Two flea markets opposite each other, from back copies of *Time Out* to missing mannequin limbs. This end of Canal has cheap art shops, wholesale rubber and plastics dealers, also shops selling surplus surplus.

Greenwich Village Flea Market, PS 41, Greenwich St., at Charles St (open 12–7, Sat. Small, pricey, interesting.

1S 44 Greenflea Market, Columbus Ave., between 76th and 77th Sts, (open 10–6, Sun). Antique clothes, Art-Deco furniture and costume jewellery—amusing to pore through but expensive.

Orchard Street, between East Houston and Canal Streets (Sun–Thurs). Turns into an outdoor clothes market, with prices slashed on designer labels. The shops on the sidestreets round about have bargains in fabrics and clothes.

Police Department Auction, Pierson Warehouse, 4715 Pierson Place, Queens, ✆ 406 1369. Lost or confiscated goods auctioned in a fiendishly complicated procedure which involves viewing the merchandise the day before and buying a $20 paddle for making bids.

Post Office Monthly Auction, GPO, 380 West 33rd St., ✆ 330 2932. Mountains of undelivered year-old parcels on auction also involving crowds and paddles. Arrive on the dot for 'viewing' the unopened mystery boxes.

SoHo Antique Fair and Collectibles Market, Grand St., at Broadway (open 9–5, Mon–Sat). Small but decently priced.

Food

markets

Throughout the year farmers come into New York to sell locally grown produce at lovely open-air **Greenmarkets**, based in locations all over the city, with the biggest of all in Union Square. Despite the dreary image, these are hugely popular with New Yorkers, and surprisingly entertaining. An astonishing variety of produce (plus free samples) is on sale, all of it of the highest quality and at the lowest possible prices: you'll find baked goods, cut flowers, wild foods and such curiosities as gourds, indian corn, blue mint leaves, iced mint tea on tap, homemade cider, maple syrup from Vermont, cacti, squash, dandelion leaves, celery knobs, cut grass, pheasant sausage, even something called vermi-compost.

Greenmarkets: Union Square, at East 17th St and Broadway (Mon, Wed, Fri and Sat); ⑧⓪ and other locations, including City Hall (Tues and Fri), Tompkins Square (June–Dec, Sun) and IS 44, at West 77th St and Columbus Ave (Sun). Call ✆ 477 3220 for more information.

A 5am visit to the **Fulton Street Fish Market** near South Street Seaport, or the **Gansevoort Meat Market** is a robust way of beating the insomnia blues. If you're still awake later on in the day, you could also visit Manhattan's most raucous and colourful market **La Marqueta**, up on Park Avenue and 110th Street under the tracks of the Penn Central railroad in El Barrio, or Spanish Harlem. Meanwhile, for late risers a visit to Kamman Supermarket and the Hong Kong Egg Lady in **Chinatown** (*see* below) is one of New York's most exotic food adventures.

One of the best ways of familiarizing yourself with the city's amazing variety of ethnic foodstores is to walk down **Paddy's Market** , at first sight a rather grubby stretch of 9th Avenue which runs from 54th Street to 38th Street. Here you'll find every kind of foodstore: fish shops, fruit and veg shops, Greek, French and Italian pastry shops, Pakistani rice and spice shops, Filipino grocers and Italian coffee and pasta shops, and the world's best bakeries. Every May, 9th Avenue hosts an International Food Festival attended by 750,000 New Yorkers, where international food-sellers from all over the city set up stalls down 9th Avenue (in 1984, Bruno the King of Ravioli broke all known records when he sold 200,000 pasta squares).

gourmet delicatessens

Balducci's, 424 6th Ave., at West 9th St. Established in Greenwich Village in 1947, **81** the family business is nowadays the most luxurious and lovable of New York's delis; even if you can't afford anything, a walk round the brightly coloured, friendly delicatessan will make life seem worth living after all.

Citarella Fish Bar, 2135 Broadway, 2135 Broadway, at 73rd St. Excellent seafood, **82** oysters and fish, as well as gourmet appetizers and breads.

Dean & Deluca, 560 Broadway, at Prince St. Displays of miniature fruit, veg and **83** muffins elevated into a mesmerising art form in SoHo, often slightly more diverting than the artworks on show in neighbouring galleries (for a catalogue call ✆ 1 (800) 221 7714).

Fairway, 2127 Broadway, at 72nd St. Grubby-looking, but actually a much-loved gourmet deli selling excellent fresh produce (grown on its own farm in Long Island), also bread, olive oil and cheese.

Kamman Supermarket, south side Canal Street at Mulberry St. From dried jellyfish **84** and bird's nest to the completely ambiguous; Chinatown's biggest, most various and cheapest supermarket.

Macy's Cellar, Herald Square, between 34th St. and 7th Ave. The most accessible part of Macy's, with all kinds of foods, and excellent kitchenware.

Russ & Daughters, 179 East Houston St., at 1st Ave. Lox, sturgeon, fancy chub, kip- **85** pered salmon, five varieties of caviar, cream cheese, dried fruits and chocolates, all of the highest quality, in a tiny delicatessan on the Lower East Side.

Zabar's, 2245 Broadway, at 80th St. Mecca for connoisseurs of the New York deli: **86** salmon, caviar, cheese and all kinds of sausages, at quite good prices too.

specialist food stores

Amy's Bread, 9th Avenue between 48th and 49th Sts. The best wholemeal and sour **87** dough bread in Manhattan—distributed from here to all the gourmet delis.

Aux Delices des Bois, 4 Leonard St., between West Broadway and Hudson St. Fresh and dried mushrooms, toadstools and truffles, imported from all over the world.

Ben's Cheese Shop, 181 East Houston St., at Allen St. The best cream cheese, farmer's cheese and pot cheese in the city—next door to Russ & Daughters.

Bruno the King of Ravioli, 653 9th Ave., between 45th and 46th Sts, also 2204 **88** Broadway between 78th and 79th Sts, and 249 8th Ave between 22nd and 23rd Sts. Bruno Cavilli emigrated to America in 1905 and was the first to intro- duce ravioli to New York. Still family-run, and with spectacular range of cheap raviolis packed in boxes of 50, sauces by the pint or gallon, home-made pesto and 'novelty' pasta in shapes such as parrots and bicycles.

Economy Candy, 108 Rivington St. Sweeties of every description, some from Europe, also halva and Tiptree jams, all as cheap as the name implies.

The Erotic Baker, ✆ orders only: ✆ 721 3217. Unconventional buns and doughnuts.

The Hong Kong Egg Cake Lady, on Mosco St, near Mott St., in Chinatown. A **89** delightful New York secret and one that's definitely worth revealing, this is a stand on Mosco Street with a permanent queue of people waiting patiently for the incredibly delicious griddled sponge cakes: cooked single-handedly on several irons at once by the lovely Hong Kong Egg Lady.

The Italian Food Centre, 186 Grand St., at Mulberry St. Heroes stuffed with mozzarella balls and prosciutto in Little Italy.

Guss Pickles, 35 Essex St., between Grand and Hester Sts. Pickles straight from the barrel: half-sours and sours, sauerkraut and pickled melons; you can smell the pickle-whiffs three blocks away.

Kossar's Bialys, 367 Grand St., between Norfolk and Suffolk Sts. Chewy, flour-dusted bialys and delicious bagels—some say the best in New York. **(90)**

Petrossian, 182 West 58th St., and 7th Ave. Expensive imported Russian caviar: *beluga, sevruga, osetra.* **(91)**

Poseidon Greek Bakery, 629 9th Ave., at 44th St. Established 1922: delicate, delicious filo pastries, cherry strudels and spinach pies, or *spanakopita*, on 9th Avenue.

Pozzo's Pastry Shop Inc., 688–90 9th Ave., between 47th–9th Sts. Exquisite Italian and French pastries and breads, biscuits, croissants and cannoli.

Vesuvio Bakery, 160 Prince St., between West Broadway and Thompson St. Good bakeries are scarce in Manhattan: this one in SoHo bakes wonderful crusty Italian bread and rolls.

Yonah Schimmel, 137 East Houston St., between 1st and 2nd Aves. The best kasha, potato, cherry and spinach knishes on the Lower East Side for those in the knish. **(92)**

English groceries

Myers of Keswick, 634 Hudson St., between Horatio and Jane Sts. For Manhattan's 350,000 British exiles: Ambrosia Creamed Rice, Marmite, HP Sauce, Ploughman's Pickle, Ribena, Flakes and Smarties.

Funeral Parlours

Frank E. Campbell, 1076 Madison Ave., corner of 81st St., ✆ 288 3500. Funerals for the rich and famous, including Rudolph Valentino, Montgomery Clift, James Cagney and Damon Runyon and scene of the funeral dance in Woody Allen's *Everyone Says I Love You.* **(93)**

Hairdressers

Atlas Barber School, 32 3rd Ave., between 8th and 9th Sts. Cheap but frightening.

Astor Place Hair Designers, 2 Astor Place, near Broadway. Experimental haircuts for $10 or less, which explains the no appointments policy, loud music, permanent queues outside and young people inside. **(94)**

Peppe and Bill at the Plaza Hotel, 5th Ave and Central Park South, mezzanine, ✆ 751 8380. Haircuts and manicures for men, supposed to be the best and most expensive in the world. **(95)**

Hats

Amy Downs Hats, 103 Stanton St., between Ludlow and Houston Sts. Recycled hats made of plastic bags and straw.

The Hat Shop, 120 Thompson St., between Spring and Prince Sts. Hats, from bonkers to normal, by fifty local milliners.

Household Products and Furnishings

ABC Carpet & Home, 888 and 881 Broadway, at 19th St. Enormous, sprawling emporium of carpets from antique to modern: on ten floors, with a treasure-house opposite decked out like a maze of walk-through apartments with furniture, linen, antiques, lighting and elegant in-store café.

American Craft Museum Shop, 40 West 53rd St., between 5th and 6th Aves. Tasteful quilts, weavings and lamp shades: which depending on your point of view are the acme or the acne of American artistic endeavour.

Apartment 48, 48 West 17th St., between 5th and 6th Aves. More 'home-shopping'—this time a single apartment and garden owned by someone called Ray Man Boozer, where everything, even oddments in cupboards, is for sale.

Bridge Kitchenware Corp., 214 East 52nd St., between 2nd and 3rd Aves. Twenty thousand kitchen utensils in deeply satisfying kitchen supplies shop.

Crate and Barrell, 650 Madison Ave., at East 60th St. Low-cost, tastefuly designed household products.

Handblock, 487 Columbus Ave., between West 83rd and West 84th Sts. Handblocked Thai and Indian linens, pillowcases, tablecloths, duvet covers etc., in traditional and modern designs.

Kentucky, 137 Duane St., © 349 6577, by apppointment only. TriBeCa home of photographer Kathy Storr, with everything inside it, from folk art to crockery and carpets, on sale.

MoMA Design Store, 44 West 53rd St., between 5th and 6th Aves. The apotheosis of consumer art: designs and reproductions inspired by the Museum of Modern Art's collection, and including such delights as Frank Lloyd Wright cherrywood writing desks, elegantly dull Charles Eames chairs and Surrealist household goods.

Mxyplyzyk, 125 Greenwich St., near Morton St. Furniture by LA designer Lisa Krohn.

Pandora's Box, 153 Prince St. Kitsch home decor, cheap and mostly featuring Elvis.

Portico, 379 West Broadway, between Spring and Broome Sts. First rate American design: beautiful reproduction furniture and antiques, plus crockery and household goods, and round the corner on Spring Street, at Portico Bed, fine frette bed linen.

Pottery Barn, 117 East 59th St., between Lexington and Park Aves. Basic but tasteful bowls, mugs, glasses, furniture and rugs. Good for setting up an apartment on a budget.

Williams-Sonoma, 20 East 60th St., near Madison Ave. The New York branch of the smart kitchen-equipment store in San Francisco—pasta machines, ovenware, knives, etc—similar to David Mellor or Habitat in England but superior.

Jewellery

Cartier, 2 East 52nd St., near 5th Ave. Classy but conventional.

Harry Winston Inc, 718 5th Ave., at West 56th St. The grandest jewellers in Manhattan, also the snootiest and much frequented by the Hollystocracy.

Tiffany and Co., 727 5th Ave., between 56th and 57th Sts. Even the 'At Home' cards are beyond your budget.

Leather Goods

Leather World, 652 Broadway, between Bond and Bleecker Sts. Leather jackets for 'guys and girls', patronized by cricketers Ian Botham and Alan Lamb.

Mark Cross, 645 5th Ave., at 52nd St. Elegant handbags.

Lingerie

Pink Pussycat Boutique, 167 West 4th St., between 6th and 7th Aves. Indecent para- 99 phernalia at decent prices.

Victoria's Secret, 34 East 57th St., between Park and Madison Aves. For an insight into the enigmatic sexual mores of smart New Yorkers.

Luggage and Discount Stores

8th Avenue, between West 42nd and 30th Sts., also 14th St. A string of bargain stores, 100 with dirt cheap prices on practically everything, from electricals to shoes, clothes, handbags and luggage. Not the most elegant street in New York, so be prepared for a certain amount of grottiness and peep shows.

Newsstands

Indians and Pakistanis bought up many of Manhattan's news-stand concessions when immigrants from the subcontinent were first allowed into the US in large numbers in the 1960s and 70s. Nowadays they own nearly all the news-stands above ground and on subway stations (*see* 'Newspapers', pp.41–2).

Gem Spa, 131 2nd Ave., at St Mark's Place, 24 hours. Legendary for its egg creams, 101 though the 24-hour news-stand itself is excellent, particularly for magazines, fanzines, comics and local community papers.

Hotalings Foreign News Depot, 142 West 42nd St., between 6th Ave and 102 Broadway, open Mon–Fri 8am–9.30pm. 'You mention it, we got it', is the motto—over 800 foreign titles at New York's oldest news-stand.

Nueva Vista, 146 9th Ave., between 50th and 51st St. Also specializing in exploding pens and edible napkins.

Tompkins Square News-stand, Avenue A, between 6th and 7th Sts, Mon–Sun 8am– 10pm. Polish-run and managed by a man who wears red leather trousers.

Universal Café, 977 8th Ave., between 57th and 58th Sts. Over 7000 domestic and international magazines to buy in café serving coffee and sandwiches from $6 or $90 for a 6ft hero.

Occult

There are hundreds of tarot card, palm, tea-leaf and New Age crystal readers, psychics, numerologists and astrologists all over the city. Many are Spanish or Latin American (*see* also 'Botánicas'); the cheapest are often in the East Village and on 14th Street.

Enchantments, 341 East 9th St., between 1st and 2nd Aves. Herbs, cauldrons and brooms for practising witches.

Magickal Childe, 35 West 19th St., between 5th and 6th Aves. Anything relating to the occult, including scented gem stones.

Wanko's Tea Cup Readings, 136 West 34th St., near 6th Ave. Tea-leaves and numerology.

Opticians

'Spectacles' sounds quaintly old-fashioned to Americans, who mostly use 'glasses'.

Studio Optics, Rockefeller Center and at *www.io.com/~vampyre/CONTACTS. html.* Expensive customized contact lenses including amazing 'cat', 'lizard' and 'wolf' styles.

Cohen's Optical, 117 Orchard St., at Delancey St. Cheapest opticians in the city.

The Glass Eye Shop, 31st St., between 6th Ave. and Broadway. Thousands of glass eyes.

My Optics, 42 St Mark's Place, at 2nd Ave. Dark glasses in every shade of black.

Personal Shoppers

As well as selecting outfits for every occasion, shoppers will sort out Christmas and birthday presents and even mail out reminders of looming anniversaries.

Barney's New York, ✆ 929 9000 ext 505.

Bloomingdale's At Your Service, ✆ 705 3135.

Macy's By Appointment, ✆ 560 4181.

Saks' 5th Avenue Club Executive Service, ✆ 940 4200.

Pharmacists

By far the cheapest pharmacists in Manhattan are in Chinatown where you'll find handsome reductions on popular brands of shampoo, cosmetics and loo paper etc.

Caswell-Massey, 518 Lexington Ave., at 48th St. Manhattan's oldest apothecary, dating from 1752, and selling elegant beauty products, also snuff, pomander balls, whalebone nail files, rice face powders and 'Washington's' shaving cream.

Kaufman Pharmacy, 557 Lexington Ave., at East 50th St. 24-hour pharmacy.

Kiehl's, 109 3rd Ave., near East 13th St. Established in 1853, and still making a superb range of natural beauty treatments: henna, musk oil, botanical drugs, herbal laxatives and lovely and rejuvenating rose water.

Condomania, 351 Bleecker St., at 10th St. 'Fun' condoms.

Records, Tapes, CDs

New York has the best collectors' record shops in the USA.

Bleecker Bob's Golden Oldies, 118 West 3rd St., between MacDougal St and 6th ⬤105
Ave. Rare punk, new wave and electronic music, as well as fifties and sixties
oldies. The best of the collectors' stores.

Dance Tracks, 91 East 3rd St., between 1st and 2nd Aves. New and obscure dance tracks
with an in-house DJ and sofas. Loft, garage, house, etc.

Footlight, 113 East 12th St., between 3rd and 4th Aves. Good for obscure filmtracks.

Golden Disc, 239 Bleecker St., near Leroy St. Range of limited edition and imported LP
and 45 rpm records.

Gryphon, 251 West 72nd St., between Broadway and West End Ave. Rare classical LPs,
also jazz and the spoken word.

House of Oldies, 35 Carmine St., between 6th Ave and 7th Ave South. Over a million
rock 'n roll 45s and over 10,000 78s, also R&B and soul.

Tower Records & Video, 692 Broadway at East 4th St and other locations, ✆ 1 800 ASK
TOWER. Huge, open until midnight every day and with a good jazz department
and large discounts on classical CDs.

Virgin Megastore, 1540 Broadway, at 47th St. The biggest in the world, including a ⬤106
café and cinema.

Shoes

Manhattan has more shoe shops than seems likely or possible. Some are concen-
trated on West 34th Street between 5th and 6th Avenues, and West 8th Street
between 5th and 6th Avenues.

Lace-Up, 110 Orchard St., near Delancey St. Hefty reductions on designer shoes.

McCreedy & Schreiber, 37 West 46th St., between 5th and 6th Aves. Quality men's
shoes, including Lucchese boots in lizard and crocodile skins.

NikeTown, 6 East 57th St., off 5th Ave. So far the largest NikeTown in the world: a ⬤107
five floor 66,500 ft^2 superbrandstore where the glorified gymshoes are delivered to customers via 26 pneumatic tubes. Machines on every floor will digitally
scan feet and spew out an electronic print-out of just how flat those arches are.
There are turnstile, flipper boards, sports memorabilia, shoe galleries and the
depressing atmosphere of endless gimmicks calculated to send consumers into a
frenzy of spending.

Otto Tootsi Plohound, 413 West Broadway, between Prince and Spring Sts. Reasonably
priced designer men's shoes from Europe and the US with rubber platform soles
and other chunky styles.

Sigerson Morrison, 242 Mott St., near Prince St. Elegant calfskin shoes in subtle pastel colours.

Susan Bennis/Warren Edwards, 22 West 57th St., between 5th and 6th Aves. Extremely fashionable shoe designers using fake or obscure skins: ostrich, emu, baby snakes and crocs. Sandals and boots.

Tucson Leather, 128 Thompson St., between Prince and Houston Sts. Cowboy boots from Texas and Arizona.

Tailors

There are tailors scattered all over the city; in the cheaper areas they will restore an almost threadbare garment for next to nothing.

Toys and Games

Abracadabra, 10 Christopher St., near Greenwich Ave. Increase your popularity in one step with a comprehensive selection of jokes including squirting flowers, rubber roaches and doggy doo foam.

Big City Kite Company, 1210 Lexington Ave., at East 82nd St. 150 different kites.

The Compleat Strategist, 11 East 33rd St., at 5th Ave. Wargames, board games, windproof magnetic playing cards.

Enchanted Forest, 85 Mercer St., between Broome and Spring Sts. Defiantly cute SoHo toy shop filled with single-celled adults.

F.A.O. Schwarz, 745 5th Ave., at 58th St. The biggest and most expensive toy shop in NY, also filled with shoppers yearning for whimsy in their lives. Inside: Statue of Liberty Barbie dolls and New York City Edition Monopoly boards.

Village Chess Shop, 230 Thompson St., between Bleecker and West 3rd Sts. Open until midnight: customers can drop by for a game of chess at around $2 an hour.

Unclassifiable, Specialist, Outlandish

Aphrodisia, 264 Bleecker St, between 6th Ave and 7th Ave South. A full range of medicines and 'cures'.

Big Joe Tattooing, 27 Mount Vernon Ave., Mount Vernon. Freehand and standard designs, executed with sterilized or disposable needles.

Bowery Restaurant District, between East Houston and 4th Sts. Shops, catering to the restaurant trade, where you can buy greasy spoon cutlery and crockery: glass cruet sets, Buffalo China mugs, and big kitchenware (10-gallon coffee machines and industrial-size wafflemakers and colanders), all at wholesale prices. Further down the Bowery you can buy horrible chandeliers from the stretch between Great Jones Street and SoHo known as the **lighting district**.

Bird Jungle, 401 Bleecker St., at West 11th St. Literally a jungle: toucans and mynah birds flapping over the customers.

Canal Rubber, 345 Canal St., near Greene St. Every kind of rubber, also mirrored disco globes, at wholesale prices.

Canal Surplus, 363 Canal St., between Wooster St. and West Broadway. The most fas- �110 cinating shop in Manhattan, specializing in industrial junk: stethoscopes, motors, magnifying glasses, clockwork mechanisms, selenium mirrors, aluminum sheets, titanium, magnets, dentists' drills, goggles, cauterizers, pendulums, doll's limbs—and beautiful but ambiguous objects that even the manager can't identify.

Evolution, 120 Spring St., between Greene and Mercer Sts. Skulls and bones—from alligator's feet to racoon's penis bones—all from animals, the shop assistants assure us, who died of natural causes.

Foster-a-pet, ✆ 387 2011.

Hammacher Schlemmer, 147 East 57th St., between 3rd and Lexington Aves. Gadgetry, from the essential to the preposterous: electric self-stirring saucepans, solar-activated garden-sprayers, bicycle-mowers.

H. Kauffman & Sons Saddlery & Co., 139 East 24th St., between Lexington and 3rd Aves. Full range of Western riding equipment.

International Boutique, 500 La Guardia Place. Anything military, including grenades.

Jeff's Baseball Cards, 150 2nd Ave., between 9th and 10th Sts. Baseball cards from 1910 to now, bought and sold.

Let there be Neon, 38 White St., between Broadway and Church St. Neon lights, signs and sculptures, founded by top American neon artist Rudi Stern.

Little Rickie, 49½ 1st Ave., at East 3rd St. New York's 'Cathedral of Kitsch': Pope � paraphernalia, Barbie dolls and the last black-and-white photo booth in New York City.

Luther Music Corp., 341 West 44th St., between 8th and 9th Aves. As well as fine � guitar strings, this sells beautifully made miniature musical instruments, from mandolins to harps, around $15–20.

Maxilla & Mandible, 451 Columbus Ave., between West 81st and 82nd Sts. Animal, � human and insect skeletons, teeth and bones in a shop smelling of camphor and relaxing fluid. Also, do-it-yourself skeleton assembly kits, human pelvises, moose antlers, porcupine quills, and every kind of beetle.

Petland Discounts, 734 9th Ave., between 49th and 50th Sts. As well as a full range of pet accessories, flexible transparent tubes for imaginatively adapting your mouse or hamster cages.

Star Magic, 743 Broadway, near West 8th St. Caters to astronomers, dinosaur-fans � (there are lots in New York), New Age faddists and the merely curious. One of the few places in Manhattan where you can get hold of universal Read-in-the-Dark Spectacle Attachments, torches which fit on to any pair of glasses.

Sports and Activities

Americans like to think that their sports reflect their attributes. Baseball has traditionally been associated with the patriotic virtues of teamwork, equality and patience, while the faster-paced sports of American football and ice hockey prize struggle, speed and fearlessness. To the uninitiated, American sport can seem a closed and secret world. Fortunately, most New Yorkers are high connoisseurs of American sport and will gladly enlighten neophytes. Unfortunately, though, these explanations are sometimes in such copious detail and involve such complicated terminology that they may end up leaving you in an even more confused state than you were to begin with. The sports pages in the papers, filled with statistics like 'Devils have lost 4 of last 5 on road, Penguins 7 of last 9, Nuggets 10 of 41 (24 per cent) in last 6', are even more bemusing. The only solution is to take yourself off to a match, preferably with someone who knows what's what. Sometimes the audience itself is the most entertaining spectacle of all.

For those wanting to participate, the 1.7 million square foot **Chelsea Piers Sports & Entertainment Complex** (Hudson Piers between West 17th and 23rd Sts, ✆ 336 6666) is the biggest in the USA and includes two year-round ice rinks, two open-air roller-blading rinks, New York State's largest gym, a quarter-mile running track, a whirlpool, a sundeck, lacrosse courts, volley ball sandcourts, a massive outdoor golf range and the largest rock climbing wall on the Northeast seaboard. Elsewhere in Manhattan you can play bowls, hire a horse, swelter in a Turkish bath or sail a J22 yacht. Roller blading is still Manhattan's favourite fad, and if you're skilled enough, the ultimate way to see the city would be to join a night-skate through the city (leaving from various locations, *see* below).

Baseball for Birdbrains

Baseball is the national obsession, and outsiders who aspire to understanding anything about America must first of all learn the complexities of this hallowed game. The sport has its place in the American psyche alongside Hollywood and doughnuts. Its heroes—Babe Ruth, Joe Di Maggio, Willie Mays—are as famous as any movie stars. Its history has inspired a wealth of literature, legend and argument. Its terminology has infiltrated everyday speech (as in 'home run', 'in the ballpark', 'strike out'). Baseball has a singular hold on the collective consciousness.

Some still insist on blaming all New York's ills and failures on the Brooklyn Dodgers and the New York Giants, who abandoned the city for greener fields in the late 1950s. During the 1960s, the Mets stepped into the gap, taking the Dodgers' blue and the Giants' orange as their colours, and since then they have been increasingly successful; in 1997 they were one of the top four teams in the National League. Both teams attract devotion in equal measures, but the reigning monarchs of New York baseball are the Yankees, whose dynasty stretches back seven decades. In October 1996 the Yankees won the World Series for the first time since 1981, an event of such cataclysmic import that it was celebrated with a tickertape parade along Lower Broadway.

Major League games are played and televized almost every day of the long season, which runs from April until October. The easiest tickets to get are 'bleachers'— unshaded seats in the rowdiest part of the stadium, which cost half the price of a regular ticket. Here you will hardly be able to see the match, but you're more likely to discover a real *aficionado*—someone who goes to 50 games a year—who will be delighted to explain it all.

The Mets, Shea Stadium, 126th St and Roosevelt Ave., Flushing, Queens, ✆ 1 (718) 507 TIXX.

New York Yankees, Yankee Stadium, West 161st St. and River Ave., Bronx, ✆ 1 (718) 293 4300 for information or ✆ 1 (718) 293 6000 for tickets. In 1989 the stadium lost 5000 seats when it was renovated to accommodate a corresponding increase in the size of the average New Yorker's behind.

Basketball

Under team captain Patrick Ewing, the Knicks had a good year in 1997, making it to the quarter finals. They still attract fanatical followers who studiously ignore the Nets across the river in New Jersey. There are basketball courts in parks all over the city: getting into a game is tricky unless you're six-foot-six. Watching, however, is great fun as tempers always flare, and usually the play is quite violent with arguments and brawls over fouls and cheating. The season lasts from winter till spring.

New York Knicks, Madison Sq Garden, corner W. 34th St. and 7th Ave., ✆ 465 JUMP.

New Jersey Nets, Meadowlands Arena, East Rutherford, New Jersey, ✆ 1 (201) 935 8888 for information or ✆ 1 (201) 935 3900 for tickets.

Bicycle Hire

Cycling is probably the fastest way to get yourself flattened in New York, and the types who go in for it are combative or reckless spirits with a devil-may-care approach to life. On the other hand cycling is an ideal way of getting around the city, especially in the outer boroughs, where bus systems can be mind-bending. At weekends thousands of bicyclists plough up the Ramble in Central Park, and the 7.2 road loop winding through the park is closed to vehicles. Hiring bikes can be quite pricey (up to $30 a day) and sometimes requires hefty security deposits.

Bicycles Metro, 1311 Lexington Ave., at East 88th St., ✆ 427 4450.

Loeb Boathouse, Central Park, 5th Ave., at East 72nd St., ✆ 861 4137.

Billiards and Pool

New Yorkers play pool and billiards round the clock, and especially in the small hours of the morning. Most bars have pool tables, but if you don't observe the etiquette of waiting your turn, you'll find yourself in a sour-tasting pickle.

Julian's Billiard Academy, 138 East 14th St., between 3rd and 4th Aves., ✆ 598 9884 *(open daily 10am–2am, Fri and Sat 10am–4am)*. Old-fashioned parlour filled with a fog of cigarette smoke and 29 tables.

Chelsea Billiards, 54 West 21st St., between 5th and 6th Aves., ✆ 989 0096 *(open 24 hours)*. Fifty-one quality pool and snooker tables, and two billiard tables.

Beaches

Most people go to the beautiful beaches on Long Island, a 2-hour trip by car or train. Only those with a taste for the outlandish brave the 80-minute subway trip to the pongy coastline of New York City.

Coney Island, Brighton Beach and Sheepshead Bay, ✆ 1 (718) 946 1350, all accessible by subway from Manhattan. A pleasant boardwalk, a freak show, a mermaid parade, a petrifying roller coaster—the rickety old Cyclone—and murky sea water. Walk along the boardwalk and after a few hundred yards you'll get to Brighton Beach or 'Little Odessa by the sea', inhabited since the 1970s by the largest community of Russians outside the Federation, and with shops and cafés selling delicious food and a general atmosphere of frenzied or dodgy activity. Sheepshead Bay (on the D or M subway line) is a lot quieter as well as rather more of a walk away, about 15 minutes down Brighton 11. The incongruous fishing harbour is inhabited mostly by retired people: there are quaint clam bars, tackle shops, ice-sellers and hundreds of fishing boats and yachts with names like *Windy-Breeze* or *Fire-fly*.

Jones Beach, Jones Beach State Park, Long Island. Pristine sands and clean sea water. Trains from Penn Station, ✆ 1 (718) 217 5477 for schedules.

Orchard Beach, Pelham Bay Park, Bronx, ✆ 885 2275. An enormous beach divided into 15 sections, at the far northeastern end of the Bronx, with curiously laval and unnatural-looking green rock.

Robert Moses Park, Fire Island, off Long Island, ✆ 1 (718) 217 5477 for train schedules. The best of the lot: wild, windswept and white-sanded, accessible from Manhattan via Penn Station. The island also includes two exclusively gay beaches: Cherry Grove and The Pines.

Rockaway Beach, Beach 1st St., to Beach 109th St., Beach 126th St., to Beach 149th St., Queens, ✆ 1 (718) 318 4000, take the A, C, or H train to Rockaway Park Beach. On a spectacular nature reserve near JFK. The subway there passes through Broad Channel—a curious swamp village built on stilts. Crowded in the summer and best out of season when it's deserted.

Boating

Loeb Boathouse, Central Park, near 5th Ave., and East 74th St., ℗ 517 4723. About $10 an hour for a rowing boat, with a $20 deposit.

Bocce

Youngsters, as well as crusty Italians, play *bocce* all over the city. The courts on Roosevelt Parkway, between Canal and Houston Streets and on 2nd Avenue and Houston Street, are popular, and sometimes passers-by are encouraged to join in.

Boxing

Madison Square Garden, 7th Ave and 32nd St., ℗ 465 6741. WBA, etc.

The Chelsea Piers (*see* 'Health Clubs', below): professional male and female boxing.

Bowling

Bowling is so straightforward and easy that even novices can land themselves a lucky strike. There are only two 'alleys' left in Manhattan but both stay open late.

Bowlmor Lanes, 110 University Place, near 12th St., ℗ 255 8188 *(open until 4am Fri–Sat)*. Loveable alley with 44 lanes, a bar and **Disco Bowling** (*10.30pm to 4am Mon*) with house by DJ Walter V.

Leisure Time Bowling, 625 8th Ave., between 40th and 41st Sts., ℗ 268 6909 (open until 1am Fri–Sat). Hardcore bowling with loud R&B music, a rowdy bar and television screens showing movies. On the west side of Midtown, reasonably near Times Square, with friendly league games on Thursdays.

Cricket and Rugby

Van Courtlant Park, Parade Ground, near Broadway, North Bronx, ℗ 1 (201) 343 4544. Weekend cricket and rugger, especially popular with local West Indians.

Croquet

New Yorkers insist on having a go, with a celebrity tournament every May.

Central Park Croquet Lawn, W. 67th St., and the West Drive, Central Park, ℗ 572 4345.

Flotation

Tranquility Tanks, 141 5th Ave., ℗ 475 5225. When New York becomes really unbearable there's always total sensory deprivation—floating with your ears plugged with wax, in a darkened room in a tank of salt water.

Football

Tickets for the Giants sell out years ahead, and although it's easier to get tickets for the less popular Jets, you'll probably end up watching American football on TV. The game is stupendously violent; a kamikaze version of rugger which is thrilling to watch. The season lasts from September until the Super Bowl championship game on the last Saturday in January.

Jets and Giants Information, Giants Stadium, Meadowlands Sports Complex, East Rutherford, New Jersey, ☎ 1 (201) 935 3900.

Golf

For golf in Manhattan, *see* Chelsea Piers, under 'Health Clubs', below.

Van Courtlandt Golf Course, Van Courtlandt Park, Park South and Baily Ave., Bronx, ☎ 543 4595. New York's oldest golf course, short but tricky.

Handball

Like squash and played against a wall with two goals. There are courts in Central Park, John Jay Park and Tompkins Square Park. Call the Park Rangers for more information, ☎ 360 2774.

Health Clubs: Gyms, Weight-training and Aerobics

'Body-conditioning' is a fetish for most New Yorkers, who must punish their bodies before they can enjoy themselves. A lot of hotels have private health clubs or off-premises gyms. The city is seething with health clubs, but most require annual membership. You can enlist by the day or the hour at the following:

Chelsea Piers Sports & Entertainment Complex, 59–62 Hudson Piers, between West 17th and 23rd Sts., ☎ 336 6666. New York State's largest gym and rock climbing wall (*see* above, p.298).

The Exercise Exchange, 236 West 78th St., at Broadway, ☎ 595 6475. Aerobics at standard rates.

Reebok Sports Club, 160 Columbus Ave., at West 20th St. Six floors, with a rooftop running track, four-storey rock-climbing wall and ski-simulators.

Hot Air Ballooning

Black Tie, 320 Red Lion Rod, Southampton, New Jersey, ☎ 1 (609) 859 9600. Hour-long balloon rides over the Rancocas Creek from around $140 per person. Includes a balloon big enough to take 20 people.

Horse Racing

Racing, or rather, betting, is immensely popular throughout the US, and the *Racing Times* is said to be the best-selling weekly in the country. If you don't make it to the racecourse, you can place a bet at any of the OTB or Off Track Betting parlours scattered all over Manhattan. Yonkers Raceway has harness racing.

Aqueduct Racetrack, 108th St., and **Rockaway Boulevard**, Jamaica, Queens, ☎ 1 (718) 641 4700.

Belmont Park, Hempstead Turnpike and Plainfield Ave., Belmont, Long Island, ✆ 1 (718) 641 4700. Travel by Belmont Special Train from Penn Station.

Horse Riding

Claremont Riding Academy, 175 West 89th St., at Amsterdam Ave., ✆ 724 5100. Fearfully expensive lessons (around $70 an hour) or rentals (around $30 per hour) for riding English-style in Central Park.

Jamaica Bay Riding Academy, 7000 Shore Parkway, Brooklyn, ✆ 1 (718) 531 8948. Lessons in English and Western-style riding and guided 45 minute trail rides through the Jamaica Bay Wildlife park for around $23.

Ice Hockey

The principal entertainment of Madison Garden ice-hockey matches is observing the Rangers' entrenched hatred for the Islanders. In 1994, after over half a century of failure, the Rangers won the Stanley Cup Championship, silencing at last taunts of 'Nineteen-forty, Nineteen-forty!' from fans of the Islanders.

Islanders Information, Nassau Coliseum, Hempstead Turnpike, Uniondale, ✆ 516 794 4100.

Rangers Information, Madison Square Garden, 7th Ave., between 31st and 33rd Sts., ✆ 465 MSGI or 465 6468.

Massage

Swish hotels offer massage in your room for around $100 an hour. Anyone who doesn't have access to this can try a chain of massage parlours called **The Great American Back-rub**. This has franchises all over Manhattan, including 162 Spring St., at West Broadway and 574 Columbus Ave, at 85th St. A 10-minute back rub or foot rub costs around $15, and a head rub (aka 'deluxe scalp treatment') about $6.

Spa 227, 227 East 56th St., ✆ 754 0227 *(open 24 hours; men only)*. Salt-glo scrubs, facials, roman steam baths and massage for men only.

Racewalking

Park Racewalkers, Central Park, E. Park Drive at 84th St., ✆ 628 1317 *(Wed 7pm and Sat–Sun 8am; membership $20)*. Monty Python-style walk-races in Central Park.

Racquetball

Softball played on a squash court with racquets.

Manhattan Plaza Racquet Club, 450 West 43rd St., between 9th and 10th Aves., ✆ 594 0554 *($10 guest fee on top of the normal rates)*.

Roller-blading, Quad and Ice-Skating

If you can blade or skate, you'll be able to enjoy one of Manhattan's quintessentially urban experiences. New Yorkers are the world's keenest skaters: excellent routes exist down the East River Park and round South Street; up Battery Park Esplanade; on the Central Park road loop (closed to traffic on weekends); along Riverside Park on the Upper West Side, and from Carl Schurz Park to John Jay Park on the Upper East Side. So many Manhattanites of varying abilities have taken to roller blades that a special patrol has now been set up giving skaters free lessons on how to stop. Old-fashioned skates, meanwhile, are so passé that they're scornfully referred to as 'quads'.

skate meets

Central Park Roller Disco and SkateOut, Literary Walk near 72nd St and 5th Ave, ✆ 486 1919 *(every Sat at 1.30pm)*. Where Central Park's bladers and skaters congregate: fascinating to watch even if you can't skate.

Night Blade Manhattan, steps to Union Square Park, West 14th St and Broadway, *(Wed 9–10.30pm; free)*. Up to a hundred people glide through the nighttime streets.

Skate under the Stars, Metropolitan-Manhattan Skate Club, Chelsea Piers, 23rd St at West Side Highway, ✆ 336 6200 *(Sat 11.30pm–3am; adm $8)*. Quad skating through the night.

Tuesday Night Skate, New York Road Skaters Association, Blades West, 120 West 72nd St, between Broadway and Columbus Ave, ✆ 929 0003 *(Tues 8pm; free)*. Fast and furious, gliding as far as New Jersey and Coney Island. Free, but you must be good.

rink skating

Not so thrillingly urban as gliding through Manhattan streets, but safer.

Chelsea Piers, 23rd St and West Side Highway, ✆ 336 6200. Music and cheap skate hire.

Wollman Memorial Rink, Central Park, 830 5th Ave., at 59th St., ✆ 517 4800 *(ice skating Oct–Mar, roller skating, blading and miniature golf April–Sept)*. A huge outdoor skating rink in Central Park, large and noisy, with disco music. Blades and ice skates are cheap to hire and you can skate for as long as you can stand it.

Rockefeller Center Ice Rink, 1 Rockefeller Plaza, 5th Ave., ✆ 757 5731/0 *(open Oct–April, 9am–10pm)*. A lot of people will be watching as you keel over on this famously small rink.

Riverbank State Park, West 145th St at Riverside Drive, ✆ 694 3600. Very cheap skating on a big, beautiful rink built over a sewage plant in Harlem.

Roxy, 515 West 18th St., between 10th and 11th Aves., ✆ 645 5156 *(adm $12 not including skate or blade rental)*. Roller blader disco, with gay/drag night on Tuesdays.

skate races

Speed Rollerblading, Prospect Park, Breeze Hil, near the boathouse and lake, ✆ 1 (718) 282 7789. Weekend races with prizes up to $500.

blade hire

Blades West, 120 West 72nd St., at Columbus Ave., ✆ 787 3911.

Blades East, 160 East 86th St., between 3rd and Lexington Aves., ✆ 996 1644.

Rollerblades, ice skates, snowboards and, more importantly, pads for hire and for sale, and within easy access of Central Park.

Roller Hockey

For a fee you can join one of the roller hockey league teams at the Chelsea Piers, ✆ 336 6200. Alternatively you can attempt to muscle your way into a park game in Tompkins Square Park (10th St and Ave A), Union Square Park (14th St and Broadway) or Carl Schurz Park (East 85th St and York Ave) *(daily from 5pm on)*.

Running

clubs

New York Road Runners Club, 9 East 89th St., between 5th and Madison Aves., ✆ 860 4455 for advice on races, finding a safe running partner and group runs. The club organizes the New York Marathon in May, and group runs around the Central Park reservoir (think *Marathon Man*) *(Mon–Fri, 6.30pm and 7.15pm; free)*.

Central Park Track Club, Central Park, Daniel Webster statue, 72nd St and West Park Drive, ✆ 838 1120 *(every Thurs 7pm)*.

Front Runners, Central Park, Daniel Webster statue, 72nd St and West Park Drive *(Sat 10am)*. Gay and lesbian club.

deep water

John Jay College, 899 10th Ave., between 58th and 59th Sts., ✆ 222 0720. Classes teaching New Yorkers how to run in a swimming pool. Flotation belts provided.

Sailing

New York Harbor Boating, The Enterprise, North Cove Yacht Harbor, World Financial Center, ✆ 786 0400 *(open dawn–dusk)*. Sail boats for hire from around $100 per half day. You need documentation to prove that you can sail.

Skiing

There are people who insist the 'slopes' of Central Park are better than those in Vermont. The nearest resort is **Great George** in New Jersey, ✆ 1 (201) 827 6000.

Skydiving

Skydive Long Island, East Moriches, Long Island, ✆ 1 516 878 5867. Includes expensive 5-hour training sessions.

Softball

Baseball for scaredy-cats, using a larger, softer ball on a smaller court. There are courts on the Great Lawn and Hecksher Field in Central Park, and in Riverside Park at 102nd Street and at the Boat Basin. You should purchase a season's permit from the Parks Recreation Department *(see* 'Tennis')*.

Squash

City Hall Squash Club, 25 Park Place, between Church St. and Broadway, © 964 2677. A guest's fee of around $30.

Swimming

Swimming in Manhattan is a palaver. Some hotels have private pools but if you want to use these you will probably have to pay a membership fee. If you want to use the free **municipal pools** you'll need photographic ID, an address in New York City and $25, payable to the Parks Dept by money order only; call © 1 (800) 201 PARK for more information. They will give you a list of city-run pools—the nicest of which are in Hamilton Fish Park (a monumental beaux-arts pool) and John Jay Park (an outdoor pool on the Upper East Side).

Tennis

To play on city-owned courts you must purchase a $50 permit from the Parks Department in the Arsenal Building at 64th St. and 5th Ave., © 360 8111. They'll give you a list of courts in Central Park, East River Park, and Riverside Park. The permit lasts for the season from April to Nov.

Turkish Baths

Tenth Street Russian-Turkish Baths, 268 East 10th St., between 1st Ave. and Ave. A, © 674 9250 *(open 8am–10pm; adm $20; massages from $26)*. There's a women-only day (Wed) and two men-only days (Thurs and Sun), as well as mixed days when everyone wears loincloths. Includes a vodka bar, a Russian Radiant Heat room and brushes made of oak branches. If it's all too much for you, there's a dormitory on the first floor.

Wrestling

Wrestling at the Madison Avenue Garden is the ultimate trash spectator sport, a cross between vaudeville and slapstick. Red-white-and-blue ice-creams, singalongs to the national anthem, and fights between 'Macho Man Randy Savage', 'Gold dust' the drag queen and 'Mankind'.

Wrestling Information, Madison Square Garden, corner of West 34th St. and 7th Ave., © 465 6000.

Yoga

Integral Yoga Institute, 227 West 13th St., between 7th and 89th Aves., © 929 0586. Reasonably priced classes (about $8 a go).

Living and Working in Manhattan

One belongs to New York instantly. One belongs to it as much in five minutes as in five years.

Thomas Wolfe

New York is not constructed to be lived in.

Wyndham Lewis, *America and Cosmic Man*

In the USA an average 20 million people move each year. Millions of people, not just the annual influx of 17 million tourists, are utterly new to Manhattan. Finding a niche, a home and a job takes stamina, plus a degree of scrabbling around and not a little cunning.

Getting a Visa

To work legally in the States, you need to get an American company or a relative living in America to sponsor you by letter. After that you can apply for a special work permit from the American embassy or consulate in your own country. Visas are notoriously hard to come by: it helps if you have a skill or professional qualification, for example, in architecture, computers or academia.

Students can apply for an **Exchange Visitor Programme**. Successful applicants will get a social security number and a short term J-1 visa entitling them to work in the US. These kind of visas are issued through bodies like BUNAC in London, ℂ (0171) 251 3472 (and usually charge a registration fee of around £60). In return, BUNAC gives students free accommodation for their first night in New York, followed by a morning's 'orientation'.

Finding Casual Work

Picking up casual work without a visa is possible though illegal—if you're caught without a visa you will be deported and your employer fined $10,000. To work illegally, most people invent a social security number, although since fines were introduced employers are a lot more conscientious about rules and regulations.

The best places to look for casual jobs are the classified advertisements in the *Village Voice* and the *New York Times*, and on noticeboards in bars, cafés and supermarkets or else at the *Village Voice* (36 Cooper Square in the East Village). If you're looking for work waiting on tables, go straight to a restaurant and ask. Basic jobs like baby-sitting, au-pairing, telephone sales, temping, hotel reception, dog-walking, life modelling and painting and decorating are low-paid but available.

An English accent will be appreciated, especially if the job you're trying for involves telephone work (with **telephone sex lines** it's practically a passport). If you're really down on uppers, remember you can sell **blood** to a blood donor centre or get money working as a guinea pig in one of the **cold clinics** and medical research centres advertising in the *Voice*.

This can be more of a headache. Minuscule rented apartments can be ridiculously expensive. **Sub-lets**—varying from a few weeks to a year or two—are cheaper, especially if you're looking for somewhere just for the summer. For those on a low budget, one of the best options is a 'share' (moving in with someone who already has an apartment), advertised in the *Village Voice* or the *New York Times*. Make sure you get hold of the *Voice* as soon as it comes out—at dawn on Wednesday morning (people advertising shares get as many as 500 calls in a few days). (If you want to arrange an apartment or house exchange, it's possible to get copies of the *Village Voice* and *Time Out New York* in some newsagents in Central London—try Leicester Square and SoHo.) In Manhattan, competition for apartments is worst at the beginning of the academic year and after Christmas: a good time to look is in the summer when people leave the city. Expect to pay a month's rent as deposit, plus the first month's rent in advance.

Before you start phoning, have a vague idea of the area you want to live in. The Upper East Side, the Upper West Side, SoHo and the West Village are the most expensive; the East Village, TriBeCa, the Lower East Side, Chelsea and Chinatown less expensive. 'Cheap' rents do exist—but usually outside Manhattan in unsmart parts of Brooklyn, New Jersey and Queens: for example Williamsburg, Hoboken or Long Island City. If you have time to pick and choose, it's an excellent idea to consult local newspapers, as well as advertisements pinned up in neighbourhood bars, restaurants and on noticeboards on campuses like Cooper Union in the East Village, Columbia on the Upper West Side, and NYU in Washington Square. Alternatively there are **roomate agencies**, like *Roomate Finders* (250 West 57th St., ✆ 489 6942) or *Gary's Gay Roomate Service*, who will fix you up with like-minded roomates for a substantial flat fee. Avoid **realtors**—real estate agencies who charge about 15 per cent of a year's rent in return for finding you a 'perfect' apartment.

Internet sublets

Sublets are just beginning to be advertised on the net. Try:

    Rent Online: *www.aptsforrent.com*
    Rent Net: *http://rent.net*
    Manhattan Apartment Guide: *www.aptguides.com*

landlords and renter's insurance

After you've moved in, you might think about getting insurance. The cheapest policies are offered by Allstate and Prudential, but you may have problems taking out a policy if your building lacks fire alarms or elevators. If you have problems with your landlord you can get advice as well as a copy of the *Tenant's Handbook* from the Open Housing Center, 594 Broadway, Suite 608, ✆ 941 6101.

Useful Numbers

Battered Women Hotline: ✆ (1 800) 942 6906

Borough president: ✆ 669 8300

Business Information: try the New York Chamber of Commerce and Industry, Battery Park Plaza, between State and Whitehall Sts., ✆ 493 7500, or the NYC Department of Business Services, 110 William St at Fulton St., ✆ 696 2442.

City Car Pound: ✆ 971 0770.

Children: the **Parents' League of New York** (115 East 82nd St., NY NY 10028, ✆ 737 7385, open Sept–June) has advice on schooling and cultural events for children who are new to New York; *Parentguide Magazine* (419 Park Ave South, NYNY 10016, ✆ 213 8840) is published every month and can be helpful as well. The 92nd Street Y (1395 Lexington Ave, at 92nd St., ✆ 415 5650) organizes day classes in Manhattan and some summer camp programmes outside of Manhattan. To join one of these write or telephone well in advance. **WonderCamp Entertainment** (27 West 23rd St at 5th Ave., ✆ 243 1111) is an indoor playground for young children. The **Avalon Nurse Registry and Child Service**, ✆ 245 0250, or **The Baby Sitters Guild**, ✆ 682 0227 can help out with babysitters and nannies. The **Runaway Hotline**, ✆ (1 800) 246 4646, will help in emergencies.

Complaints: when provoked, New Yorkers are hardly shy about complaining. The **Better Business Bureau**, ✆ 533 6200, gives paid advice on consumer complaints; the **New York City Department of Consumer Affairs**, ✆ 487 4444, receives complaint reports on shops and services in Manhattan, and **Rent-A-Kvetch**, ✆ 463 0960, will take on consumer complaints for people who don't have the time to make them in person. Alternatively call the **Bella Thomas Dial-a-Philosophical Debate** line on ✆ 792 5508.

Computer Repairs: RCS Computer Service Center, ✆ 949 6935.

Consumer Protention Board: ✆ 1 (518) 474 8583.

Costume Hire: Allan Uniform Rental Service, ✆ 529 4655, hires out a complete range of animal outfits including chicken suits. Frielich Police Equipment, 211 East 21st St., sells genuine NYPD uniforms and 'equipment'.

Crime Stoppers: ✆ 577 TIPS, rewards for information.

Death Certificates: ✆ 788 4520.

Despatch deliveries: Breakaway, 17 Varick St., ✆ 219 8500. Delivery within the hour using cycles, vans and motorbikes.

Dial-A-Doctor: ✆ 971 9692, 24-hour house or hotel calls.

Dial-A-Mattress: ✆ 1 (718) 628 7377, same day mattress delivery and assembly.

Dial-A-Secretary: 521 5th Ave., ✆ 348 9575. Your fantasy come true: hundreds of Miss Jones', some with bionic typing speeds up to 170 words a minute.

Dirtbusters: ✆ 721 HELD/4357, specializing in crisis cleaning at two hours' notice.

Domestic Staff: Edwina Ashton Maids Unlimited, ✆ 838 6282, can supply you with any kind of help, from a professional spring clean to tidy-ups after a rowdy party. Butler, bartender, maid and window cleaner-hire too.

Electrolysis: Ivan O'Hare, 18 West 21st St., ✆ 645 9212.

Exterminators: landlords are supposed to send round exterminators to cope with New York's thriving cosmopolis of rats, squirrels, mice, cockroaches, bed bugs and termites. If you need an exterminator quickly, try Roach Busters' 24-hour service line: 1 718 232 5507.

Family Planning: Planned Parenthood, 380 2nd Ave., at 22nd St., ✆ 677 3320. Sympathetic advice on birth control, sexually transmitted diseases and abortion.

Food and Hunger Hotline: ✆ 533 7600.

Furniture Rental: Churchill, 44 East 32nd St., ✆ 686 0444. Furniture rented out for up to five years.

Garage Parking: phone Kinney Inc for 150 Manhattan garages, ✆ 1 (800) KNY PARK.

Gay Events: are listed in the gay entertainment and resource guide *Metrosource*, available on news-stands.

Greenpeace: ✆ 941 0094.

Heat Complaints: ✆ 960 4800.

Hire-a-Concert-Pianist: Marcelo Bratke, ✆ 23PIANO.

Image Consultants: ✆ 1 (610) 867 4582. Improve your image and become more popular.

Immigration and naturalization:, ✆ 206 6500.

Laundry: Midnight Express, ✆ 921 0111: 24-hour dry-cleaning service specializing in smoke-damaged clothes. Free pick-up and delivery night and day.

Legal Aid: ✆ 577 3300.

Lesbian Herstory Educational Foundation: PO Box 1258, New York, NY 10116, ✆ 1 (718) 768 3953. Lesbianism archive in Brooklyn.

Libraries: New York has the most egalitarian public library in the world: anyone residing in the city can join, take out books and return them to any branch in Manhattan. Best of all anyone can use the magnificent Research Library on 42nd Street and 5th Avenue. Take along a letter addressed to you as proof that you live in the city, and the library will issue a membership card. Telephone ✆ 869 8089 to find your nearest branch.

Lotto: ✆ 976 2020 (you pay for the service) to find out the day's winning number. The lottery is a notorious scam.

Mail Fraud: ✆ 330 3844 complaints, chain letters, and obscene letters.

Marriage licenses: ✆ 669 2400.

Parking Regulations Information: ✆ 442 7080.

Parking Violations: ✆ 477 4430.

Parks Department: ✆ 360 1333 for the latest calendar of events.

Pay phone complaints: ✆ 526 2000.

Pets: the **American Society for the Prevention of Cruelty to Animals**, ✆ 1 (718) 257 6000 has advice on strays and adoption. If you walk your dog, you must scoop up after him. If you don't you'll get fined or, more likely, savaged by an infuriated New Yorker. If you can't face walking the dog, **Pet Patrol**, ✆ 924 6319, is a recommended dog-walking and pet-sitting service, and **Dog-O-Rama**, 123 4th Ave., ✆ 353 9186, supervises dog obedience-training and grooming for problem breeds and also sells a complete range of boutique accessories for dogs. The **Pet Department Store** on 233 West 54rh Ar., between Broadway and 8th Ave., ✆ 489 9195, includes a photographical studio and café and stocks a complete range of pet products, from fashions to 'pup' corn. **NYC Animal Rescue** has orphan pets for adoption, ✆ 387 2011. The **Animal Medical Care Center**, ✆ 838 8100, provides emergency 24 hour pet care. **Aldstate** in Brooklyn takes care of pet cremations, ✆ 1 (718) 748 2104.

Plant and Flower Hotline: c/o Harry Cotbean, ✆ 220 8681.

Pot Hole Complaints: ✆ 768 4653.

Private Detectives: Shirley Locke Inc., 210 East 35th St., ✆ 889 1656, specializing in 'difficult and unusual investigations' and electronic debugging.

Pothole complaints: ✆ POT HOLE.

Rent Control District Office: 1 (718) 739 6400.

Sexually Transmitted Diseases: ✆ 1 (800) 9000HIV, open 7 days a week. No appointments necessary and while you wait test results on HIV, chlamydia, syphilis and hepatitis.

Steak Delivery: ✆ 1 (800) 228 9055. Filet-mignons from Omaha delivered in 3 business days or less.

Taxes: ✆ (1 718) 935 6436.

Telephone Answering Services: Media Response, 1713 3rd Ave., ✆ 246 7676. Pay someone to receive and take down messages for your business, rather than rely on an impersonal answer machine.

Theater and TV Tickets: Audience Extras, ✆ 989 9550, has a scheme for selling left-over seats for all kinds of events for less than $3 to members who have paid an annual registration fee of around $80. *See* also **Practical Information** p.39.

Toupées: try Ira Senzuma, 13 East 47th St, ✆ 752 6800.

Traffic reports: call Jocelyn Faure-Spaize, ✆ 235 8226.

Transportation: ✆ 1 (718) 330 1234 (or 1 (718) 330 4847 for non-English speakers) for information about bus and train schedules and ✆ 1 (800) AIR RIDE for information about transportation to airports.

Visas: Visa Express Inc., 21 East 40th St., between Madison and 5th Aves., ✆ 532 9437. Visas for all countries. Also try **It's Easy**, 10 Rockefeller Center, ✆ 586 8880.

Vocational Assessment: aka career counselling, ✆ 880 2607.

Voter Registration: ✆ 1 (800) FOR VOTE.

Wardrobe Psychology: by appointment ✆ 289 7807. Psychological assessment and tips on how to improve your appearance.

Weather Information: Claudia Leighter, ✆ 738 0239.

Women's Health Line: ✆ 230 1111. Low-cost referrals to hospitals in Manhattan, for women only.

The Americans are going to be the most fluent and melodious voiced people in the world—and the most perfect users of words. Words forming character—nativity, independence, individuality.

Walt Whitman, *An American Primer*, 1855–60

New Yorkers speak a different language from everyone else. The fact that both of you think it's the same one only makes matters worse. The distinctive New York accent is delivered with a swaggering nasal twang; New Yorkers talk faster than other people and interrupt each other at the slightest opportunity; they say *wassermajawidgiu?* when you can't understand.

The so-called Brooklyn argot, which has Brooklynites referring to 'de goils on toid and toid-toidy street' and 'de toikeys in Joisey', was the invention of generations of comedians: in fact the dialect is indigenous to the entire Metropolitan area, and was first spoken before the Civil War by Manhattan gangs with names like the Plug-Uglies and the Bowery B'hoys. Over the years the accent been honed into the timeless squawking we hear in films and on streets today. More curiously still, the average New Yorker's vocabulary is stocked with words like like sleigh, stoop, cookie, coleslaw, boss, dope and nit wit (from the Dutch 'Ik niet wiet' meaning 'I don't know') which arrived here in the 17th and 18th centuries via the first Dutch settlers.

Noo Yawkers love tawking, above all else. Cecil Beaton once described their use of language as Elizabethan, and certainly to outsiders the average New Yorker's use of slang is attractive and often infectious blend of imagination and florid adjectives. In recent years, apart from a strong Yiddish input, the black community has had by far the most pervasive influence on New York slang.

Like most things in the city, slang comes and goes. Nevertheless the glossary below will give you an invaluable head start: British visitors,

Glossary of Slang

in particular, are advised to study those problematic everyday idioms which have other meanings in America. To 'knock someone up', for example, means to get them pregnant; while to 'blow someone off' is a mild phrase, meaning to cut or avoid someone.

Key to abbreviations

n: noun
v: verb
adj: adjective
interj: interjection

n phr: noun phrase
v phr: verb phrase
adj phr: adjective phrase

Assawayigoze—*interj* That's life, or *c'est la vie*

Babycakes—*n* Sweetheart

Barn-burner—*n* Something sensational or exciting

Bat one's gums—*v phr* Talk flippantly or frivolously

Bazoo—*n* The mouth

Belle-boy—*n* Gay prostitute

Bin-wacker—*n* A habitual drunkard

Biseeinya—*interj* I'll be seeing you again soon

Bodacious—*adj* Extremely blatant or audacious

Brewskies—*n* Beers

Brodie—*n* A total fiasco and or suicide (after Steve Brodie who leapt off the Brooklyn Bridge in 1886 but mysteriously failed to have the jump witnessed).

Bronx cheer—*n phr* A gusty flatulating noise made with the tongue, cheeks and lips

Bug off—*v phr* To leave or depart

Catch some rays—*interj* A parting salutation

Caveman—*n* A masterful man

Cheesy—*adj* Lacking in taste; kitsch or shoddy

Cha'abolt—*interj* 'What are chattering about?' [West Indian], i.e. What do you mean?

Chill—*v* Relax

Chill out—*v phr* Relax and enjoy yourself

Chim—*n* A good fellow

Chum the waters—*sentence* Throw out some bait and see how many (figurative) fish rise to take it.

Chutzpah—*n* Hubris; extreme and arrogant brashness, epitomised, according to travel writer Bill Bryson, in the 'old joke about the boy who kills his parents, then begs mercy from the court because he has only recently been orphaned'.

Clever cock—*n phr* A know-it-all

Clothears—*n phr* Someone who is paying so little attention that they seem to be hard of hearing.

Clover hole—*n phr* Irish bar

Cool breeze—*v phr* Don't hassle me

Craven—*adj* Greedy

Crib—*n* House

Crucial—*adj* Brilliant or excellent

Ditsy—*adj* Vapid and silly

Ditz—*n* A frivolous ninny; flighty or fey

Does Howdy Doody have wooden balls?—*sentence* What a stupid question to ask

Doggie—*n* A $10 bill

Don't dis me—*v phr* Don't show me any disrespect

Douche bag—*n* An unpleasant woman.

Duhshuh-ul—*n* The shuttle connecting Times Square and Grand Central Terminal

Duplex—*n* The ultimate in Manhattan apartments: on two floors, or occasionally on one floor but with a ceiling two floors high.

Dyawanna brr?—*sentence* Would you like a beer?

Excuse me—*v phr* 'Get out of my way now.'

Fanny pack—*n* Bum bag, considered safer than knapsacks by the NYPD.

Flaky—*adj* Exuberantly eccentric, insane, or dizzily bewildered

Frantic—*adj* Excellent, cool

Funk—*v* To panic and fail

Funky—*adj* Quaint and attractively eccentric, or repulsively smelly

Furburger—*n* An alluring woman

Futon-potato—*n* Yuppie stay-at-home and kill-joy

Geddowdedewai—*v phr* Excuse me, please

Get the matches—*interj* Let's have some fun

Get your gummies on—*interj* Move it, because the police are coming

Ginchy—*adj* Admirable or sexy

Gizmo—*n* A fellow, or 'bloke'

Glop-pads—*n* Marks left on a floor by sweaty feet

Go for a steak out—*v phr* Go out for a big meal, usually of steak

Go to business—*v phr* Go to work

Goof around—*v phr* Potter about

Goop—*adj* An idiotic person

Grand Central Station—*n phr* Anywhere excessively crowded or busy

Gumball—*n* The lights on top of a police-car

Gussy up—*v phr* Dress up in one's best, or refurbish

Gutsy—*adj* Assertive and strong

Happy talk—*n phr* Informal chat among newscasters during a broadcast

Have some buttons missing—*v phr* To be eccentric and whimsical

Heaving—*adj* Excellent, wonderful or 'groovy'

Heavy duckets—*n phr* Lots of money

Hefty—*n* A fat person

Helluvalot—*n* A large amount

Hizzoner—*n* The mayor

Ho—*n* Prostitute or slapper type of woman

Hokum—*n* Poppycock, nonsense

Homeboys, *Hos*, or *Homes*—*n* Neighbour, compatriate or buddy

hooch—*m* Strong liquor, from brews made by the *Hoochinoo* Indians of Alaska.

Hootoadjadat?—*sentence* What you're saying is rubbish

How're you hangin?—*interj* How do you do?

Humpy-bumpy—*n* Intercourse

Jeepers creepers—*interj* An exclamation of surprise

Juiced up—*adj phr* Full of energy

Kazoo—*n* Backside or lavatory

Khazeray—*n* Odious, worthless material

Kibitz—*v* To give unwelcome and intrusive advice

Kishkes—*n* Guts or innards

KISS—*sentence* Keep it simple, stupid

Kissyface—*n* Cuddling and hugging

Kitten—*n* $50 bill

Klutz around—*v phr* Behave in goonish manner

Kneesies—*n* Clandestine friction of the knees

Kneesup—*n* A fun-loving person

Kvell—*v* To beam with pride or satisfaction

Kvetch—*v* To complain or be consistently pessimistic, a favourite occupation

Laugh–riot—*n* A jolly person, as in 'She's a real laugh-riot'.

Later—*interj* A casual farewell

Leg-biter—*n* A small child or infant

Let's break the cake—*interj* It's time we left this place

Let's make time—*interj* Hurry up

Love-puppet—*n* Sweet and irresistible boyfriend

Marker—*n* An IOU (from gambling) or a score (from sports)

Mashuggah—*adj* Crazy.

Melthead—*n* Dim-witted person

Mynjabak—*v phr* Please get out of my way

Momser, *Mofo* or *Mucker*—*n* Contemptible or despicable person

Moocher—*n* A beggar or parasite

Moore?—*interj* Score, as in what's the score?

Moosh someone—*v phr* To attack someone vigorously, to let them have it

Moxie—*n* Gumption, guts or shrewdness

My posse—*n phr* My crowd of people

No soap—*negation* Absolutely not, no way

Out of the loop—*phr* Someone who has left New York to live in Northwest America.

Penthouse—*n* A smart name for an apartment on the top floor of a tower block.

Pesky—*adj* Irritating and annoying

Pol—*n* A politician

Rat around—*v phr* Loaf around

Ratchet-mouth—*n* A blabberer

Righteous—*adj* Excellent/genuine/the greatest

Rusty-dusty—*n* The buttocks or rump

Sass—*n* Impudence

Sausage-jock—*n* Taxi-driver

Savvy—*n* Intelligence, nous, brains

Schikse—*n* A Christian female

Schlemiel—*n* A victimized oaf

Schlep—*v* To carry with difficulty, or lug, or *n* a stupid person

Schlock—*n* Rubbish or shoddy, vulgar merchandise

Schlok shop—*n* Fancy-dress shop

Schlub or *Zhlub*—*n* A boorish, coarse-tongued person

Schlubette—*n* A silly girl

Schmaltz—*n* Cloying sentimentality, literally meaning 'chicken fat'

Schmear—v To bribe, flatter or soft soap, or smear on thickly, or n A scam

Schmeck—n A soupçon, a taste

Schmegeggy—n A fool

Schmendrick—n A gangly, inept person

Schmo or Joe Schmo—n An undistinguished, backward or hapless character

Schmooz—v Cosy conversation

Schmuck—n An obnoxious person

Schmutter—n Clothes

Schnorrer—n A sponger or niggard

Schnozzola—n The nose

Shoot one's cookies—v phr To vomit

Shtarker—n A tough, a swell or a very important person

Shtick—n A small theatrical role, or a characteristic trait

Sissified—adj Timorous and spineless

Slap the plank—v phr To greet with mutual palm-slapping

Slooper—n A sneak or a gossip

Smokes—n Cigarettes

Snake-bitten—adj Hopelessly incapacitated

Spiffed-out—adj Dressed to the nines

Spiffy—adj Elegant and snazzy

Spunker-master—n Someone who is full of beans

Stop dissing me—v phr Stop distressing me

Studio-apartment—n Usually a bedsit with no separate bedroom and sometimes a kitchenette instead of a kitchen.

Studmuffin—n A gentle and attractive man with a great deal of sex-appeal, or n a transvestite husband

Swashle the swoosh—v phr Pilfer from a shop or till

Talk turkey—v phr Speak lucidly and candidly

Taykdiway—v phr I've finished, thank you

Taykideezy—v phr Don't let things get on top of you

That's stoopid—interj That's absolutely wonderful

Tittermouse—n A giggling chatterer

Yang-allure—n Masculine sex appeal

Yo—interj Hail

You-know-what-I'm-saying?—v phr Do you read me?

Wannamaiksumpnuvvit?—v pht Do you want to get involved in a brawl?

Walk heavy—v phr To be important

Walk-Up—n An apartment in a building without an elevator.

Washyerstep—v phr Mind where you are going

Way-hip—adj Very fashionable

Weenie—n Frankfurter, or an ineffectual person

Whadayyawant?—v phr Can I help you?

What can I do you for?—interj Hello

What gives?—interj What's going on? How are you?

Whazzitooyuh?—v phr Stop irritating me

Whazzup?—interj What's going on?, or hello

Whooper-dooper—n A wild party

Wussy—n A very weak person

Asbury, Herbert, *The Gangs of New York* (Alfred A. Knopf, Incl, 1928). An arresting account of the New York underworld, from the early gangs of the Revolution to the '20s.

Botkin, B. A., *New York City Folklore* (Random House, 1956). A wonderfully entertaining compendium of tall stories and anecdotes about New York, compiled from diaries, gossip columns, literature and letters, as well as travel books.

Capote, Truman, *Breakfast at Tiffany's* (Abacus, 1991). Warm and witty tale of Miss Holly Golightly's 'travels' through the glitter of New York's social scenery in the '50s.

Caro, Robert, *The Power Broker: Robert Moses and the Fall of New York* (Vintage, 1975). A vast, obsessed and enthralling tome, portraying the imperious Evil Gnome, for nearly half a century the most powerful man in New York and the one who shaped the city we see today—with $27 billion.

Charyn, Jerome, *Metropolis: New York as Myth, Marketplace and Magical Land* (Putnam, 1986). Engaging and occasionally rather fey tour through 1980s New York, from the sex booths on Times Square to a TV supper with Ed Koch.

Cohen, Barbara, Steven Heller and Seymour Chwast, *Trylon and Perisphere* (Abrams, 1989). A glossy poster-sized encyclopaedia of a high-point in American design, the 1939 World's Fair.

Cohen, Barbara, Steven Heller and Seymour Chwast, *New York Observed* (Abrams, 1988). An adventurous anthology of New York from 1650 to the '80s, with a good selection of illustrations ranging from Diego Rivera to Cecil Beaton and Thomas Nast.

Conrad, Peter, *The Art of the City* (OUP, 1984). An eloquent dissection of the city using its artists and writers as scalpels.

Dos Passos, John, *U.S.A.* (Penguin, 1938). An Olympian attempt to capture the first bewildering three decades of the century.

Edmiston, Susan and Linda D. Cirino, *Literary New York* (Houghton Mifflin, 1976). Well-written and copiously researched geographical guide to historical and literary New York, from Washington Irving to the Beats.

Feininger, Andreas and John Von Hartz, *New York in the Forties* (Dover, 1978). Extraordinary photos of New York taken when its serrated skyline looked best.

Galbraith, John Kenneth, *The Great Crash* (Penguin, 1979). Engrossing investigation into the causes of the Wall Street Crash, written with zest and panache.

Goldberger, Paul, *The City Observed* (Vintage Books, 1979). A perceptive guide to the buildings of the city by the architecture critic of the New York Times. Cheeky at its best, though every so often it teeters into sententiousness.

Further Reading

Green, Martin, *New York 1913* (Scribners, 1988). An erudite account of pre-War radicalism in New York, focusing on the Armory Show and the Paterson Strike Pageant of 1913 as a sea-change in politics and art.

Jones, Pamela, *Under the City Streets* (Holt, Rinehart & Winston, 1978). Crisply and intelligently written, an intriguing journey into the murk of underground New York.

Kessner, Thomas, *Fiorello H. La Guardia, and the Making of Modern New York* (McGraw-Hill, 1989). An illuminating biography of the New York's best-loved mayor, and a thorough analysis of the politics of liberalism in the '30s and '40s.

Koolhaas, Rem, *Delirious New York* (OUP, 1978). Iconoclastic, fantastical, and entirely convincing—a bracing and highly entertaining explanation of New York's predilection for insanely congested streets and delirious architecture.

Moorhouse, Geoffrey, *Imperial City* (Hodder & Stoughton, 1981). A fresh-faced view of New York by the English travel writer.

Morris, James, *The Great Port* (Faber, 1970). Apologetically romantic account of New York Harbour and the Port Authority.

Newfield, Jack and Wayne Barrett, *City for Sale* (Harper & Row, 1988). An absorbing chronicle of corruption and double-dealing in the Koch administration, focusing on the dramatic suicide of Donald Manes, the Queens borough president, in 1986.

Plath, Sylvia, *The Bell Jar* (Faber, 1963). Taut account of Esther Greenwood's visit to New York in 1953, the summer they electrocuted the Rosenbergs.

Salinger, J. D., *The Catcher in the Rye* (Penguin, 1951). The story of the wry adolescent, Holden Caulfield, who runs away from a Pennsylvanian boarding school to New York, and his fears about the ducks in Central Park.

Sanders, Ronald, and Edmund V. Gillon, *The Lower East Side; a Guide to its Jewish Past* (Dover, 1979). An unusual set of photographs and a brief history of the Lower East Side, past and present.

Still, Baynard, *Mirrors for Gotham* (New York University Press, 1956). A meaty anthology of New York as contemporaries have described it from Dutch days to 1956.

Talese, Gay, *Honor Thy Father* (Dell, 1981). Talese's gripping study of the rise and fall of the Bonanno organization, and the mafia in New York.

Trollope, Frances, *Domestic Manners of the Americans* (Alfred A. Knopf, 1949). Terse and often funny first-hand account of 19th-century New York.

Van Dyke, John C., *The New New York* (Macmillan, 1909). A daring commentary on the architecture of New York in 1909, with extraordinary illustrations of a wrecked Piranesian New York, by Joseph Pennell.

Wharton, Edith, *The Age of Innocence* (Appleton, 1920). Set in tight-legged turn-of-the-century upper-class New York, an account of Newland Archer's frustrated passion for the separated wife of a Polish count.

White, Norval, *A Physical History of New York* (Atheneum, 1987). An extremely good architectural history including digressions on pipes, drains, transits and elevators.

White, Norval and Elliot Willensky, *AIA Guide to New York City* (Macmillan, 1989). An indispensable geographical gazetteer of literally every single structure in the city, with brief and distinctly camp remarks on each item.

Wolf, Reinhart, *New York* (Tuschen, 1980). A tray-sized coffee-table book of Reinhart Wolf's spectacular photographs of skyscraper crowns in dawns and sunsets, and at night.

Page numbers in **bold** refer to main entries; page numbers in *italic* refer to maps.

Index

Vaux, Calvert 75, 129
Verrazano, Giovanni da **52–3**, 158
Verrazano–Narrows Suspension Bridge 161
View, The 101
Village Square 154
Village Voice **42**, 246
Villages walk *138–9*, 138–56
visas 12, 308
waiters 195
Waldorf-Astoria Hotel 82, 95, **109–10**
Walker, Jimmy 61
Walker, Ralph 166
walking 14, 87–8
  Midtown *90–1*, 90–114
  Staten Island, Wall Street, Brooklyn Bridge 158–74, *159*
  tours 20–1
  Upper West Side, Upper East Side *116–17*, 116–36
  Villages *138–9*, 138–56
Wall Street 158–9
  Federal Hall (No 28) 166–7
  40 Wall Street 167–8
  hotels 242
  Irving Trust Company (No 1) 165–6
  Morgan Guaranty Trust Company (No 23) 166
  New York Stock Exchange 167

Wall Street Crash 62, **167**
Warren, Whitney 77
Warren & Wetmore 77
Washington, George 56
Washington Mews 154
Washington Square 152–3
Washington Square Arch 153
Washington Square Art Show 153
weight-training 302
weights and measures 273
West Village 140, **152–6**
  bars 223
  cafés 141–2
  clothes shops 280–1
  hotels 241
  restaurants 206–8
  tea rooms 208
where to stay **226–44**
  bed and breakfast 243–4
  finding somewhere to live 309
  gay and lesbian 243
  home exchange 244
  hostels 242
  renting 244
  student accommodation 242
  sublets 244, 309
  women only 243
  see also hotels
White, Stanford **77–8**, 153
Whitney Museum of American Art 112, 183–4

Wildlife Conservation Center 133
'Wildman' Steve Brill 130–1
Williamsburg 264
'Window on the World' 105–6
Winter Garden 85, 170
women only accommodation 243
Wood, Fernando 58
Woolworth Building 60, 81, **170–1**
Works Project Administration 62–3
World Fairs 63, 76–8
World Financial Center 85, **170**
World Trade Center 84, 160, **169–70**
wrestling 306
Wright, Frank Lloyd 84
Yacht Club 102–3
yoga 306
Yonah Schimmel's Knishes 147
Zabar's 125–6
Zangwill, Israel 59–60
Zenger, Peter 55
Zito's 156
Zoning Law (1916) **81**, 82
zoo 133

Accommodation

Aaah! Manhattan Bed & Breakfast, and Self Catered Registry,
342 W 46th Street, New York, NY 10036.
Tel: 212 246 4000, Fax: 212 765 4229.

Off SoHo Suites Hotel, 11 Rivington Street, New York, NY 10002.
Tel: 212 979 9808, Fax: 212 979 9801.
Elegant two and four guest suites, from: US $89.00.

Tour Operators

Travel By Design, 28 London Rd, Alderley Edge, Cheshire, SK9 7DZ.
Tel: 01625 584195, Fax: 01625 586629.
Design your own New York holiday with us.